Contemporary Literary Theory

Contemporary

Literary

Theory

Edited by

G. Douglas Atkins and Laura Morrow

MACMILLAN

1989

Copyright © 1989 by The University of Massachusetts Press

All rights reserved

Printed in the United States of America

LC 88–14692

British Library Cataloguing in Publication Data

Contemporary Literary Theory.

1. Literature. Theories.

I. ATKINS, G. Douglas (George Douglas) *1943–*

II. MORROW, Laura *1953–*

801

ISBN 0–333–49657–4

0–333–49658–2 (pbk)

Contents

Preface

This book relates contemporary theory to critical and pedagogical practice. That it has no single identifiable origin suggests (better, allegorizes) the way theory and practice are intertwined and interimplicated. The joint labor of two editors and twelve (amazingly cooperative) contributors, *Contemporary Literary Theory* is actually a creature of multiple origins. In one sense, it derives from several years of teaching graduate courses in criticism and theory by one of the editors, me, who came late but happily to this burgeoning subdiscipline, and from the recent—and equally happy—discovery of the "field" by my coeditor. Laura, who remains, she insists, a close reader rather than a theorist, convinced me of the need for such a textbook— for herself as teacher and for the students she and so many others encounter. In another sense, this text derives from a semester-long symposium held at the University of Kansas in fall 1985 on literary theory, critical practice, and the classroom, which week in and week out attracted dozens of teachers and students from English and the other languages and literatures as well as from history, philosophy, anthropology, and various other (sometimes surprising) disciplines. In still another sense, *Contemporary Literary Theory* derives from the dawning recognition, abetted by the experience of codirecting that symposium and team-teaching a seminar offered in conjunction with it (a recognition now shared by many other critics and theorists), that, as prominent, influential, and important as theory has become in the last few years, it has not significantly affected classroom teaching, particularly at the undergraduate level. This is so for a number of reasons, one of which has to do with an expressed and powerful resistance to theory, particularly by those ill informed about its work. Another reason involves the proliferation of theories, with which even the growing number of specialists in criticism and theory are hard-pressed to keep up. If even the specialists find the array of competing theories bewildering, what of the "general reader," who often is a teacher at the college and university level? And even worse, what of the student, graduate or undergraduate, confronted with so many theoretical positions, strategies, and terminologies, some of them (at least) certain to appear alien if not alienating, many being foreign imports?

Let us not mislead, however: As much as one may be desirable, ours does not seek, or pretend, to be a contemporary, or poststructuralist, counterpart to the widely influential textbooks *Understanding Poetry* and *Understanding Fiction*, written by Cleanth Brooks and Robert Penn Warren, and *Understanding Drama*, by Brooks and Robert B. Heilman, which, with admirable clarity and enviable success, taught hundreds of thousands of students the principles and practices of close reading characteristic of New Criticism. As William E. Cain pointedly observes in *The Crisis in Criticism*, "the New Critics succeeded in revolutionizing English studies" in large part "because they devoted themselves as much to pedagogy as to criticism and scholarship." Though it certainly hopes to direct attention to pedagogy, *Contemporary Literary Theory* is a different kind of (text)book from those mentioned. Nor is it a handbook of theories (often called "approaches" or, worse, "methods"), providing step-by-step directions for the *application* of one or more of them to the task of interpreting particular texts, in the (vain) hope of soliciting them to yield up their meanings. Instead, our text is a series of essays, individual though related, on the twelve most prominent, influential, and far-reaching theoretical positions currently available: each is written by a different author, who is not only an expert on the theory discussed but also an experienced and successful classroom teacher. We offer these essays not as a substitute for reading the theorists themselves but as an aid in doing so. Though the discussions contain much of interest and value to specialists in criticism and theory, few of whom can claim to be deeply read in all twelve positions represented, our essays are directed to and written expressly for the non-specialist, teacher, student, and "general reader," still in need of succinct but detailed, clear, and accessible introductions to the theoretical positions that clamor for attention and claim privilege—and that have so much to offer. Our effort was prompted by the desire to provide discussions that straightforwardly describe the primary features, background, strategies, and implications of the theories most influential now and likely to remain so for some time. We elected to leave our contributors free to present their accounts in the form each thought most appropriate given inherent differences among the theories included.

Given in roughly the chronological order of their appearance on the critical scene, British as well as American, the theories represented are New Criticism, archetypal criticism, structuralism/semiotics, reader response, phenomenology, hermeneutics, deconstruction, psychoanalysis, feminism, political, dialogical criticism (inspired by Mikhail Bakhtin), and the work associated with Michel Foucault and the so-called New Historicism. These theories vary, of course, in degree of current and likely influence and importance, and there is inevitably some overlap among them, most notably between phenomenology and hermeneutics. Though we have tried to present a comprehensive survey of the contemporary theoretical field, we grant certain omissions: for example, the (quite different) work of Harold Bloom, Kenneth Burke, René Girard, and Geoffrey Hartman. Important as the work of each of these has proven, none has developed into anything like a school or tradition. Whereas most other major contemporary theorists are assimilable within the theories represented here, Bloom, Burke, Girard, and Hartman are, each of them, *sui generis*. Arguably, their individuality constitutes their undeniable importance, but it makes it impossible for us to consider them here, beyond certain "uses" in the Introduction.

A few words more may be in order concerning the mode of presentation we have adopted: "Farming out" the discussions, we agreed from the beginning, has far more advantages than disadvantages. Neither of us—nor both of us together—possesses the knowledge to treat all twelve positions with the informed awareness, breadth of reading, and depth of (sympathetic) understanding displayed by our contributors. Thus we invited an expert—though not always a specialist—on each theory to join in our effort. We are convinced that the achieved diversity of viewpoint and degree of expertise represented more than compensate for any loss of consistency or singleness of perspective. As a matter of fact, we assert the value of precisely this diversity of perspective. Of course, our strategy and that result may suggest to some a certain pluralism, a laissez-faire attitude, or the appearance that all theories are equally valid. Such an interpretation of our procedure would be unfortunate, for we in fact believe that the theories represented here differ considerably in conceptual rigor and consistency, power, self-consciousness, and value for literary studies, as well as for contemporary thought generally. Rather than embrace an easy pluralism, whose hegemony over college and university curricula remains virtually unchallenged, I for one subscribe in general to

Frank Lentricchia's combative and unfortunately polarizing distinction between "the debased humanist sentiment that all points of view are valid, [and]
the historical consciousness that any point of view—opinion, belief, theory—
about literature and literature itself are [*sic*] alike in this crucial way: both are
bound over to contexts and forces not in their autonomous control; both
express something else besides themselves; neither is freely originary."

   Still the question imposes itself: Confronted by the bewildering array of
theoretical possibilities (options? opportunities?), what is a reader to do? Even
if *we* do not advance an argument for any of the theories represented here, *you*
will ultimately have to make some choices, and choices entail consequences.
And even if we choose not to *advance* here an argument for deconstruction or
psychoanalysis, each of us has, in our own life and work, made a choice, and
we may as well divulge our theoretical investments: One of us was brought up
on New Criticism, became attracted to poststructuralist thinking, but holds
many reservations about theory and the teaching of theory, whereas the other
(I) was weaned on New Criticism, imbibed Hirschian hermeneutics in graduate school, later became a card-carrying deconstructionist, and now finds
himself drawn to Hartman's style of literary work. Such shifts, developments,
and evolving consciousness probably represent the careers of most professional
students of literature. In providing under one cover access to the major
contemporary theories, our text will, we hope, enhance the evolutionary
process of understanding and foster critical growth. It is not, in any case, far
from Gerald Graff's recent call, in *Professing Literature*, for openness regarding
the disagreements and disputes that activate us, indeed for making public the
conflicts and controversies that we all too often hide from students. Presenting
theories in open conflict, as we do here, can—and, we hope, will—have a
stimulating and productive pedagogical effect.

   A couple of related points: In order to make clear that theories inhabit a
richly integumented field, forming an intricately woven text(ile), rather than
function as self-contained, autonomous, and isolated entities, we have asked
our contributors to discuss both internecine disagreements (for example, the
way the New Critic John Crowe Ransom differs from the New Critic Cleanth
Brooks) and some of the differences from other theories. In addition, we have
asked contributors to situate themselves within the particular theoretical
framework discussed, indicating the specific slant given to the theory, the
position taken vis-à-vis the internecine struggles, and the stance assumed in
the heterogeneous thinking that parades under the umbrella of, for example,
deconstruction, psychoanalysis, Marxism, and feminism. Far from being an
ethereal or transcendent matter, safely isolated from the contingencies of

human existence, theory is mottled through and through with history, context, and personal preference and prejudice. Theory is, in short, a matter of practice.

With this last sentence at least my own particular position on theory begins to emerge. That position, which the Introduction tries to make clear, is but one of several possible, and in the Introduction I take up questions of theory as such, consider some of the different meanings now being given to theory, and ask how particular theories relate both to a possible common enterprise and to each other. In arguing that *theory* functions as more than a set of directions or principles for the (presumably better) interpreting of particular texts, I offer something like a counterpoint to the discussions of *theories*. The *unsettling* nature of such a juxtaposition is, I maintain, characteristic of the theoretical.

G. Douglas Atkins

Acknowledgments

More often than not, we hear, coeditors of essay collections must contend with disregard for deadlines, resistance to criticism, and illness of temper. Of such experience we can tell you little. Manuscripts of impressive grace and clarity came promptly from Minnesota, from Texas, from Taiwan. We had no differences with our deconstruction worker, nor did we experience oral sadistic behavior from our psychoanalytic reader, and our phenomenologist fulfilled the horizon of our greatest expectations. Others may have lost friends in such projects; we have gained many and are most grateful to them.

Bruce Wilcox, Director of the University of Massachusetts Press, deserves our sincere thanks: he has been supportive of our efforts from the day we approached him with the idea of such a textbook. We are grateful for his wisdom, his encouragement, and his genuine kindness.

We wish to extend special thanks to Beth Ridenour and Pam Lerow, gracious and expert processors of words at the University of Kansas, and to Mary Pate and Susan Jusselin of Louisiana State University in Shreveport, for the skill and good humor with which they typed our correspondence and assembled our manuscript.

Doug would like to indicate other debts as well: to those at the University of Kansas, especially Michael L. Johnson, chair of the English department, who supported, in various ways, a semester-long symposium in 1985 on literary theory, critical practice, and the classroom; to an appreciative audience at the University of South Florida who responded helpfully to a version of the Introduction; and to Patricia L. Douglass, who brought to the project—and to his life—new meaning, purpose, and joy.

My own debts are few but substantial: to my father, Harry Rutherford Powers, whose loving wisdom sustains me still; to my mother, Helen Smith Powers, whose wit is exceeded only by the generosity of her spirit; and to my husband, Edward Morrow, "susceptor meus . . . / Gloria mea et exaltans caput meum."

L.P.M.

Contemporary Literary Theory

G. DOUGLAS ATKINS

Introduction: Literary Theory, Critical Practice, and the Classroom

The good critic cannot stop with studying poetry, he must also study poetics. If he thinks he must puritanically abstain from all indulgence in the theory, the good critic may have to be a good little critic. . . . Theory, which is expectation, always determines criticism, and never more than when it is unconscious. The reputed condition of no-theory in the critic's mind is illusory.

John Crowe Ransom, *The World's Body*

One would expect that our libraries would be full of works on the theory of interpretation, the diagnosis of linguistic situations, systematic ambiguity and the function of symbols. . . . [But] there is no other human activity for which theory bears so small a proportion to practice. Even the theory of football has been more thoroughly inquired into.

I. A. Richards, *Practical Criticism*

Mere reading, it turns out, prior to any theory, is able to transform critical discourse in a manner that would appear deeply subversive to those who think of the teaching of literature as a substitute for the teaching of theology, ethics, psychology, or intellectual history.

Paul de Man, "The Return to Philology"

Taken together, the three quotations above are meant to suggest the *unsettling* nature of theory. That is, unlike the "cold pastoral" of Keats's Grecian urn, which "teases us out of thought," theory makes us think, forcing us to examine our assumptions; it thus constitutes, contrary to our expectations, fun as well as an effort of potentially the highest value. In the quoted passages the unsettling or at least the unexpected, appears in the following way: That Ransom and Richards extol the virtues, indeed admit the inescapability, of theory is as important as it may be surprising. Begetters of the (now old) New Criticism, frequently cited as antithetical to the work of theory, or at best unself-conscious in its reputed claims that close reading, aided only by a good dictionary, will unlock a text's secrets, Ransom and Richards upset our assumptions and expectations, perhaps deflating a myth or at least problematizing our understanding. No less surprising is the way that, in the third quotation I provided, Paul de Man, the major American de-constructionist and one of the most distinguished and influential theorists of the twentieth century, claims that close reading, virtually synonymous with the New Criticism that Ransom and Richards promulgated, (in every sense) precedes theory. A baffling situation is thus traced in these brief passages, an allegory, in other words, of the bewildering turn of events in which one side to a dispute seems to occupy the position of the other, exchanging places with its apparent opposite. Unsettling, to be sure, this structure (re)calls us to thought and a more rigorous examination of what we thought we knew. Truth thus *turns* out to be more complex than we assumed. 'Twas ever thus, and it is theory that helps us to see that it is so.

Surprisingly, theory can be fun. In the hands of writers as different as William H. Gass, Susan Sontag, Roland Barthes, Jacques Derrida, Harold Bloom, Geoffrey Hartman, Barbara Johnson, and Jane Gallop, theory may actually *become* literature, self-consciously displaying its fictive nature and exploiting an impressive arsenal of stylistic devices.[1] But no matter how self-conscious or mannered the writing, crucial is the attitude we as readers bring to theory. Pleasure derives not just from the skillful writing of the more artful critics and theorists but also from the decision readers are free to make to regard "criticism informed or motivated by theory [as] part of literary crit-icism (rather than of philosophy or an unknown science) and . . . literary criticism [as] within literature, not outside it."[2] Read as we do *other* literary forms and texts, theory offers many pleasures as well as insights, themselves pleasurable, of course.

Implicit here is the important theoretical point that, contrary to assump-tions still prevalent in classroom practice, "there really is no way to read a text in and for itself":

Only a repetition of every word in its "original" sequence could represent the work in its purity, and even then, as Borges's Pierre Menard learned, the act of writing and its local circumstances alter what the text signifies. Every critical reading, then, necessarily casts the work within another narrative: in a story of moral values, psychologies, societies, religious and philosophical truths, editorial procedures, political conflicts, or aesthetic techniques. Many have pointed out that the very quality of "literariness," that essence we need in order to say what is or is not literature, depends on a framework of presuppositions that cannot (without going in circles) be construed as simply literary.[3]

Rather than free-standing, every reading is thus framed. And theories are among the most important frameworks, allowing us to *see* the "meaning" of/in texts—including the texts of theory.[4] Etymologically, there is a crucial link "between 'theory' and 'seeing' (Greek *thea* = spectacle)," a link that "becomes a forgotten or sublimated metaphor underlying the certitudes of science."[5]

Though the notorious Hellene Ezra Pound thought, in more or less New Critical fashion, that literature gives us eyes to see with, it is actually theory that does so.[6] That some theory is always in place and at work, whether we know it or grant it or not, raises at least two major questions. One concerns the relation of theory to practice, and my argument will be that not only does practice always imply its own theory but "theory exists only as a form of practice."[7] The other major question concerns *theory* itself: what it is and how it relates to the various competing *theories* regarding texts.

The Function of Theory at the Present Time

The emergence of theory has been frequently and well chronicled, and so there is no need to repeat here the story of its meteoric rise to prominence in the academic community, in this country as well as abroad.[8] If there is not yet the situation I. A. Richards expected, whereby our libraries "would be full of works on the theory of interpretation," the past ten or fifteen years have certainly witnessed an outpouring of books on theory and its relation to various "primary" texts, the establishment of major journals devoted to theoretical issues, and the creation of jobs for theorists, in all kinds of institutions, from the Ivy League to small colleges and regional universities. Noting the intensity associated with theory as well as its invigorating features, William E. Cain writes in *The Crisis in Criticism: Theory, Literature, and Reform in English Studies* of the way theory has succeeded in becoming a subdiscipline of considerable power and promise, whose major practitioners, who are eagerly sought for lectures, conferences, and positions and whose books actually sell, enjoy a remarkable "degree of privilege."[9]

Whether or not Howard Felperin is right to locate a "paradigm-shift toward theory" and an "institutional turn toward theory as the new common denominator of our activity,"[10] the (armed) resistance to it indicates well enough its achievement of power, place, and prestige. In an essay first published in the (London) *Times Literary Supplement*, Paul de Man grants that "the quarrelsome tone that hangs over the debates on the teaching of literature" stems from "the advent of contemporary literary theory." This, he writes, "is certainly not surprising. Whenever new approaches or techniques are being advocated, a very understandable ill-humor overcomes those who feel they may have to modify or to reconsider well-established pedagogical habits that served them well until the most recent troublemakers came along." But, de Man continues, "the polemical response in the case of contemporary theory, and especially of some of its aspects, runs deeper." The widespread polemic, he surmises,

feeds not only on civilized conservatism but on moral indignation. It speaks with an anxiety that is not only that of a disturbed tranquillity but of a disturbed moral conscience. Nor is this mood confined to the opponents of theory. Its protagonists, in most cases, are just as nervous. When they appear not to be, their self-assurance often seems to be dependent on utopian schemes. The well-established rationale for the professing of literature has come under fire. Small wonder that it chooses to shoot back.[11]

Important, if not surprising, is de Man's criticism of the proponents of theory as well as its antagonists.

Perhaps more shrewdly than anyone else, de Man has written of "the resistance to theory," the title, in fact, of a posthumous volume of his essays. In the *TLS* discussion, de Man confronts one of the most strident and unfortunate polemics, an essay published in the *Harvard Magazine* by the distinguished scholar Walter Jackson Bate. According to Bate, joining a chorus of often shrill voices raised in anger in the popular media, the humanities are "in the weakest state they ever suffered—bent on a self-destructive course, through a combination of anger, fear and purblind defensiveness."[12] The main cause for this lamentable decline Bate attributes to "the increasing concentration on literary theory." That decline culminates, as de Man puts it, paraphrasing Bate, "in the final catastrophe of the post-structural era, the invasion of departments of English by French influences that advocate 'a nihilistic view of literature, of human communication, and of life itself.'"[13] Bate denounces Jacques Derrida as the ruthless, unprincipled antagonist in this tragedy, misidentifying him as a " 'puckish Parisian' (he is neither), 'who never turns to the really major philosophers except to snatch at stale pessimisms' (e.g., Nietzsche)." De Man adds that this strange remark "suggests that Professor Bate, a careful scholar and brilliant teacher, has this time confined his sources of information to *Newsweek* magazine." Moreover, de Man reasons that "one must be feeling very threatened indeed to become so aggressively defensive."[14]

Much more interesting, de Man finds, than such "local manifestations" of the resistance movement are the systematic implications they reveal. He proposes that "resistance may be a built-in constituent" of theory's discourse.[15] Since "literary theory can be said to come into being when the approach to literary texts is no longer based on non-linguistic, that is to say historical and aesthetic, considerations," the resistance to theory is "a resistance to language itself or to the possibility that language contains factors or functions that cannot be reduced to intuition."[16] More specifically, de Man continues, "the resistance to theory is a resistance to the rhetorical or tropological dimension of language, a dimension which is perhaps more explicitly in the foreground in literature (broadly conceived) than in other verbal manifestations or—to be somewhat less vague—which can be revealed in any verbal event when it is read textually."[17] The resistance to theory is, therefore, according to de Man, a resistance to reading, or at least to reading that attends to language's rhetorical or tropological features. That all means, de Man rather dazzlingly—or dizzyingly—concludes, that "nothing can overcome the resistance to theory since theory *is* itself the resistance. . . . Yet literary theory is not in danger of going under; it cannot help but flourish, and the more it is resisted, the more it flourishes, since the language it speaks is the language of self-resistance."[18]

The resistance to theory has, in any case, assumed many forms, some of it, like Bate's, deriving from a lack of understanding of what it is and what it does. There is, one feels sure, some nationalism, and parochialism, in this resistance movement, alarmed that the literary economy is being overrun by foreign imports, many of them from France (notably structuralism, deconstruction, Lacanian psychoanalysis), some from Germany (including hermeneutics and forms of reader response), and at least one (God save us!) from Russia (Bahktinian dialogical criticism). In a conservative political climate and an age of retrenchment, with (at least until very recently) few jobs being available in the academy, professional anxiety is certainly understandable. After all, "student head count" is crucial to institutional and individual survival, and courses in criticism and theory do draw students away from *literature* courses (more interested in intellectual issues than professors often grant, students are attracted to theory because it transcends narrow disciplinary limits to raise large and important questions). Beleaguered, ill paid, often anxious about their work, its importance, and its lack of recognition, literature professors especially worry about the sometimes extravagant claims and imperialistic designs of theory. And when, as more and more often happens, theorists claim (like me) that criticism and theory are inside literature, differing from supposedly more creative forms in degree rather than kind, then professors feel especially threatened, theory unsettling the professional and personal stability to which academics passionately cling.

By no means all the resistance, or the most important, has come from "outside" theory, however. Probably the most notable, if not the most notorious, such opposition appears in a 1982 essay "Against Theory," written by Steven Knapp and Walter Benn Michaels and published in *Critical Inquiry*. Indebted to the American pragmatist tradition (e.g., the work of John Dewey), Knapp and Michaels conclude, intemperately and melodramatically, that "the whole enterprise of critical theory is misguided" and "should therefore come to an end."[19] Their reasoning is complicated, the argument subtle and not without allure. Basically it consists of the claim that theory is possible *only* as a mistake: Believing it possible to get away from intentionality "makes theory possible because it creates the illusion of a choice between alternative methods of interpreting." The following paragraph nicely summarizes the particular antitheoretical position assumed by Knapp and Michaels: "To be a theorist," they begin, "is only to think that there is such a choice" as they have mentioned "between alternative methods of interpreting." They continue:

In this respect intentionalists and anti-intentionalists are the same. They are also the same in another respect: neither can really escape intention. But this doesn't mean the intentionalists win, since what intentionalists want is a guide to valid interpretation; what they get, however, is simply a description of what everyone always does. In practical terms, then, the stakes in the battle over intention are extremely low—in fact, they don't exist. Hence it doesn't matter who wins. In theoretical terms, however, the stakes are extremely high and it still doesn't matter who wins. The stakes are high because they amount to the existence of theory itself; it doesn't matter who wins because as long as one thinks that a position on intention (either for or against) makes a difference in achieving valid interpretations, the ideal of theory is saved. Theory wins. But as soon as we recognize that there are no theoretical choices to be made, then the point of theory vanishes. Theory loses.[20]

But of course theory does not lose. As various respondents to Knapp and Michaels have pointed out, despite the claims made, there *are* theoretical choices. Without engaging all of the arguments made in "Against Theory" or offering a comprehensive rejoinder, I might note that Knapp and Michaels proceed from an unnecessarily limiting definition of theory: "the attempt to govern interpretations of particular texts by appealing to an account of interpretation in general."[21] Their sense of intentionality is also simplistic and mechanical. Regarding meaning "as just another name for *expressed* intention"[22] reveals an ultimately untenable belief in thought as existing outside of and apart from language. One does not need Derrida's elaborate deconstruction of *expression* to realize Knapp and Michaels's mistake, for we all find that it is precisely in the process of writing that we discover the meaning we intended. Intention does not, then, precede language or writing, as the authors of "Against Theory" claim; instead, it occurs in and simultaneously with language. As a final point against Knapp and Michaels, I note that in arguing against theory they are nothing if not theoretical—still another (not so surprising) crossover, in other words.

Other internal or "family" resistances to theory are less stridently antitheoretical. There is now a good deal of concern with and worry about the dangers resulting from the *institutionalization* of theory. For example, the theorist Edward W. Said has distinguished between theory and "critical consciousness" in an effort to prevent theory from contenting itself "with being purely theoretical, never making contact with society and culture because its own fascinations prove so arresting," as Cain says; needed, argues Said, is

a sort of spatial sense, a sort of measuring faculty for locating or situating theory, and this means that theory has to be grasped in the place and (of course) the time out of which it emerges as a part of that time, working in and for it, responding to it; then, consequently, that first place can be measured against subsequent places where the theory turns up for use. The critical consciousness is awareness of the differences between situations, awareness too of the fact that no system or theory exhausts (or covers or dominates) the situation out of which it emerges or to which it is transported. And above all, critical consciousness is aware of the resistances to theory, reactions to it elicited by those concrete experiences or interpretations with which it is in conflict. . . . It is the critic's job to provide *resistances* to theory, to open it up toward historical reality, toward society, toward human needs and interests, to point up those concrete instances drawn from everyday reality that lie outside or just beyond the interpretive areas necessarily designated in advance and thereafter circumscribed by every theory.[23]

Like Said, and others, William E. Cain recognizes theory's potential, granting that it is "intense and invigorating," but it is so, he laments, only "within its own boundaries."[24] For Cain, theory fails to achieve its potential, which is, in fact, to be the very critical consciousness Said summons, "when it divorces itself from practice, when its rigors and difficulties acquire a kind of privilege and fail to connect with anything else."[25] That failure constitutes a major "crisis in criticism," theory having "come close to exhausting itself": "becoming increasingly *less* critical, less skeptical, about itself and its reason for being," the "theory industry grinds along, and books, articles, and symposia multiply, but much of the material seems arid and unreal, out of phase with concrete issues in critical practice and pedagogy, and out of touch with human needs and interests."[26] The regrettable inclination has been, Cain laments, "to post boundaries around [the space of theory] and transform it into a special 'field' where theorists address each other—and sometimes, it seems, meditate upon themselves—in clannish and self-congratulatory terms."[27]

If this is an accurate representation of the current condition of theory, what should be done? Certainly it seems unprofitable to give aid and comfort to the enemy by turning "against theory" or to wring our hands in impotent rage over what might have been. Better is the effort being waged by a number of critics to recall theory to its work, proposing to *use* its powerful resources, turning it away from an inclination to become metatheory toward actual practice.

This effort stems from the recognition, as described by Daniel T. O'Hara, that "the elusive, purely theoretical quest for the hidden rules governing *the system* of production, dissemination, and interpretation of texts, a quest generally informed by an essential concern to revise the academic study of literature, can lead only to the foolish positing of some single, all-determining principle of critical practice (Language, Power, Influence, etc.)—that is, to a speculative trap of self-indulgent rarefaction, in short, to an intellectual dead end."[28] In opposition to such "hermetic" criticism emerges what Robert Scholes misleadingly calls "secular criticism."[29] According to Gregory Jay and David L. Miller, writing in the Introduction to *After Strange Texts: The Role of Theory in the Study of Literature*, theory may now be seen as "turning in many ways toward the 'extratextual' dimensions of discourse, those intangible as well as material institutions that house or imprison what can be known and done."[30] This is an assessment in general shared by Howard Felperin, who writes in *Beyond Deconstruction: The Uses and Abuses of Literary Theory* of the way theory is now frequently regarded "as a means of transforming material, political, or sexual relations within the wider culture."[31] Indeed, Felperin claims, "one common denominator of all the schools of theory is the conviction that their thought, and the language of their thought, is consequential in real social terms, that their relation to society is not that of a passive reflex or mechanistic response."[32] Instead, then, of the understanding expressed by Knapp and Michaels (as interpreted by Cain) that theory gives us "techniques that adjust and update methods of 'close analysis' of masterpieces," we have a definition such as Cain develops of theory as "intellectual work."[33]

By that notion, Cain denotes an effort that is "flexible, strategic, and provisional," theory being more specifically understood as an analytical, critical, and at times polemical force; it does not seek to fashion a grand system for "interpretation in general," one that somehow could transcend history and appraise practice from "the outside." In positive terms, theory . . . does aim to affect interpretation, exposing, for example, the limits of the traditional canon, disputing the distinction between literary and nonliterary texts, and identifying other groups of texts that critics should examine and that students should study. Theory aims to criticize and reorient practice, not prescribe once and for all or dictate what in some final, authoritative sense "interpretation" should be.[34]

In short, as Cain defines it, theory is "the critique of established practice and the beliefs and values (usually concealed) that justify this practice, and second, the inspection of new theories and forms of practice that get proposed as substitutes for what has formerly been in place. Theory exposes errors in what has been done in the past, highlights mistakes and unexamined assumptions in what is being done in the present, and remains skeptical, if also hopeful, about alternatives for the future."[35] Theory thus acts as critique and always in relation to practice—indeed as critique of practice, including its own. Theory contests itself, as a matter of fact.

Thoroughly pragmatic, Cain specifically argues that theory "ought to be slanted towards questions of pedagogy, education, social and cultural practice, and should be placed in dialectical relation with research."[36] Such efforts constitute "intellectual work," which involves "productive questioning and committed thinking, a willingness to be skeptical but not a refusal to affirm the truth of one's position."[37] In terms I have frequently used, that entails, in turn, a willingness and a capacity to read both *with* and *against* the grain.[38] Still, despite all the work that needs to be done *within* the discipline, probing its "taken-for-granted business," "at the present time," writes Cain, "we need, perhaps above all else, to articulate the continuities between 'English' and the wider world, between literary expertise and social, political, and cultural analysis and understanding."[39]

Despite some significant differences, Frank Lentricchia, author of the well-known *After the New Criticism* and *Criticism and Social Change*, agrees that "literary theory is always more than literary theory. . . . literary practice is a social practice and theory is a way of critically engaging the cultural work of both literature and literary criticism within a given social whole."[40] Despite its impatience and occasional intemperance, Lentricchia's work exemplifies the power within theory to effect significant institutional change. A far cry this from either the "Natchez-Augustan manor" of the New Critics or the stridently antitheoretical stance of Knapp and Michaels.[41] Quoting "the father of American pragmatism," C. S. Peirce, who "attacked the stance of the anti-theorist as one of the traditional expressions of irrationalism, a non-method of fixing belief . . . with bullheaded tenacity and, at its worst, with willful ignorance," Lentricchia offers an effective conclusion to our consideration of what theory is as he further undermines the position of the antitheorists: "If Peirce is right," he continues, "then theory is not the pointlessly specialized activity of disengaged intellectuals; it is rather the fundamental obligation to live self-reflectively and even . . . a condition of democratic community."[42] Lentricchia's conclusion is trumpeted and directed against Knapp and Michaels:

> So to be against theory, in this latest, perverse version of pragmatism and American anti-intellectualism, is to court the mindless life that those who like things just as they are hope we in America's colleges and universities will continue to cultivate. To be against theory is to be against self-examination—against raising and exploring questions about how texts and selves and societies are formed and maintained and for whose benefit. To be against theory is to take everything at face value and never to be suspicious.[43]

In differing degrees, the theories represented here, and the writers who represent them, do the "intellectual work" that Cain calls for. Whether or not they make explicit the relation to the world beyond the narrowly textual, all of these theories bear implications for culture, society, and pedagogy. This is true even of probably the least manifestly extratextual theory represented, the New Criticism, which not only flourished in a climate of political conservatism (the Eisenhower era) but also coexisted with a vigorous rejection, on the part of several of its prominent advocates, of the values of secular, pluralistic, and industrial modernism. At the other end of the political spectrum, Marxism looks, of course, toward—and expects nothing short of—the total reshaping of society. Among the less "extreme" positions, some versions of deconstruction, for example, appear closer to New Critical formalism, whereas other versions actually link up, as do varieties of psychoanalysis, with Marxism, including in the work of one of our contributors, Michael Ryan.

Whatever their relation to extratextual matters, implicit or explicit, individual *theories* stand to benefit from—and indeed need—the work of theory, as defined above. There is a difference, in other words, between *theory*, understood as "an extremely sophisticated and powerful set of procedures" for opening assumptions up for scrutiny, and *a theory* functioning as a particular and competitive reading strategy (even if not necessarily a set of directions for the better "processing" of texts).[44] This distinction is hardly an absolute difference: That theory reads texts, literary as well as institutional, whereas individual theories actively engage extratextual issues indicates that the distinction is a moving difference. Simply put, there neither is nor can be a "metatheory" to deliver us from the exigencies of practice and transport us to an ethereal realm of pure theory: "What we call theory and practice borrow from each other in an economy neither can comprehend."[45] Being interimplicated, theory and practice seem to "cross over," upsetting the line we tend to draw between them.

Refusing to identify itself with, or commit itself to, any one position, and being promiscuous enough to consort with several, theory exists as a principle, strategy, and *practice* of both self-consciousness and self-criticism. Theory thus allows the various theories to *see* their own stance as interested, positional, and strategic rather than objective, natural, or true. In short, without itself escaping critique, theory prevents particular theories from evading the question of their own framing. Even "deconstructive framing cannot . . . be offered as a representation of the truth about framing, since in practice it defers the question of its own essence." This point is important, for it indicates "the uncanny way that interpretive devices allow for truth and presence only in the moment of their own disappearance." This situation carries great importance for critical practice. Indeed, as a result of "the theoretical revolution" and the self-consciousness and self-criticism it has advanced, "critical texts have increasingly become two-handed engines"; that is, "a theory is proposed whose use in practice is either implied or demonstrated; at the same time, the theory of the theory is itself so scrutinized that its claims are unsettled and a different field of practice created."[46]

Inter-section

It seems, then, that, as Geoffrey Hartman has written, "the rift between theory and practice" is based on "a false perception."[47] But what about the divide, implicit in the foregoing discussion, between historical and formal modes of interpretation, which Jay and Miller predict will likely constitute "the major point of disagreement for some time to come" in theoretical discussions? The issue concerns, as Robert Scholes has noted, "the relationship between text and world," and Scholes, following Edward Said, has identified the oppositions as *secular* and *hermetic*: In his polarized (and therefore misleading) account, the "secular or worldly critics" are represented as seeing texts "historically grounded in public occasions and socially supported codes. The hermetic interpreters [on the other hand] see texts as radically self-reflective and nonreferential—and therefore beyond the reach of criticism."[48] But as my mention of Hartman here is intended to suggest, a crossover occurs, problematizing an absolute difference: That that formalist or hermetic critic (as he is frequently labeled) actually hopes to bring theory and practice together, being himself increasingly attracted to *cultural* criticism, suggests that the apparent rift between formal and historical modes of interpretation may be posited as greater than it actually is, if not, like that between theory and practice, based on a "false perception." The real issue, in any case, I suggest, is not so much *whether* formal and historical perspectives, procedures, styles, and goals come together but *how* they do so. Like all other differences, including theory and practice, the formal and the historical are "always already" *related*. To oppose such differences, to regard them as locked in combat, *is to lock* them in combat, freezing differences into and as differences.

As a side but related and important issue, I want to consider the apparent opposition between *"creative"* criticism and *critical* theory (I intend no opposition of criticism and theory). Whether by those who consider criticism as secondary and subservient to so-called imaginative writing (i.e., literature) or by theorists who (rigidly) distinguish between them, creative criticism and such worldly, committed work as I have discussed and advocated are regarded as opposed to each other. Even William E. Cain, though as committed to institutional, cultural, and social criticism as anyone else, grants that advocates and practitioners of "creative criticism" like Hartman and Bloom "are right to contend that criticism and theory are 'creative' forms, involving an exploratory and meditative relation to the subject at hand."[49] Hartman especially is well known for arguing that a "crossover" occurs between "primary" and "secondary," between "literature" and that form of "imaginative reason" known as criticism and theory: "criticism as commentary *de linea* always crosses the line and changes to one *trans lineam*. The commentator's discourse, that is, cannot be neatly or methodically separated from that of the author: the relation is contaminating and chiastic; source text and secondary, though separable, enter into a mutually supportive, mutually dominating relation."[50] For Hartman, in fact, the critical essay becomes, in the hands of Lukács, Benjamin, Barthes, Bloom, and others, nothing less than an "intellectual poem." Hartman has reminded us of criticism's long-standing if oft-forgotten indebtedness to the familiar essay as well as the tradition regarding the critical essay as tentative, open, *and* ironic in claiming only to be about art without itself being art.

Might a relationship, rather than an absolute difference, exist between the creative aspect of criticism, the critical essay, and theory itself? Though I can only be suggestive here, let me try to explain why I raise the question. As Jonathan Culler has written, theory now constitutes an impressive genre of heterogeneous texts distinguished by "their ability to function not as demonstrations within the parameters of a discipline but as redescriptions that challenge disciplinary boundaries"; theory consists, according to Culler, of texts having "the power to make strange the familiar and to make readers conceive of their own thinking, behavior, and institutions in new ways."[51] Now it is the case that for a number of reasons recent critics, of different persuasions, have found the essay form congenial to and appropriate for their work: Open, tentative, and exploratory, the essay, rather than either "the definite article" or the comprehensive and closed book, has been preferred by such different critics as Stanley Fish, Derrida, Bloom, and Hartman. But there is more, linking the critical to the familiar essay, which in its rich tradition has been personal, sometimes confessional, and roundabout rather than linear in development, presenting the play of the writer's mind and the subsequent course of his or her interpretive discovery, as the critical essayist often shuttles between theory and particular critical analyses.[52] The history of the essay allows us to make the connection to the work of theory, as we have come to understand it. From its "beginnings" in fact, as W. Wolfgang Holdheim has argued, the essay has been "less a genre than quite deliberately an antigenre, designed to flaunt the prescriptiveness in literary matters which had been inherited from a rationalistic rhetorical tradition." Holdheim claims, in fact, that Montaigne himself was "engaged in an *Abbau* of his tradition . . . an active deconstruction in the genuine sense: a clearing away of rubbish, of reified sedimentations, so that issues may once again be laid bare in their concreteness. His radical presentation of discontinuity is very much a reaction against uncritically accepted accumulations of continuity; his insistence on the uniquely diverse and particular is directed against too exclusive a concern with universals." In short, Holdheim concludes, "the essay is in its very essence the form of the problematical."[53] It thus joins with theory itself, which always, everywhere, problematizes, unsettling, calling into question our assumptions. Both Montaigne, then, and the essay form he inaugurated bear striking and important parallels not just with deconstruction but with theory itself.

The Teaching of Theory/The Theory of Teaching

Accepting William E. Cain's challenge to slant theory toward pedagogy and so to "contest the 'ground' that traditional modes and customs have occupied," I want, in the remaining pages of this essay, to look at that particular practice.[54] Clearly, the classroom is one of those places, arguably the most important one, where the future of theory is being played out. I will claim that teaching bears a special relationship to theory and, further, that a crisscrossing of teaching and theory occurs. The form and style of this section will be somewhat more essayistic than that of the first, for reasons hinted at in the Inter-section. I will, in short, be more personal and familiar than formal and objective, offering you something other than the scholarly "definite article." I suspect that you will prefer such an effort, for all its imperfections, to what I might have inflicted upon you. And I hope you won't be put off by the title I have given this section, one that I alternately regard as clever, merely cute, and appropriate (as well as accurate).

Before launching into my argument that teaching bears a particular relationship to theory, a couple of distinctions: My position accepts but goes beyond the claim, already noted, that a theory is always at least implicit in every critical or pedagogical effort (perhaps never more so than when we deny, in the name of innocence and purity, that we have a theory). In maintaining, moreover, that teaching is inseparable from theory, I mean something other than the truism, bequeathed by the New Criticism, that pedagogy and criticism are virtually synonymous and indistinguishable. Not a small point this latter, for it is unfortunately true, as Gerald Graff and Reginald Gibbons lament in *Criticism in the University*, that "the very word 'criticism' has become synonymous with 'academic criticism,'" a situation that requires attention and response rather than mere lamentation;[55] correction would, I think, best be effected via a criticism, informed by theory, that acknowledges the need to reach a large, *general* audience. It is precisely here that theory and the essay, comprehended within the long and distinguished tradition of familiar writing, might productively come together.

In any case, it appears that for some time the classroom has exercised *too much* power over critical practice, even to the point of determining its nature and limiting its role. Too often, criticism carries the imprimatur of the classroom: Wishing to accommodate, criticism remains, long after the heyday of the New Criticism and the dissemination of structuralist, reader-response, and deconstructionist procedures, mainly explication, concerned to transport a "message" in language accessible to an audience seduced by "the dream of communication," increasingly insensitive to language, and impatient for "the meaning." Goal-oriented, students, as well as many teachers, show little patience with the wilderness that is language, regarding it as a mere transparency in which objects appear truly and unobstructed and which is impervious to their will and manipulation. Only if it plays in the classroom is the hermeneutical effort deemed successful and significant. *There*, it seems, it can't be particularly demanding, nor can it be *either* creative *or* culturally and radically critical. Subservient to the pedagogical situation and the exigencies of the classroom, criticism can little afford to privilege the strangeness of individual texts or to brood upon the extraordinary language events that great poems are. A reduction has occurred, as Geoffrey Hartman maintains in *Criticism in the Wilderness: The Study of Literature Today*, a reduction that shrinks the dimensions of language—and the soul.

At heart genuinely critical, theory blasts apart the chains of reduction that have confined *both* criticism *and* the teaching of written texts. As Hartman maintains, "practical criticism," which we have so narrowly defined, restricting its function and limiting it to classroomlike explication, is now free to "grow up," to leave behind the mainly pastoral activities, and to take on at last the mature (if not epic) tasks of hermeneutics and cultural criticism, which are neither quickly foreclosed nor easily accommodated. At least as I understand it (and I recognize that I run here the risk of reductiveness myself), recent theory, particularly the structural and poststructuralist varieties, has emphasized difference and its cousin relation. Deriving, of course, from Saussure's conclusion that "in language, there are no positive terms, *only differences*," deconstruction has been concerned to show how meaning arises only because a "trace" of the "one" always already inhabits "the other," revealing a *difference within* that makes possible *relation between*, "the other" being not absolutely different or totally other, after all.[56] The relational, or differential, thinking that Saussure inaugurated and that Derrida has pursued (with a difference!) carries far-reaching implications that are only now beginning to be explored, for example in religion and theology, via the work of Mark C. Taylor and Robert Magliola, so-called deconstructive theologians like Thomas J. J. Altizer (famous, or infamous, since the sixties for his contributions to "Christian atheism"), and yours truly.[57]

That differential, or relational, thinking also bears great potential importance for teaching, as Michael L. Johnson and I try to show in our collection of essays *Writing and Reading Differently: Deconstruction and the Teaching of Composition and Literature* and as Jasper Neel brilliantly shows in his recent book.[58] In the brief space available here, I want to take a somewhat different and rather specific tack in suggesting how this is so. I begin with Shoshana Felman's provocative essay "Psychoanalysis and Education: Teaching Terminable and Interminable." Drawing on the work of Jacques Lacan (the "French Freud"), Felman defines the unconscious as "precisely the discovery that human discourse can by definition never be entirely in agreement with itself, entirely identical to its knowledge of itself, since, as the vehicle of unconscious knowledge, it is constitutively the material locus of a signifying difference from itself."[59] Moreover, like Socrates, as Plato depicts the famous teacher in the *Meno*, psychoanalysis teaches, surprisingly enough, that "there is no such thing as teaching, only recollection."[60] Proceeding "not through linear progression, but through breakthroughs, leaps, discontinuities, regressions, and deferred action, the analytic learning-process puts . . . in question the traditional pedagogical belief in intellectual perfectibility, the progressistic view of learning as a simple one-way road from ignorance to knowledge."[61] In this formulation, teaching becomes not "the transmission of ready-made knowledge," as we often assume, but rather "the creation of a new *condition* of knowledge—the creation of an original learning-disposition," one that understands how ignorance is "an integral part of the very *structure* of knowledge," ignorance being inseparably "linked to what is *not remembered*" but repressed.[62] In analysis, as Felman explains, it is "out of the patient's active ignorance, out of the patient's speech which says much more than it itself knows, that the analyst will come to *learn* the *patient's own* unconscious *knowledge*, that knowledge which is inaccessible to itself because it cannot tolerate knowing that it knows; and it is the signifiers of this constitutively a-reflexive knowledge coming from the patient that the analyst *returns* to the patient from his different vantage point, from his non-reflexive, asymmetrical position as an Other." Making specific the connection with teaching, Felman argues that

the position of alterity is therefore indispensable: knowledge is what is already there, but always in the Other. Knowledge, in other words, is not a *substance* but a structural dynamic: it is not *contained* by any individual but comes about out of the mutual apprenticeship between two partially unconscious speeches which both say more than they know. Dialogue is thus the radical condition of learning and of knowledge, the analytically constitutive condition through which ignorance becomes structurally informative; knowledge is essentially, irreducibly dialogic.[63]

Somewhat like the classicist William Arrowsmith, writing from a very different perspective, Felman proceeds to deny that teaching is "a purely cognitive, informative experience"; it is, she asserts, "also an emotional, erotical experience." Moreover, Felman claims that it is "as of the moment the student recognizes that *learning has no term*, that he can himself become a teacher, assume the position of the teacher. But the position of the teacher is itself the position of *the one who learns*, of the one who *teaches* nothing other than *the way he learns*. The subject of teaching is interminably—a student; the subject of teaching is interminably—a learning." This, Felman concludes, "is the most radical, perhaps the most far-reaching insight psychoanalysis can give us into pedagogy."[64]

Among the important results of the application Felman makes of psychoanalysis to pedagogy is an understanding of the student–teacher relationship, often figured, unfortunately, as an opposition. In her words: "Psychoanalysis as teaching, and teaching as psychoanalysis, radically subvert the demarcation-line, the clear-cut opposition between the analyst and the analysand, between the teacher and the student (or the learner)—showing that what counts, in both cases, is precisely the transition, the struggle-filled *passage* from one position to the other. But," she quickly adds, "the passage is itself interminable; it can never be crossed once and for all." Not unrelated is another lesson psychoanalysis teaches: Like that of theory, "its *teaching* does not just reflect upon itself, but turns back upon itself so as to *subvert itself*, and truly *teaches* only insofar as it subverts itself. Psychoanalytic teaching," Felman perhaps extravagantly claims, "is pedagogically unique in that it is inherently, interminably, self-critical. Lacan's amazing pedagogical performance thus sets forth the unparalleled example of a teaching whose fecundity is tied up, paradoxically enough, with the inexhaustibility—the interminability—of its *self-critical potential*."[65] An interesting, if much less sophisticated, parallel to Felman's description of teaching as the creation of a "learning-disposition" occurs in the work of the priest/educator/writer Henri J. M. Nouwen, who believes that "we have paid too much attention to the content of teaching without realizing that the *teaching relationship* is the most important factor in . . . teaching." Though I applaud Father Nouwen's emphasis on "our fundamental human condition . . . as the foundation of all learning in which both students and teachers are involved," I do not want to privilege *either* the "teaching relationship" or "the content," since I believe them to be of equal importance.[66]

Agreeing with Felman that the "teaching relationship" is dialogical, I suggest that teaching, in its various aspects, involves not just a delicate balance between the (apparently competing) interests and needs of teacher and student but also a particular structure. Less committed to (Lacanian) psychoanalysis than Felman, whose account of teaching I do not pretend to follow in all its particulars, I would describe that structure as resembling Wordsworth's resolution, in a fine surmise, of "mutual domination" and "interchangeable supremacy" as occurring between the demands of, and the opportunities presented by, the forces of imagination and nature.[67] In teaching, that structure, which involves an oscillation of power and authority, entails the aggrandizement of neither student nor teacher, content nor form (or style), at the expense of the other. No master–slave relationship here, then. To put it differently: Teaching occurs in and as a play of differences that neither becomes absolute nor collapses into identity. (If at this point you are wondering whether I'm talking about teaching or theory, you have understood. My argument involves the claim that teaching consists of principles and strategies notably similar to those that characterize poststructuralist theory.)

Allow me now, please, to slip into something more comfortable, personal, and confessional and comment on my own experience as a teacher. The desire to do so, by the way, is not at all unusual, a number of writers finding it helpful to wax autobiographical in discussing theory and teaching (the reasons why are perhaps structural—as well as implicit in what I have already written).[68] At any rate, since I began working in a serious way with theory, about ten years ago, my teaching has improved markedly, in large part because, contrary to what happens to many (most?) teachers, I am now, after eighteen years in the classroom, much more interested in teaching. In my case, I may as well admit, teaching and theory have proceeded in conjunction with enlightened self-understanding to produce significant changes in the person that I am, one now far less (concerned with the) proper. Indeed, I maintain that theory and especially deconstruction deserve considerable credit for helping to effect those changes. My experience thus mounts a not insignificant challenge to the familiar, if mistaken, assumption that theory functions in a realm safely removed from the flesh and blood of quotidian existence and human suffering, which it supposedly never touches. It was only when theory jolted me into recognizing (Felman would say *re*-cognizing) that human beings exist *in*, *through*, and *as* a play of differences and a field of relations that I was able to break out of the pernicious trap of binary-oppositional thinking, which is ineluctably hierarchical and maintained by violence and in which self is always engaged in fierce competition with other. To quote Jonathan Culler writing on the relationality that Saussurean linguistics teaches, I had to become interested "not so much in the properties of individual objects or actions as in the differences between them."[69] Influenced by theory, I began to conceive of teaching as something other than and different from the (monological) communication of truth from "the one who knows" (I deliberately use the Lacanian terminology) to an ignorant, enslaved, and completely different other. Education then began to appear as a process of discovery, for teacher no less than student, in a situation involving the affective as well as the intellectual. To privilege the latter, if it entails sacrificing the affective, constitutes an act of disembodiment such as recent theory has not only tried to avoid but opposed. As theory teaches us in its interimplication with practice, there is no escaping the muck, mire, and muddle—the misery—of human existence, no way to avoid the meanness, recalcitrance, and—for all that—the beauty of human beings and their daily affairs. Theory and teaching alike involve us *in* texts and *with* each other, implicating us, whether we like it or not, in the very content we teach (and make). Not for the faint of heart, teaching comes fraught with risk but also with opportunity. Much the same can be said of theory.

In brief, theory effected certain changes of attitude in me. In teaching, of course, attitude is crucial, the teacher's attitude toward students, toward teaching itself, toward the texts studied having immeasurable if not determining effect upon the learning situation; and deconstruction in particular "inevitably involves a certain *attitude*, a word that bears the etymological inscription of 'action' and that, like *strategy*, is relatively free of the logocentric baggage of words such as *method, technique*, and *approach*." That attitude "is simultaneously both skeptical and tolerant, both questioning and affirmative."[70] Allowing me to see relations where mainly objects had appeared, theory eventually crumbled the hierarchization whereby I occupied the position of "the one who knows," without, however, allowing students to assume that vacated authority. Dialogue resulted, not in any cheap ed-school or touchy-feely sense, for in that, I think, the teacher is mainly manipulative, if no longer authoritarian. I refer, instead, to a teaching that is *personal*, the teacher as *person* engaged in a situation with other *persons* that can only be described, as Hartman has taught me via Wordsworth, as one of "mutual domination" or "interchangeable supremacy."

And so the teaching of theory? What, if anything, can you extract from my lucubrations that might bear on the undergraduate or graduate curriculum? Let me repeat, to begin with, that I share Culler's sense that theory represents a new, burgeoning, and significant genre deserving significant curricular recognition. I also share Hartman's view of the critical essay as being ironic in pretending only to be *about* literature and of the "mutually supportive, mutually dominating relation" that exists between "primary" text and "secondary." Teaching intellectual prose, such as the theory and criticism of Barthes, Benjamin, Derrida, and Hartman, among others, leads to an opening of the canon as it effectively questions rigid distinctions between "primary" and "secondary" texts and at the same time confronts students with large and important questions too long ignored in classrooms.

In my classes I exploit these notions concerning theory and the essay. I assume, moreover, that students come to classes in criticism and theory with preconceived notions (no one is a *tabula rasa*, of course), some valid, some not, about the difficulty of this abstract, abstruse stuff and that I must somehow help them to feel less intimidated. I must, in short, create both an effective "teaching relationship" and a "learning disposition." From the beginning, accordingly, I work on what educationists call classroom climate, trying to establish an atmosphere at once collegial and rigorous, professional and humane. No either/or choice here. Key to the goals I have in mind is humor. As the popular writer and former editor of the *Saturday Review* Norman Cousins has long maintained, laughter can be quite effective, even therapeutic. In the theory classroom, humor is particularly effective when it emerges from play *with* language. That play is itself an enormously important, though little-used, pedagogical device that directs students' attention *to* language. While—*mirabile dictu*—the students are having some fun, they are also becoming aware of the richness and equivocalness of language. Even when egregiously bad, as mine almost always are, puns directly illustrate that equivocalness, as well as allow us, if we wish, to consider Hamlet's belief that "we must speak by the card, or equivocation will undo us." Play, I thus suggest, is neither licentious nor irresponsible; rather, it is intimate with the weightiest concerns.

As I hope is obvious to my students, I enjoy criticism, I enjoy reading and teaching it, and I think I've had some success introducing others to its delights and pleasures. This stress on enjoyment has *in no way* diminished the quality of the work expected—*and* (thus?) performed—in my classes; on the contrary, it may have enhanced the quality. As Hartman writes, "instruction has to find a way to become art, a pleasurable and responsive activity."[71] In an effort, then, to teach students to read even more closely, and tapping literature students' interests, I insist that, and demonstrate how, criticism and theory may be read *as literature* and *for enjoyment*. Teasing metaphors, attending closely to structure, rhetorical patterns, and textual dynamics, we linger over style, brooding upon the letter, rather than rush to penetrate the text (with its sexual implications, the verb I've chosen is significant) and to transcend language in favor of spirit, idea, or meaning.[72] But even as I teach the literary nature of theoretical texts, I stress the theoretical and critical implications of literary texts, as my mention above of *Hamlet* was intended to suggest.

For a number of reasons, therefore, some of them deriving from my experience as a teacher, I believe that criticism and theory have a major role in the curriculum. I started to write "their own place," but that would identify and freeze them, constituting marginalization via establishment as just another field or area, one among many in the current curricular smorgasbord of literature and language offerings, confined, specialized, and pigeonholed. Better, then, a dissemination, with theory permeating the curriculum and working to make it conscious of its arbitrary and conventional nature, its history, and its function within the network of power relations that constitute our social being/our being social. Inveterately self-conscious, theory is allied with that sacred discontent that keeps us Western men and women forever unsettled.[73]

Notes

1. See the important study by Elizabeth W. Bruss, *Beautiful Theories: The Spectacle of Discourse in Contemporary Criticism* (Baltimore: Johns Hopkins University Press, 1982).
2. Geoffrey H. Hartman, *Criticism in the Wilderness: The Study of Literature Today* (New Haven: Yale University Press, 1980), p. 298.
3. Gregory S. Jay and David L. Miller, "The Role of Theory in the Study of Literature?" in their collection *After Strange Texts: The Role of Theory in the Study of Literature* (University: University of Alabama Press, 1985), pp. 3–4.
4. On framing, see Jacques Derrida, *La vérité en peinture* (Paris: Flammarion, 1978); and Barbara Johnson, "The Frame of Reference: Poe, Lacan, Derrida," *The Critical Difference: Essays in the Contemporary Rhetoric of Reading* (Baltimore: Johns Hopkins University Press, 1980), pp. 110–46. In *Professing Literature: An Institutional History* (Chicago: University of Chicago Press, 1987), Gerald Graff chronicles some of the effects of assuming that a text can be studied and taught "in itself."
5. Christopher Norris, *Deconstruction: Theory and Practice* (London: Methuen, 1982), p. 82.
6. See esp. Ezra Pound, *ABC of Reading* (New York: New Directions, 1960).
7. Jay and Miller, "Role of Theory," p. 2.
8. See, e.g., William E. Cain, *The Crisis in Criticism: Theory, Literature, and Reform in English Studies* (Baltimore: Johns Hopkins University Press, 1984); *Criticism in the University*, ed. Gerald Graff and Reginald Gibbons (Evanston, Ill.: Northwestern University Press, 1985); Terry Eagleton, *Literary Theory: An Introduction* (Minneapolis: University of Minnesota Press, 1983); and Paul A. Bové, *Intellectuals in Power: A Genealogy of Critical Humanism* (New York: Columbia University Press, 1986).
9. Cain, *Crisis in Criticism*, p. 247.
10. Howard Felperin, *Beyond Deconstruction: The Uses and Abuses of Literary Theory* (Oxford: Oxford University Press [Clarendon Press], 1985), pp. 1, 200, 211.
11. Paul de Man, "The Return to Philology," *The Resistance to Theory* (Minneapolis: University of Minnesota Press, 1986), p. 21.
12. Bate, quoted in de Man, "Return to Philology," p. 22. See also Bate's letter in *Critical Inquiry* 10 (1983): 365–70. Though various reactions to theory, and especially deconstruction, similar in tone and understanding to Bate's might be cited, I shall mention only that by James A. Winn, "Some Doubts about Deconstruction," *Scriblerian* 17 (1985): 117–21, a response to my essay "Going against the Grain: Deconstruction and the Scriblerians," in the same issue of that journal, pp. 113–17.
13. Bate, quoted in de Man, "Return to Philology," p. 22.
14. de Man, "Return to Philology," pp. 22–23. The reference to *Newsweek* concerns an ill-informed article that appeared there in 1981.
15. de Man, "The Resistance to Theory," *Resistance to Theory*, pp. 7, 12.
16. Ibid., pp. 7, 12–13.
17. Ibid., p. 17.
18. Ibid., pp. 19–20.
19. Steven Knapp and Walter Benn Michaels, "Against Theory," *Critical Inquiry* 8 (1982): 724, 742.
20. Ibid., p. 730.

21. Ibid., p. 723. For an excellent definition of theory, in line with that offered in this introduction, see Graff, *Professing Literature*, esp. pp. 252–53.

22. Knapp and Michaels, "Against Theory," p. 742.

23. Cain, *Crisis in Criticism*, p. 9, and Said, quoted in Cain, *Crisis in Criticism*, p. 9, from "Travelling Theory," reprinted in Edward Said, *The World, the Text, and the Critic* (Cambridge, Mass.: Harvard University Press, 1983), pp. 241–42.

24. Cain, *Crisis in Criticism*, pp. 247–48.

25. William E. Cain, "Reply to Lentricchia's 'On Behalf of Theory,' " in Graff and Gibbons, *Criticism in the University*, p. 222.

26. Cain, *Crisis in Criticism*, p. ix.

27. Cain, "Reply to Lentricchia's 'On Behalf of Theory,' " p. 222.

28. Daniel T. O'Hara, "Revisionary Madness: The Prospects of American Literary Theory at the Present Time," *Critical Inquiry* 9 (1983): 726.

29. See Robert Scholes, *Textual Power: Literary Theory and the Teaching of English* (New Haven: Yale University Press, 1985), esp. pp. 75 ff.

30. Jay and Miller, "Role of Theory," p. 17.

31. Felperin, *Beyond Deconstruction*, p. 213.

32. Ibid., p. 216.

33. Cain, *Crisis in Criticism*, p. 249.

34. Cain, "Reply to Lentricchia's 'On Behalf of Theory,' " pp. 221–22.

35. Ibid., p. 221.

36. Cain, *Crisis in Criticism*, p. 249.

37. Ibid., p. 256.

38. See G. Douglas Atkins, *Quests of Difference: Reading Pope's Poems* (Lexington: University Press of Kentucky, 1986), esp. pp. 1–15.

39. Cain, *Crisis in Criticism*, pp. 275, 273–74. Cf. Felperin, *Beyond Deconstruction*, pp. 1, 2, and "The Anxiety of Deconstruction," in *The Lesson of Paul de Man*, Yale French Studies, 69, ed. Peter Brooks, Shoshana Felman, and J. Hillis Miller (New Haven: Yale University Press, 1985), p. 265.

40. Frank Lentricchia, "On Behalf of Theory," in Graff and Gibbons, *Criticism in the University*, p. 106. See also Lentricchia, "On the Ideologies of Poetic Modernism, 1890–1913: The Example of William James," in *Reconstructing American Literary History*, ed. Sacvan Bercovitch (Cambridge, Mass.: Harvard University Press, 1986), pp. 220–49.

41. Hugh Kenner, writing about "the professional Popeans," in "In the Wake of the Anarch," *Gnomon: Essays on Contemporary Literature* (New York: McDowell, Obolensky, 1958), p. 176.

42. Lentricchia, "On Behalf of Theory," p. 107.

43. Ibid., p. 109.

44. Scholes, *Textual Power*, p. xi.

45. Jay and Miller, "Role of Theory," p. 6.

46. Ibid., p. 7. Several books have recently appeared relating theory and pedagogy, including Scholes, *Textual Power*; G. Douglas Atkins and Michael L. Johnson, eds., *Writing and Reading Differently: Deconstruction and the Teaching of Composition and Literature* (Lawrence: University Press of Kansas, 1985); and Cary Nelson, ed., *Theory in the Classroom* (Urbana: University of Illinois Press, 1986). See also Mary Ann Caws, ed., *Textual Analysis: Some Readers Reading* (New York: MLA, 1986); Chaviva Hosek and Patricia Parker, eds., *Lyric Poetry: Beyond New Criticism* (Ithaca, N.Y.: Cornell University Press, 1985); and Richard Machin and Christopher Norris, eds., *Post-Structuralist Readings of English Poetry* (Cambridge: Cambridge University Press, 1987). Finally, see Graff's important history of the profession, *Professing Literature*.

47. Hartman, *Criticism in the Wilderness*, p. 297.

48. Scholes, *Textual Power*, pp. 75–76.

49. Cain, *Crisis in Criticism*, p. xiv.

50. Hartman, *Criticism in the Wilderness*, p. 206.

51. Jonathan Culler, *On Deconstruction: Theory and Criticism after Structuralism* (Ithaca, N.Y.: Cornell University Press, 1982), p. 9.

52. See Hartman, *Criticism in the Wilderness*, e.g., pp. 5–6; and Paul H. Fry, *The Reach of Criticism: Method and Perception in Literary Theory* (New Haven: Yale University Press, 1983), esp. p. 200.

53. W. Wolfgang Holdheim, *The Hermeneutic Mode: Essays on Time in Literature and Literary Theory* (Ithaca, N.Y.: Cornell University Press, 1984), pp. 20, 21.

54. Cain, *Crisis in Criticism*, pp. 249, 276.

55. Graff and Gibbons, Preface, *Criticism in the University*, p. 7.

56. For elaboration on these points, see my *Reading Deconstruction/Deconstructive Reading* (Lexington: University Press of Kentucky, 1983).

57. See, e.g., Thomas J. J. Altizer et al., *Deconstruction and Theology* (New York: Crossroad, 1982); Mark C. Taylor, *Erring: A Postmodern A/theology* (Chicago: University of Chicago Press, 1984); Robert Magliola, *Derrida on the Mend* (West Lafayette, Ind.: Purdue University Press, 1984); and various of my essays forthcoming in a volume on relations of literature and religion "in the wake of deconstruction."

58. Atkins and Johnson, *Writing and Reading Differently*. Jasper Neel's book is *Plato, Derrida, and Writing* (Carbondale: Southern Illinois University Press, 1988). See also Gregory L. Ulmer, *Applied Grammatology: Post(e)-Pedagogy from Jacques Derrida to Joseph Beuys* (Baltimore: Johns Hopkins University Press, 1984).

59. Shoshana Felman, "Psychoanalysis and Education: Teaching Terminable and Interminable," in *The Pedagogical Imperative: Teaching as a Literary Genre*, Yale French Studies, 63, ed. Barbara Johnson (New Haven: Yale University Press, 1982), p. 28.

60. Plato, *Meno*, quoted in Felman, "Psychoanalysis and Education," p. 21.

61. Felman, "Psychoanalysis and Education," p. 27.

62. Ibid., pp. 31, 29.

63. Ibid., pp. 32, 33.

64. Ibid., pp. 35, 37. For Arrowsmith's view, see "Mediating the Classics: A Conversation with William Arrowsmith," *CEA Forum* 15 (1985): 1–7.

65. Felman, "Psychoanalysis and Education," pp. 38, 39.

66. Henri J. M. Nouwen, *Creative Ministry* (1971; New York: Doubleday, 1978), pp. 5 (italics added), 19.

67 This interpretation of Wordsworth, with all its rich suggestiveness, derives from Geoffrey Hartman's *Wordsworth's Poetry, 1787–1814* (New Haven: Yale University Press, 1964).

68. See, e.g., Gerald L. Bruns, "Literary Study without Aims or Methods," *ADE Bulletin* 81 (1985): 26–31.

69. Jonathan Culler, *Structuralist Poetics: Structuralism, Linguistics, and the Study of Literature* (Ithaca, N.Y.: Cornell University Press, 1975), pp. 10–11.

70. Atkins and Johnson, *Writing and Reading Differently*, p. 11.

71. Hartman, *Criticism in the Wilderness*, p. 2.

72. For an excellent analysis of the metaphors we use, and the implications they bear, see Keith Fort, "The Psychopathology of the Everyday Language of the Profession of Literary Studies," *College English* 40 (1979): 751–63.

73. Cf. Herbert N. Schneidau, *Sacred Discontent: The Bible and Western Tradition* (Baton Rouge: Louisiana State University Press, 1976).

JOHN R. WILLINGHAM

The New Criticism: Then and Now

The term *formalism*, broad if not ambiguous, refers to the many critical dogmas and related "practical criticism" that accompanied the sea change from Anglo-American romanticism to the modernist avant-garde. Typically, formalism asserts the autonomy of the artifact, the preeminence of form and style over relationships of the work to "life," and the irrelevance of older doctrines like mimesis or any idea that poetry's highest value is its reflection of the "real world." Emphasizing *form* as what Mark Schorer memorably called "achieved content," the twentieth-century formalists have opposed the separation of form and content. From epistemological bases in Kant and Coleridge and with the examples of Poe and Henry James often on their minds, they have erected systems upon idealistic concepts of the imagination and organic form, asserting the superiority of the language of art to that of science because art "transcends the limitations which are constitutionally a part of the language of science."[1] Within such a context, questions of form and technique become paramount if not exclusive, for they embrace the special structures achieved only in art. By fiat, implication, or practice, formalists try to resist tainting the aesthetic dimension by moralism, didacticism, or intellectualism; their central concern is only *form*, the unifying principle within the work.

Emerging in London as early as 1907, out of the somewhat thin air of Pound's protomodernist effusions, formalism prospered throughout the first half of this century and dominated Anglo-American critical discourse for twenty-five years, since about 1935. Its major practitioners include T. S.

Eliot, I. A. Richards, John Crowe Ransom, Allen Tate, Robert Penn Warren, Cleanth Brooks, and William K. Wimsatt; often the names of Yvor Winters, Kenneth Burke, R. P. Blackmur, F. R. Leavis, and William Empson are added, although the case for these five critics is fraught with abundant qualifications and their influence on "practical criticism" has been relatively slight. Ransom and the other American, or Southern, "New Critics" became familiar names, especially in academic parlance, and their critical theories and approaches apparently continue to guide, to "correct" classroom literary study.

All twentieth-century formalism has generally responded to intense pressures for explanations of Anglo-American avant-garde works, the modernist anthology or canon, and to derive from those explanations some coherent theoretical core. Such drives appear in the conversations of the Poets' Club in London about 1907, especially in the dicta of T. E. Hulme, F. S. Flint, and Ezra Pound. Pound from the beginning of his campaign sought to force dramatic changes in English poetry, to justify repudiation of threadbare romanticism ("spilled religion," Hulme called it) and decadent Victorianism (a deadly amalgam of predictable technique and tiresome didacticism). Apparently no one noticed the paradoxical denunciation of romanticism despite heavy leaning on its poetics.

Nevertheless, the resulting theory, the fragmentary cumulations under Pound's hand, was doggedly formalistic and at least partly Coleridgean. In Pound's Imagist "manifesto" in *Poetry* (January 1913), the doctrine of the Image announced the priority of formal considerations—"direct treatment of the 'thing,'" rigid economy in diction, organic rhythm, and the "image" itself, a highly charged fusion of idea and emotion—as the proper goal of the poet. Impatient with details of exposition or professional protocols and pressed for time to write his own ambitious, exploratory poems, however, Pound as theorist settled for aphoristic bits and pieces and simply promised that the new poetry would supply ample models of what "the age demanded."

Eliot, with tidier habits and academic stance, reworked some of Pound's elliptical pronouncements, aligning them with his own disdain for romanticism, acquired mainly from Irving Babbitt at Harvard, from French symbolism mediated by Remy de Gourmont, and from his own discoveries as he worked out his poems before 1920 and the many essays he wrote in England. For Eliot, such combination was salutary, as is shown in his "position papers" in *The Egoist* and later in *The Criterion*, in which Eliot synthesized the London "vortex" of 1915–20.

Eliot's critical prose nearly always focused upon a single work or author;

but the focus was reinforced by naming and defining basic modernist concepts like "tradition," "objective correlative," and "dissociation of sensibility"; by urging poets to ransack non-English literature for techniques; by advocating the poet's duty of "stealing" from other poets to gain a heavily allusive texture; by proclaiming the elevation of the English metaphysical poets and the consequent dismissal of Milton and Shelley; by persuading his readers to make the "correct" response to religious poetry and to see criticism as creative union with artists and the literary tradition as a simultaneous order. Eventually Eliot, of course, became the guru of modernist formalism; and every other critic would have to reckon with, if not defer to, Eliot's perspectives and to treat Eliot's poems as particularly privileged. His adroit irony further enhanced his appeal to other modernists. But even Eliot produced no systematic theory, no "practical" system for close, critical reading of texts.

About a decade after Pound's first literary high jinks in Kensington and alongside Eliot's emergence from obscurity, I. A. Richards began at Cambridge experiments linking psychology and literature, focusing on the *act* of reading poetry and the degree of success the reader objectively might claim in achieving what Richards called "balanced poise." To some degree foreshadowing reader-response theory, Richards's investigations seemingly offered solid ground for at last a more "scientific" analysis of poetry. Collecting, classifying, and defining his subject-readers' responses to texts he had chosen, Richards developed in the 1920s the foundation for an otherwise absent "practical criticism" (a term later to be synonymous largely with New Critical "explication" and the title of Richards's most influential treatise on the analysis of poetry). In controlled experiments with students at Cambridge, Richards asked them to record faithfully their responses to "neutral texts" (unfamiliar poems without identification of authors, dates, or oddities of spelling and punctuation). Out of their responses, Richards sifted and identified the problems poems present to readers—problems of interpretation and of relationships between techniques and meanings. He identified the most successful texts as "poetry of inclusion," which, he said, is inevitably characterized by the presence of an "irony" that allows successful readers to reach a state of "internal equilibrium" or "synaesthesia."[2]

In *Practical Criticism* (1929), Richards identified for readers the levels of meaning in particular texts; kinds of problems readers of varying abilities encounter; use or misuse by poets of their creative liberty; the poet's deference or indifference to readers; relationships of thought and emotion; implications of variant readings; and, above all, benefits of meticulous scrutiny of texts. He warned against naive faith in the poet's "intention," superficial awareness of techniques, or expectations of results.[3] Ultimately, said Richards, poetry might replace religion—a kind of "positivism" abhorrent to Eliot.[4] Richards did not burden his readers with any arcane critical vocabulary; he simply and gracefully endorsed and demonstrated critical exactness based in the details of the text.

More than a decade after his important work lay behind him and still without a strong following, Richards was identified by John Crowe Ransom as *the* "psychological critic" but denied, along with all the critics Ransom discussed in *The New Criticism* (1941), the stature of "ontological" or complete critic. Among Richards's shortcomings, Ransom pointed out his emphasis upon the reader's feelings and his admitted failure to settle on a method for analyzing the "opposed impulses" within the "poetry of inclusion."[5]

But even as Richards was setting up his first experiments and in mutual unawareness, a beast in Nashville, Tennessee, was poised to spring. For in 1919 three enthusiastic teachers of English at Vanderbilt University, a fluctuating number of bookish townsmen, and eventually some bright undergraduates formed a little club to discuss topics of mutual, mainly philosophical, interest. These were the "Fugitives" of later renown. Gradually their discussions began to narrow to poetry and, finally, to the writing and criticism of their own poems. The senior faculty member, Ransom, shortly became the central figure.

Although he had drifted into teaching English instead of philosophy, his major in college, and lacked the usual academic background for a scholar-teacher of English literature, Ransom had long been thinking about and writing poetry. About 1912, while reading philosophy as a Rhodes scholar at Oxford, Ransom had become intrigued by what he saw as a crucial but generally unremarked dichotomy between a poem's subject and its sounds (as tallied in diction, meter, and rhyme)—a duality always to be a central part of his own poetics and therefore naturally discussed by the club members. This preoccupation with poetry's dualities would be common as well to the formation of the critical school of "New Criticism," though usually the other members of the group emphasized some means of resolution for the duality.

Between 1920 and 1925, even as he was writing his few most memorable poems—"Blue Girls," "Captain Carpenter," "Bells for John Whiteside's Daughter," "Necrological," "The Equilibrists," and "Dead Boy"—Ransom solidified his serious commitment to the aims of the Fugitives by his theoretical insights rather than his creativity. One can scarcely avoid suspecting that all along Ransom's poems, fine as they are, were for him primarily experiments for testing and refining a poetics forming for him since about 1912. Once their purpose was achieved, he seemed to lose interest in his poems despite considerable praise from their readers and turned exclusively to critical prose.

The group's distinguished little magazine, *The Fugitive*, published between 1922 and 1925, required editorial duties of all the club members. Consequently, all perforce wrote on occasion short quasi-critical editorials and essays, which reflect the cumulative refinements in discussing their own and others' poems. In a series of articles under the collective title of "The Future of Poetry" (1924), Ransom formulated his basic ideas and an approach to criticism reflecting not only the mode of club discussions but a classroom manner—that of the subtly questioning *eiron*. Sounding sometimes like a testy Frost, he professed serious reservations about the abandonment by Imagists, Amygists, and "prairie poets" of traditional conventions, particularly meter. He was now ready to declare publicly that successful poetry has a dual nature: It produces "tension" between "logical sequence" (i.e., meaning) and "objective pattern" (sounds). Although clearly distinct, these two parts of the poem coexist successfully only through the "miracle," which occurs with "the adaptation of the free inner life to the outward necessity of things."[6] By "miracle," Ransom clearly meant something like what most New Critics would later call "form." Ransom's insistence upon duality in poetry was to remain basic for him and set him accordingly apart from the later, younger New Critics, occasionally causing disagreements between him and the others. He anticipated a basic aversion of all the New Critics toward "microscopic analysis" of a poem for meaning alone, as if the poem were prose and had no "metrical distractions."[7] (Later, the New Critics would call such sole concern with "meaning" "the heresy of paraphrase.")

A little earlier, in a review of Eliot's *Waste Land* for the *New York Post* in 1923, Ransom had advanced another principle adumbrating later New Criticism—the insistence that there is a profound distinction between the processes of art with their reliance upon the imagination and those of science with their incessant drive toward abstraction.[8] In a testy, public exchange with Tate after the review appeared, Ransom made the distinction even more emphatic: Poetry, he declared, should never have as its primary goal the "pure presentation of ideas and sensations."[9]

Allen Tate, then still an undergraduate studying under Ransom and Donald Davidson, almost immediately after joining the Fugitives in 1921 took up the role of gadfly, especially to Ransom. Even after Tate had received his degree and left Nashville, he would force Ransom in exchanged letters to clarify ideas but also to grumble rather helplessly about youthful zeal and resentment of former masters. Tate discovered French symbolism and the work of Eliot for the Fugitives and thereby brought into the Nashville ferment the avant-garde of London and, later, New York. By 1923 Tate had written two or three successful poems; and when one was published in *The Double Dealer*, elicited a letter of praise from Hart Crane observing Tate's apparent debt to Eliot, who was as yet quite unknown to the Nashville group. Tate immediately acquired and responded with delight to Eliot's poems, becoming overnight an ardent disciple of the London "vortex." As a convert to Eliotic irony, allusiveness, textural density, and preference for metaphysical poetry and Jacobean drama and dramatic lyric, Tate found not only his own direction as poet and critic but also the compulsion to convert his fellow Fugitives.

Tate's intense partisanship led to the rift with Ransom over the latter's disapproving review of *The Waste Land*, in which he denounced the betrayal of Eliot's own prescriptions for form and the example of modernism's flagrant indifference to meter and traditional techniques generally. The ensuing heated exchange not only divided old friends for a time but also underscores the lasting distinction between the essentially conservative Ransom and the younger Fugitives and future New Critics. Ransom always preferred traditional conventions; the others, including Brooks, who joined the group after the breakup of the Fugitive Club, found that they shared ideas and attitudes with expatriate camps in London and Paris.

During the remainder of the 1920s, however, the Fugitives and reinforcements like Brooks and Andrew Lytle supplemented literary intensity with the defense of the South against what they interpreted as Northern subversion and the gradual replacement of the Southern way of life by the "American way," attuned to capitalism and industrialism and consequent enmity toward traditional Southern culture. Out of the Fugitive stage had come, despite some amateurishness and controversy, general agreement about the dangers of an industrial order to poetry and art generally. Moreover, the Nashville poets began to associate their literary principles—technical integrity in poetry, the necessity of structure, a preference for the lyric mode and the ironic manner— with the "Southern way" they had all grown up with. They saw parallels between manners and meters, the agrarian life and religious values, precision in art and cultural integrity—all imperiled by a baneful "American way."

Identified in the early 1930s as the "Southern Agrarians" because of their spirited defense of the South, the former Fugitives and future New Critics now embraced economic and social issues. They tried to point out that only a homogeneous culture like the South's, which honored tradition and rural life, could offer a favorable climate for the imagination, poetry, and religion. Only in the South could the correct relationship between God and man, between man and nature, between the individual and society exist and encourage the free play of the imagination, checked only by religion, tradition, and a code of manners. In *The Critique of Humanism* and the rather belligerent "manifesto," *I'll Take My Stand* (both in 1930), the Agrarians pro tem challenged the forces they saw as enemies—the Marxists, the New Dealers, the neohumanists, the "boosters" of a mongrelized "New South," and representatives of the "American tradition" claiming their descent from Emerson and Whitman—and by association lambasted liberalism, impressionism, sentimental "appreciation," and journalistic superficiality. This short period of intense regional piety (it was over by 1935) was good preparation for the Nashville group's metamorphosis as New Critics: Their unity had been reinforced, and their sense of duty to Southern letters (specifically, to themselves) found them ready for serious criticism and pedagogy as antidotes to a national pursuit of mediocrity.

Moreover, discovering in rather short order that neither the South nor the nation at large felt much need for their socioeconomic leadership, the former Fugitives turned again to specifically literary preoccupations and to academic careers. As ardent pedagogues by the mid-1930s, they sought but could not find suitable textbooks for the courses in literary studies that they were assigned to teach, especially introductory courses to the literary genres. Brooks and Warren accordingly chose to write their own materials for their classes. Thus the mimeograph machines at Louisiana State University brought forth the first versions of a line of distinguished, exemplary textbooks, of which *Understanding Poetry* (1938) and *Understanding Fiction* (1941) were the first.

Brooks's extended essay about contemporary poetry, *Modern Poetry and the Tradition* (1939), begun while he was still at Oxford and including the work of his old friends at Vanderbilt, appeared appropriately as a kind of prospectus for the New Criticism and for the textbooks he and the others would write. The timing was perfect for the alliance of impressive pedagogical pragmatism and scholarly theoretical substance—and for a quiet revolution in the study and teaching of literature at American colleges and universities. Literary studies have never been the same.

The series of textbooks—unpretentious, well-written, sequential, pragmatic—persuaded students and teachers to pay closer attention to the language of literary texts; to form habits of identifying and justifying their identifications of tone, mood, voice, metaphors and symbols; to perceive how formalizing principles unify content and meaning; to share the creative process that brought the work into existence; and to celebrate organic wholeness when it was discovered. Even the latest edition of *Understanding Poetry*—the fourth, in 1976—still asserts the original aim:

To begin with as full an immersion in the poem as possible; to continue by raising inductive questions that lead students to examine the material, the method, and their relations in the poem—that is, to make an appeal to students' "understanding" of the poetic process; then to return students as far as possible to the innocent immersion—but now with a somewhat instructed innocence to make deeper appreciation possible. [10]

The final incomplete comparison seems deliberate: Such responsible, sometimes rigorous study of a poem gives students (and teachers!) more insight into its formal dynamics than can any other approach, especially an approach that leaves the student with merely a "set of cliches that may be parroted about any poem."[11]

In the foreword to chapter 1, "Dramatic Situations," the authors distinguish between journalistic or historical treatment of human experience and the "form" that only poetry may confer. This distinction strengthens and clarifies the contrast between poetry and science observed by Ransom early in the Fugitive years. Brooks and Warren argue that "form does more than 'contain' the poetic stuff: it organizes it; it shapes it; it defines its meaning." Indeed, their whole critical system becomes an extension of that central concept of "form" permeating *Understanding Poetry*.

Brooks and Warren place the burden of careful reading and interpretation directly upon the student, who with some nudging by the editorial apparatus must work incrementally toward the integration of all technical features by and into form, the "governing idea of the massive unity of the good poem." Searching questions surround poems carefully selected by the author-critic-pedagogues to reveal special properties of poetry—analogical language (metaphor and symbol), theme, tone, dramatic structure, and so on; to the book's appendixes are relegated concern with the poet's "intention" and metrics (far less important here than in Ransom's theory). Throughout the book appear concise instances of the kind of critical analysis, incrementally more complex, ultimately expected of the student. *Understanding Poetry* is another American "how-to-do-it" manual; and by way of emphasizing the necessity of the student's finally becoming independent of book and teacher, Brooks and Warren present an abundance of poems without editorial apparatus or pedagogical nudge (perhaps a recognition of Richards's effort) as materials for which students will construct their own analyses and interpretations. *Under-*

standing Poetry is unremittingly student-centered: The teacher's role is assumed to be that of the patient, quizzical, genial *eiron* (like Ransom at Vanderbilt), who almost imperceptibly guides the initiate toward the understanding and *discovery* of form.

Understanding Fiction (third edition, 1971) has always seemed less intense, less stylized, less adroit, even less consistent about the primacy of form, than its predecessor. It is more obviously an anthology; and the authors have less to say about the properties of fiction than they had about lyric poetry. Its intensity and precision, indeed its unique success, reinforces the frequent charge that the New Criticism is grounded in a poetics of lyric and that its application to other genres, fiction and drama, is often seemingly forced. After all, the foundations of the New Criticism came from the table talk of practicing poets and devotees of poetry, of whom only two—Warren and Tate—ever wrote fiction. Nevertheless, Brooks and Warren again tried to lead students (and their teachers) to discover *how* literary works *mean* by questions and brief discussions. Perhaps the strongest testimonial to the worth of *Understanding Fiction* is the endless stream of textbooks introducing fiction for freshmen and sophomores by other hands that have followed it. Moreover, early imitations came from ardent disciples of the New Criticism—for example, *The Art of Modern Fiction* (1949) by Robert Wooster Stallman—and from old friends—*The House of Fiction* (1950) by Caroline Tate with her then husband, Allen Tate.

With their two successful textbooks (followed by the collaboration of Brooks and Robert B. Heilman in *Understanding Drama* in 1948), Brooks and Warren had naturalized criticism in the college classroom, an impressive feat from any perspective and without previous parallel in the United States. They had created and packaged a totally new way of approaching literature that was pedagogically sound, attractive, pragmatic, productive of analysis, and to an impressive degree self-teaching. They made New Criticism famous by 1940, and they made responsible, painstaking analysis of literary texts the central, most attractive feature of English studies at both undergraduate and graduate levels. And they set off a burgeoning academic industry in literary studies that scholarly societies and journals alone never could have effected.

By the mid-1940s, as veterans of World War II swarmed onto campuses and into graduate programs in literary studies, young English faculty (many of them veterans too) were enthusiastically promoting and using the textbooks of Brooks and Warren or their imitators and the classroom devotion to the analysis of literary texts they sanctioned. New quarterlies espousing the New Criticism sprang up: At Baton Rouge, Brooks and Warren coedited the new *Southern Review*, established in 1936; Ransom founded and edited the *Kenyon Review* (1939); older journals such as the *Sewanee Review*, *South Atlantic Quarterly*, and *Virginia Quarterly Review* welcomed all the New Critics as contributors. In 1940 the *Southern Review* and the *Kenyon Review* jointly featured a symposium on the revolution in criticism and teaching methods in literary studies.

Special summer schools in English spread the principles and critical methodology of the Southern New Critics, explication, to faculty and graduate students from all over the United States. Enrollments in English courses increased sharply after 1945, and the waning of positivistic "scholarship"— philology, literary biography and history, and influence tracing—became a rout by the end of the forties. Criticism, now not only dominant in the classroom but also increasingly defiant of traditional scholarship, soon invaded conservative journals like *PMLA*, *Modern Philology*, and *American Literature*. The New Criticism competed with philology and history and usually won at regional and national meetings of the scholarly societies.

In the 1940s Cleanth Brooks appeared to be the quintessential New Critic, as even he has ruefully acknowledged in a recent essay.[12] In addition to collaborating on the textbooks, coediting the *Southern Review*, writing essays for the other quarterlies, and being increasingly the spokesman for New Criticism at professional and scholarly meetings, Brooks wrote two major statements of the new poetics, the previously mentioned *Modern Poetry and the Tradition* (1939) and *The Well Wrought Urn* (1947). In the first, he was anxious to connect his old friends, the Fugitive poets, with the work of Richards and Eliot and the "great tradition" of English poetry and to promote what Frank Lentricchia identifies as "an idealistic theory of [literary] history through Eliot's notion of 'unified sensibility.' "[13] The chapters develop and synthesize not only Brooks's ideas but those of others he had adopted after his undergraduate days at Vanderbilt (i.e., since 1925): from Ransom, the view of poetry as the complex language of complex experience, the distinctions between abstract science and concrete poetry, and irony as the indispensable stance; from Tate, a Poesque insistence on meticulous craftsmanship and scorn of allegory; and from Eliot, the dramatic possibilities of the lyric, the poet's impersonality, and wit as the guarantee of seriousness.[14] Tate later spoke in admiring wonder at Brooks's remarkable achievement in writing the book: It was, he said, a surprising but convincing synthesis of Eliot, Richards, Ransom, and Tate himself, which could not have been believed possible and which only Brooks could have brought off.[15] Bradbury has called the book "all but indispensable for the comprehension of the ways and means of aesthetic formalist criticism."[16] A half-century later it still strikes us as a remarkably good study and, if one must choose among the many excellent critical works of the New Critics, it is the most satisfactory exhibit of the most influential critical movement of this century in the United States.

By 1942, when he turned to work on *The Well Wrought Urn* (1947), Brooks was no longer a junior camp follower of the Nashville Fugitives and Agrarians but the most systematic, committed, comprehensive exponent of New Criticism. His position, curiously and perhaps pointedly unremarked by Ransom in *The New Criticism*, turned out to be something of a boon, for it allowed him to distance his version of New Critical strategy and his authority from Ransom's. Clearly, Brooks seems in *The Well Wrought Urn* to have escaped Ransom's insistence on the "ontology" of the poem, the duality of structure and texture, or the superiority of Donne to Shakespeare. In minimizing what Ransom had called "logical unity" (and what Yvor Winters had called "rational meaning"), Brooks stresses "imaginative unity" and warns against the "heresy of paraphrase." Characteristically, he insists that the "language of paradox" inevitably appears in mature poetry as the means by which a poem achieves structural unity.[17] Brooks, already perhaps sensitive to charges that the New Critics were indifferent to or did not know literary history, took pains in this second treatise to include representative poets of each literary era since the Middle Ages: Shakespeare, Milton, Herrick, Pope, Gray, Wordsworth, Keats, Tennyson, and Yeats. Each poem he considers is "successful," because Brooks's analysis inevitably uncovers the presence of irony, paradox, ambiguity, dramatic context, and organic structure. Structural unity of a poem, he assures us, lies in its "unification of attitudes into a hierarchy, subordinated to a total and governing attitude."[18] "Attitude" thus becomes the emphatic control of all other features, the local equivalent of *form*, in his masterful disclosure of dramatic context in Keats's "Ode on a Grecian Urn."

Although the theory of New Criticism was complete with *The Well Wrought Urn*, Brooks turned even more noticeably toward literary history in *The Poems of Mr. John Milton* (1951), which he and John Edward Hardy edited and for which they wrote analytical commentary on the individual poems. This work has been apparently, perhaps deliberately, overlooked by foes of the New Criticism eager to make the familiar, reductive charge that the New Critics ignore or do not know literary history and cannot cope with "scholarship." Brooks further demonstrated his respect for and command of literary history with *Literary Criticism: A Short History* (1957), written with William K. Wimsatt; in his two volumes on Faulkner in 1963 and 1978; and in his multivolume edition of the letters of Thomas Percy. Such use of traditional scholarship surprises only those who fail to look beneath the surface of the writings of the New Critics or who know only the work of some of their less responsible disciples. All of the Nashville group had rigorously and thoroughly studied literary history and consequently buttressed their critical writing with historical detail whenever they wished; they opposed only the usurpation of texts by literary history and its substitution for close reading and painstaking analysis.

Throughout the New Criticism's long hegemony, Ransom was, at least to "watchers" of New Critics, the conservative voice, if not always the preferred spokesman. Two others from the Fugitive period—Warren and Tate—became increasingly vocal. In the 1930s Warren wrote two essays on Southern poets: one about Ransom's facility with irony; the other, comparing John Gould Fletcher's poetry with Davidson's and Ransom's. Fletcher, also a Southerner but a follower of Amy Lowell's reductive Imagism, wrote inferior verse, said Warren, because he lacked the technical grasp of irony and therefore failed to give "structure" to emotion and ended up with a poetry of "almost pure texture."[19] Davidson, though not an "ironist," gives the effect of "shock and desperation" and therefore must be given to "ironic contemplation." But Ransom's poetry succeeds because of his technical assurance—as we might expect, his skill with irony.[20] The old Fugitive predilection for irony had become a cardinal principle of New Criticism.

In the 1940s, in an essay contrasting "pure poetry" (that which "tries to be pure by excluding, more or less rigidly, certain elements which might qualify or contradict its original impulses") and "impure poetry" (that which willingly and generously complicates its entire context with the wide range of complex human experience, thus necessarily summoning irony), Warren, like Brooks before him, and the Fugitives before Brooks, expressed his wholehearted agreement with the New Critical conviction that irony is the best guarantor of sincerity and vision.[21] Still later, Warren too appears to have been somewhat anxious to demonstrate his command of conventional scholarly procedure; hence his long essay appended to a handsome edition of *The Rime of the Ancient Mariner*, illustrated by Alexander Calder.[22] Commending *The Rime* as "a poem of pure imagination," Warren surveyed all the available scholarship on the poem to show that it had been seriously misinterpreted as lacking "meaning" or, worse, as embodying allegory; he argued that the poem is, however, "thoroughly consistent with Coleridge's basic theological and philosophical views as given to us in [his] sober prose, and that, without regard to the question of self-consciousness on the part of the poet at any given moment of composition, the theme is therefore 'intended.' "[23] Armed with impeccable, even formidable scholarly apparatus—notes on Coleridge's life and abundant references to scholarship about Coleridge's canon—Warren unfolded a detailed analysis of the poem's symbolic system to bolster his discovery that indeed the Mariner's journey, far from being either allegorical or meaningless as interpreted by the scholars innocent of New Criticism, is a tightly, richly organized "paradoxical process" of the creative experience.[24] The essay of course evoked anger and derision from "the scholars" but served notice that New Critics did not feel obliged to limit themselves to the text but were quite capable of using "traditional" resources as they chose to strengthen explication.

As I stressed earlier, it was Allen Tate who established and strengthened the crucial link between the Fugitives in Tennessee and the modernists in London, Paris, and New York. His poetry and his other prose (he wrote two novels and two biographies) garnered adequate though restrained critical attention; but as literary commentator and critic—actually, man of letters— he has been highly respected. As poet, he is remembered mainly for "Ode to the Confederate Dead," which he finally and notoriously had to explicate. As critic he was somewhat limited by his regional and philosophical prejudices, as in the case of his vicious attack on Hart Crane's *Bridge*, which Tate really did not understand and to which he curiously neglected to apply the principles or methodology of the New Criticism (Crane, he said, was simply allied with the wrong literary gang—Emerson, Whitman, etc.).

Tate defined one useful New Critical concept—that of "tension" in poetry—which resembles Ransom's notion of opposition between "structure" and "texture," Brooks's emphasis on "paradox" and "irony," and Warren's distinction between "pure" and "impure" poetry. But Tate's term and its application point more precisely to the healthy balance between a poem's "extension" (the body of abstraction, denotation, and literalness) and its "intension" (the concrete, the connotative, and the figurative details).

No account of the New Criticism and its immense (and, I believe, continuing) contribution to the prosperity of literary studies since World War II would be complete without mention of two late arrivals and major allies, William K. Wimsatt and René Wellek, both colleagues of Brooks's after he moved from Louisiana State University to Yale in 1947. Wellek, a distinguished literary historian, comparativist, scholar, and critic of critics, endorsed the New Criticism in his and Austin Warren's *Theory of Literature* (1949)—for two decades a basic textbook for graduate students in English— by praising an "intrinsic," or contextual, approach in literary studies over "extrinsic," clearly inferior biographical, historical, sociological, or psychological approaches. There and elsewhere Wellek lent his immense prestige to the clarification of terminology and issues in ways clearly favorable to the New Criticism.

Wimsatt helped by elaborating upon, with Monroe C. Beardsley in *The Verbal Icon* (1954), the "affective fallacy" and the "intentional fallacy," both of constant, often implicit, concern to the New Critics. Moreover, in *Literary Criticism: A Short History* (1957), written in collaboration with Brooks, Wimsatt, who wrote twenty-five of the thirty-two chapters, adroitly persuades his reader to agree that formalistic criticism is the desired end toward which all earlier critical theory has been tending. He tries to bolster formalistic considerations by drawing an analogy between the poem as reconciliation of opposites in its text to an understanding of the dogma of the Incarnation.

Something also should be added about the roles of Yvor Winters and William Empson in New Criticism's heyday. Both are often associated with the movement, largely because Ransom included them in his purview called *The New Criticism* (which, however, declared that *the* New Critic had yet to appear). Winters can hardly be called a "compleat formalist" because of his demand that a critic is obliged to discover the "best poems" of all time, that the poet *must* make good sense and thus avoid technical arcana like Eliot's or Hopkins's. Moreover, as Hart Crane discovered traumatically, Winters took for the critic's duty the detection and denunciation of a poet's "immoral" tendencies.

Empson, Richards's student at Cambridge and excited by the work of Robert Graves and Laura Riding in analyzing "in word-by-word collaboration" English poems written since 1918, turned to the kind of scrupulous analysis we find in *Seven Types of Ambiguity* (1930), in which he, indeed formalistically, probed for tensions between words and for clues to structure. Subsequently, however, Empson found Marxist and Freudian issues quite as intriguing as formal considerations. And neither Winters nor Empson ever became resources for the classroom. F. R. Leavis is sometimes called a New Critic, but he was really always *sui generis* in practical criticism, and his idiosyncracy may be gauged by his enthusiasm for Lawrence and hostility to Joyce. Substantially, we are left with the Nashville group and their best disciples, almost altogether teachers and students, as the definitive voices of the New Criticism.

These days—since the early 1970s—formalism, especially the New Criticism, is often patronized and sometimes ridiculed. It has been declared intellectually naive and methodologically fruitless. Its putative aversion to extrinsic, extratextual, possibilities for illuminating the literary work (the old charge of omission of history and biography from the 1930s and 1940s); indifference to author and reader; undemocratic and elitist aura and protection of the teacher against the hapless student; ruthless drive to demonstrate organic unity; "privileging" of Elizabethan, metaphysical, and modernist lyric poetry; employment of mysterious terms (presumably, like *structure*, *tension*, *tone*, and *texture*)—all these charges are solemnly leveled and elaborated. Perhaps worst of all, the New Criticism has been called "boring" because it is tied to one interpretation, discourages students who do not perceive or care about a "right reading" or the process of responsible reading, finds irony, ambiguity, and paradox in unlikely places. It discourages students by requiring close reading. And it does not allow for "creativity" of the reader.

The vast, seemingly obvious, contributions by the New Critics to literary studies are increasingly denied or simply unmentioned. Perhaps many partisans of other approaches simply do not perceive that only after the New Criticism flowered did academic "literary" sovereignties—departments of English, modern languages, comparative literature, women's studies, black studies, even biblical studies—undertake some significant degree of literary discipline, flourish, and become bustling academic empires at the universities. The climate for the proliferation of scholarly associations, literary journals, foundations, and grants supporting literary scholars and endless projects in research is, in large part, the legacy of the New Criticism, which makes possible the kind of speculation and textual studies emerging as structuralism, reader response, and deconstruction. If their demand for responsibility in reading and interpretation be seen as authoritarian, then the New Critics may be fairly called "undemocratic," but so may be any critical discipline requiring rigorous attention to words and their often mysterious interplay.

Late in these years of its "eclipse," the New Criticism has been defended, effectively and appropriately, by its most enduring spokesman, Brooks himself. As in any respectable New Critical statement, the critic (unlike most structuralists and poststructuralists) turns quickly away from theory and toward explication. Although declaring that he writes in *apologia* for the enterprise called (wrongly, as he points out) the New Criticism, Brooks's point depends ultimately upon a successful demonstration of pure praxis—a methodical reading of Hardy's "Channel Firing"—to show how New Critics generally and simply tried only to achieve "a special emphasis on the literary work as distinguished from an emphasis on the writer or the reader."[25]

Briskly, he identifies the dramatic situation—context, setting in time and place, level and tone of dialogue: The dead in a particular churchyard comment wryly upon the monstrous machinery of the living combatants in World War I. Brooks finds the poem's effect dependent, not surprisingly, upon *irony*, verbal and dramatic; the most precise possible accounting for allusions to times and places—Stonehenge, Camelot, Stourton; the possible significance of Parson Thirdly's name in view of his utterance; possible, even likely, echoes from Swift and the Bible (even the easily overlooked choice of "Ha, Ha" for God's response to modern warfare instead of the less precise, less dramatic "No, No" in an earlier version of the poem); the relationship of metrical pattern and variation to "the effect of solemnity"; and thematic possibilities restricted in the light of the poem's texture and progression.

Moreover, Brooks shows that "outside" considerations—popular tropes (e.g., loudness that would awaken the dead, the poverty of church mice); historical facts ("Mad as hatters"); Mrs. Hardy's identification of the particular churchyard, Stinsford Church, correctly and reasonably close to Portsmouth, Stonehenge, and Camelot; textual changes—are quite compatible with an otherwise purely textual analysis. They need only the scholar's patience, intellectual assay, and pertinent associations. Having led his reader through careful examination and synthesis of all its details, Brooks concludes his task. He refuses to tell readers how they *must* judge the poem, for, as he remarks, readers who observe the meanings of words and deliberate upon figurative structures, modulations of tone, relationship of rhythm to "total effect," will certainly know how to judge the poem for themselves. Thus Brooks disposes of attacks upon himself and the other New Critics.

If their approach seems always to "privilege" the text, to expect that careful readers will always arrive approximately at the same interpretation, and to see literature as more complex yet more precise than casual speech or the writing of most journalists, the New Critics never suggested otherwise. They merely taught, after all, that literature requires and deserves responsible reading and readable response.

Notes

1. William J. Handy, *Kant and the Southern New Critics* (Austin: University of Texas Press, 1963), p. 10.
2. William K. Wimsatt, Jr., and Cleanth Brooks, *Literary Criticism: A Short History* (New York: Random House, 1957), p. 621.
3. I. A. Richards, *Practical Criticism* (New York: Harcourt Brace, 1929; rpt., New York: Harvest, n.d.), p. 183.

4. David Ward, *T. S. Eliot between Two Worlds: A Reading of T. S. Eliot's Poetry and Plays* (Boston: Routledge and Kegan Paul, 1973), pp. 55–56.

5. John Crowe Ransom, "Roads Taken and Not Taken," in *Directions for Criticism*, ed. Murray Krieger and L. S. Dembo (Madison: University of Wisconsin Press, 1977), p. 39.

6. John Crowe Ransom, "The Future of Poetry," *The Fugitive*, February 1924; quoted in Louise Cowan, *The Fugitive Group: A Literary History* (Baton Rouge: Louisiana State University Press, 1959), p. 142. Later, of course, Ransom would refine his terms into "structure" and "texture," though the meanings are essentially unchanged.

7. Ibid. Ransom also lamented the modern poets' lack of their predecessors' "sense of miracle" at the fusion of "inner meaning" and "objective form," declaring that neither art nor religion is possible until we suppress "the *enfant terrible* of logic that plays havoc with the other faculties."

8. Thomas Daniel Young, *Gentleman in a Dustcoat* (Baton Rouge: Louisiana State University Press, 1976), p. 152.

9. Cowan, *Fugitive Group*, p. 154.

10. Cleanth Brooks and Robert Penn Warren, *Understanding Poetry*, 4th ed. (New York: Holt, Rinehart and Winston, 1976), p. ix.

11. Ibid., p. 18.

12. Cleanth Brooks, "In Search of the New Criticism," *American Scholar* 53 (Winter 1983/84): 41–53.

13. Frank Lentricchia, *After the New Criticism* (Chicago: University of Chicago Press, 1980), p. 109.

14. John M. Bradbury, *The Fugitives: A Critical Account* (Chapel Hill: University of North Carolina Press, 1958), p. 231.

15. Allen Tate, "What I Owe to Cleanth Brooks," in *The Possibilities of Order: Cleanth Brooks and His Work*, ed. Lewis P. Simpson (Baton Rouge: Louisiana State University Press, 1976), p. 126.

16. Bradbury, *The Fugitives*, p. 231.

17. Ibid., p. 240.

18. Cleanth Brooks, *The Well Wrought Urn: Studies in the Structure of Poetry*, rev. ed. (London: D. Dobson, 1968), p. 104.

19. Bradbury, *The Fugitives*, p. 232.

20. Ibid., p. 240.

21. Robert Penn Warren, "Pure and Impure Poetry," *Kenyon Review* 5 (Spring 1943): 229–54.

22. Robert Penn Warren, ed., *The Rime of the Ancient Mariner* (New York: Reynal and Hitchcock, 1946), pp. 61–148.

23. Ibid., p. 65. Warren assails the interpretations of the two foremost Coleridge scholars of that day, Earl Leslie Griggs, who had declared the poem to be a "journey into the supernatural for the sake of the journey," and John Livingston Lowes, who had seen the poem as an "illusion for the sake of illusion."

24. Ibid., pp. 1–6.

25. Brooks, "In Search of the New Criticism," p. 47.

Selected Bibliography

Bradbury, John M. *The Fugitives: A Critical Account*. Chapel Hill: University of North Carolina
   Press, 1958. A fine supplement to Louise Cowan's history of the Fugitives, Bradbury's
   approach analyzes their ideas and their critical statements. His book maintains an admirable balance between praise and disagreement.

Cowan, Louise. *The Fugitive Group: A Literary History*. Baton Rouge: Louisiana State University Press, 1959. Without peer as a complete chronicle and definition of the Nashville poet-critics from their first collegial stirrings of creativity and thought through their emergence as important modernist poets and theorists. Cowan has made the most of the rich archives at Vanderbilt and her friendships with the subjects themselves.

Elton, William. *A Glossary of the New Criticism*. Chicago: Modern Poetry Association, 1949. Originally published serially in *Poetry* from December 1948 through February 1949 and revised and enlarged for this printing as a pamphlet, the *Glossary* may seem odd and perhaps pretentious today, but its appearance and revisions reflect an extensive and genuine concern with understanding the large body of terms generated by New Critics by the end of the 1940s. Still a useful reference for those making a study of the movement.

Handy, William J. *Kant and the Southern New Critics*. Austin: University of Texas Press, 1963. A relatively rare effort to track the epistemological backgrounds of Ransom's, Tate's, and Brooks's theories—"the direct influence of the Kantian generative idea," which emphasizes "the celebration of man's qualitative experience." Stresses ideas rather than practice.

Karanikas, Alexander. *Tillers of a Myth: Southern Agrarians as Social and Literary Critics*. Madison: University of Wisconsin Press, 1969. A history usefully supplementing Cowan's book by concentration on the interim between the Fugitive days and the New Criticism. Generous notes and bibliography take the reader fully into the Nashville group's ventures into social, economic, and political polemic and spirited *apologia* for the "Southern way" and consequent myth making which reinforced their ultimate return to and concentration upon literature from the mid-1930s onward. A final chapter charts the smooth transition from Agrarianism into full-fledged New Criticism.

Ransom, John Crowe. *Beating the Bushes: Selected Essays, 1941–1970*. New York: New Directions, 1972. These graceful essays span the thirty years including Ransom's command post as editor of the *Kenyon Review* and his occasional pieces afterward. They show Ransom's differences with the other New Critics as well as the many points of total agreement. Contains the indispensable "Wanted: An Ontological Critic" (1941), which largely defined the concerns of the just emerging New Criticism, and the previously unpublished, late essay on Hegel, "The Concrete Universal" (1970).

Schorer, Mark. "Technique as Discovery." *Hudson Review* 1 (Spring 1948): 67–87. A concise, spirited, and very lucid statement of the central meaning of New Criticism and a relatively rare application of its methods to fiction. Schorer predictably claims the superiority of novels of "thickness and resonance" (i.e., the lineage of Henry James) to those of Fielding, Defoe, and H. G. Wells.

Simpson, Lewis P., ed. *The Possibilities of Order: Cleanth Brooks and His Work*. Baton Rouge: Louisiana State University Press, 1976. Tape-recorded conversations between Warren and Brooks, essays and affectionate recollections of other old friends, and critical assessments by eminent scholars (including Walter J. Ong, René Wellek, Thomas Daniel Young, and Monroe K. Spears) are assembled by Simpson to trace the career of Brooks, his ultimate role as chief spokesman for the New Criticism (especially for the academic community), and the durability of his work beyond the 1950s.

RICHARD F. HARDIN

Archetypal Criticism

Because archetypes, primordial images that seem to reside deep in the self or the civilization, often find expression in works of art and in rudimentary folk stories, the criticism centering on them usually transcends "literature" as formalism conceives it. Work of otherwise limited imagination can assume great significance for the archetypal critic. The approach is almost synonymous with "myth criticism," in that myths are the purest expression of such images in most human experience. The interplay of archetype and myth will necessitate some overlap of the terms in the following discussion, which deals with a powerful movement in the history of recent literary theory. Especially from the 1950s to the 1970s, criticism in this country was virtually on an archetypalist binge. This critical label actually defines several different approaches, as exemplified in the pains taken by its foremost practitioner, Northrop Frye, to distance himself from its foremost philosopher, Carl Jung. Despite the relative paucity of such work by major critics in the last decade or so, archetypal criticism still prospers in some fields, such as the still embryonic work on children's literature and science fiction and the more voluminous and impressive critical texts of feminism. The most recent available subject index of the annual *MLA International Bibliography* contains nine columns of entries under the headings "archetype" and "myth."

Certain texts, such as the following poem, lend themselves readily to archetypal treatment. The author of this poem is unknown, and even the century of composition remains doubtful. Like other Scottish ballads it exists in several texts, none of which is clearly primary. The poem is usually called "The Twa Corbies" (The Two Crows):

As I was walking all alane,
I heard twa corbies making a mane;
The tane unto t'other say,
"Where sall we gang and dine to-day?"

"In behint yon auld fail dyke,
I wot there lies a new slain knight;
And naebody kens that he lies there,
But his hawk, his hound, and lady fair.

"His hound is to the hunting gane,
His hawk to fetch the wild-fowl hame,
His lady's ta'en another mate,
So we may mak' our dinner sweet.

"Ye'll sit on his white hause-bane
And I'll pike out his bonny blue e'en;
Wi' ae lock o' his gowden hair
We'll theek our nest when it grows bare.

"Mony a ane for him makes mane,
But nane sall ken where he is gane;
O'er his white banes, when they are bare,
The wind sall blaw for evermair."

Like other ballads, the poem is an admirable feat of condensation. The knight's tragedy could not be told more succinctly with more emotional force. Along with its acknowledged mastery of understatement, the ballad's strength resides in stark images of death: the two birds of prey, the bones, the eternal wind, the lock of hair in the birds' nest, the blue eye pecked from the skull. Such images can be called archetypal in that they speak the same meaning to almost any culture, any time. The universal experience of death in nature insures this universality of image. It also overrides any unfamiliar particulars of the poem, such as its medieval context, its references to hunting practices that are unknown to many cultures, its peculiar dialect, its use of crows or ravens rather than, say, buzzards (generally much uglier and more frightening birds for Texans or Mexicans, who tend to think of crows as agricultural pests).

The situation of the poem has equally deep appeal: the hero slain by treachery (he is "new slain," and his lady already has "another mate") appears in almost all literatures of the world. Not only the images and plot but the characters, undeveloped though they are, are also archetypal: the handsome, competent knight-hero; the shadowy femme fatale and her lover. The "I" of the poem and the talking birds also find counterparts in poems and stories throughout the world. Archetypal qualities may even seem to occur in the colors (blue, gold, white) and the numbers (two, the number of division and duplicity; three, of completeness and finality), though agreement on such points can scarcely be found outside of Western European conventions.

The peculiar slant of archetypal criticism is shown when the foregoing comments are compared with a New Critical or formalist reading of roughly the same poem—"roughly the same" because the texts of early ballads are seldom identical, owing in part to their oral origins, their identification with a community rather than an author. In "The Three Ravens" ("There were three ravens sat on a tree") the story changes so that the ravens report the hounds' guarding of the knight's corpse while the hawks ward off the birds of prey; the lady (in the guise of a "fallow doe") buries her man before dying herself:

> She lift up his bloudy hed,
> And kist his wounds that were so red.
>
> She got him up upon her backe,
> And carried him to earthen lacke.
>
> She buried him before the prime,
> She was dead herself ere even-song time.
>
> God send every gentleman,
> Such haukes, such hounds, and such a leman.

Although the sentiment of this poem contrasts sharply with the bleakness of "The Twa Corbies," the imagery and situation are close enough to indicate that both texts might have come from the same stock. The analysis of this poem by Cleanth Brooks and Robert Penn Warren in their classic New Critical textbook underscores the "ironic contrast" that is heightened "when the ravens themselves, examples of mere brute appetite, comment on the hawk and the hounds, examples of a fidelity that reaches beyond such appetite."[1] Something similar might be said of "The Twa Corbies," regardless of the bleaker ending. The crows exemplify appetite; the woman, hounds, and hawk, the tenuousness of loyalties in nature on account of appetite. As formalist critics, Brooks and Warren observe qualities of the poet's voice and details that uphold contrasts and ironies in the poem. Although allowing for the role of the reader's experience and feelings in their criticism, they prefer to emphasize internal features of the text (voice, contrast or paradox, arrangement of images—e.g., the climactic ordering of hounds, hawks, and lady). Archetypal criticism, by contrast, looks outward from these details to wider levels of human comprehension and sensibility. The image of the bones may be related to the valley of bones in Ezekiel 37, the *dans macabre* of late medieval culture, or the gravediggers' scene in *Hamlet*. "The Twa Corbies" evokes the same sense of hopelessness, grim playfulness, and fatalism that occurs in these other sources. It matters little to the archetypal critic that the author of this ballad never read *Hamlet* or that he never intended an allusion to Ezekiel. All poets, especially those who have written works that stand the test of time, possess a special sense for these widely recurring, deeply felt kinds of imagery.

Because archetypes find expression in myths, it is reasonable to look at "myth criticism" as a species of the archetypal approach. In "The Three Ravens" one could draw parallels between the lady/doe and the shape shifter of myth and folklore, or between the knight mourned by nature and the dead young hunter Adonis or the shepherd Daphnis in classical mythology. In "The Twa Corbies" the brief but ominous appearance of the faithless lady recalls the fatal woman of Western myth and legend, whose love is death. Her counterpart exists in Keats's "La Belle Dame sans Merci" or in Spenser's evil fairy Acrasia, who drives her human lover Mordant and his wife to a bloody death. Often the victims of these women undergo an especially oblivious kind of death, as if their souls are forgotten the moment their bodies are abandoned to nature. The crows or ravens resemble mythical insatiable devourers like the Harpies in the *Odyssey*. Not unlike these creatures is the figure of Cerberus, the three-headed dog of Hades, which some medieval interpreters saw as the three elements that devour our bodies after death.

Such considerations take us repeatedly back to the thought of death in nature that lies at the core of both "The Twa Corbies" and "The Three Ravens." Concerning the last couplet of the second poem, Brooks and Warren state that it is in a sense the theme of the ballad: "The poem, taken as a whole, makes a contrast between two ways of looking at life. The ravens represent one way, the hawks, hounds, and 'doe' the other. One view regards life in a purely materialistic way; the other finds an importance in life beyond mere material circumstances" (p. 46). An archetypal reading of the poem, rooted in the experience of death in nature, would find perhaps less to hope for: God *may* send us such loyal servants, but these can do nothing for us, finally, except to create a momentary illusion. The doe and her unborn child die, depriving the knight even of posterity. The gifts of God seem ineffectual against the overwhelming fact of death. In "Corbies" nature does not care about the human tragedy; in "Ravens" (as in Milton's *Lycidas*) nature is sympathetic but finally impotent.

The outward movement of the archetypal approach is at once its chief attraction and its principal deficiency as an aesthetic instrument. We may be impressed by the wide range of correspondences or analogues that can be found in the images and characters of widely divergent texts but may soon find that such associative efforts have drawn us completely away from the text itself. The contours and nuances of feeling that make a poem or narrative unique can quickly drown in the sea of the collective unconscious.[2] Perhaps for this reason archetypal critics tend to write about "literature" rather than specific literary works, or to use literature chiefly as a means toward cultural criticism. Although both literature and culture are entirely worthy objects of thought, such thought is bound to find expression in very different ways from a formalist explication of a poem or novel. Archetypal criticism lets us see the text in its family portrait or its genealogical tree, but the text is simply a face in the crowd, a dot on the diagram. Formal criticism presents us with the close-up or portrait, "the thing itself" (if such there be), as archetypal criticism never will. Either version of the text, though, is incomplete in itself because it must isolate some feature of text, audience, or milieu.

Some idea of the aims and results of archetypal criticism is conveyed in the history of the movement beginning in the late nineteenth century with the work on classical drama of the so-called Cambridge anthropological school. To a great extent the *fons et origo* of this school is Sir James Frazer's *Golden Bough*, the remarkable encyclopedia of world mythology that is still revered by folklorists and literary people. A good Victorian rationalist, Frazer was out to show the common patterns of human delusion as expressed in the rituals and myths of religions around the world, not excluding the religion of Roman Catholicism. He had little use for some of the more mystical notions of the Cambridge school and later dissociated himself from them. The Cambridge school followed Frazer and other nineteenth-century ethnologists in believing that a myth was "a fiction devised to explain an old custom, of which the real meaning and origin had been forgotten."[3] From this was derived "the ritual theory of myth," the idea that a myth existed only to justify the celebration of a rite whose original meaning had been lost. Undoubtedly there are such myths. Swinging from trees, for example, is a fertility rite in a number of unrelated cultures. In the Dionysian festival of Aiora, young women would swing in tree swings, supposedly commemorating the myth of Erigone, who hanged herself after neighbors murdered her father. In fact, that story seems to have been invented or imported for the sake of the rite. As a universal theory of myth, however, the ritual explanation has few adherents among modern anthropologists, having been attacked by several generations of scholars, including Andrew Lang (in a lengthy early review of *The Golden Bough*), Clyde Kluckhohn, and Joseph Fontenrose. The theory suited the evolutionary ideas of the age, however: Wordless ritual becomes hazy myth, which finally develops into epic or drama.

At the center of the Cambridge school was the charismatic figure of Jane

Ellen Harrison, one of the first women to be celebrated as a scholar at the university. Her views on art, religion, and ancient culture were first publicized in her *Mythology and Monuments of Ancient Athens* (1890). Her more significant work in the history of archetypal theory is *Themis: A Study of the Social Origins of Greek Religion* (1912), to which the young Cambridge classicist Francis M. Cornford contributed a chapter on the origin of the Olympic games, and the Oxford graduate Gilbert Murray added "An Excursus on the Ritual Forms Preserved in Greek Tragedy." Both men were younger friends of Harrison: Cornford called her "Aunt Jane," and on her death in 1928 Murray gave an address at her college.

Properly speaking, all three of the chief members of the school (to whom a fourth member, A. B. Cook, should be added) are not primarily literary critics. Like many other archetypal theorists they were, or soon became, cultural, especially religious, historians and commentators. Literature was for them a means to an end. All three held unorthodox beliefs (Cornford and Harrison belonged to a Cambridge club called the Heretics; Murray had a rationalist's aversion to organized religion). All were seriously concerned about the plight of civilization and wrote tracts and essays supporting humanitarian causes. Jung was a common resource for them but not really a source. They saw him as developing ideas that they had already stumbled upon, partly as a result of reading earlier anthropologists like E. B. Tylor and J. J. Bachofen, as well as the philosopher Nietzsche's ideas on the Apollonian and Dionysian spirit in *The Birth of Tragedy*. In accepting some of Jung without becoming disciples, they resemble the later mythographer and critic Joseph Campbell: "Archetypal" does not always mean "Jungian." Murray became the first school dropout, perhaps regretting his association with the controversial Miss Harrison (he does not mention her in *An Unfinished Autobiography*, nor is there evidence of his anthropological theories in his Oxford inaugural lecture as Professor of Greek in 1909), though one still finds him quoting Jung in 1944.

Cornford seems to have held his ground. An insight into the archetypal method is revealed in his apologetical essay (originally read before the Classical Association in 1921), the very title of which suggests Freud's and Jung's influence upon his beliefs at this time.[4] "The Unconscious Element in Literature" presents two salient features of archetypal criticism as it later develops: the tendencies to allegorize and to discard material peculiar to the author's life in studying his text. Biographical criticism had dominated literary study for more than a century, so it was a novel approach that set out to disregard the author on purpose. Without the biographical distractions one may then examine, as Cornford had in his controversial *Thucydides Mythistoricus*, the universally held preconceptions or myths that shape the work. This critical strategy may be called "backing up." Cornford applauds the efforts of the critic who, *Golden Bough* in hand, backs up to see the root structures of character and action in Greek tragedy: "How can any modern critic be positive that, in that concrete region of the mind where concrete images take the place of discursive thought, there were not still links of association, however obscure or unexplicit, connecting (say) the figure of Jocasta with the earth-mother, and the figure of Oedipus with the divine king" (p. 6). A second strategy noted in this essay, and indicated in the foregoing question, is that of allegorizing and flattening out characters and events in interpretation. Like Jung, Cornford believed that "philosophy is internally nothing else but a refined and sublimated mythology." Such thinking was hardly new, having been developed two centuries earlier in Giambattista Vico's *Scienza Nuova*. What is modern is the tracing of poetry, mythology, and thus philosophy to what Cornford calls "the impersonal unconscious," so that the translation of poetry into philosophical concepts is simply another way of conveying the archetypes.[5]

The Cambridge school anticipates later archetypalists like Northrop Frye in their emphasis upon the structure or paradigm typical of certain literary works. Murray's excursus on tragedy argues that the tragic plot conceals the older practice of ritual fertility drama involving (1) the Agon or struggle of the Year Spirit against its enemy (darkness or winter); (2) the *pathos* of the Year Spirit enacted in a sacrificial death (often of a *pharmakos* or scapegoat); (3) the messenger who announces the death; (4) the lamentation (*threnos*); (5) the discovery (*anagnorisis*) of the slain Year Spirit; (6) his resurrection and epiphany or revelation to the faithful. It should be noted that we have no evidence of any Greek ritual that took this precise form. Murray found corroboration for his theory in English mummers' plays (as described by his friend E. K. Chambers in a work on early English drama that influenced half a century of scholars) and in modern Greek folk drama. In a famous essay, "Hamlet and Orestes," Murray even extends his pattern to Shakespeare, noting the intriguing parallels between these two famous heroes, in whose creation there was supposedly no chance of direct influence. Forty years later this approach to *Hamlet* reached a wide audience through Francis Fergusson's *Idea of a Theater*.

Cornford followed Murray in treating Aristophanic (old) comedy as yet another outgrowth of fertility ritual, taking as his starting point the observation that each of the surviving comedies ends with a festive union of the hero with a female figure in a kind of marriage. Like tragedy, old comedy developed an agon, but this was interrupted by a *parabasis*, a long choric address to the audience, then a sacrifice, a feast, and finally a marriage procession (*komos*).

Cornford attends as much to character types as to plot in his *Origins of Ancient Comedy*, roughing out notions that will later be refined by Frye and others. A principal type is the *alazon* or impostor, like the hack poet who offers an ode on the founding of the new city in *The Birds*. The impostor is often victimized or revealed by an *eiron* (one who deprecates himself and thereby shows up conceit and affectation in another), "a fox in the sheep's clothing of a buffoon." A third type is the mere buffoon (*bomolochos*), "the ungentlemanly person who makes fun for the amusement of others." Cornford sees the conflict between *eiron* and *alazon* as parallel to that between hero and antagonist, the *alazon* in fact being a "double" of the antagonist. Cornford's source for these labels is an ancient, perhaps not classical, tract of two or three pages, called the "Tractatus Coislinianus"; Greek dramatists and Aristotle did not use these terms to describe characters.[6] Cornford's purpose was to find the origins of Attic comedy, not merely to analyze its structure. Yet, if classical scholars no longer accept his ideas (the Cambridge school lost its accreditation with Arthur Pickard-Cambridge's thorough 1927 study, *Dithyramb, Tragedy, and Comedy*), they remain indebted to his stimulating analysis of Aristophanes' characters and plots. Cornford raised questions about the nature of comedy and dramatic form analogous to those of Aristotle on tragedy in the *Poetics*.

It is a revealing fact about the state of literary criticism, especially in English, that despite the efforts of classical scholars from Pickard-Cambridge to William Arrowsmith and Gerald Else, Cambridge school theories are periodically resurrected like the dying and rising gods of which Frazer, Harrison, and Cornford were so fond. The persistence of this idea attests to the strength of the kindred idea, romantic in origin, that the aesthetic has somehow supplanted the religious in human life.

Some such idea underlies Keats's comment in a letter to Shelley that "My imagination is a monastery and I am its monk," and Stephen Dedalus's lecture on art in Joyce's *Portrait*. As children of romanticism, archetypal theorists of literature have perpetuated the view that art has evolved from the sacred. Cave paintings, for instance, are supposed to have been addressed to primitive religious needs and were not objects of beauty in themselves. The mistake is in separating the religious, the aesthetic, and other spheres of primitive culture in the specialized way that is done with modern culture. A tribal dance in a traditional society can be simultaneously a political activity, a source of conviviality and aesthetic pleasure, and a guarantee of crops, fertility, or rain. The same dance can also communicate with the spirit world. To say that art originates in religion, in other words, is nothing more than to say that it originates in culture, of which "religion" is a fairly recently separated department. The early history of art discloses an analogy with that of science.

Historians of science find that medicine, chemistry, and even physics have roots in the religious or magical activities of early civilizations; but the "religious" underpinnings of science are really the whole cultural fabric that to modern eyes is virtually tainted by its indiscriminate commingling with "religion." Thus the Cambridge school was only partly right in saying that drama evolved from ritual or that a certain kind of character originated with the scapegoat. In most parts of the world rituals and scapegoats are simply inevitable constituents of human culture during its traditional phase. To say that art originates in religion is another way of saying that it is human.

Archetypal criticism can be developed from a psychological as well as an anthropological perspective, as was demonstrated in Maud Bodkin's *Archetypal Patterns in Poetry*,[7] a book that enjoyed a wide readership in this country on its republication during the 1950s, the high point of the archetypal movement. Bodkin was educated as a psychologist, lecturing on her subject at a teacher-training college in Cambridge. She was considerably younger than Jane Harrison and her circle and does not seem to have had any direct association with them, though it is clear from autobiographical statements in *Studies of Type Images in Poetry, Religion, and Philosophy* (1951) that the works of Cornford and Harrison strongly shaped her views on literature and art. She writes that she, like Harrison, was raised in a strict religious environment, against which she rebelled in adolescence. An income on her parents' death allowed her to leave teaching and devote herself wholly to reading and writing. *Archetypal Patterns* was written after a return to Christianity (she had read Schweitzer's *Quest of the Historical Jesus*), when she had acquired "a fuller sense of the unexplored wealth of the heritage communicated through language and custom, influencing unawares all our conscious individual thoughts and actions."[8] In other words, she approached literature with a fully Jungian sense of the archetype and with little formal education in literary studies.

Archetypal Patterns sets out to test Jung's hypothesis (explained in his essay, "On the Relation of Analytical Psychology to Poetic Art") that certain poems derive their power to stir us from their appeal to "primordial images" (p. 1). She recalls Gilbert Murray's exploration in "Hamlet and Orestes" of the peculiar power still retained by themes that moved primitive people. An "archetypal pattern" is "that within us which, in Gilbert Murray's phrase, leaps in response to the effective presentation in poetry of an ancient theme." She goes on to say that in poetry "we may identify themes having a particular form or pattern which persists amid variations from age to age, and which corresponds to a pattern or configuration of emotional tendencies in the minds of those who are stirred by the theme" (p. 4). Thus the archetypal pattern corresponding to tragedy is "a certain organization of the tendencies of self-assertion and submission. The self which is asserted is magnified by the same collective force to which submission is made," and the tension between these two impulses gives rise to "the tragic attitude and emotion" (p. 22). The view that the archetypal pattern is in the self rather than on the page necessitates an approach not unlike that of recent affective or reader-response criticism. A difference, though, is that Bodkin's subject is herself, and her discussion of literary works contains numerous references to her own dreams and experiences. She is quite familiar with I. A. Richards's psychological investigations but differs with him on this point—insisting, for example, that in a reading of Dante the reader must take account of "one's individual experience" of certain words and their power to "mediate any realization of heavenly joy" (p. 133). Her method does not attempt to judge the text but "is concerned with emotional response only, not with opinion. It is akin to the method proposed by Keats [Keats to Reynolds, 18 February 1818] that one should read a page of poetry, or distilled prose, and wander with it, muse, reflect, and prophesy, and dream, upon it" (p. 28).

Such an approach can lead to an undisciplined impressionism occasionally in Bodkin's discussion of texts, but as a rule she is as interested in the whole as in its parts. She explores Coleridge's *Rime of the Ancient Mariner* from the standpoint of its following the rebirth archetype in structure and discusses the capacity of certain images (wind, storm clouds, slime, the color red) "to enter into an emotional sequence" (p. 52), so that context and ordering of images are valued over the image itself as having power to influence feelings. The chapter on "The Image of Woman" (pp. 148–210) is the stuff of which books have been made in recent years. Here Bodkin explores the especially important Jungian concepts of the anima (the female soul mate present to the unconscious of every male) and the mother-imago in her discussion of Virgil's Dido, Dante's Beatrice, and Milton's Eve and Muse. The rich suggestiveness of her allegorizations may be sampled in her comments on Virgil's tale of Orpheus and Eurydice (in *Georgics* 4) as a myth about poetry (p. 197).

Bodkin's last chapter, on contemporary literature (Lawrence, Eliot, Woolf), serves as a reminder that anyone who takes the archetypal approach to twentieth-century literature may be in the position, as Stanley Edgar Hyman has said, of digging for gold at Fort Knox. We know from such scholarly studies as John B. Vickery's *Literary Impact of "The Golden Bough"* that Jung and Frazer, no less than Freud, were seminal influences on the minds of Eliot (whose notes to his *Waste Land* are redolent of Frazerian myth and anthropology), Faulkner, Joyce, Yeats, Lawrence, and other writers of the World War I generation and after. Younger writers of the American South, like Eudora Welty, Tennessee Williams, Shirley Jackson, and even Flannery O'Connor, were strongly attracted to the vogue for myth, though with varying results. Still more recent writers have followed a more explicitly archetypal path: Diane Johnson's *The Shadow Knows* and Margaret Atwood's *Surfacing* both make use of Jungian ideas in subtle ways (the "shadow" is the archetype of the villain or the person we most fear in our unconscious). Both these authors were enrolled in graduate study in English at a time when archetypal criticism was virtually inescapable in the classroom, a fact that raises interesting questions about the relation between creativity and theory in our time.

One of the strongest links between Frazer and modern literature, T. S. Eliot, ends his essay, "Tradition and the Individual Talent," "at the frontiers of metaphysics or mysticism." Eliot claims that the poet must escape from his personality (adding that he must of course first have a personality) into the stream of tradition that is poetry without poets. The paradox of poetry living apart from poets might very well be resolved in the notion of Jungian archetypes, though Eliot believed that "tradition" was acquired rather than implanted in the psyche. The most successful of archetypal critics, Northrop Frye, continues in this belief and is not surprisingly the author of one of the best introductions to Eliot, a book in which tradition looms large. Unlike other archetypal critics, Frye sees literature as a system closed off from the author's psyche, even from history itself. An archetype is not an image derived from Jungian racial memory—or, rather, it makes no difference whether it is so derived or not. It is principally "A symbol, usually an image, which recurs often enough in literature to be recognizable as an element of one's literary experience as a whole."[9] It is "a symbol which connects one poem with another and thereby helps to unify and integrate our literary experience" (*Anatomy of Criticism*, p. 99). Frye's widely read *Anatomy of Criticism* follows Eliot and the New Critics in removing authors from the centrality they had occupied in earlier literary discussion. He shows, too, the midcentury penchant for scientific method and anticipates the structuralists in seeking to organize a model of the whole literary tradition across historical boundaries—"synchronically," as social scientists would say. But Frye also echoes the views of the Cambridge school in seeing myths, ultimately religious rituals, at the core of literary composition.

We have already noticed the tendency in archetypal criticism to back up from the text so as to apprehend underlying mythic or imagistic patterns. Frye compares this process to a viewer's moving away from a painting:

At a great distance from, say, a Madonna, we can see nothing but the archetype of a Madonna, a large centripetal blue mass with a contrasting point of interest at its center. In the criticism of literature, too, we often have to "stand back" from the poem to see its archetypal organization. If we stand back from Spenser's *Mutabilitie Cantoes* [*sic*] we see a background of ordered circular light and a sinister black mass thrusting up into the lower foreground—much the same archetypal shape that we see in the opening of the Book of Job. If we "stand back" from the beginning of the fifth act of *Hamlet*, we see a grave opening on the stage, the hero, his enemy, and the heroine descending into it, followed by a fatal struggle in the upper world. [P. 140]

This process describes what Frye calls "displacement," by which an abstract myth becomes a narrated myth, then a romance, then a realistic narrative. The example from *Hamlet* shows how standing back can reveal the mythic in the mimetic. But it is the constituents of the narrative, the myths (or, to use structuralist terminology, the "mythemes," persons and images that make up myths) and images, that interest Frye.

Frye equates the meaning of a poem with its structure of imagery, setting the possible number of structures at five. One extreme on the spectrum contains apocalyptic images or symbols that embody the fulfillment of desire (e.g., biblical images of "heaven"); at the other lies the demonic imagery of "the world that desire totally rejects" (p. 147): Marvell's "Garden" versus Orwell's *1984*. Moving from the higher end of the spectrum we encounter the imagery of romance, high mimetic, and low mimetic (examples of water imagery in each category are the enchanted fountain, the Thames of English lyric and epic, and the awful sea of Conrad's novels, respectively); these correspond to the recession from innocence to experience. The five structures of imagery are compared to the keys in a single musical composition. A whole work will occupy one of four phases: an upward kind, the comic, corresponding to spring; the romantic, corresponding to summer; a downward shift, the tragic, corresponding to autumn; the satire or irony, for winter. These *mythoi* (the Greek plural of myth) are pregeneric: They can occur in any of the usual genres of lyric, drama, or narrative.

It is perhaps evident by now that Frye's method is one of classifying rather than analyzing, and his treatment of comedy typifies this approach. Moving into spring, we have the "earliest"—in the sense that it is nearest to the ironic and winter—phase of comedy, as in Jonson's *Alchemist*, where "a humorous society triumphs or remains undefeated" (p. 177). Each of the next four stages is like "a sequence of stages in the life of a redeemed society" (p. 185), culminating in the fifth phase, which moves away from human experience toward the kind of pensive, spiritual perspective revealed at the end of Shakespeare's romances. Frye is obviously indebted to Cornford for his discussion of plot and character in comedy, as we meet again with the *eiron*, *alazon*, and *bomolochos*, and as we consider the analogy (though *only* an analogy) between comedy and a ritual contest of summer and winter, in which winter occupies the middle action. He avoids the pitfalls of Cambridge anthropological criticism by adhering to his principle of the literariness of literature. The archetypes manifest themselves in literature; they may do so in corresponding ways in religion or artistic design, but these in no way concern the critic.

As an anatomist of the huge body of literature, Frye is not inclined to analyze specific texts. By 1960 or so, New Criticism had already generated a vast number of these anyway. When he does apply his theories, however, the results are not unlike Maud Bodkin's analyses, though more disciplined. In "Literature as Context: Milton's *Lycidas*" (collected in his 1963 book *Fables of Identity*), Frye begins by describing the drowned Edward King as a displaced Daphnis or Adonis figure, from which he deduces an association with the cycles and rhythms of nature. Myth, in other words, is the starting point for author and critic, the pregeneric principle or seed of the work. King also has secondary roles of poet and priest, embodied in the figures of Orpheus and Saint Peter. In the rondolike structure of the poem, described as ABACA, the two minor figures preside over B and C, while the main A-theme of premature death is repeated twice. Woven into the poem (from the possible five structures of imagery in the *Anatomy*) are image groups centering on four levels of existence: Christian, human (i.e., society fallen but retaining its potential for good), natural, and the disorderly unnatural level of sin and death. These are identified, respectively, with the apocalyptic, high mimetic, low mimetic, and demonic. Considering this analysis, we may feel that we are being told in a new way what we have long known; yet this is perhaps always the response to any good essay on a much discussed text. When Frye moves away from *Lycidas* to examine larger issues raised in his discussion (true to his inclinations, he cannot stay on a single text for an entire essay), he indicates some critical principles that fit neatly into the program of literary theory about 1950–60, the time of this essay's composition.

First, says Frye, literature transcends even the language in which it is written: "every problem in literary criticism is a problem in comparative literature, or simply in literature itself." This is a commonsense response to the linguistic interests that had dominated, perhaps tyrannized over, literary study for centuries. It also speaks to the "intertextuality," in recent terminology, of every literary work. Next, consistent with the "organicism" of the formalists, Frye points out how the analysis has shown the unity of the poem, seeming to suggest that the single-myth theory helps us to see that unity. For Frye and the New Critics unity is perhaps the only indisputable criterion of value. The analysis also weakens the claims of literary historians and biographers on the text. Questions about Milton's relations with King, his sincerity, his knowledge of certain sources for the poem are all extraneous to our understanding and appreciation of the elegy.

Why this should be so is not entirely clear. No one needs to know what porridge had Keats, but John Updike begins a recent essay with the question "What did Hawthorne believe?" and a good many doors would be opened (or closed) in Hawthorne scholarship if we knew the answer to this question. Also, one could argue that Frye's own approach is a form of the much maligned source study. No one remembers the inane articles that prove Shakespeare to have been a hack who got all his ideas from one obscure novella, but there have been milestones of the genre, like James Holly Hanford's 1910 essay on *Lycidas* (which lurks somewhere at the back of Frye's own essay) or John Livingston Lowes's *Road to Xanadu*. Frye's impatience with source hunters, like Bodkin's criticism of Lowes in her Coleridge chapter for his positivism and intellectualism, addresses the reductive, simplistic attitude they often bring to their task. But even more than Bodkin (for whom the source is in the poet's psyche all along), Frye is a student of literary sources. If all texts have as their source the literary tradition, then he is free of the source hunter's historical constraints and may range widely in the hunt for analogues in any number of texts. We might well call such work synchronic source study.

If critics, like everyone else, are condemned to repeat the mistakes of the past, the one new thing about archetypal criticism at its inception was its wide, liberating perspective on literature, a reaction in part to the formalist's intense scrutiny of the isolated text. In psychologically based criticism (which continues, e.g., in the recent books of Annis Pratt) the movement is outward to kindred phenomena in art and literature in order to illuminate the hidden corners of both reader's and writer's psyches. Such criticism requires an outside specialist like Carl Jung or, most recently, James Hillman to guide us through the science of the mind. Frye's protostructuralist approach has the advantage of needing no philosopher to set the stage. The *Anatomy* sets out to study the whole body of literature, not to plot its evolution along the Darwinian path to fitness, as did the Cambridge school, but to appreciate the continuity of forms and images across widely disparate cultures and times. In either case the aims of archetypal criticism are well within the limits of the proper study of mankind.

Notes

1. Cleanth Brooks and Robert Penn Warren, *Understanding Poetry*, 3rd ed. (New York: Holt, Rinehart and Winston, 1960), p. 45.
2. The notion of a "collective unconscious" that transmits the typical experiences of our

ancestors was formed by Carl Jung and developed in relation to his theory of archetypes in *Archetypes of the Collective Unconscious* (Princeton, N.J.: Bollingen, 1969). Jung's psychology is the subject of Joland Jacobi, *The Psychology of C. G. Jung* (New Haven: Yale University Press, 1962). For Jung, the artist is peculiarly attuned to the unconscious, which manifests itself in his visions. Unlike Freud, Jung believed that such visions were not personal but transcended the artist's experience. See his "Psychology and Literature" (1930); trans. and rpt. in *20th Century Literary Criticism*, ed. David Lodge (London: Longman Group, 1972), pp. 175–88.

3. Sir James Frazer, *The Golden Bough* (London: Macmillan, 1915), 4: 153, quoted in Stanley Edgar Hyman's informative "The Ritual View of Myth and the Mythic," in *Myth: A Symposium*, ed. Thomas A. Sebeok (Bloomington: Indiana University Press, 1958).

4. Francis M. Cornford, "The Unconscious Element in Literature," rpt. in Cornford, *The Unwritten Philosophy and Other Essays*, ed. W. K. C. Guthrie (Cambridge: Cambridge University Press, 1950), pp. 1–13.

5. Guthrie, *Unwritten Philosophy*, intro., p. x; Cornford, "Unconscious Element," p. 13.

6. A text of the "Tractatus" is in Lane Cooper, *An Aristotelian Theory of Comedy* (1922; rpt., New York: Kraus, 1969).

7. Maud Bodkin, *Archetypal Patterns in Poetry* (1934; rpt., New York: Random House [Vintage Books], 1958).

8. Bodkin, *Studies of Type Images in Poetry, Religion, and Philosophy* (London: Oxford University Press, 1951), p. 9.

9. Northrop Frye, *Anatomy of Criticism: Four Essays* (1957; rpt., New York: Atheneum, 1967), p. 365. Most of my discussion refers to Frye's third essay, "Archetypal Criticism: Theory of Myths," pp. 131–239.

Selected Bibliography

Adams, Hazard. *Philosophy of the Literary Symbolic*. Tallahassee: University Press of Florida, 1983. A tough-minded critic, Adams provides valuable assessments of some of the leading figures in archetypal or myth criticism: Campbell, Eliade, and Wheelwright in a chapter entitled "Sentimental Archaism," Frye in a separate chapter. A number of critics could be said to share the blame that Adams lays on Wheelwright for "his efforts to keep poetry and religion together in spite of their apparent desire for an amicable separation" (p. 262).

Antczak, Janice. *Science Fiction: The Mythos of a New Romance*. New York: Neal-Schuman, 1985. Included here as a good recent specimen of applications of concepts from Frye and other archetypalists to both children's literature and science fiction.

Bodkin, Maud. *Archetypal Patterns in Poetry*. 1934. Reprint. New York: Random House (Vintage Books), 1958. Discussed in text.

Brewer, Derek. *Symbolic Stories: Traditional Narratives of the Family Drama in English Literature*. Cambridge: D. S. Brewer, 1980. On fairy tales, medieval literature, Shakespeare, Austen, and Dickens. Making no pretense at theoretical innovation, the book provides an accessible, credible argument for stories as both reflecting and originating in enduring psychological needs. The "family drama" refers not to Freudian ideas (Brewer belongs to no school), but to the viewpoint of the child growing up. The "inner drama" of *Cymbeline* is the quest to integrate family and self. Brewer also appeals to the essential humanity of stories in his presidential address for the English Association, *Traditional Stories and Their Meaning* (London: English Association, 1983).

Campbell, Joseph. *The Hero with a Thousand Faces*. 2nd ed. Princeton, N.J.: Bollingen, 1968. Notable for its attempt to define the role of the hero in all world mythology and literature, this book resembles most of Campbell's in subordinating literature to larger human issues such as the enduring conflict between violence and the quest for peace. A good introduction to this major thinker is Robert A. Segal's *Joseph Campbell* (New York: Garland, 1987), especially valuable for its bibliographies. Segal distinguishes Campbell's thought from that of Jung: The former tends toward mysticism, the latter toward rationalism in the treatment of archetypes. In his work, Campbell has sought a scientific model of concrete symbols that arouse archetypes as stimuli activating "innate releasing mechanisms," which in turn provoke certain emotions.

Duncan, Robert. *The Truth and Life of Myth: An Essay in Essential Autobiography*. Freemont, Mich.: Sumac Books, 1968. The poet's point of view from one of his generation's most distinguished poets. Myth "is not only a story that expresses the soul but a story that awakens the soul to the real persons of its romance, in which the actual and the spiritual are revealed, one in the other" (p. 42).

Fisch, Harold. *A Remembered Future: A Study in Literary Mythology*. Bloomington: Indiana University Press, 1985. Considers the displacement of such archetypes as the double, Abraham and Isaac, and the wasteland in a wide range of texts from the Bible and Shakespeare to works by John Barth and contemporary Israeli authors.

Frye, Northrop. *Anatomy of Criticism: Four Essays*. 1957. Reprint. New York: Atheneum, 1967. Discussed in text. Almost all of Frye's many books show something of his own brand of archetypal criticism. He is one of the most readable and stimulating critics of our century.

Gould, Eric. *Mythical Intentions in Modern Literature*. Princeton, N.J.: Princeton University Press, 1981. The long first chapter treats myth and archetypal criticism. Gould dislikes "the deliberate mystification of the essentialist viewpoint on myth and archetype, especially in the work of Jung." Jungianism fails to realize that "the archetypal significance of myth must be a language event" (p. 86). (The reaction against "essentialist" belief in something like Platonic ideas is a frequent theme in current theory, especially in critiques of authors like Jung and Wheelwright. Compare Adams.) Principal subjects in ensuing chapters are Joyce, Eliot, and Lawrence. Not easy reading.

Jung, Carl Gustav. (See also Kerenyi.) *The Spirit in Man, Art, and Literature*. 1967. Reprint. London: Routledge and Kegan Paul (ARK Paperbacks), 1984. This, one of many collections of Jung's writings available, provides texts of some of the classic statements of the author: "On the Relation of Analytical Psychology to Poetry," "Psychology and Literature," "Ulysses: A Monologue," and "Picasso," among others.

Kerenyi, Carl, and C. G. Jung. *Essays on a Science of Mythology*. Translated by R. F. C. Hull. Princeton, N.J.: Bollingen, 1950. A meeting of minds and disciplines: classical scholarship with psychology.

Kirk, G. S. *The Nature of Greek Myths*. Harmondsworth: Penguin Books, 1974. Provides thoughtful assessments of various theories of the origin and purpose of mythology, as well as accounts of most of the important myths, including a long chapter on Herakles (Hercules). For his account of the tree swingers of the Aiora, see p. 231.

Lauter, Estella, and Carol Schreiner, eds. *Feminist Archetypal Theory*. Knoxville: University of Tennessee Press, 1985. These seven essays use literature mainly in the service of psychological theory. Critical of the masculine bias in Jung, the authors both reassert and redefine concepts like archetype, individuation, and the unconscious. They approach their topic from the standpoint of art history, religion, therapy, and literary theory (see discussions of Frye and Lévi-Strauss). Good bibliography, pp. 266–70.

Lentricchia, Frank. *After the New Criticism*. Chicago: University of Chicago Press, 1980. Begins with a chapter on Frye's *Anatomy*, seen as helping to liberate poetry from "the hegemony of New Criticism," even though Frye retained a formalist's belief in the autonomous status of literature.

Lockerd, Benjamin G. *Psychic Integration in "The Faerie Queene."* Lewisburg, Pa.: Bucknell University Press, 1987. Studies Spenser's poem from the perspectives of both Renaissance religion and Jungian psychology, with special attention to the masculine-feminine dynamic in the poem.

Lucente, Gregory L. *The Narrative of Realism and Myth: Verga, Lawrence, Faulkner, Pavese.* Baltimore: Johns Hopkins University Press, 1981. The centerpiece for this largely structural approach to myth in literature is an analysis of Giovanni Verga's "She-Wolf" (text of this brief story included). Lucente explores the way realism and myth interact in modern fiction. Though subordinated to realism, myth helps unify plot, shapes character, and focuses the narrative subject's (the narrator's) perceptions. Clear but freighted with citations. The second chapter neatly surveys theories of myth since Vico.

Maud, Ralph. "Archetypal Depth Criticism and Melville." *College English* 45 (1983): 695–704. Urges the application of the post-Jungian depth psychologist James Hillman's ideas to literature.

Murray, Gilbert. "Hamlet and Orestes." In his *The Classical Tradition in Poetry*, pp. 205–40. Cambridge, Mass.: Harvard University Press, 1927. Discussed in text. This reprints "with a few changes" a British Academy Shakespeare lecture given in 1914.

Parabola: The Magazine of Myth and Tradition. Published quarterly for a decade now, this handsomely printed journal embraces a wide variety of disciplines, including literature, art history, and anthropology. Like much transliterary discussion in this field, its articles stop short of critical engagement with their assumptions.

Pratt, Annis, et al. *Archetypal Patterns in Women's Fiction.* Bloomington: Indiana University Press, 1981; Brighton: Harvester Press, 1982. Discusses mostly modern fiction by women from the standpoint of key concepts: self, patriarch, eros, and rebirth. Author of a number of books and articles relating archetypalism and feminism, Pratt believes that "the novel performs the same role in women's lives as do the Eleusinian, dying-god, and witchcraft rituals—a restoration through remembering, crucial to our survival" (p. 176).

Righter, William. *Myth and Literature.* London: Routledge and Kegan Paul, 1975. In the Concepts of Literature series, this little book provides the best general treatment of the subject, with an incisive discussion of Frye. Like Gould, Righter emphasizes that myths, like all experience, are mediated by language.

Strelka, Joseph P., ed. *Literary Criticism and Myth.* Special issue of the *Yearbook of Comparative Criticism* 9 (1980). Authors consider a variety of subjects, mostly non-Anglo-American, from classical antiquity to Proust and Mann. John Vickery's essay is the exception to the foreign emphasis, though almost all his examples of myth criticism are from the 1960s and earlier.

Vickery, John B., ed. *Myth and Literature.* Lincoln: University of Nebraska Press, 1966. An immensely valuable collection of leading myth critics. It includes Hyman's essay, mentioned in n. 3, above, and a preliminary article to Vickery's own valuable chronicle of Frazer's influence, *The Literary Impact of "The Golden Bough"* (Princeton, N.J.: Princeton University Press, 1973). Vickery also provides several essays critical of the premises of myth criticism.

Wheelwright, Philip. *The Burning Fountain: A Study in the Language of Symbolism.* Bloomington: Indiana University Press, 1954. Except for Frye, probably the most fully developed theory of literature by a critic fundamentally in accord with archetypalism. Wheelwright's concept of "plurisignification" differs from William Empson's more formalist "ambiguity" in that literature acquires its multiple meanings not from the play of language but from the unconscious apprehension of spiritual resonances; in other words, his theory is grounded in a religious idea of human nature. Discussions of the *Oresteia* and Eliot's poetry are especially valuable. See also two chapters, "The Archetypal Symbol" and "On the Verge of Myth," in his *Metaphor and Reality* (Bloomington: Indiana University Press, 1962), pp. 111–52.

Ziolkowski, Theodore. *Disenchanted Images: A Literary Iconology*. Princeton: Princeton University Press, 1977. Traces the way certain images, originally bearing magical and religious associations, survive in literature despite their "disenchantment." Images of Venus and the ring, the haunted portrait, and the magic mirror are examined in about one hundred texts from many authors, mostly over the last two centuries. In modern literature these images cluster in fantasy, horror fiction, and travesty. While not strictly an archetypal critic, Ziolkowski often provides material for this approach.

The study of the influence of a single myth on many literary works is a natural project for critics working in comparative literature. Some notable books of this kind written in English are: Honor Matthews, *The Primal Curse: The Myth of Cain and Abel in the Theatre* (New York: Schocken Books, 1967); Patricia Merivale, *Pan the Goat-God: His Myth in Modern Times* (Cambridge, Mass.: Harvard University Press, 1969); Walter A. Strauss, *Descent and Return: The Orphic Theme in Modern Literature* (Cambridge, Mass.: Harvard University Press, 1971). The last three sections of Hans Blumenberg's weighty excursion into "philosophical anthropology," *Work on Myth*, trans. Robert M. Wallace (Cambridge, Mass.: MIT Press, 1985), survey the myth of Prometheus in thought and literature from antiquity to Goethe to Nietzsche, Joyce, and Mann. The distinguished classicist Charles Segal has a study of the Orpheus myth in ancient and modern literature forthcoming from Johns Hopkins University Press.

LORI HOPE LEFKOVITZ

Creating the World: Structuralism and Semiotics

Preview

Because things are not necessarily what they seem, we are always decoding our
world. We interpret gestures; we translate simple remarks: "The weather
looks lovely" may mean "I would rather not go to the movies." Because people
obey certain rules (of grammar, of etiquette, of artistry, or, more deeply, of the
subconscious) in producing texts (whether verbal, visual, or other), we are
always encoding our world. Some of these operations are so basic to the lived
experience of people who share a culture that the rules seem self-evident and,
therefore, natural. The structuralist or semiotician takes a few steps back to
scrutinize that which seems self-evident, because if things need not be what
they seem, neither must they necessarily be the way they are. Standing at a
remove from the text, one questions the apparent naturalness of cultural
manifestations and artifacts, for example, the seemingly self-evident value of
such aesthetic objects as the much taught poem. In contrast with the practice
of New Criticism, current in the academy through the 1950s and sixties,
semiotics ceases to define art as *mimesis*, as the representation of reality,
concentrating instead upon *semeosis*, the process of recovering from a text a
secondary, deeper level of signification.

In *The Semiotics of Poetry* Michael Riffaterre accordingly describes two
stages of reading poems. First we read *as if* the language were ordinary
language, and then we return to gaps in the text, the moments when the poem
defies usual logic. Looking for method in the madness of language gone awry,
we discover the code that generates and will make sense of apparent nonsense
(what Riffaterre calls "ungrammaticalities"). Roland Barthes's analyses of
fiction, rather than beginning from the assumption that a realistic fiction

imitates reality, ask how fiction creates the "effect-of-the-real" and how art has taught us to imagine reality in the way that we do. Because reality is mediated by signs, the critic uses textual knowledge to identify the codes to which the writer has appealed.

Literary criticism asks *what* texts mean. Semiotics and structuralism are among the theories that first ask *how* language and literature convey meaning. Different theories respond differently to this question. Structuralism and semiotics recognize that communities that share a textual history reach a consensus about meaning because they share codes and conventions of expression. That consensus is limited to the extent that individual experiences of codes vary. Thus, although you and I share a basic notion of what the word *friend* means, a different idea, image, person undoubtedly comes to each of us when we think of the word. Moreover, the world has not always been encoded in the same way by all people in all places at all times. A text's meaning derives from its place within a system of texts.

Meaning is intertextual; that is, a given text always refers us to other texts, which explains why readers are able to infer meaning from sparse information.[1] The reader makes the meaning from the signs. Umberto Eco describes an unwritten cultural encyclopedia that we all consult as we make sense of texts, as texts necessarily contain references that we grasp without ostensible effort. Some semiotic critics (Riffaterre, for example) go so far as to say that the system of reference is closed; language refers only to itself and to no world beyond itself. Others (Lotman and Scholes, for example) claim that our understanding of meaning derives from both our linguistic and our extralinguistic experience.[2] In either case, the more familiar we are with the relevant codes (linguistic, generic, historical, social), the richer and more complete our experience of a particular text will be. Hence, semioticians attend to the distinction between denotation (a word's dictionary definition or a situation's ostensible meaning) and connotation (the associations that words carry). Denying the New Critical position that it is possible to look at a work independent of its contexts, semiotics finds meaning only relationally and restores literature to its many contexts. Moreover, within a single text, meaning is also expressed only relationally, and structuralists and semioticians therefore look to those internal structures, asking what the categories are within which meaning is expressed and how they are organized.

History

Structuralism and semiotics are presented together, here and in other expositions of literary theory, because they are closely related enterprises, and both are related as well to the development referred to as poststructuralism.[3] *Structuralism, semiotics,* and *semiology* carry different connotations because they are sometimes associated with different founding figures, precursor movements, practitioners, or with different academic disciplines, though everywhere in this history there is cross-fertilization and overlap.[4] Although my purpose here is not so much to render these fine distinctions as to describe broadly those concepts of semiotics and structuralism that have been most important to literary studies, a sketch of the movements' histories can usefully introduce basic concepts and shared premises that were later elaborated in a variety of ways.

Ferdinand de Saussure, the founder of structural linguistics, observed that except for rare onomatopoetic coinages, words stand in arbitrary relation to the things that they name. We understand each other only because we agree about the meaning of sound combinations. Moreover, we understand something only insofar as we perceive that it is different from something else. (*Car* is not *cat* because we distinguish the *r* from the *t*.) The crucial insight here is that meaning is located where difference is perceived. Saussure further observed that speakers of a language can generate an infinite number of different utterances (*paroles*) but that all of these utterances obey the rules of the language system (*langue*). Behind the infinity of possible statements is a more limited system of enabling rules. Saussure distinguished between syntagmatic and paradigmatic relations. A word in a sentence acquires meaning from its position in the sentence, syntagmatically, in relation to what it precedes and follows; and from other words that might have stood in its place, paradigmatically, in relation to the array of words (synonyms, antonyms, alternative utterances) that the speaker could have chosen but did not choose. For example, in the sentence "John hit the ball," *John*'s meaning here comes both from his position *before* the word *hit* and from the fact that the word in that position is neither *Joe* nor *a boy*. Saussure developed an approach to the synchronic study of language (how language works at a particular moment in time) that radically departed from the historical linguistics (which Saussure called diachronic linguistics) current when *Cours de linguistique générale* (a compilation of Saussure's lecture notes reconstructed by his students) was published in 1915.

Moving beyond the level of sentences to larger units of speech and writing, structuralism identifies the *underlying* structures shared by the individual *surface* manifestations of a system. It provides methods of analysis. Structural anthropology, particularly Claude Lévi-Strauss's work with myth, was an important application and extension of structuralism. Discovering the structural similarities among myths rewarded analysts with discoveries about the larger social functions of mythmaking. Working from Saussure's perception that meaning is relational, structural anthropology identifies the binary oppositions in a culture as they are manifested in story and ritual. Insofar as stories mediate between irreconcilable oppositions, mythmaking is a survival strategy.[5]

Saussure imagined that his work could provide a basis for a larger study of psychology. Having understood language as a process of signification in which words (signifiers) arbitrarily refer to things (signifieds)—the two in combination forming a sign—Saussure imagined the possibility of studying many different sign systems (symbolic rites, military signals, for example). He coined the term *semiology* to designate the science of signs (from the Greek *sēmeîon*, meaning "sign"), which would show "what constitutes signs, what laws govern them." Linguistics was to be but one branch of the science that Saussure envisioned but did not develop.

As these insights came to be applied to literature, the notion of making humanistic study "scientific" troubled humanists, who were reluctant to apply rigorous methods of analysis to art. No critic works without a method, however, and one important advance of semiotics has been that readers are learning to specify the rules and beliefs that inform their readings. Because it asks readers to identify themselves, semiotics is particularly respectful of individual expression, though it challenges a traditional humanist assumption by treating even "individuality" as a cultural product.

Although Saussure saw linguistic products as but one small branch of semiology, many semioticians have since come to the conclusion that language is primary and that other signifying systems are modeled on the structure of languages. Some semiotic schools resent this so-called logocentrism. Because our perception of all reality seems to be structured by language, the evidence for asserting the primacy of language seems to me compelling, and this position has been the more influential in the field of literature.[6] The science of signs has since developed principally into the study of codes, of the manner in which information is organized so that communities achieve consensus about meaning.

In literary studies, Saussure's impact was immediately felt by the critics who came to be called the Russian formalists and the Prague School linguists. Formalism, which looked at literary forms and reduced narratives to basic functional units, may be said to be the antecedent of literary structuralism. An exemplary work of formalism is Vladimir Propp's *Morphology of the Folktale* (original Russian text, 1928). Propp isolates key features common to folk-tales, identifying a variety of narrative functions performed by characters and discovering underlying formal similarities among superficially dissimilar stories. In England, and independent of the efforts of Russian formalism, Lord Raglan's book *The Hero* (1936) comparably identified features common to literary heroes. Though his work is less systematic than that of the formalists, it was influential in the English tradition, especially on Northrop Frye's *Anatomy of Criticism* (1957), which broke with New Critical emphases. By identifying five narrative possibilities for heroic action (myth, romance, high mimesis, low mimesis, and irony), Frye's protostructuralism became part of mainstream criticism in the Anglo-American tradition.

Formalism differs from later structural studies in that it rarely attends to the significance of difference among like structures. The charge of reductionism is still sometimes leveled against structuralist theory, though semiotic and structural applications to texts (such as Barthes's reading of a story by Balzac in *S/Z* or Scholes's analyses in *The Semiotics of Interpretation*) provide clear evidence against this charge. The profound aim of structuralism was to discover the structure of the human psyche, that is, the minimal basic structures that we transform to generate unique expressions (all human products being but variations on a limited number of themes). The more practical result has been the discovery of a culture's abiding premises, prejudices, and myths (*myth*, understood in Barthes's sense, as those commonplaces that so pervade a culture as to seem invisible). In *Mythologies*, Barthes unpacks our culture like a suitcase, displaying our wares in endlessly surprising ways; the topics of Barthes's essays include the meaning of wrestling matches, Einstein's brain, soap, wine and milk, and magazine ads. The reader sees the complexity of connotation, and in a concluding major theoretical statement, "Myth Today," Barthes shows us his technique for determining second-level significations.

This immensely fruitful result of semiotic analysis also derives from another notion first expressed by Russian formalism: Victor Shklovsky's concept of *defamiliarization*. Shklovsky meant by this term that it is art's job to revitalize our experience of the familiar world so that we can see it more clearly, from a new perspective. In his words, art should make the stone stony. Barthes, among other semiotic literary critics, goes further and uses *criticism* to defamiliarize. Reading literature as participant in the systems of conventions and codes, the semiotic critic exposes the literary conventions that have come to look like truth. From this perspective of outsider to the work, the critic can both read the page and notice what or who is consistently relegated to the margins.

In narrative theory, formalism distinguished between story and plot. The story is the order in which the events of a narrative actually occurred, and the plot is the often jumbled chronology in which these events are presented to the reader. This distinction enabled critics to comment more precisely about how narrative effects are achieved. Later structuralists, Gérard Genette in particular, refined and systematized these distinctions, observing that there is the story, the narration presented to the reader, and the actual discourse that the narrator presents. The usefulness of these refinements can best be appreciated as we see them applied in Genette's readings of fiction, specifically that by Proust.

The last contribution of formalism and structural linguistics that I will introduce is Roman Jakobson's influential model of communication:

```
                          context
                          message
        addresser----------------------------------addressee
                          contact
                          code
```

To be understood, every act of communication requires someone who sends the message and someone who receives it, the message itself, knowledge of the context in which the message is conveyed (the same words mean different things in different contexts), knowledge of the code (the English language or the language of science, if the message is a medical prescription), and a method of contact (the words on the page, the telephone line). Jakobson's model directs our attention to the ways in which messages vary according to their emphasis on a particular aspect of the communication situation. For example, a diary focuses on the sender of the message, an advertisement on the receiver, the question "Can you hear me?" on the contact, and so on. Jakobson accordingly schematized the possible functions that correspond to his model of communication:

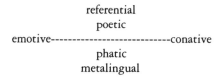

```
                        referential
                          poetic
        emotive--------------------------conative
                          phatic
                        metalingual
```

Although these schematizations cannot account for all of the elements or subtleties of meaningful expression, they do provide a way of describing and distinguishing among texts and parts of text. These models facilitate the teaching of reading and writing by providing a vocabulary that can clearly express the different emphases of modes of discourse. Critical discourse, for example, devotes most of its attention to the code (the genre, the use of language) and is largely metalingual (language about language). Beginning with formalism through contemporary developments in semiology, Saussure's legacy has been rich.

Roughly contemporary with Saussure, but independently, the American philosopher Charles Sanders Peirce developed a science of signs that he named "semiotics." Peirce's semiotics is the far more detailed, though the two men shared an impulse to discover the rule-governed characteristics of signifying systems. Peirce names three kinds of signs: icon, index, and symbol. An icon resembles its object (a drawing, a photograph, a graph). An index is connected to its object because the interpreter recognizes connecting functions (as we know to look in the direction that a finger points, as we know that a particular skin rash signifies poison ivy). Finally, a symbol stands in arbitrary relation to its object (words being the best example).

Peirce also describes another triad of relations: the sign, the interpretant, and the object. The sign stands for something, its object, *to someone*. How the sign for the object is understood by a particular someone is the interpretant. Peirce thus focuses attention on *the relay of thoughts* that signs generate. In so doing he begins to describe an infinite process of signification: An interpretant becomes a sign of another object, which in turn generates another interpretant. According to Peirce, the world can be known only indirectly, through this signification process, and the process depends upon community.

Peirce's most radical extension of this principle is his statement that "man himself is a sign." Each human subject is constituted in language and by language; we are each the sum total of our utterances because all of life and all of reality are composed of only trains of thought. The psychology of Jacques Lacan begins from this premise, and Michel Foucault's dramatic claim that the age of man is nearing its end also depends upon our ability to imagine that the human subject is not inevitable in the way that we understand it today but is also a *product* of signifying systems.[7] Contemporary semioticians are indebted to the basic insights of both Saussure and Peirce, and the international community has adopted the term *semiotics*, though *semiology* is sometimes used in deference to the French founder.

Constructs

The most important contribution of structuralism and semiotics to literary studies has been the discovery that rules govern the production and consumption of texts. Because meaning can be expressed only within and through systems of relations, all communication, all literature, is necessarily systematic. Texts are cultural artifacts that participate in and express the values of the system out of which they emerge. One consequence of this contribution has been the removal of textual processes from the domain of the mysterious; the "magic" or "mystique" of literature becomes suspect. Semiotic and structural studies demystify literature and the procedures of reading and writing.

Umberto Eco, in *A Theory of Semiotics*, defines a sign system as anything that can be used to lie. Language is one such system, literature another. Genres of literature, as well as other modes of communication, comprise signifying systems. By implication semiotics teaches one how he or she is lied to or how to lie. (Advertisers have long understood a practical application of semiotic theory as they manipulate codes to create desire in consumers in order to sell products.) An alternative to describing a sign system as something that can be used to lie, the metaphor of seduction has been used by semiotic critics such as Barthes and Julia Kristeva. We can see stories as seductive insofar as realist literature lulls us into a receptive posture: Everyone loves a good story; and many people go to the movies for passive escape into the fiction displayed before them. Indeed, semiotic theory has been especially important to the fast-developing field of film studies, as film yields to a theory that can distinguish among its several systems (script, sound track, moving images, edits). Especially exciting are developing theories of the psychology of spectatorship. As we consume any story before we subject it to semiotic analysis, we accept the assumptions, morals, and values of the writer (some of which may be subconscious, which is why psychoanalysts can surprise us with readings of our own stories). The goal becomes overcoming the pleasure of the text to achieve mastery over it.[8]

To the extent that they describe rules that govern the relation between a deep structure and a surface manifestation, the basic insights of Freudian psychology (subconscious/conscious) and Marxist economic analysis (base/superstructure) exemplify not only what has retroactively been called early structuralism but also how a construct with effective explanatory powers soon comes to be seen as self-evident.[9] Freud, for example, organized his own and his patients' experiences into narrative form. His readings of these narratives point up connections between superficially inexplicable physical symptoms and deeper psychological causes. The slippery nature of language—its potential to conceal as well as to reveal—provides the necessary clues, and, to interpret such overdetermined psychic events as dreams, the analyst decodes the symbols. Where a Victorian reader would not have found Oedipal explanations, most of us are ready discoverers of Freudian meanings. So, too, Marx explained economic relations by pointing to other kinds of displacements and equivalences.

The semiotician might step back and pose a few questions of the culture that produced such early semioticians as Freud and Marx: Why does structuralism emerge at this juncture? Why did thinkers in unrelated disciplines both come to wonder about how one thing stands in for another? Why did both speak of fetishism (sexual or commodity)? And it is a small step from noting these similarities to questioning the seemingly natural divisions within the academy: Theology, once the queen of the disciplines, today hardly exists as an academic department in American liberal arts institutions; Freud is taught in psychology and literature programs, rarely in economics departments, though his work clearly shares something with the thinking of Marx. There is arbitrariness in this compartmentalization of learning. Over time, classification systems change, the governance of academic disciplines changes, and ideals of beauty change; what we take for granted at one moment as universal, explicable, reasonable, and natural may be easily explained away as the mistaken notions of the past a moment later, only to resurface still later as partial rediscovered truth.

Semiotics and structuralism, as theoretical sciences, are methods with corresponding ideologies that cross and challenge traditional academic divisions. The very designation of disciplines has been called into question by structuralists. Because semiotics is a transdisciplinary field, its vocabulary is not always received comfortably. An oft-heard complaint against these theories has been the tendency of some semioticians to rely upon jargon. Though I am no fan of jargon, it should be recognized that, just as a Freudian or Marxist literary critic trains in the terminology of medicine, psychology, or economics, so a basic vocabulary of semiotics and structuralism derives from the originary fields of linguistics and philosophy. These theories have had impact on all academic disciplines, the natural and social sciences as well as the humanities and the arts.

In the habit of asking about cultural responses, a semiotician wonders about the wide appeal of semiotic theory itself. Semiotics and structuralism appeal to our wish to organize the increasing vastness, even chaos, of information in our world. It is not surprising that a theory that claims that literature, fashion, language, and even the human psyche are informed by an essential universal organization, rule-governed in its transformations, should have taken hold at the beginning of our century of technological revolution. In George Eliot's *Middlemarch*, the unsympathetic Casaubon looks for a "key to all mythologies," and the reader is impressed with the misguided nature of his effort. Along with other collapses in faith, nineteenth-century humanism could not believe in the possibility of such systematizing. Some have said that today's structuralists share Casaubon's mistake.

Ironically, structuralism has had to sustain the opposing charges that it (1) lacks humanity because it subjects literature to scientific analysis and (2) is overidealistic because it searches for universals and gives greater privilege to synchronic systems than to historical change. The latter charge comes principally from Marxist critics.[10] It seems to me, however, that semiotics and structuralism are liable to neither accusation because the two accusations are mutually exclusive. Saussure offered us the concept of diachronic as well as synchronic study, and the analysis of codes recognizes the historical and necessarily evolving character of systems of meaning. The traditional conception of humanism is challenged because our humanity is recognized as a product of culturally changing situations even as the recognition of universality among our organizing systems affirms cultural and communal connections that can be made visible only through systemic analyses.

Opening Lessons

Two parables about coding: (1) Rubin applies for a job and wants to convey the message that he is terrific, the most talented, the most hard-working, the best applicant. He says so in so many words in a first letter of application, which conveys not the message that he intended but the message that he is conceited, or overeager, or immature, or simply that he does not understand the rules that govern the writing of job letters. Consequently, he loses the job to a better-trained writer.

(2) Simone spends her first weekend in college partying. To atone, she decides to fulfill two promises to stay in touch. She describes the same evening twice, once in a letter to her best friend from high school and again in a letter to her grandmother. As you can imagine, the two letters are quite different, though neither is, strictly speaking, dishonest. Simone's roommate gets a good laugh when she reads the letters over Simone's shoulder, and each of her correpondents gets a letter from the woman she remembers and likes best. Simone becomes feature editor for the college paper.

Invented for use in the writing classroom, these stories suggest that the better we are able to manipulate codes, the better able we are to succeed in such cultural institutions as the family, friendship, school, and business.[11] Good readers and writers imitate and modify discourses that are recognizably effective because they resemble other valued discourses. It is the job of professional readers and teachers to teach these codes, that is, to teach how to reproduce what is valued. Rubin is not forever doomed to lose jobs because he lacks the talent with which Simone was supposedly born. Indeed, so-called talent may be acquired through familiarity with discursive modes. Familiarity with the rules of discourse paradoxically frees us from the constraints of those rules: We are defamiliarized. Even a successful writer may find that because she has never been much for reading poems she cannot produce a poem to save her life. She may not need to do so, but we often have to manufacture appropriate selves for different occasions, and sometimes knowing the rules of a discourse can save one's life or one's job or one's face.

The rules of discourse can and do change, and what we call truth changes accordingly. In this sense, and in other ways as well, our use of language creates the world and the people who populate it. We create ourselves by the language that we use, and we create others in the language that we use to characterize them. As Roland Barthes says, of characters in literature, people in books are nothing more than proper nouns with adjectives and other connotative words attached to the proper name. [12]

Structuralism and semiotics have methodological and ideological implications for the study of literature, both of which have been resisted by traditional humanists. Moreover, those who define themselves (or are defined by others) as structuralists or semioticians or semiologists disagree on methodological and ideological grounds. [13] Marshall Blonsky's recent collection *On Signs* exemplifies both the range within the field and how semiotics has opened itself beyond its own early limits, as identifying limits has allowed for the possibility of straining against them. Blonsky writes in his introduction that "Modern semiotics was founded to enable myth to be read *simply*. . . . For semiotics postulated that natural language mediated the process of decoding the world; only that which can be verbalized has been thought" (p. xvii). He goes on to identify a second stage in the evolution of semiotics: "the heady days of seeing the functioning of the (respectable) world's semantic organization; of catching not the meaning, but the production of meaning, the *signification*, the decisive statements of architecture, urban studies, painting, poetry, narrative, cinema, gestures, rites—their deep being, their truth, their official meaning." With the self-consciousness appropriate to semiotics, Blonsky collects the work of authors who now turn "their intelligence onto the body, onto laughter, onto space and land, the intentionality of the right and left, the machinery of success and failure, the apparatus of governing and selling."

Humanists have been disturbed by the enterprise's apparent irreverence with respect to great individuals: If Tolstoy simply knew the rules of a code, then his novels are less the product of an individual genius who expresses universal truths than the product of a man who is himself a product of his culture. For the semiotician, the success of Tolstoy's artistry may be measured by his ability to make the truths of his culture *seem* universal. Literature generates the readers' expectations and then delights them by effectively meeting or by surprising those expectations.

Delighting the reader in this way can, of course, be accomplished by popular as well as "high" art. *War and Peace* is a more valued text than *Peanuts* because powerful communities of readers have agreed to prefer epic novels to comic strips. Discomforted by this challenge to established values, some have said that semiotic criticism is best applied to popular culture rather than to art. Semiotics denies, however, the sanctity of any text. The result has been an effort to discern *why* the literary establishment canonized the texts that it did and exiled others to silent realms. One measure of the influence of structuralism on English departments has been the challenges to the literary canon by groups who have reason to resist the status quo (feminist critics, for example). The job of criticism is not art appreciation but demystification. Semioticians do not look for universal beauty and truth but rather tell us how we have come to see something as beautiful or true and whose interest this aesthetic has served.

Structuralism and semiotic studies have gone in several directions as critiques have developed into independent but related literary theories. Lacanian psychoanalytic criticism develops from the notion that the subject is constituted in language; the reader-response theories of Iser or Fish develop from notions of communal consensus and the subjectivity of a message's receiver; feminist theory has been able to use the idea of coding to explain how the female body has been negatively inscribed in a culture that creates binary oppositions and hierarchies that have consistently worked to oppress women in text and in life; Derrida's deconstruction finds in texts not one but several competing signifying systems that are often in contradiction with each other, so that texts undercut their own meanings. The recognition that discourse is a matter of codes has revitalized genre criticism, exemplified in Tzvetan Todorov's work on the fantastic or Scholes's work on science fiction. The structural Marxism of Althusser and Jameson also departs from, but therefore acknowledges the contribution of, semiotic and structuralist principles.

Rereading the Beginning: A Semiotic Application to Genesis 1–3

Beginnings, like endings, assume special status in structural analyses. Silence or a blank page is rich in potential, but how we break the silence establishes expectations for what will follow. Setting out in a direction limits the possibilities for what may be said thereafter. The wealth of potential, a meaningless void, yields at the same time to form and meaning. Because what we designate as beginnings has this rhetorical importance, culture inevitably tries to go back on them, to rewrite them, to re-create the start in conformity with changing values. As layers accrue, it becomes difficult to read the beginning as once it was, but there is, finally, no going back on the beginning. Every backtracking acquires its significance in relation to what was already said.

The Bible is such a beginning, as it has conventionally been read as the start of one branch of the Western textual tradition. Since the first account of creation, there have been innumerable retellings, interpolations, interpretations, commentaries, drawings, paintings, sculptures, movies, and advertisements that shroud our reading of the text in veils of revision. According to the story's self-understanding, here people are inscribed into the world for the first time, and according to literary criticism (Frye) people are inscribed into the Great Code for the first time. It is a momentous occasion, a cosmic semiotic event.

The book opens with the phrase "In the beginning," but since we cannot imagine a moment before which there was no before, the story assumes that this was the beginning because the world as we know it did not yet exist, nothing had meaning, and what did exist was "formless void." Creation and valuation occur through the agency of language. The hero, God, names things, they come into being, and they are good. The act of naming is an act of making distinctions, as God's voice reaches into the chaos and separates the light from the darkness, the heaven from the earth, the earth from the water. Creation occurs in language, is a matter of naming, of making distinctions, and more specifically, creation is a matter of articulating opposites.

These oppositions, light and dark, heaven and earth, and so on, organize the chaos as God creates a system of classification that makes sense of nonsense by mapping the world. These oppositions, after these many years, seem to us natural enough. Nonetheless, there is nothing inevitable about the choice of opposites here named, each acquiring its identity and value only in relation to that to which it is opposed. Dry earth below, for example, first opposes heaven above and later stands distinct from the wet water. Earth need not have been opposed to heaven; hell, had it been the relevant opposition in the mind of this author, might have been created to oppose heaven. In each instance, meaning is determined on the basis of where difference is perceived. Further, where there is difference, there is hierarchy. In each case of an opposing pair, the reader meets a meaningful distinction because we know which half of the pair is superior, which is inferior: Light is preferred to dark, heaven to earth, sun to moon, and so for each named and created thing.

Near the end of this process the most important act of creation occurs. Against the creation of animal life is produced humanity: "male and female created He them." No significant distinction, no hierarchy is established between the sexes because humanity is given but one name. It is not until the second chapter of Genesis, when another creation story is introduced, that the first human is identified as male. In chapter 1 the text specifies the simultaneous creation of both sexes of each species.

In Genesis 2:5, the redactor goes back on the beginning by retelling the story, and the reader is presented with a second, but earlier, version of the creation story. The map gets infinitely smaller as we are removed from the cosmos and placed on a pinpoint on earth, the Garden of Eden, a microcosm of the world. From this utopia, all human history will emanate. The garden story adds two more oppositions, which are central and meaningful ever after, the opposition between man and woman and, more deeply, the opposition of knowledge and nakedness. Even Freud's account of the psyche will obey these Edenic divisions.

In this story man, not humanity (male and female), is formed from dust and placed in Eden. Here, man is primary. What follows this verse is a history of the present. The story tells not only why things are the way they are but also why they must be the way they are. Creation, the making of meaning, is a practical business. The story dictates to its readers how we organize our lives in a post-Edenic state, and the hierarchy known as the Great Chain of Being is established: vegetable life, animal life, woman, man, God, each, in turn, serving the other. Man's fate will be to toil cursed ground and earn the family's keep; woman's fate is pain in childbirth and to yearn toward her husband who will lord over her.

In this second beginning, the earlier story of creation, Adam is given the divine prerogative of naming as God parades the animals before Adam and invites Adam to identify them. Adam will own the world as God owns the cosmos that he named. As Adam creates his universe on earth he looks for a companion, but none is found suitable. God puts Adam to sleep and, significantly, removes the first woman from the belly of the man. Adam names her and thus owns her, too. In this story of creation, in particular of the creation of human sexuality and sexual difference as a meaningful fact of culture, God's principle function is to create life. In an overwhelming counterfactual moment, God insures that life does not first develop from the body of woman. Reversing the biology of hereafter, the first woman is born out of the belly of a man. When Eve becomes a childbearer at the story's conclusion, childbearing is suitably identified not as her blessing but as her curse. Beneath the story lies a fear and suspicion of female sexuality, and each opposition generates a reversal designed to allay that fear, to soothe the anxious psyche of the primitive mythmaker.

God admonishes Adam not to eat of the tree of knowledge, declaring that eating will result in death. At that moment, the reader knows that Adam will do so, because where there is an admonition so must follow a transgression or there would be no story. Eve is thus created to instigate the crime. The snake comes and declares that eating will bring divine knowledge, not death. But when Adam and Eve do eat they neither die nor acquire any immediate divine knowledge; when their eyes are opened they do not learn astrology or physics or any specialized agricultural formulas. The only knowledge that they acquire is knowledge of their nakedness, knowledge of their own sexuality. The text establishes an equivalence: Death equals knowledge equals sex. This equation has been sustained linguistically as "to know in the biblical sense," as the euphemism "to die" in Elizabethan English or the euphemism *un petit mort* in French all of which refer to sexual engagement. And sex was for a long time thereafter imagined to be a slow suicide: Biology taught that man lost his life fluid and gave it to woman.

Even as female sexuality tempts man and ruins his Edenic peace, driving him out to labor, the story displays some unease about which sex does the tempting. The serpent, a talking, walking serpent, an erect snake tempts Eve. From the perspective of the story, which is male, woman brings the greatest threat to obedience to God and to personal peace; she brings knowledge of the body in its nakedness. At the same time in the story's subconscious, male sexuality first tempts woman. On the surface, man yearns to woman and falls; in God's punishment the facts are again unceremoniously reversed as God declares that woman will do the yearning while man will do the lording.

After all of the oppositions of chapter 1 of Genesis (sky, earth; land, sea; day, night; sun, moon), chapter 2 makes the most important cultural distinction of all. Man opposes woman, innocence then opposes experience, and woman destroys innocence and gives it another opposite (guilt). In the chain of signification, experience is equivalent to guilt. In all the world of man's possessions, woman is a threat to male piety. It is a moral with which we are well familiar. Man must master woman not because she sinned but, more deeply, because the story suggests that if literature does not keep female sexuality under control, woman has the power to destroy continually.

The value of structuralism and semiotics as theories does not lie exclusively in the interpretive readings that structural critics produce. Instead, the theories suggest a way of seeing by challenging the classification systems of humanism. If the theories also provide us with readings that can enable us to be free of cultural assumptions that harm, that is good. But where we expose one set of assumptions, we miss others, and undoubtedly we create some of our own.

Notes

1. Cf. Umberto Eco, *The Role of the Reader: Explorations in the Semiotics of Texts* (Bloomington: Indiana University Press, 1979), especially the discussion in chap. 8, "Lector in Fabula," of inferential walks and ghost chapters.

2. For a discussion of the debate on referentiality (which is argued for important stakes), see Robert Scholes, *Semiotics and Interpretation* (New Haven: Yale University Press, 1982), pp. 37–56. Scholes persuasively reasons that our experience of literature should bring us to a better understanding of the world. The argument about reference has given rise to the concern from social critics that structural and semiotic theories encourage complacency. See Scholes, "The Text and the World," *Textual Power: Literary Theory and the Teaching of English* (New Haven: Yale University Press, 1985), pp. 74–85.

3. See, e.g., Terence Hawkes, *Structuralism and Semiotics* (Berkeley: University of California Press, 1977), or Terry Eagleton, *Literary Theory: An Introduction* (Minneapolis: University of Minnesota Press, 1983), chap. 3, "Structuralism and Semiotics."

4. Though Hawkes, among others, points out that semiotics and structuralism are roughly coterminous, Thomas Sebeok regards this as a fundamental misconstrual of the facts, the history, and the development of semiotics. The collection *Frontiers in Semiotics*, ed. John Deely, Brooke Williams, and Felicia K. Kruse (Bloomington: Indiana University Press, 1986), represents the latter point of view, tracing a philosophical lineage for semiotics different from the perspective that I offer here. The contributors to this volume consider sign systems in nature (animal signing, that is, zoosemiotics) among various other signifying systems. My own exposition, which aims to present the theories that have most influenced literary critics, is less than sympathetic with the perspective offered by Deely et al. The editors define their own purpose: "We aim at nothing less that a full-scale 'paradigm shift,' in the popular consciousness, from the exclusively literary, structuralist, and Saussurean *pars* to the inclusive biological, philosophical, and Peircean *totum*." In my view, the popular consciousness referred to here is unfairly represented. Biological studies have not been the subject of literary semiotics for reasons other than this mistaken distinction between Saussure and Peirce. Faulting Saussure for roots in linguistics is misguided at best. Certainly Peirce devoted himself to the development of a semiotics that Saussure did not attempt. I am convinced that human language informs and provides the basic structure for all other communication systems.

5. See also the work of the structural anthropologist Mary Douglas.

6. That names create thought and that language structures our very perception of reality are an insight of the linguist Benjamin Lee Whorf, who discovered that the Eskimos have many more words for snow than do speakers of English. Because their language makes these fine distinctions, the Eskimos *see* differences in snow that we cannot see. Language and its conventions both create and restrict our vision. What should perhaps be added is that while there are social reasons that account for the Eskimos' having to distinguish among snows, there may be any number of other *unseen* things that it would be useful to distinguish and reclassify if only we could reimagine the world that is already structured by our language. Thomas S. Kuhn in *The Structure of Scientific Revolutions* (Chicago: University of Chicago Press, 1962) demonstrates that the scientific enterprise is often a matter of breaking out of a classification system that limits laboratory observations.

7. For the best exposition of these developments in semiotics and their application to works of literature and film, see Kaja Silverman, *The Subject of Semiotics* (New York: Oxford University Press, 1983).

8. Dubious about genre boundaries, semiotic theorists often make this point by being linguistically playful, writing criticism that is art. The most threatened critics of semiotics simply assert that the enterprise is not serious. See, e.g., Harold Brodkey's review of Roland Barthes, *The Rustle of Language*, in *New York Times Book Review*, 20 April 1986, p. 13.

9. See, e.g., the collection of *The Structuralists from Marx to Lévi-Strauss*, ed. Richard and Fernande De George (Garden City, N.Y.: Doubleday [Anchor Books], 1972).

10. See Eagleton, *Literary Theory*, or Frederic Jameson's critique in *The Prison-House of Language: A Critical Account of Structuralism and Russian Formalism* (Princeton, N.J.: Princeton University Press, 1972).

11. A writing textbook that makes use of semiotic principles is Robert Scholes and Nancy Comley, *The Practice of Writing*, 2nd ed. (New York: St. Martin's Press, 1986).

12. Barthes, *S/Z: An Essay* (New York: Hill and Wang, 1974), p. 67; earlier, E. M. Forster, *Aspects of the Novel* (New York: Harcourt Brace, 1927), p. 44, makes a similar observation.

13. De George and De George, *Structuralists from Marx to Lévi-Strauss*, write in their introduction: "To the extent that structuralism is a movement, it is multi-dimensional with several independent leaders, each disowning any relation to the others and each carrying along with him a group of devoted and enthusiastic followers. . . . If each disowns the others as brothers-in-arms and struggles to get free of invidious labels, scores of lesser figures fight to be included in the group, to learn the terminology, and to apply and misapply the techniques at random and at will in order to be associated with the fashionable successor of existentialism."

Selected Bibliography

Because the literature on structuralism and semiotics is vast, I do not include articles or journals devoted to the subject. Instead, I have favored anthologies that collect major statements, introductory texts (including those with which I do not agree), historical surveys, foundation texts, and works particularly valuable for literary studies. Only representative works of prolific authors are cited, and the work of theorists who have come to be more closely associated with poststructuralism than structuralism (such as the Yale critics) is omitted here.

Abel, Elizabeth, ed. *Writing and Sexual Difference*. Chicago: University of Chicago Press, 1980. A collection of feminist essays, but as the title suggests many of them take a semiotic approach to texts and feminist analysis.

Bailey, R. W., L. Matejka, and P. Steiner, eds. *The Sign: Semiotics around the World*. Ann Arbor: Michigan Slavic Publications, 1978. Most valuable for its collection of international contributions to semiotics.

Bakhtin, Mikhail. *The Dialogic Imagination: Four Essays by M. M. Bakhtin*. Edited by Michael Holquist. Austin: University of Texas Press, 1981.

———. *Rabelais and His World*. Translated by Hélène Iswolsky. Cambridge, Mass.: MIT Press, 1965. Bakhtin's theories of literature, his notion of carnival, and his discussion of texts as participants in dialogues are acquiring increasing importance in recent years. A fascinating study of Rabelais.

Barthes, Roland. *Elements of Semiology*. New York: Hill and Wang, 1967. A brief study that includes consideration of the garment system and the food system. Basic concepts are introduced, but this work is not a primer.

———. *Image–Music–Text*. New York: Hill and Wang, 1977. A collection of essays including analyses of photographs and films as well as "The Death of the Author," "Writers, Intellectuals, Teachers," and "Introduction to the Structural Analysis of Narrative."

──────. *Mythologies*. New York: Hill and Wang, 1973. Short, lively essays on popular culture followed by a statement of theory and method.

──────. *S/Z: An Essay*. New York: Hill and Wang, 1974. A book-length analysis of Balzac's short story, "Sarrasine." Barthes divides the text into codes and demonstrates the semiotics of fiction. An essential work.

Benveniste, Emile. *Problems in General Linguistics*. Coral Gables, Fla.: University of Miami Press, 1971. The linguistic background.

Bersani, Leo. *A Future for Astyanax: Character and Desire in Literature*. Boston: Little, Brown, 1969. Applications of theory to literature. Bersani reads fiction beautifully and argues an effective case.

Blonsky, Marshall. *On Signs*. Baltimore: Johns Hopkins University Press, 1985. A collection of important recent contributions.

Chatman, Seymour, ed. *Approaches to Poetics*. New York: Columbia University Press, 1973.

──────. *Story and Discourse*. Ithaca, N.Y.: Cornell University Press, 1978. As Chatman both clarifies and applies semiotic theory to fiction, this work is both basic and valuable criticism.

Coward, Rosalind, and John Ellis. *Language and Materialism: Developments in Semiology and the Theory of the Subject*. London: Routledge and Kegan Paul, 1977.

Culler, Jonathan. *The Pursuit of Signs: Semiotics, Literature, Deconstruction*. Ithaca, N.Y.: Cornell University Press, 1981. Culler does here for semiotics what *Structuralist Poetics* did for structuralism. A strong case for teaching theory is made.

──────. *Structuralist Poetics: Structuralism, Linguistics, and the Study of Literature*. Ithaca, N.Y.: Cornell University Press, 1975. Here Culler introduces structuralism to the American academy, clearly, well, and critically. Winner of MLA's Lowell Prize, this is the most influential book of its kind.

Deely, John. *Introducing Semiotic: Its History and Doctrine*. Bloomington: Indiana University Press, 1982. Deely disapproves of the "logocentrism" of linguistics-based semiotics and consequently his work has not been central to literary studies.

Deely, John, Brooke Williams, and Felicia E. Kruse. *Frontiers in Semiotics*. Bloomington: Indiana University Press, 1986. The introduction to this collection defines the divide between those who use semiotic theory to study human language and culture and those who study animal behavior as well as other "natural" signifying systems as coequal with the linguistic. The editors here, writing in the tradition of Thomas Sebeok, favor the latter approach. The collection is uneven but contains some valuable theoretical statements.

De George, Richard T. and Fernande M., eds. *The Structuralists from Marx to Lévi-Strauss*. Garden City, N.Y.: Doubleday (Anchor Books), 1972. Well introduced, this collection defines structuralism broadly, including essays by Freud and Marx beside the work of the pioneering structuralists, Saussure, Jakobson, and Lévi-Strauss. Also represented are Barthes, Althusser, Foucault, and Lacan.

Detweiler, Robert. *Story, Sign, and Self: Phenomenology and Structuralism as Literary-Critical Methods*. Philadelphia: Fortress Press, 1978.

Eco, Umberto. *The Role of the Reader: Explorations in the Semiotics of Texts*. Bloomington: Indiana University Press, 1979. Essays distinguish among open, closed, and "open/closed" literary works and the reader's position with respect to each.

──────. *A Theory of Semiotics*. Bloomington: Indiana University Press, 1976. A major work, wide-ranging in its references and applications. Eco tackles the issues and develops a comprehensive theory of semiotics.

Ehrmann, Jacques, ed. *Structuralism*. Garden City, N.Y.: Doubleday, 1970. Contains influential essays in a variety of fields; the significant contribution to the debate in literary studies is Riffaterre's response to Lévi-Strauss and Jakobson's reading of Baudelaire, *Les chats*.

Empson, William. *Seven Types of Ambiguity*. New York: New Directions, 1947. Foreshadows later developments in structuralism.

Erlich, Victor. *Russian Formalism*. The Hague: Mouton, 1955. Introduces formalism. Standard text.

Foucault, Michel. *The Archaeology of Knowledge*. New York: Pantheon Books, 1970. With *The Order of Things*, Foucault's statements of theory. Difficult reading.

————. *Discipline and Punish: The Birth of the Prison*. Translated by Alan Sheridan. New York: Random House (Vintage Books), 1977. A nonstandard history of prisons, exemplary of the author's other histories of sexuality, madness, and so on. This work is particularly surprising and readable. Because Foucault charts historical process in terms of changes in discourse and linguistic classifications, this is structuralist history. Foucault did not admit the structuralist affiliation.

————. *The Order of Things: An Archaeology of the Human Sciences*. New York: Pantheon Books, 1970.

Fowler, Alastair. *Kinds of Literature: An Introduction to the Theory of Genres and Modes*. Cambridge, Mass.: Harvard University Press, 1982. A theory of genre informed by structuralist work.

Frye, Northrop. *Anatomy of Criticism: Four Essays*. Princeton, N.J.: Princeton University Press, 1957. Shifted the emphasis in American criticism to structure.

Garvin, Paul L. *A Prague School Reader on Esthetics, Literary Structure, and Style*. Washington, D.C.: Georgetown University Press, 1964.

Genette, Gérard. *Figures of Literary Discourse*. New York: Columbia University Press, 1982. Eleven essays selected from three of Genette's books and translated into English. Genette uses structuralism to revitalize poetics and rhetoric.

Gombrich, E. H. *Art and Illusion*. Princeton, N.J.: Princeton University Press, 1961. Because Gombrich analyzes the spectator's role in the making of meaning and the evolution of the real, his consistently brilliant books are in the semiotic tradition.

Guillén, Claudio. *Literature as System*. Princeton, N.J.: Princeton University Press, 1971. A major statement and contribution to structuralism in relation to genre theory.

Guiraud, Pierre. *Semiology*. New York: Routledge, 1975.

Hawkes, Terence. *Structuralism and Semiotics*. Berkeley: University of California Press, 1977. A brief, clear introduction that includes discussions of Vico, Piaget, Jakobson, Greimas, Todorov, and Barthes. Good bibliography.

Innis, Robert E., ed. *Semiotics: An Introductory Anthology*. Bloomington: Indiana University Press, 1985.

Jakobson, Roman. *Selected Writings*. The Hague: Mouton, 1971.

Jakobson, Roman, and Morris Halle. *Fundamentals of Language*. The Hague: Janua Linguarum, Mouton, 1956.

Jameson, Frederic. *The Prison-House of Language: A Critical Account of Structuralism and Russian Formalism*. Princeton, N.J.: Princeton University Press, 1972. The criticism is from a Marxist perspective. Interesting and provocative.

Kermode, Frank. *The Genesis of Secrecy*. Cambridge, Mass.: Harvard University Press, 1979. Not explicitly a semiotic study of the Bible but extraordinary and informed by semiotic theory.

Krieger, Murray, and L. S. Dembo. *Directions for Criticism: Structuralism and Its Alternatives*. Madison: University of Wisconsin Press, 1976. Essays by Hazard Adams, René Girard, Edward Said, Hayden White, et al.

Kristeva, Julia. *Desire in Language: A Semiotic Approach to Literature and Art*. New York: Columbia University Press, 1980. A collection of extraordinary and wide-ranging essays. Kristeva is a major and unique thinker.

Kuhn, Thomas S. *The Structure of Scientific Revolutions*. Rev. ed. Chicago: University of Chicago Press, 1970. A structural approach to the history of scientific discoveries.

Kuhns, Richard. *Structures of Experience: Essays on the Affinity between Philosophy and Literature*. New York: Basic Books, 1970.

Lane, Michael, ed. *Introduction to Structuralism*. New York: Harper Torchbooks, 1972. Crosses disciplines. Bibliography.

————. *Structuralism, a Reader*. London: Cape, 1970.

Leach, Edmund. *Claude Lévi-Strauss*. New York: Viking Press, 1970. Explanation and critique of Lévi-Strauss's thought.

Lévi-Strauss, Claude. *Structural Anthropology*. Translated by Claire Jacobson and Brooke Grundfest Schoepf. New York: Basic Books, 1963.

Lodge, David. *Working with Structuralism: Essays and Reviews on Nineteenth- and Twentieth-Century Literature*. Boston: Routledge and Kegan Paul, 1981.

Lotman, Yuri. *Analysis of the Poetic Text*. Ann Arbor, Mich.: Ardis, 1976. Includes analyses of Russian poetry. A major work in the Soviet semiotic tradition. Includes bibliography of Lotman's work in Russian.

————. *The Structure of the Artistic Text*. Ann Arbor: University of Michigan Press, 1977.

Macksey, Richard, and Eugenio Donato, eds. *The Structuralist Controversy: The Languages of Criticism and the Sciences of Man*. Baltimore: Johns Hopkins University Press, 1970. Papers from an important international conference at Hopkins. Girard, Goldmann, Todorov, Barthes, Lacan, Derrida, and others.

Matejka, L., and K. Pomorska, eds. *Readings in Russian Poetics*. Cambridge, Mass.: MIT Press, 1971. Collection of essays by Russian formalists.

Mukarovsky, Jan. *Structure, Sign, and Function*. New Haven: Yale University Press, 1978. Representative work of Prague circle structuralism. Essays on film and theater.

————. *The Word and Verbal Art*. New Haven: Yale University Press, 1977. Essays on literature.

Peirce, Charles Sanders. *The Collected Papers of Charles Sanders Peirce*. 8 vols. Cambridge, Mass.: Harvard University Press, 1931–58. Peirce is the American founder of semiotics.

Pettit, Philip. *The Concept of Structuralism: A Critical Analysis*. Berkeley: University of California Press, 1975. Examines structuralism from perspective of philosophy.

Piaget, Jean. *Structuralism*. Translated by Chaninah Maschler. London: Routledge and Kegan Paul, 1971. This major theoretical statement discusses the importance of structuralism in mathematics, logic, the natural and social sciences.

Prince, Gerald. *Narratology: The Form and Functioning of Narrative*. New York: Mouton, 1982. A schematic approach to narrative theory. Lots of diagrams.

Propp, Vladimir. *Morphology of the Folktale*. Austin: University of Texas Press, 1970. Basic and influential work of early formalism.

Riffaterre, Michael. *Semiotics of Poetry*. Bloomington: Indiana University Press, 1978. Pedagogically fascinating as it provides a method for reading poetry. Riffaterre is an exceptional reader of the French poetic tradition.

Robey, David, ed. *Structuralism: An Introduction*. New York: Oxford University Press, 1973. This book gathers the Wolfson College lectures for 1972, lectures designed to introduce and explain important current trends in scholarship. The volume includes essays by Culler, Eco, Lyons, Todorov, and others.

Said, Edward. *Beginnings*. New York: Basic Books, 1975.

Saussure, Ferdinand de. *Course in General Linguistics*. Translated by Wade Baskin. New York: McGraw-Hill, 1959. The founding work of structural linguistics compiled by the author's students from his lecture notes.

Scholes, Robert, *Semiotics and Interpretation*. New Haven: Yale University Press, 1982. This lucid work first explains and then proves the importance of semiotics for students of narrative with analyses of stories by Joyce and Hemingway. Scholes also uses semiotics to analyze poems and to consider the treatment of the female body in our textual tradition, as he consistently exemplifies the value of semiotic theory for textual practice.

————. *Structuralism in Literature: An Introduction*. New Haven: Yale University Press, 1974. The best single-author introduction of structuralism to students of literature, this book provides the historical background against which structuralism emerged as an important trend in critical theory. Critically summarizes the early contributions to the field and provides a good bibliography with historical emphasis.

————. *Textual Power: Literary Theory and the Teaching of English*. New Haven: Yale University Press, 1985. Brings theory to bear on pedagogy. Clear, persuasive critique of institutional and classroom practices.

Sebeok, Thomas A. *Style in Language*. Cambridge, Mass.: MIT Press, 1960. A fine collection that includes analyses and readings by Beardsley, Roger Brown, Seymour Chatman, Benjamin Hrushovski, Jakobson, I. A. Richards, and many others.

Seung, T. K. *Structuralism and Hermeneutics*. New York: Columbia University Press, 1982.

Silverman, Kaja. *The Subject of Semiotics*. New York: Oxford University Press, 1983. An introduction to semiotics that emphasizes a psychoanalytic approach. Includes readings of literature and film.

Smith, Barbara Herrnstein. *On the Margins of Discourse: The Relation of Literature to Language*. Chicago: University of Chicago Press, 1978.

————. *Poetic Closure: A Study of How Poems End*. Chicago: University of Chicago Press, 1968. Analyzes poetic structure by examining possibilities for closure. Clear persuasive argument and readings.

Sturrock, John. *Structuralism and Since*. New York: Oxford University Press, 1979. Essays on Lévi-Strauss, Barthes, Foucault, Lacan, and Derrida, each written by a major writer. This book provides a unique service.

Suleiman, Susan Rubin, ed. *The Female Body in Western Culture: Contemporary Perspectives*. Cambridge, Mass.: Harvard University Press, 1986. This collection of feminist essays includes several semiotic approaches.

Todorov, Tzvetan. *The Fantastic: A Structural Approach to a Literary Genre*. Ithaca, N.Y.: Cornell University Press, 1973. True to promise of title.

————. *Introduction to Poetics*. Minneapolis: University of Minnesota Press, 1981. A fine introduction to the field of structuralist poetics.

————. *The Poetics of Prose*. Ithaca, N.Y.: Cornell University Press, 1977. By one of the foremost semiotic critics of fiction, these essays present their arguments with clarity and force.

Uspenski, Boris. *A Poetics of Composition*. Berkeley: University of California Press, 1973.

Whorf, Benjamin Lee. *Language, Thought, and Reality*. Cambridge, Mass.: MIT Press, 1956. Establishes importance of language in the perception of reality.

Wollen, Peter. *Signs and Meaning in the Cinema*. Bloomington: Indiana University Press, 1969.

PETER J. RABINOWITZ

Whirl without End: Audience-Oriented Criticism

"One might very roughly periodize the history of modern literary theory in three stages: a preoccupation with the author (Romanticism and the nineteenth century); an exclusive concern with the text (New Criticism); and a marked shift of attention to the reader over recent years."[1] Terry Eagleton's observation may be, as he says, only rough, but it does point to a swing in critical orientation that is increasingly difficult to ignore. In sharp contrast to the period when New Criticism provided the dominant model for American critical practice, it is now hard to find serious literary theorists who do not, in one way or another, feel the need to account for the activities of the reader. From Wolfgang Iser (who sees literature as a set of directions for the reader to follow) to Roland Barthes (who, in his later years, saw the best texts as unlimited opportunities for orgasmic free play), from narratologists like Gerald Prince to subjectivists like David Bleich, a wide range of contemporary critics ground their arguments in the reader as a perceiving subject rather than in the text as an autonomous object.

This explosion of interest has made reader-response criticism (or, as it might more broadly but more accurately be called, audience-oriented criticism)[2] especially important to understand. But it also makes it especially difficult. Granted, discussing *any* "school" of critics—be they the Chicago Aristotelians or the Yale deconstructionists—as a group necessarily exaggerates their similarities and minimizes their differences. Still, the Chicago critics did at least have a mode of discourse in common. That is, they shared a view not only of what constitued literature but also of what sorts of things one might appropriately claim about it and what sorts of evidence and arguments would validate those claims. Similarly, whatever their disagreements, feminist critics (like Freudian critics) share enough assumptions about procedures and goals to provide a stable ground on which those disagreements can be debated. That is not true of audience critics. Audience theorists are not working together from the same assumptions toward some common end; they have neither a shared methodology nor a clear pattern of growth.[3] Rather, reader-critics combine an interest in reading with a wide variety of other critical and political concerns. Thus, whereas Jonathan Culler in *On Deconstruction* sees the study of strategies for reading as an appropriate first step toward an exploration of poststructuralism, Judith Fetterley in *The Resisting Reader* sees reading primarily as a source of feminist insight. Neither can be seen as a development of or a variation on the other. What reader-critics share, at most, is a word (reader)—and as we shall see, even that word does not have a fixed definition.

Rather than consider reader criticism, therefore, as a unified body of theory (a collection of little fish who, for all their individual darting, follow a uniform route when considered as a school), it is more profitable to envision it as an amusement park tilt-a-whirl, a collection of small, independent groups in their own cars, swirling about their own axes, while the whole set of cars in turn revolves around a central core.[4] The central core, consideration of the reader, has arisen to fill the void created by the collapse of a basic New Critical premise: that a literary text is an autonomous object that can and should be analyzed without regard to its context. There are any number of reasons why this premise has lost its appeal. There is, for instance, the powerful (if often only implicit) theoretical influence of structuralism, which starts with the counterpremise that the observer creates, rather than finds, his or her world. There is, in addition, the recent revival of interest in the relationship between literature and history. On a more pragmatic level, there is mounting research pressure on young scholars, coupled with the growing recognition that New Criticism has worn thin and no longer provides a mechanism through which substantially new (that is, publishable) literary insights can be generated. For these and other reasons, more recent literary theorists have been increasingly willing to trade in that article of faith for another, more suited to the slipperiness of the times: the belief that meaning is context-dependent.

Consequently, more and more critics have begun to turn their attention from the "text itself" to the contexts in which it is embedded—both the contexts of its production and (what concerns us here) the contexts of its reception. More specifically, audience critics have engaged in a series of heterogeneous but interlocking debates centering on three related questions: Who is the reader? Where are the locus of meaning and the authority for interpretation? What kind of experience is the act of reading?[5] Yet, though the resulting critical whirl does not have any agreed-upon end (in the sense of goal)—though audience critics are united more by their questions than by the directions they follow in trying to answer them—their work, as a totality, is more than simply a dizzying free-for-all with no concrete consequences. Merely by asking new sorts of questions, audience critics have succeeded in altering literary criticism—both as an aesthetic practice and as a political institution—in substantial ways.

A *text* can exist (and, for the New Critics, largely did exist) without a reader. But as soon as we begin to talk about a text's reception, we come up against our first basic question. *Reading* requires a reader. But when we talk about readers, whom or what are we really talking about? Recent theorists have posited a surprisingly large number of answers, but they can be divided into two basic categories: hypothetical and real.

Hypothetical Readers. The first group includes all those "ideal" readers whose existence is created by a critic himself or herself—for instance, as a model to explain the ways that texts ideally operate or as an ideal for us to copy. Included in this category, for example, is the *narratee*, a term popularized by Gerald Prince. The narratee is the fictional counterpart of the narrator, the person to whom the narrator directs the story. The narratee is sometimes explicitly addressed (e.g., the internal audience that listens to Marlow's narration in *Heart of Darkness*) but is often only implicit. Indeed, as Prince points out, "the variety of narratees . . . is phenomenal,"[6] and it is possible to characterize narratives in part according to the ways in which their narratees differ from a neutral reference point, what Prince calls the zero-degree narratee. This kind of characterization of narratives is central to Prince's enterprise: The narratee is important not so much because "he" is intrinsically interesting but rather because he is *useful* as a concept to help analyze the structure of texts.[7] As Prince puts it, "The thorough examination of what he represents, the study of a narrative work as constituted by a series of signals addressed to him, can lead to a more sharply delineated reading and a deeper characterization of the work"—as well as to better typology and history and ultimately to "a better understanding . . . of all acts of communication."[8]

Although study of the narratee is traditionally considered part of audience criticism, Prince is careful to distinguish the narratee from readers, both real and hypothetical. Indeed, the narratee, whether explicit or implicit, is, like the narrator, closer to being a character in the text than to being a reader, even a model for the reader to emulate. The narratee is always perceived by the reader as someone "out there"—someone who often serves to mediate between author and reader.

For this reason, the narratee differs substantially from the kind of idealized reader usually covered by the rubric *implied reader*, the reader who engages in those activities that seem to be called for by the strategies a particular text has adopted. Although this term is most closely associated today with the German critic Wolfgang Iser, the concept is actually used by a wide variety of critics. Walker Gibson, for instance, developed the similar notion of the "mock reader," a "fictitious reader . . . whose mask and costume the individual takes on in order to experience the language" of a given text.[9] Even Wayne Booth's *Rhetoric of Fiction*, which developed the notion of the *implied author* (the authorial voice that can be gleaned from the particular textual choices he or she has made, as opposed to the biographical author), can be seen as an early instance of audience criticism as well, for its arguments depend on an implied reader who charts out a path we are expected to follow as we attempt to engage the text.

Two closely connected objections have been leveled against the concept of the implied reader. First, the term *implied* reminds us that this idealized reader's characteristics can be extracted from the text itself. For this reason, the notion of the implied reader (and even more the notion of the narratee) lays itself open to the charge made by Mary Louise Pratt that "much reader-response criticism turns out to be a notational variant of that very formalism so roundly rejected."[10] And it is certainly true that the concept of the implied reader is entirely consistent with the premise that texts are closed, autonomous objects. As a result, such criticism grounded in the implied reader offers little more than a new vocabulary for dressing up insights that are equally accessible through familiar formalist methods. Indeed, Iser essentially says as much when he distinguishes his own work (a theory of response) from what he calls theories of reception. "A theory of response has its roots in the text," he assures us; "a theory of reception arises from a history of readers' judgments."[11] Thus, for all of Iser's claims of novelty, most of his analyses in *The Implied Reader* are traditional explications with a new terminology; Iser's analyses, in other words, are sheep in wolf's clothing, which may help explain why Iser is so often acceptable to the conservative pastors of literary culture.

Second, by charting out the perspective that seems to be "demanded" by the text in question, critics who talk about implied readers run the risk of privileging that one perspective and failing to notice the ideological implications of doing so. This risk *can*, of course, be avoided; as we shall see, Judith Fetterley uses an implied-reader approach precisely to uncover the covert ideological structures of literary texts. Nevertheless, the New Critical heritage is not easy to escape; even many critics who have theoretically abandoned the principle of textual autonomy find that they still, in practice, award primacy to the text. As a consequence, an interpretation grounded in an implied reader seems privileged, and we are more prone to accept than to contest it.

From this perspective, the apparently similar concept of the *intended reader* (or, as I have termed it elsewhere, the *authorial audience*)[12] has substantially different implications. The intended reader—the hypothetical person who the author hoped or expected would pick up the text—may not be marked by or "present in" the text at all but may rather be silently *presupposed* by it. The intended reader, therefore, is not reducible to textual features but can be determined only by an examination of the interrelation between the text and the context in which the work was produced. The intended reader, in other words, is a *contextualized* implied reader, and studies of reading that start here have the potential to open up new questions of history, culture, and ideology.

The intended reader varies from text to text. Jonathan Culler has moved to the next level of generality with his notion of "literary competence." The competent reader is not text-specific but is rather someone who has learned certain socially determined skills of interpretation, skills more broadly defined than—and potentially even in conflict with—those the particular author might have expected.[13]

Real Readers. Whatever their differences, all of the aforementioned "readers"—narratees, implied readers, intended readers, competent readers, informed readers—are hypothetical constructs, products of the theorist's mind. Critics who focus on them thus differ markedly from those concerned with *real* readers, the actual people who pick up texts. Introducing real readers, of course, disrupts traditional New Critical poetics even more than introducing hypothetical readers. The New Critics, for a variety of reasons, wanted to establish literary criticism as an independent discipline, neither a supplement to nor even significantly supplemented by history, sociology, anthropology, psychology, or other fields. As actual readers have been admitted as legitimate objects of literary inquiry, however, the boundary lines of the discipline have begun to dissolve, and it is increasingly difficult to tell where literary criticism ends and history, sociology, anthropology, and psychology begin.[14]

Even among critics who center on actual readers, however, there are substantial theoretical and methodological differences. Some critics focus on individual readers and their responses. In *5 Readers Reading*, for instance, Norman Holland analyzes the ways particular students interpret Faulkner's story "A Rose for Emily" in order to uncover the psychological mechanisms that determine their responses. He concludes that response depends more on the reader's own "identity theme" than on any characteristics of the text itself. This position has been vigorously attacked; but significantly, the most persuasive arguments have criticized Holland's *psychology* more than his literary criticism. Many have found it odd, for instance, that in order to attack the belief that real unity can be found in texts, Holland relies on the even more dubious notion that unity can be found in people, specifically in their identity themes. Culler, in addition, perceptively points out that Holland's subjects report their responses in terms of "the clichés of the various subcultures and cultural discourses that work to constitute the consciousness of American college students." Holland's research, he concludes, therefore points not to the individuality of his students but to the way their "individuality" is in fact a "product" of their cultural situation. [15]

In *Readings and Feelings*, David Bleich takes an approach toward the real reader that differs from Holland's. Although he too is interested in individuals, his primary concern in this book is with pedagogy rather than psychology; he therefore examines the ways in which meanings are constructed in a classroom environment, with particular emphasis on the ways in which a group can negotiate among competing interpretations. Yet a different direction is taken by Janice Radway in *Reading the Romance*. She is interested in the way actual readers perform as members of a group that shares a *social* context, rather than as individuals or as members of an academic group. She therefore works with the notion of the "composite" reader—an abstraction, to be sure, but one developed out of the empirically determined responses of actual readers. [16]

In New Criticism, the "text itself" provided the locus of meaning and had the authority to settle interpretive disputes. As soon as the literary paradigm is opened up to include readers as well as texts, however, the source of meaning becomes problematical. Do readers make meanings, or do texts? Or authors? Indeed, New Critics legislated the reader out of critical discussion precisely to avoid these questions, to sidestep the embarrassing problems of "relativity" of interpretation and judgment that inevitably result when readers read.

Unlike New Critics, most audience critics would probably agree that on some level readers "construe" or "construct" meaning. But the difference in the terminology employed by various audience-centered critics is revealing.

Many of those who prefer the "construing" metaphors—who see readers as "decoding" or "realizing" texts or as following directions—stress the undeniable fact that, for all their individual differences, readers really *do* agree about a great deal when they interpret and evaluate texts. Such critics often posit the text itself as the governing structure that explains this agreement. This is especially likely to be the case among critics who are charting the activities of implied readers. Indeed, as Pratt's criticisms suggest, when one talks about implied readers, to ask whether the meaning lies in the text or is "produced" by the reader is to ask a pseudoquestion. Since the implied reader is him/herself a product of the text, the text itself always provides the ultimate control over meaning. Thus, for instance, while Iser talks a great deal about indeterminacy, about gaps in texts that must be filled by the imaginative activity of the reader, he sees those gaps as rhetorical devices that in fact direct the reader and force his/her activity in particular ways. The reader may have, to use a James Bondian phrase, license to fill—but that license is ultimately granted by the authority of the text.

At the opposite extreme are those who insist that readers *construct* the meaning of the text. These critics typically stress the equally undeniable fact that, for all their interpretive agreement, readers really *do* disagree in substantial ways when they interpret and evaluate texts. Such critics often look to the readers themselves for the explanation of this disagreement. Critics like Bleich, Holland, and Robert Crosman—whatever their differences—stress the radical individuality of readers and insist that there are no ultimate grounds on which to argue for one interpretation over another. As Bleich provocatively puts it, "Reading is a wholly subjective process and . . . the nature of what is perceived is determined by the rules of the personality of the perceiver."[17]

Other critics have tried to mediate between these two poles, to find some source of meaning whose primary locus is neither in the text nor in the individual reader. Many such critics have been concerned with "intertextuality," with the ways in which a literary text takes on meaning through its intricate relationship with other texts, both literary and nonliterary. More generally, many audience theorists have moved out from the text to the community norms (the interpretive conventions, the reading strategies) that allow the act of interpretation to take place. This is the approach encouraged by Culler's notion of literary competence, developed further in my own *Before Reading*, which examines the socially determined "rules" of interpretation that a reader has to have learned before picking up a text. Pratt's *Toward a Speech Act Theory of Literary Discourse* falls into this category, too, even though it does not explicitly present itself as audience criticism. Starting out with the observation that literature is not a particular "kind" of language (as many formalists have insisted) but rather a particular "use" of language, Pratt shows how modern linguistics—specifically, the "linguistics of use" developed by such theorists as Austin and Grice—can provide insight into the shared procedures that allow literature to work.

Since she wrote *Toward a Speech Act Theory*, however, Pratt has become rightfully wary of the ways in which the study of social norms of reading can seduce us into believing "that tacit or informally acquired knowledge has a kind of natural validity beyond socialization."[18] In other words, concepts like literary competence can depoliticize the study of literature by veiling the social and political implications of the ways in which "competence" is defined. Such mystification, however, is not inevitable, especially if the responses of so-called competent readers are contrasted with the responses of other readers employing different strategies.

Stanley Fish has moved in this direction by stressing the community context in which reading takes place. Although he agrees with the subjectivists that the reader does not decode some preexisting text but rather makes the text according to prior interpretive assumptions, he counterbalances this apparently skeptical stance by insisting that reading always takes place within some "interpretive community" and that reasoned choices are always possible *within* an interpretive community. By juxtaposing the interpretations of different interpretive communities, he demonstrates that each community creates its own texts and hence its own standards of competence; he thus undermines any belief that literary competence has a "natural validity beyond socialization." Unfortunately, Fish consistently backs off from the political implications of his theories, even arguing that they really have no consequences at all, skimming over the reasons why people choose one interpretive community over another.[19] Thus he does not explain why people change. Nor does he deal adequately with the costs and benefits that might accrue to someone by joining one interpretive community rather than another (the pressures, for instance, that might dissuade a young graduate student in a conservative department from becoming a Marxist or even a deconstructionist).[20]

Whether we think of readers as hypothetical abstractions or flesh-and-blood human beings, whether we think of them as construing texts or constructing them, the swing from the study of texts to the study of readers has been accompanied by a shift from the consideration of the text as "object" to an engagement with literature as an experience or activity. But here, too, different paths are charted by different audience critics. Some, for instance, focus their attention on reading as a "horizontal" activity, studying the reader's experiences over time. Stanley Fish's early notion of "affective stylistics," for instance, was based on the assumption that "the experience of an utterance . . . is its meaning."[21] Although his description of those experiences is less rich than that of Kenneth Burke, who had made a similar claim with more subtlety many years before,[22] Fish was influential in reminding the critical community that there is a shape to the experience of art, a shape that is not reducible to any propositional content that the text might convey or even to the formal features of the text itself. Iser, too, has examined the temporal interaction between reader and text, although his phenomenological perspective illuminates the process with a different light. Iser gives special emphasis to the relation between the explicit and the implicit in the text, arguing that the reader's place is "marked by the gaps in the text" and that "whenever the reader bridges the gaps, communication begins. The gaps function as a kind of pivot on which the whole text–reader relationship revolves."[23]

Alternatively, one can look at the activity of reading "vertically" by examining the simultaneous roles a reader plays at a given time. My own model, for instance, distinguishes four levels on which readers operate when they read fiction. First, they can never escape themselves as "actual audience," in a particular historical and cultural context. Second (and simultaneously), readers often try to take on the characteristics of the "authorial audience" (that is, the intended readers), in order to determine the intended meaning. Third, since fiction generally imitates some nonfictional form (such as history or biography), the narrator (implicit or explicit) generally imitates an author and writes for an imitation "narrative audience." This is an audience that a reader must *pretend* to join for the fiction to work (we pretend to believe, for instance, that the murder of Jay Gatsby really took place). Finally, unreliable narrators often hope for audiences ("ideal narrative audiences") that will accept their judgments, even when neither the narrative nor the authorial audience does; to feel the irony of such texts, we must "try on" that role too, even though we ultimately discard it.

Whether they think of reading vertically or horizontally, however, most critics tend to think of the act of reading as synonymous with the intellectual process of interpretation. But while reading inevitably involves interpretation, it is also an event, a *physical* activity that requires a book, a place to read, light, and leisure time—things that are not uniformly available to all people under all conditions. Ian Watt, in *The Rise of the Novel*, showed how economic, physical, and social conditions worked together to nurture the particular "readership" that in turn fostered the development of the English novel as it came to be. More recently, Radway has pointed out that "the simple event of picking up a book" inevitably involves a choice not to perform some other act, like taking care of children or doing the laundry. In her ethnographic study of a group of avid romance readers, she discovered that reading romances actually provides a double escape. For her informants, reading is an escape not only in the metaphorical sense of "identifying with a heroine whose life does not resemble their own in certain crucial aspects" but also in the more literal sense of "denying the present" by engaging in a private act that "takes them away from . . . the psychologically demanding and emotionally draining task of attending to the physical and affective needs of their families."[24]

Radway's work reminds us that, whether viewed as a horizontal or as a vertical activity, reading always takes place in a broader social and cultural context, and it is in the study of the ideological components of that context that we see the most far-reaching implications of audience criticism. To be sure, audience critics have not always faced up to the challenges they raise. Indeed, some of the strongest critiques of reader criticism—Pratt's in particular—attacked it precisely for failing to take the social and political context sufficiently into account. But in the years since Pratt's essay, audience criticism, like much American criticism, has become increasingly political.

Few critics have done an in-depth study of reading as an "event" in quite the same way that Radway has. For the most part, when critics have investigated the historical and cultural implications of the act of reading, they have centered on the implications of *interpretation* as a socially defined practice. In so doing, they have moved, to use Jonathan Culler's phrase, "beyond interpretation,"[25] from hermeneutics to poetics—that is, from the generation of new readings of texts to an examination of the grounds on which such readings are produced.[26] Of course, any audience-oriented poetics, having rejected pure description of the "text itself," must *start* with interpretations, with the ways in which readers have construed or constructed texts. But instead of taking those interpretations as the *end* of inquiry (as something to be attained), much reader criticism has taken them as the *starting point* (as something to be explained—and perhaps as something to be altered as well). That is, we can consider the interpretive conventions that readers use when they confront texts not as a means of arriving at newer and "better" interpretations but as objects of investigation in their own right. Thus, for instance, Culler has examined conflicting interpretations of Blake's "London" not in order to choose the best among them but in order "to make explicit the interpretive operations" beneath them, to show "what conventions and interpretive procedures enable critics to draw the inferences and make the statements they do."[27]

Some of this exploration of the grounds of interpretation has been historical. The German critic Hans-Robert Jauss's work has been especially visible in this regard. Jauss has popularized the notion of the reader's "horizon of expectations"—the set of expectations, both literary and cultural, with which a reader approaches a text. By examining the ways that the horizon changes over time, we can understand the consequent changes in the ways different audiences in different historical situations understand a text. This leads us to recognize not only that "a literary work is not an object that stands by itself and that offers the same view to each reader in each period" but also that literary history itself requires an "ever necessary retelling," since the history of literature is not a fixed sequence of " 'literary facts.' " "The *Perceval* of Chrétien de Troyes," he writes, "as a literary event, is not 'historical' in the same sense as . . . the Third Crusade. . . . *Perceval* becomes a literary event only for its reader. . . . A literary event can continue to have an effect only if those who come after it still or once again respond to it."[28]

Some of the exploration of the grounds of interpretation, though, has been more overtly political and ideological then Jauss's. Indeed, because it explicitly confronts the ways in which different readers interpret differently, reader criticism opens up ways to talk about the impact of race, class, and gender on the processing of texts. It has thus provided considerable support for Marxist and especially for feminist inquiries. In *The Resisting Reader*, for instance, Fetterley uses a reader-oriented approach to explain the ideological power of the central male texts in the American literary canon. Specifically, she demonstrates that the interpretive strategies demanded by the canon do not "emasculate" female readers so much as *immasculate* them—that is, force them to identify against themselves by identifying with male experience and interests. Women, she argues, need to become "resisting readers" who actively refuse to engage in the interpretive activities that the texts expect. Jean Kennard, starting with a similar recognition that the canon is both masculinist and heterosexist, suggests an alternative strategy, what she calls "polar reading," in which "we redefine aspects of ourselves through contrast with the opposite aspects in a fictional other which we have temporarily experienced."[29] And Annette Kolodny has used insights gained from reader criticism to help explain why these male texts dominate the canon in the first place. Her arguments suggest a paradoxical reversal of the commonly ac-

cepted cause-and-effect relationship between aesthetic value and canon formation. As she puts it, "We read well, and with pleasure, what we already know
how to read." Male readers brought up on male texts will lack knowledge of
the literary conventions and traditions informing women's writing, just as
they will lack experience of the real-world contexts such as the lying-in room
from which the action of such writing is likely to take much of its meaning.
As a result, they will simply "lack the capacity to fully interpret" those texts
and will assume that the fault lies in the writers rather than in the inadequacy
of their own reading strategies.[30]

In its critique of the canon, audience criticism leads to precisely the
consequences that the New Critics were trying to avoid when they originally
insisted on centering literary study on the text as an object. That is, whatever
the beliefs of particular critics, audience criticism as a whole has a strong
tendency to undermine the stability not only of literary interpretation but of
literary evaluation as well. Evaluation has always been a more sensitive issue
than interpretation. Although in theory New Criticism supports the principle
of "correct" readings, in practice it produces the opposite—a series of competing interpretations of the same texts. Indeed, New Criticism as an academic
practice depends on that kind of competition, for without it one soon runs out
of things to say. Evaluation, however, is something else again, and for critics
like Cleanth Brooks the solidity of the canon was essential for meaningful
literary study.

It is important to realize what is at stake in these recent attacks. In one
sense, of course, the canon has never really been stable. Changing literary
interests have always resulted in the reshuffling of the respective rankings of
various authors. Mass taste has on the whole tended to prefer the new and has
been little concerned with finding concrete and lasting values in texts (Richard Ohmann provocatively notes that "it is hard to think of a novel more than
25 years old, aside from specialist fiction and *Gone with the Wind*, that still
commands a large readership outside of school and college").[31] Among academics, of course, there is more commitment to *enduring* aesthetic values; but
here, too, changing perspectives have regularly been accompanied by consequent changes in the contents of curricula and anthologies. Even the rise of
New Criticism itself brought a reevaluation of the metaphysical poets. What
is notable about the most recent attacks on the canon, then, is not that former
literary favorites have been demoted, or even that former aesthetic creeds have
been replaced, but that many audience critics have become increasingly aware
of relationships between canonical choices and ideology. As a consequence,
the very belief that there *is* "enduring value" in texts—that there ought to be a
canon at all—has come to be questioned.

Not all reader-critics, of course, have undertaken such critiques of literary value; and those who have done so pursue the issue in various ways. Jauss, for instance, is clearly comfortable with the fact that the particular texts esteemed by a culture will vary with time. But he wants to smuggle some unchanging values back into his system, too. He does this by asserting that aesthetic value depends on "the distance between the horizon of expectations and the work." In the end, then, Jauss's arguments vary only slightly from traditional elitist New Critical aesthetics; like the New Critics, he divides texts into great texts that challenge readers and make them work, and " 'culinary' or entertainment art" that does little to change the reader.[32] Granted, he admits that the character of a given work will vary according to the reader's perspective; but while the membership of each category is fluid, the categories themselves seem to reflect enduring values.

Although Iser's position is superficially similar to Jauss's in that he associates quality with literature's power to disrupt the reader, Iser locates that power more firmly in the text. He does (grudgingly) admit literary quality in some texts like courtly romances that "shore . . . up" the "weaknesses of the prevailing system," but he gravitates primarily to novels that have many gaps and that undermine social norms. For the most part, he argues, works that "support prevailing systems" are "of a more trivial nature, as they affirm specific norms with a view to training the reader according to the moral or social code of the day."[33]

But if we have learned anything from the criticism of the past two decades, it is that even the distinction between the contestatory and the supportive (whether those qualities are found in the reader or in the text) is ideological rather than neutrally aesthetic. The very notion that people need to be "challenged" more than they need to be confirmed in their beliefs implies a whole set of assumptions about culture and human behavior, assumptions that are necessarily ideologically charged; as Eagleton argues in his Marxist critique of reception theory:

Iser's reception theory, in fact, is based on a liberal humanist ideology. . . . He writes that a reader with strong ideological commitments is likely to be an inadequate one, since he or she is less likely to be open to the transformative power of literary works. What this implies is that in order to undergo transformation at the hands of the text, . . . [the] reader would *already* have to be a liberal. . . . The reader is not so much radically upbraided, as simply returned to himself or herself as a more thoroughly liberal subject.[34]

Fetterley, writing from a feminist position, similarly questions the notion that "great" literature is really transforming: "If a white male middle-class literary establishment consistently chooses to identify as great and thus worth reading those texts that present as central the lives of white male middle-class characters, then obviously recognition and reiteration, not difference and expansion, provide the motivation for reading."[35] One need not, of course, be a Marxist or a feminist to see a paradox in the position represented by Iser: Teaching people to doubt and to be skeptical, as Wayne Booth pointed out in *Modern Dogma and the Rhetoric of Assent*, is itself training them according to the moral and social code of the day.

Whatever individual practitioners may think about literary value, therefore, the questions raised by audience-oriented criticism have put considerable pressure on the belief that the academic canon simply represents "the best" that has ever been thought and written. For once you take seriously the notion that readers "construct" (even partially) the texts that they read, then the canon (any canon) is not (or not only) the product of the inherent qualities in the texts; it is also (at least partly) the product of particular choices by the arbiters of taste who create it—choices always grounded in ideological and cultural values, always enmeshed in class, race, and gender. My own work, for instance, has shown how the canon gives priority to those texts that respond well to particular reading strategies, strategies that always have an ideological underpinning.[36] And Tompkins argues that Hawthorne's reputation is not the result of some inherent quality in his writings; rather, his "work, from the very beginning, emerged into visibility, and was ignored or acclaimed, as a function of the circumstances in which it was read."[37] She goes on to offer a spirited reader-oriented defense of such writers as Harriet Beecher Stowe and Susan Warner.

There is yet another step in the subversive tendency of reader criticism: Like feminist and Marxist criticism, it has begun to challenge not only the endurance of particular interpretations and evaluations put forth by the establishment but also the way in which literary criticism is constituted as a profession. Thus, while in 1980 Pratt was able to criticize reader-critics for failing to question the implications of the notion of literary competence, since then literary criticism itself has been increasingly scrutinized as a political institution, as critics have directed their attention to the mechanisms by which literary competence is taught and "certified" and to the ideological effects of our academic practices. Although Radway would not phrase it this way herself (in part because of her commitment to the Fishean notion that one cannot make any reasoned choices among interpretive communities), her work on the romance, for example, has neatly turned the literary competence argument on its head, suggesting that the kind of competence specifically taught in high schools and colleges can actually *distort* the act of interpretation. And Steven Mailloux has recently called for the development of what he calls "rhetorical hermeneutics"—a study of "acts of interpretive persuasion" viewed in the context of their "ever-changing background of shared and disputed assumptions, questions, assertions, and so forth," with special attention to "institutional politics."[38] It is hard to predict just where such arguments may lead; but we can be fairly sure that once the discursive practice of criticism itself undergoes the kind of reader-oriented contextualization to which literary texts have been subjected, substantial changes in the operation of the academy will follow.

Notes

1. Terry Eagleton, *Literary Theory: An Introduction* (Minneapolis: University of Minnesota Press, 1983), p. 74.

2. The term *reception theory* (or *reception aesthetics*, from the German *Rezeptionasthetik*) is probably best reserved for the members of the so-called Konstanz School, the most prominent of whom are Wolfgang Iser and Hans-Robert Jauss.

3. For a different view, see Jane P. Tompkins, "An Introduction to Reader-Response Criticism," in her *Reader-Response Criticism: From Formalism to Post-Structuralism* (Baltimore: Johns Hopkins University Press, 1980), pp. ix–xxvi.

4. Although her classification is entirely different, Susan Suleiman takes a similar tack in her essay, "Varieties of Audience-Oriented Criticism," in *The Reader in the Text: Essays on Audience and Interpretation*, ed. Susan Suleiman and Inge Crosman (Princeton, N.J.: Princeton University Press, 1980).

5. Jonathan Culler organizes his discussion of "stories of reading" around three central questions as well, although his questions are somewhat different from mine; *On Deconstruction: Theory and Criticism after Structuralism* (Ithaca, N.Y.: Cornell University Press, 1982), pp. 64–83.

6. Gerald Prince, "Introduction to the Study of the Narratee," in Tompkins, *Reader-Response Criticism*, p. 8.

7. In Prince's discussions, the narratee is assumed to be male unless specified as female.

8. Prince, "Introduction," p. 24.

9. Walker Gibson, "Authors, Speakers, Readers, and Mock Readers," in Tompkins, *Reader-Response Criticism*, p. 2.

10. Mary Louise Pratt, "Interpretive Strategies/Strategic Interpretations: On Anglo-American Reader Response Criticism," *Boundary* 2 11(1981/82): 201.

11. Wolfgang Iser, *The Act of Reading: A Theory of Aesthetic Response* (Baltimore: Johns Hopkins University Press, 1978), p. x.

12. Peter J. Rabinowitz, "Truth in Fiction: A Reexamination of Audiences," *Critical Inquiry* 4, 1(1977): 121–42. My own work has not been entirely consistent and has occasionally smudged the line between what is implied and what is assumed. See, in particular, my exchange with David Ketterer in *PMLA* 97, 1 (1982).

13. Jonathan Culler, *Structuralist Poetics: Structuralism, Linguistics, and the Study of Literature* (Ithaca, N.Y.: Cornell University Press, 1975), esp. chap. 7. Stanley Fish's "informed reader," similarly, has characteristics that the intended reader might not share; see "Literature in the Reader: Affective Stylistics," in Fish, *Is There a Text in This Class?: The Authority of Interpretive Communities* (Cambridge, Mass.: Harvard University Press, 1980), pp. 48–49.

14. It is indicative of a new academic climate, for instance, that the recent anthology,

Gender and Reading: Essays on Readers, Texts, and Contexts, ed. Elizabeth A. Flynn and Patrocinio P. Schweickart (Baltimore: Johns Hopkins University Press, 1986), includes, along with essays by such noted literary critics as Judith Fetterley and Susan Suleiman, an essay by cognitive psychologists Mary Crawford and Roger Chaffin, "The Reader's Construction of Meaning: Cognitive Research on Gender and Comprehension." Whether this growth of interdisciplinary study is seen as nourishment or contamination, of course, depends on your perspective and your own notions of purity—as well, perhaps, as on the political structure of your institution and your own program's security.

15. Jonathan Culler, *The Pursuit of Signs: Semiotics, Literature, Deconstruction* (Ithaca, N.Y.: Cornell University Press, 1981), p. 53.

16. Janice Radway, *Reading the Romance: Women, Patriarchy, and Popular Literature* (Chapel Hill: University of North Carolina Press, 1984), pp. 14–15.

17. David Bleich, *Readings and Feelings: An Introduction to Subjective Criticism* (Urbana, Ill.: National Council of Teachers of English, 1975), p. 3.

18. Pratt, "Interpretive Strategies," p. 217.

19. See, e.g., the final essays in Fish, *Is There a Text?*

20. Still, some of Fish's insights have been used by politically oriented critics with considerable force. By holding up the interpretations of popular romances made by academic scholars against the interpretations of the "ordinary" reader by whom they are primarily consumed, for instance, Radway, in *Reading the Romance*, has shown how the failure to take differing interpretive communities into account has obscured our understanding of what is really involved—culturally and politically—in the enormous popularity of the genre.

21. Fish, *Is There a Text?*, p. 32.

22. Kenneth Burke, "Psychology and Form," *Counterstatement* (Berkeley: University of California Press, 1968), pp. 29–44.

23. Iser, *Act of Reading*, p. 169.

24. Radway, *Reading the Romance*, pp. 86, 90, 92.

25. Culler, "Beyond Interpretation," *Pursuit of Signs*, pp. 3–17.

26. For a different point of view, see Tompkins: "Although New Critics and reader-oriented critics do not locate meaning in the same place, both schools assume that to specify meaning is criticism's ultimate goal"; "The Reader in History," in Tompkins, *Reader-Response Criticism*, p. 201.

27. Culler, *Pursuit of Signs*, p. 76.

28. Hans-Robert Jauss, *Toward an Aesthetic of Reception*, trans. Timothy Bahti (Minneapolis: University of Minnesota Press, 1982), pp. 20–22.

29. Jean E. Kennard, "Ourself behind Ourself: A Theory for Lesbian Readers," in Flynn and Schweickart, *Gender and Reading*, p. 70.

30. Annette Kolodny, "Dancing through the Minefield: Some Observations on the Theory, Practice, and Politics of a Feminist Literary Criticism," *Feminist Studies* 6, 1 (1980): 12–13.

31. Richard Ohmann, "The Shaping of a Canon: U.S. Fiction, 1960–1975," *Critical Inquiry* 10, 1 (1983): 206.

32. Jauss, *Toward an Aesthetic*, p. 25.

33. Iser, *Act of Reading*, p. 77–78.

34. Eagleton, *Literary Theory*, p. 79.

35. Judith Fetterley, "Reading about Reading: 'A Jury of Her Peers,' 'The Murders in the Rue Morgue,' and 'The Yellow Wallpaper,' " in Flynn and Schweickart, *Gender and Reading*, p. 150.

36. Peter J. Rabinowitz, *Before Reading: Narrative Conventions and the Politics of Interpretation* (Ithaca, N.Y.: Cornell University Press, 1987), esp. chap. 7.

37. Jane P. Tompkins, *Sensational Designs: The Cultural Work of American Fiction, 1790–1860* (New York: Oxford University Press, 1985), p. 5.

38. Steven Mailloux, "Rhetorical Hermeneutics," *Critical Inquiry* 11, 4 (1985): 631.

Selected Bibliography

Some of the essays listed below have been reprinted several times; in such cases, I have listed a single, readily accessible source. For further bibliographies of audience-centered criticism, see Flynn and Schweickart, Suleiman and Crosman, and Tompkins's *Reader-Response Criticism.* Culler's *On Deconstruction* has an excellent bibliography, too, although it includes a great deal of material that is not really centered on readers.

Bleich, David. *Readings and Feelings: An Introduction to Subjective Criticism*. Urbana, Ill.: National Council of Teachers of English, 1975. Develops pedagogical techniques based on the notion that reading is a "wholly subjective process."

———. *Subjective Criticism*. Baltimore: Johns Hopkins University Press, 1978. A more detailed and philosophical development of the subjectivity outlined in *Readings and Feelings*, with greater emphasis on its philosophical bases and less immediate concern with classroom practice.

Booth, Wayne C. *The Rhetoric of Fiction*. Chicago: University of Chicago Press, 1961. Although it stresses the choices of the author more than the activities of the reader, this book—because of its emphasis on techniques of persuasion and its development of the notion of an implied reader—has been an important influence on many reader-oriented critics.

Burke, Kenneth. "Psychology and Form." In *Counterstatement*, pp. 29–44. Berkeley: University of California Press, 1968. Develops the idea that form is the creation and satisfaction of appetites in the reader.

Crawford, Mary, and Roger Chaffin. "The Reader's Construction of Meaning: Cognitive Research on Gender and Comprehension." In Flynn and Schweickart, *Gender and Reading*, pp. 3–30. This essay not only provides an excellent discussion of the effects of gender on reading comprehension but also provides an introduction to recent research into reading by cognitive psychologists, including a good explanation of "schema theory."

Culler, Jonathan. *On Deconstruction: Theory and Criticism after Structuralism*. Ithaca, N.Y.: Cornell University Press, 1982. A study of poststructural critical practice beginning with a detailed discussion of theories of reading, and including an important essay on "Reading as a Woman."

———. *The Pursuit of Signs: Semiotics, Literature, Deconstruction*. Ithaca, N.Y.: Cornell University Press, 1981. An excellent collection of essays on a variety of theoretical topics; of particular interest with respect to audience criticism are "Beyond Interpretation," which argues that the study of literature should stress not interpretation of individual works but rather the conventions and operations underlying it; "Semiotics as a Theory of Reading," which shows how even apparently conflicting interpretations are often generated by shared interpretive strategies; "Riffaterre and the Semiotics of Poetry"; and a vigorous critique of Fish's work, "Stanley Fish and the Righting of the Reader."

———. *Structuralist Poetics: Structuralism, Linguistics, and the Study of Literature*. Ithaca, N.Y.: Cornell University Press, 1975. Although not focused specifically on readers, this excellent introduction to structuralism has become especially important to audience critics because of its extensive discussion of literary competence.

Eagleton, Terry. *Literary Theory: An Introduction*. Minneapolis: University of Minnesota Press, 1983. Includes a strong Marxist critique of reception theory.

Eco, Umberto. *The Role of the Reader: Explorations in the Semiotics of Texts*. Bloomington: Indiana

University Press, 1979. A semiotic study of literary texts, with special attention to the reader and the different kinds of activities he or she is called upon to perform by open and closed texts.

Fetterley, Judith. "Reading about Reading: 'A Jury of Her Peers,' 'The Murders in the Rue Morgue,' and 'The Yellow Wallpaper.'" In Flynn and Schweickart, *Gender and Reading*, pp. 147–64. An examination of three texts by women writers, seen as "stories about reading."

————. *The Resisting Reader: A Feminist Approach to American Fiction*. Bloomington: Indiana University Press, 1978. Argues that male texts force women readers to identify against themselves and that women therefore need to learn to read against the grain of the text.

Fish, Stanley. *Is There a Text in This Class?: The Authority of Interpretive Communities*. Cambridge, Mass.: Harvard University Press, 1980. A collection of Fish's major essays from 1970 to 1980, documenting his move from "affective stylistics"—in which the text was all-determining—to a more radical theoretical position in which a text is the product of the interpretive procedures brought to bear on it.

Flynn, Elizabeth A., and Patrocinio P. Schweickart, eds. *Gender and Reading: Essays on Readers, Texts, and Contexts*. Baltimore: Johns Hopkins University Press, 1986. A wide-ranging collection of essays that maps out the complex intersection between reader criticism and feminism.

Gibson, Walker. "Authors, Speakers, Readers, and Mock Readers." In Tompkins, *Reader-Response Criticism*, pp. 1–6. An early discussion of the ways in which texts call on readers to perform certain roles.

Holland, Norman N. *5 Readers Reading*. New Haven: Yale University Press, 1975. A detailed look at the ways in which specific readers interpret Faulkner's "Rose for Emily" according to their individual "identity themes."

Iser, Wolfgang. *The Act of Reading: A Theory of Aesthetic Response*. Baltimore: Johns Hopkins University Press, 1978. An account of the interaction between text and reader, with particular stress on the ways in which gaps and negativities in the text force the reader's imaginative activities.

————. *The Implied Reader: Patterns of Communication in Prose Fiction from Bunyan to Beckett*. Baltimore: Johns Hopkins University Press, 1974. More "practical" in emphasis than *The Act of Reading*, this collection of essays works toward a theory of reading through close analyses of novels.

Jauss, Hans-Robert. *Toward an Aesthetic of Reception*. Translated by Timothy Bahti. Theory and History of Literature, vol. 2. Minneapolis: University of Minnesota Press, 1982. A collection of essays with a stress on the historical dimension of reading; especially important is "Literary History as Challenge to Literary Theory," which argues that literary history must concern itself not with "objective" statements about texts but with the history of readers' experiences.

Kennard, Jean E. "Ourself behind Ourself: A Theory for Lesbian Readers." In Flynn and Schweickart, *Gender and Reading*, pp. 63–80. In contrast to Fetterley's call for "resistance," this essay develops the notion of "polar reading," through which one's sense of self is increased by the experience of otherness.

Kolodny, Annette. "Dancing through the Minefield: Some Observations on the Theory, Practice, and Politics of a Feminist Literary Criticism." *Feminist Studies* 6, 1 (Spring 1980): 1–25. Although not explicitly couched in terms of audience theory, this brilliant essay argues that when we read we engage paradigms for interpretation rather than texts themselves. Kolodny offers a strong critique of the traditional notions of literary history and evaluation.

————. "A Map for Re-reading; or, Gender and the Interpretation of Literary Texts." *New*

Literary History 11 (1980): 451–67. Argues that readers, both male and female, not only must be introduced to texts by women writers but also must "relearn" their strategies of reading so that they can read those texts in the ways they require.

Mailloux, Steven. *Interpretive Conventions: The Reader in the Study of American Fiction*. Ithaca, N.Y.: Cornell University Press, 1982. A study of the ways in which textual meaning depends on conventional activity and the ways reader-response criticism can help solve some traditional problems facing scholars of American fiction.

———. "Rhetorical Hermeneutics." *Critical Inquiry* 11, 4 (1985): 620–41. Beginning with a critique of what he calls "idealist" and "realist" theories of convention, this essay calls for the abandonment of theory and the turn toward a study of the ways in which critical "acts of persuasion" occur, with particular emphasis on "the institutional politics of interpretation."

Ohmann, Richard. "The Shaping of a Canon: U.S. Fiction, 1960–1975." *Critical Inquiry* 10, 1 (1983): 199–223. Although not reader-oriented, Ohmann's astute political analysis of the ways in which the canon is formed provides support for the questioning of the canon found in the work of many reader-critics.

Pedrick, Victoria, and Nancy Sorkin Rabinowitz, eds. Special issue of *Arethusa* 19, 2 (Fall 1986). A collection of audience-oriented essays on Greek and Latin texts.

Pratt, Mary Louise. "Interpretive Strategies/Strategic Interpretations: On Anglo-American Reader Response Criticism." *Boundary 2*, 11 (Fall/Winter 1981/82): 201–31. A strong critique of early reader-response theory, arguing that it is neither literarily nor politically as radical as it often claims to be.

———. *Toward a Speech Act Theory of Literary Discourse*. Bloomington: Indiana University Press, 1977. Using the linguistic model of speech act theory—especially Grice's cooperation principle—Pratt outlines the conventional agreements that make literary communication possible.

Prince, Gerald. "Introduction to the Study of the Narratee." In Tompkins, *Reader-Response Criticism*, pp. 7–25. Detailed discussion of the fictional addressee to whom the narrator directs his or her narrative.

Rabinowitz, Peter J. *Before Reading: Narrative Conventions and the Politics of Interpretation*. Ithaca, N.Y.: Cornell University Press, 1987. Examines the ways in which a reader's prior knowledge of interpretive conventions influences the processes of interpretation and evaluation. Emphasis on the ideological implications of traditional aesthetic practices, including canonization.

———. "Truth in Fiction: A Reexamination of Audiences." *Critical Inquiry* 4, 1 (Autumn 1977): 121–41. A study of the simultaneous roles that a fictional text calls on a reader to perform.

Radway, Janice. *Reading the Romance: Women, Patriarchy, and Popular Literature*. Chapel Hill: University of North Carolina Press, 1984. Radway begins with the assumption that "comprehension is actually a process of making meaning." Through an ethnographic study of the ways in which actual romance readers (in contrast to academic critics) attribute significance to the texts they read, she not only challenges received opinion about the meaning of the popularity of romantic fiction but also makes a substantial contribution to the theory of reading in general.

Rosenblatt, Louise. *The Reader, the Text, the Poem: The Transactional Theory of the Literary Work*. Carbondale: Southern Illinois University Press, 1978. Rosenblatt is one of the pioneers of the current wave of reader criticism; since the 1930s, she has been arguing against the notion of objective texts and for the importance of taking ordinary readers into account.

Suleiman, Susan, and Inge Crosman, eds. *The Reader in the Text: Essays on Audience and Interpretation*. Princeton, N.J.: Princeton University Press, 1980. A collection of essays, most of which were written especially for this volume, that shows something of the wide diversity of approaches to audience criticism current at the beginning of the 1980s.

Tompkins, Jane P., ed. *Reader-Response Criticism: From Formalism to Post-Structuralism*. Baltimore: Johns Hopkins University Press, 1980. A complement to Suleiman and Crosman's anthology, Tompkins's collection includes previously published essays, originally written in the 1950s through the 1970s, that have had major impact on reader-critics.

————. *Sensational Designs: The Cultural Work of American Fiction, 1790–1860*. New York: Oxford University Press, 1985. Arguing that interpretation and evaluation are always the product of the circumstances in which a book is read and discussed, Tompkins offers studies of a number of literary texts—including fiction by such noncanonical writers as Stowe and Warner—from the perspective of the historical context in which they were originally written.

Watt, Ian. *The Rise of the Novel: Studies in Defoe, Richardson, and Fielding*. Berkeley: University of California Press, 1957. Includes a detailed account of the interaction between the formal features of the eighteenth-century novel and the social, economic, and educational characteristics of the reading public it was designed to attract.

ROBERT MAGLIOLA

Like the Glaze on a Katydid-Wing: Phenomenological Criticism

THE MIND IS AN ENCHANTING THING
is an enchanted thing
  like the glaze on a
Katydid-wing
    subdivided by sun
    til the nettings are legion
        Marianne Moore

In his *Ideas*, Edmund Husserl tells us that "eidetic reduction" opens up "the realm of pure eidetic description," that is, the realm of "essential structures of transcendental subjectivity" which are "immediately transparent."[1] The nettings of mind are subdivided by that eidetic sun—to appropriate Moore's felicitous phraseology here—mind which is enchanting (noetic) and enchanted (noematic). It is to make a point, of course, that I have chosen texts that are so logocentric, with their ocular/solar imagery, their accessibility to deconstructive game-play (e.g., the equivocal use of "subdivided" here, and of "nettings," their seemingly vulnerable etymons (enchantment: to *sing* into, i.e., to *enchant* or *mystify*), and so on. For Marianne Moore's poem not only phenomenologically constitutes (and deconstructs) but also proposes a fine emblem for the phenomenological moment and that postphenomenology which is "deconstruction": In her poem the deconstructive *virtus* is called "fire in the dove-neck's iridescence." If during the decade of the 1970s deconstruction behaved like a predator taking phenomenology as its prey, the decade of the eighties has witnessed a singular abatement in the deconstructive demiurge. The fiery play of color in the plumage of a dove is, after all, 'nothing of itself'. Deconstruction is really neither predator nor even partner but the "colorful play in the plumage," or—to adopt Gianni Vattimo's usage—it is phenomenological presence 'given a twist'. In the 1980s, postphenomenological criticism still decenters, deconstructs, but is often benign, even reverential.

But why do I begin in so specialized a way what is to be a "general survey" of phenomenological criticism? For three reasons: first, to emphasize that phenomenology perdures and is relevant, even in the face of deconstruction, undoubtedly its chief antagonist—we shall not be surveying dead letters; second, to emphasize that phenomenological criticism has both stayed the same and changed and that this survey—while tracing phenomenology from its historical beginnings—must be attentive to the most recent developments, not only vis-à-vis deconstruction but also in relation to other important approaches, especially structuralism and "universal pragmatics." Indeed, it can be fairly said that phenomenological criticism in its most recent Germanic representation—that of Gadamer's disciples, that of Jauss and Iser—is pushing deconstruction aside and is *en vedette*, both because of its clash with Jürgen Habermas, who is now so much in vogue, and because of the ongoing popularity of reader-response theory. Third, to emphasize that this survey shall try to move incrementally toward notions sophisticated enough for advanced study, though the development shall be as internal to itself as possible, so that beginners do not need special or outside preparation as long as they follow step by step. [2]

The ontology of the literary work as understood by most phenomenological theorists depends on certain basic principles of phenomenological epistemology. The epistemology is first fully developed in the philosophy (or, more appropriately, in the "phenomenology") of Edmund Husserl (1859–1938). Every discussion of Husserl must pause for a moment at the term *phenomenology* itself, so entrammeled is the word's history and so prolific its use over the last several decades. *Phenomenon*, for Kant, meant the appearance of reality in consciousness, as opposed to *noumenon*, or the being of reality-in-itself (which is unknowable by man). In Hegel, phenomenology has a historical perspective: For him, it is the "science" describing the development natural phenomenal consciousness undergoes by way of science and philosophy toward absolute knowledge of the Absolute. When the early Husserl takes over the term, however, he renounces what he calls the "dualism" between phenomenon and noumenon posited by Kant, and the "constructionism" whereby Hegel dialectically moves from phenomena to the Absolute Mind they supposedly manifest. Husserl agrees with them in asserting that only phenomena are given, but he claims that in them, and only in them, is given the essence of that which is. Since by Husserl's time the philosophy of Hegel had already been tagged with other labels, Husserl felt he could legitimately appropriate the word *phenomenology* for his own philosophical approach.

The early Husserl claims that contemporary epistemology is at an impasse. His disciples often interpret this to mean that since Descartes thought and world have been falsely dichotomized, and that such a dichotomy results from regarding consciousness as self-enclosed (that is, as thought knowing itself, not knowing the outside). Consciousness is wrongly considered a *faculty* for being conscious instead of an *act* of being conscious. For example, the pure idealist, emphasizing the subject (and the subject's priority, spontaneity, and activity), maintains that subjectivity actively projects objectivity. Indeed, so much is this the case that the trend of the idealist movement is to eliminate the world as a source of knowledge. The empiricist, on the other hand, stresses the passivity of consciousness and differs from Husserl on this count. The empiricist maintains there is a reflecting image, or impressed species, lodged in the knower. The impressed species has been imprinted by physical reality and (as a "double" of reality-in-itself) becomes the immediate object of knowledge. Though opting for opposite horns of the subject–object dilemma, both idealist and empiricist agree there is no bridge between thought and world.

The early-phase Husserl rejects both these epistemologies because each fails to understand consciousness as a unified intentional act. Consciousness for Husserl at this time is not a Cartesian knowing of knowledge but a real intercourse with the outside. Consciousness is an act wherein the subject *intends* (or directs himself toward the object) and the object is *intended* (or functions as a target for the intending act, though the object transcends this act). The subject intending and the object intended are reciprocally implicated (and, it should be added, the subject is real and the object is real, that is, truly emanating from the outside). Following the lead of several historians of philosophy, I call this epistemological formula Husserlian neorealism. Phenomenology thus asserts that one can get at reality through a recognition of "essence" revealed in consciousness.

In his later phases, Husserl becomes progressively appreciative of Descartes and Kant. In what is often called his idealist period, Husserl makes subjectivity constitutive of objectivity. Unsympathetic critics lambaste this move as a "retreat to Kant." In any case, it is the earlier Husserlian formula ("the mutual implication of subject and object," or neorealism) that comes to influence both the Geneva School and the Heideggerians. The influence of Husserl's later phase on literary theory and criticism has been somewhat weaker. The outstanding exception is its impact on Maurice Natanson, who has brilliantly applied the notion of Husserl's "transcendental subjectivity" to literature and all the arts.

After Husserl, phenomenological epistemology undergoes meaningful changes at the hands of Martin Heidegger, Jean-Paul Sartre, and Maurice Merleau-Ponty. Whereas Husserl brackets out (i.e., suspends consideration of) the question of existence so that he can better isolate the essence of the intentional act, Heidegger, radicalizing the Husserlian definition of consciousness, declares that consciousness should be grasped not as a static but as a dynamic action and, indeed, as existence itself. In his own words, "the essence of human being lies in existence." The whole human being is "being-in-the-world" (*in der Welt sein*), a reciprocal relation of subjectivity and world. The human being "is there" (*Dasein*) in the world and feels thrown there (thus experiencing *Geworfenheit*, or a sense of "thrownness"). Being *is* a movement toward future possibility, a "falling back into" the past, and a "falling for" the present. Because temporality and death are threatening and man as act is fearful, the fundamental structure of being is Care (*Sorge*). Whereas Husserl's stress is on rational acts of consciousness, Heidegger's emphasis is on Care and the "moods" (*Stimmungen*). Thus the effect of Heidegger's monumental book *Being and Time* (*Sein und Zeit*, 1927) is to shift focus from intellect-consciousness to a more radical emotion-consciousness. Heidegger also charts the "field of consciousness" according to various systems of meaning, such as the generalized "other" ("impersonal humanity," or *Das Man*), and the world of physical objects experienced as either "present-at-hand" (*Vorhandenheit*) or "ready-to-hand" (*Zuhandenheit*).

Heidegger's focus on temporality, the nonrational modes of consciousness, and regionalization in the field of consciousness all influence the Geneva School. After *Being and Time*, Heidegger fixes a more direct gaze on "Being," and his philosophical approach becomes, in the eyes of orthodox Husserlians, more and more disreputable. Husserl had argued that phenomenology should see meaning *in* experience and that, before undertaking elaborate philosophical themes, it should master its own methodology. Husserlians call their movement "descriptive phenomenology" and tend to consider Heideggerian thought ("hermeneutical phenomenology") too grand, too presumptuous in its claims about being (about *ontology*). For his part, Heidegger rejects most of the methodological procedures (the "reductions") that Husserl believes can isolate the essential structures of experience. Heideggerians tend to think that Husserl mistakenly looks for essences *beneath* experience instead of *in* concrete experience.

Apropos literary theory and criticism, the dramatic difference between the Geneva School, which is more Husserlian in its assumptions, and the hermeneutical tradition (Gadamer, Jauss, Iser) is that the latter, following Heidegger, extends the principle of "mutual implication" to the relation between reader(s) and literary text.[3] This is to say, for the Geneva School the "mutual implication of subject and object" *does* characterize *intratextual relations*, and also the relation between an *author and his text*. The "phenomenological ego" or *cogito* of the text shares with the author's "empirical ego" the same deep-structured patterns, so that at least on the level of deep structure the author and his text are forever entrammeled.[4] But for the Geneva School, mutual implication *does not* characterize the relation of *reader(s) and text*, because the Geneva School demands that readers be "neutral" (or, better yet, "passive") so that they can identify completely with the experiences of the textual *cogito*. Heideggerians, instead, see readers and text as mutually implicated: A reader cannot (and, for that matter, should not) be "neutral," "objective." All readers are necessarily conditioned by their personal and communal history, so that they interpret, consciously and unconsciously, according to their *point of view* ("forestructure," "horizon of expectations").

After Heidegger, the two philosophers who most influence the Geneva critics are Jean-Paul Sartre and Maurice Merleau-Ponty. Sartre identifies intentionality with an individual's "fundamental choice," his "forward throw" or *projet*. Merleau-Ponty emphasizes the gestural function of language: Word as *parole* is not just a "sign" for meaning, but an *embodiment* of meaning. Both philosophers have a positive effect on the Geneva School's appreciation of the unity and nonconceptual role of the phenomenological ego.

Phenomenological literary theory and criticism are identified with the Geneva School, which attained maximum influence in the 1950s and sixties but still has influential representatives (see Selected Bibliography), and with some Heideggerians, both those identified with a school such as Binswangerian *Daseinanalyse* (again, see Selected Bibliography) and others deriving their inspiration from Heidegger independently. Marcel Raymond and Albert Béguin, whose most celebrated criticism was published before World War II, constitute the "first generation" of the Geneva School. Properly speaking, however, the school achieves its own definition only with the Belgian Georges Poulet (b. 1902), among whose works one should at least read, I think, *Studies in Human Time* (*Etudes sur le temps humain*, vol. 1, 1949), *The Interior Distance* (*La Distance intérieure*, 1952), and *Metamorphoses of the Circle* (*Les Métamorphoses du cercle*, 1961).[5]

Other figures of this "second generation" are the Frenchman Jean-Pierre

Richard (*L'Univers imaginaire de Mallarmé*, 1961) and the two Swiss critics Jean Starobinski (*L'Oeil vivant*, 1961) and Jean Rousset (*Forme et Signification*, 1962). At the University of Zurich Emil Staiger generates a criticism (*Stilwandel*, 1963) closely associated with the school. The school's analysis of consciousness clearly induces the later publications of Gaston Bachelard and the early writing of Roland Barthes. In America, Genevan practice becomes widely known through the early production of J. Hillis Miller (*Charles Dickens: The World of His Novels*, 1959; *The Disappearance of God*, 1963; and *Poets of Reality*, 1965) and Paul Brodtkorb's phenomenological treatment of Melville (*Ishmael's White World*, 1965). Though Miller turns to deconstruction shortly thereafter, the continuing influence of the Genevan tradition can be seen in a critic such as David Halliburton (*Edgar Allan Poe: A Phenomenological View*, 1973), and that of an independent Husserlian/Heideggerian aesthetics in critics such as Thomas J. Hines (*The Later Poetry of Wallace Stevens*, 1976) and Bruce Johnson (*True Correspondence: A Phenomenology of Thomas Hardy's Novels*, 1983).

The Geneva critics are at variance with each other just as a John Crowe Ransom is with a Cleanth Brooks in American New Criticism. But just as Ransom and Brooks hold a set of bedrock principles in common and thus can present a common front against a neo-Aristotelian such as R. S. Crane, so too can it be said that the various Geneva critics "agree on the basics." Thus we can now turn to a careful consideration of the school's theory and practice. Husserl's phenomenology is very much "in the air" during the genesis and development of the Genevan approach. It is very helpful to describe the school according to Husserlian parallels,[6] keeping in mind, of course, that literary theorists/critics are *bricoleurs*: They borrow "fast and loose" from philosophy and patch together a rationale, overt or implied, which serves their own purposes. In general, the Geneva School and its allies accept the description of human consciousness we have already encountered in our survey of phenomenological epistemology. Human consciousness is, for them, a massive self–world relation, a *Lebenswelt* ("life world") or network of personal experiences. The author of a literary work becomes, then, one whose imagination selects and transforms elements of his or her *Lebenswelt* and creates out of them a fictive construct, a fictive "universe." The creative writer develops and embodies his fictive universe in and through language. If they wish, the Geneva critics can at this point invoke the support of Roman Ingarden, the great phenomenological aesthetician who writes in the Husserlian tradition. In his monumental *Literary Work of Art* (*Das literarische Kunstwerk*, 1931), Ingarden describes the literary work as a structure of four strata which constitute a "polyphonic harmony." The four heterogenous yet interdependent strata are (1) that of "word sounds" and higher phonetic formations, (2) that of "meaning units," (3) that of "schematized aspects and aspect continua," and (4) that of "represented objectivities." The fourth or climactic level is a fictive world which "unfolds" out of the preceding levels and includes them.

The next phase of the ontological description, however, takes one a crucial step further. It states that precisely because language is gestural, is expressive, the literary work bears within itself the unique imprint of the author's own consciousness. The Geneva critics consider the author's unique imprint immanent in the literary work and critically available there. They are not, however, "biographical critics." The Geneva School, with few exceptions, agrees that biographical criticism or any critical system which treats the author's "self" in "disembodied form" (that is, as external to the work) is invalid. Because phenomenological critics operate solely within the confines of the literary structure, they consider their approach intrinsic, a parameter of phenomenological method since Husserl's day.

I might add here too a word of explanation for those who feel that talk of an "author's imprint" comes perilously close to what is called in the Anglo-American world the "intentional fallacy." When the phenomenological critic refers to the author's "intentionality" enverbalized in the literary work, intentionality means the author's multi-modal interaction with world, not just the conceptual interaction; the intentionality concerned is accessible only through internal analysis of the text. Furthermore, the author's concept of what the literary work is or will be does not necessarily identify with what of the self was actually put into the work. Intentionality in the phenomenological sense refers only to those interactions between the author's selfhood and world that actually appear in the work (whether the author knows he or she put them there or not). Thus the American "New Critical" admonition against "intentional fallacy" does not apply.

What we are calling the author's unique imprint is precisely the ensemble of "experiential patterns" which characterize his/her *Lebenswelt* but are *duplicated* in the literary work.[7] Since both Husserl and others had warned against "psychologism," or the relegation of cause to an empirical subjectivity outside the phenomenon under study, the notion of "duplication" (instead of substantive transference) is crucial here. Another important distinction is that experiential patterns are *not* experiences but *patterns* of experience which underlie the surface language of the work, giving it an *organic unity*. Just as the whole *Lebenswelt* of a human being is at bottom unified, so too is the collective work of an author unified. This unity is not "simple" but "dialectical," just like the unity of the *Lebenswelt*, so a Geneva critic often treats an author's production collectively, reconstituting it in the interpretation according to a dialectical scheme characteristic of a *Lebenswelt*. In a dramatic departure from the norms of American New Criticism, the Geneva critic thus feels free to gloss one poem with another, say, or to dissolve the surface unity of an individual work so fragments of the work can exemplify a "systemic experiential pattern" of the collective work.

In order to chart the patterns of this "field of consciousness," the Genevan employs what can be called the "modes" and the "content-categories" of consciousness. The modes designate the concretely differentiated functions of consciousness, and consciousness here means intentionality, the reciprocal implication of self and world (*not* function in a Kantian sense, where the "function" is "inside" the self). The most exhaustive classification of the modes lists seven kinds: cognition, volition, emotion, perception, time (including memory), space, and imagination. The contents of consciousness are the quiddities of self and world involved in consciousness, that is, intentionality; contents too, then, are a reciprocal implication of self and outside (thus, *not* purely "outside" the self). The most representative listing of the content-categories comprises four designations: World (non-human entities), Happenings (events), Others (other human beings), and Self (selfhood as the content of one's own intentional act). To avoid the charge that such classifications render their practice as "extrinsic" as that of Freudians or archetypalists, the Geneva critics insist the designations of the modes and contents are artificial: They are just "convenient" ways of charting consciousness, of "breaking into" the patterns so one can begin to describe them.

Though the practice of the Geneva School is often a very poetic meditation on the text (witness Poulet), the philosophical inspiration of the rigorous Husserl is indispensable for an understanding of why the school is called phenomenological. Husserl demands the "phenomenological reduction," a maneuver that in literary terms becomes the suspension of ideological presuppositions on the part of the critic, and the "bracketing out" of their so-called historical causes (though this latter application gradually weakens, so the Geneva critics sometimes perform critiques of cultural consciousness). After the interpretation of the *surface-configurations* of the text, they proceed to the unique task, the phenomenological description of experiential patterns. Husserl's "phenomenological intuition," the careful scrutiny of the individual phenomenon so one "sees" its *essential structure*, is paralleled by the Geneva critic's exposure of a literary work's *ensemble* of experiential patterns. Husserl follows phenomenological intuition by "eidetic intuition," the "seeing" of *general essences* within the structures common to all or most phenomena in the set. Circling back and forth between individual text and the collective work of an author (an "interpretive circle"), Geneva criticism parallels Husserl's eidetic intuition by the exposure of *systemic experiential patterns*, that is, patterns which often recur in the collective work. Since an author's systemic patterns usually undergo change several times in his or her life (these changes reflect a "depth change" in the author's consciousness), Geneva critics often specialize in the dialectical exposure of these "shifts." For example, in *The Interior Distance*, Poulet shows that the poetry of the French poet Stéphane Mallarmé moves through three phases. During the early phase, the visual mode experiences "the Absolute" as blocked out by "opaqueness"; during the middle phase, the Absolute is visually experienced as "unmediated light"; and in the last phase, it is experienced as "mediated light" (actualized by surface-configurations involving "translucent" images such as "fog" and "luminous curtains").

In its recovery of an author's experiential patterns (even though recuperated *in* the work and not by a presumed research of the original empirical experience), the Geneva School operates in the tradition of the nineteenth-century hermeneut Friedrich Schleiermacher and of Husserl himself and *differs from* the other great phenomenological school, the "existential hermeneutics" of the Heideggerians. What links the two schools, then, so we have a definition of "phenomenological criticism" in general? Two important features, actually. The first is that both schools take "experience" as their ground, whether that experience be prelinguistic (Husserl) or linguistic (Heidegger). Thus both phenomenologies reject the various versions of rationalism associated with Habermas ("universal pragmatics"), Lévi-Strauss (the "rational unconscious" of structuralism), or Derrida (deconstruction, whereby reason in perpetual regress forever finds its *own* "fault"). The second feature is that both phenomenologies affirm that experience is a mutual implication of subject and object (as we have already explained) and that this implication is illuminated not by empiricism or romantic subjectivity but by way of the "circle of understanding" of the Geneva School, the "hermeneutical circle" of Gadamer.

Hans-Georg Gadamer, the most influential of post–World War II Heideggerians, published *Truth and Method* (*Wahrheit und Methode*) in 1965. His position furnished phenomenology with two exciting in-house debates, that with the Italian Emilio Betti and that with the American E. D. Hirsch. Hirsch, in his *Validity in Interpretation* (1967), appropriates Husserl so as to align the "master" with what is called the older "objective hermeneutics" (Schleiermacher, etc.), arguing that the meaning of a text is the author's purposeful "intentional object." For Hirsch, Gadamer's famous "fusion of horizons" (the mutual implication of historical text and the reader's rich and variegated forestructure) produces mere "significance." Gadamerians answer that an honest phenomenological description of the "act of understanding" necessarily recognizes it as "effective-historical" (*Werkungsgeschichtliche*). That is, a text always arrives sedimented with the "effects" of intervening interpretations, so that understanding is always a creative meditation, not the retrieval of "pure authorial intention."

Two present-day thinkers in the Gadamerian tradition are especially important. Wolfgang Iser (*Der implizite Leser*, 1972; Eng. trans., *The Implied Reader*, 1974), using a combination of Ingarden ("concretization" of "schematic gaps") and Gadamer, proposes that the "implied reader" is that generated by the text through its "response-inviting" structures. The "actual reader" concretizes these structures, but always in a way possible for his or her forestructure, conditioned by past experiences. Hans-Robert Jauss, in *Literaturgeschichte als Provokation* (1970), specializes in *Rezeption-ästhetik* ("aesthetics of reception"), which focuses on *historical* discourse (and less on *individual* reception, Iser's main interest). Since readership is always in-situation, Jauss argues, a text is not accessible, in any pure and objective sense, in the way it was received by its original readership ("original horizon of expectations") nor is it perfectly subject to an alleged present-day "arbitrary" reading; rather, reading is a fusion of past and present horizons.

We can now work our way, indicatively, through the more important extramural debates in which phenomenology is engaged. The just-mentioned notion of "fusion of horizons" is the crux of a fierce debate between the Heideggerians such as Jauss and Gadamer on the one hand, and Jürgen Habermas, a descendant of the Marxist Frankfurt School, on the other. Habermas accuses Gadamer in particular of naiveté for assuming horizons necessarily "fuse." Do they not often collide because of social oppression, economic tyranny, and so on?[8] David Hoy and others defend Gadamer by arguing that Gadamerian "fusion" involves flux, tension, even discontinuity.[9] Habermas also participates in a long-standing charge leveled against Heideggerian forestructure: that it is relativistic. Gadamer and others answer that on the contrary "truth" is precisely what is disclosed by the involvement of forestructure and world. Since Habermas affirms that idea precedes word, Gadamer counterattacks by indicating the naiveté of "prelinguisticality" and "ideal rationality."

If the "universal pragmatics" of Habermas be excessively idealist and rationalist, structuralism is doubly guilty, founded as it is on an a priori "rational unconscious" and strict "binary opposition" (formulations of Lévi-Strauss). To structuralism's argument that phenomenology overestimates the directly experienced, thus slighting both logic and empirical science (Was the Ptolemaic universe "true" because it so closely approximated the "immediate experience" of the "heavens"?), phenomenology answers that by nature it is less extremist. Indeed, phenomenology has long considered itself the standard bearer of modern "humanistic value." Paul Ricoeur, whose thought is surely very moderate, provides a carefully elaborated defense of phenomenology, showing that Husserl and Heidegger give logic and science their due. And he mentions that phenomenology is more nuanced than structuralism: Doesn't a word take a qualitative leap in status, he argues, when it moves from the dictionary to a sentence? When in a sentence, doesn't it really refer to an *existential* situation, instead of functioning as a "chip" in an isolated "logical circuit?"[10]

Deconstruction challenges traditional phenomenology precisely because, on all levels, it ruptures theories of presence.[11] Thus Jacques Derrida even argues that Poulet's famous description of the image of "fold" in Mallarmé's poetry is unconsciously dissimulative: the so-called fold, which represents synthetic thinking, is neither "fold" nor "non-fold" (in my own work, I would call it an "off/fold"). And Paul de Man, claiming that critics (including himself) are "blind" to their own "insight," argues that Poulet's real contribution is that he proves the "otherness," the *unavailability*, of an experiential pattern. In so limited a space, we have only time to indicate one argument of Derrida, that of "endless metaphoricity."

Metaphysical formulas of presence, he asserts, mistakenly take as representative of an unshifting reality a set of terms that are *metaphoric*. Even the word *presence* does not make a contact with a "reality." Rather, as the Latin root reveals, *presence* is the metaphor—"that which is like a thing *before* or *ruling over*" (both themselves metaphors). So, once again, the "reality" is not really named but deferred. And so on, and on.

Phenomenology has produced two kinds of response to Derrida, the traditional and the innovative. Félix Martínez-Bonati, for example, can be our representative of the former, in that he answers that "presence" and "real communication" are undeniable *facts* of our *experience*, and as such to deny them is simply pseudophilosophizing.[12] Alternately, Paul Ricoeur's answer represents the innovative response to Derrida. While preserving the phenomenological connection, he uses the "newer linguistics," which denies that words "possess a proper, i.e., primitive, natural, original (*etumon*) meaning in themselves."[13] Thus he argues that Derrida is beating a dead horse. And, furthermore, he argues that Derrida is out-and-out wrong in thinking, say, that the word *presence* is equal to its root. Rather, when a language community wants to express a new "find," it often fabricates new words by piecing together old words. So with the philosophical community when it wanted to talk about "presence," for example. Ricoeur's innovative theory of "dynamic identity" is phenomenologically directed by experience, freeing it to follow the "intermediary course between the Charibdis of logical identity [traditional definition] and the Scylla of identity and difference [the Derridean 'sameness which is not identity']."[14]

If I may presume to close our summary with a brief indication of my own position vis-à-vis Derrida in particular and literature in general, I think there are four points to be made. First, I consider Derrida himself a residual phenomenologist, a "closet" phenomenologist if you will. For he can only know that "alternate solutions *sous rature* (under erasure)" better approximate the way life "goes on" *through experience*, since rationally the erased alternate solutions carry the "same" defects as classical solutions. Second, Derrida's constitution of off/presence can truly liberate (surely a good experience, if it is to be had), but only when *experienced mystically*, through the off/centric mysticism which we find in a kind of Buddhism called the Buddhism of devoidness (*not* centric voidness). No doubt so "alien" an experience as Buddhism causes most Westerners, even intellectuals, to cringe (often under the cloak of protesting "no interest in the subject"),[15] but how can a phenomenologist or deconstructionist really so behave? Are phenomenologists to so cramp and isolate their description of experience? Are deconstructionists to so compartmentalize a strategy that claims to rupture boundaries? Third, as argued in my *Derrida on the Mend*, the Buddhism of devoidness, historically represented by the Buddhist Nagarjuna, a thinker in the Indian rationalist tradition, offers a version of Buddhism's "two truths" which can at once restore "presence" (and therefore the practice of the Geneva School) and deconstruct "presence." Fourth, in literary criticism, the Yale School's stress on the dissolution of organic readings is not enough. More important is the second part of Derridean procedure, an accounting of the "slide," which follows upon the rupture of presence. The *experience* of this slide, with its care-filled *phenomenological description*, can open up literature to new beauty.[16]

Notes

1. Edmund Husserl, *Ideas*, trans. W. R. Boyce Gibson (New York: Collins, 1962), 1: 6, as cited in Tom Rockmore et al., *Marxism and Alternatives* (Dordrecht: Reidel, 1981), p. 259.
2. Parts of this survey are excerpted from my own *Phenomenology and Literature* (West

Lafayette, Ind.: Purdue University Press, 1977; 2nd ptg., 1978), which the reader can consult for more specialized and thorough treatment.

3. My essay aims to limit itself to phenomenological criticism. Heideggerian thought is sometimes phenomenological and sometimes not. Because the principle of mutual implication is historically so identified with phenomenology (though the how and where of its functioning are open to dispute), I am treating that part of the Heideggerian tradition which addresses epistemology. The part of his tradition which is more thematic—giving accounts of the Earth, the Holy, the Fourfold, and so on—I assign to nonphenomenological hermeneutics.

4. Deep structure for the phenomenologist is the *moi profond* ("deep ego") that is generated by "self" and "outside." It is constituted according to the radically *human* modes (cognition, volition, emotion, sensation, etc.) and contents (happenings, others, etc.) and is not at all to be confused with the binary and apersonal deep structure proposed by structuralism.

5. In what he calls the second kind of epistemology found in a literary work, Poulet seems to offer a Cartesian or late-phase (idealist) Husserlian formula. But practical critics are judged by *how they practice* their craft, not by how they abstractly define themselves. Poulet's practice is universally recognized as phenomenological. See Magliola, *Phenomenology and Literature*, pp. 21–24, for documentation.

6. This is not to deny, of course, that there are many other influences of the Geneva School, among whom we can name Henri Bergson, Wilhelm Dilthey, Karl Vossler and the Munich School, and, especially, Leo Spitzer.

7. I am here talking only of the patterns of intentionality that underlie the author's experience and pass over into the deep structure of the literary work (so they are "duplicated" there). They are not to be confused with the intentional acts whereby they "pass over," that is, the creative intentionality of the author (the latter is transitory and cannot be regained by the reader). Nor are they to be confused with the intentional acts of the reader whereby the reader experiences the intentionality embedded in the literary work.

8. Michel Foucault lodges just such an assault against Gadamer when he reads horizons as texts that wield sociopolitical power and break into each other. Terry Eagleton in England and Fredric Jameson in America deliver similar charges against Gadamer from their independent Marxist positions.

9. See David Hoy, *The Critical Circle: Literature and History in Contemporary Hermeneutics* (Berkeley: University of California Press, 1978).

10. For Paul Ricoeur's most extensive refutation of structuralism, see *The Conflict of Interpretations: Essays in Hermeneutics*, ed. Don Ihde (Evanston, Ill.: Northwestern University Press, 1974).

11. For my account of Derridean deconstruction, see Magliola, *Derrida on the Mend* (West Lafayette, Ind.: Purdue University Press, 1984; 2nd ptg., 1986), part 1.

12. See Félix Martínez-Bonati, "The Stability of Literary Meaning," in *Identity of the Literary Text*, ed. Mario Valdés and Owen Miller (Toronto: University of Toronto Press, 1985), p. 241.

13. Paul Ricoeur, *The Rule of Metaphor*, trans. Robert Czerny (Toronto: University of Toronto Press, 1977), p. 290.

14. Paul Ricoeur, "The Text as Dynamic Identity," in Valdés and Miller, *Identity of the Literary Text*, p. 175.

15. Actually, a rereading of the Orientalism pervasive in Nietzsche but now so blithely bypassed (despite the Nietzschean vogue) and a creative rereading of the Buddhism so dominant in Schopenhauer (who I believe will be soon coming into his own) lead quite inevitably to Buddhist devoidness, that is, to the version of Buddhism which tracks the "same" off/path as Derridean "trace."

16. In a paper at the Symposium in Postmodernism, Cerisy-la-Salle, France (Summer

1983), I interpreted Dickinson, Stevens, Ashbery, Mandelbaum, and others according to this new kind of "Derridean" phenomenological criticism. The paper is published in the proceedings of the Cercle International de Recherche Philosophique (Houston and Paris), *Krisis: International Journal of Philosophy* 3–4 (1985): 91–111.

Selected Bibliography

Phenomenology and Philosophy

Heidegger, Martin. *On the Way to Language*. Translated by P. Hertz. New York: Harper and Row, 1971.

———. *Poetry, Language, Thought*. Translated by Albert Hofstadter. New York: Harper and Row, 1971.

Magliola, Robert. *Derrida on the Mend*. West Lafayette, Ind.: Purdue University Press, 1984. See part 1 for a discussion of phenomenology and Derrida, and the first appendix for an evaluation of the conflict between American "analytic aesthetics" (Morris Weitz) and the hermeneutical approach.

Spiegelberg, Herbert. *The Phenomenological Movement*. 3rd rev. ed. The Hague: Nijhoff, 1982. Good introduction to Husserl, Heidegger, Sartre, Merleau-Ponty, though somewhat biased against Heidegger.

Zaner, Richard, and Don Ihde. *Phenomenology and Existentialism*. New York: Putnam, 1973.

Phenomenology and Literary Theory

Falk, Eugene. *The Poetics of Roman Ingarden*. Chapel Hill: University of North Carolina Press, 1981. Exhaustive analysis and synthesis of Ingarden's aesthetics. Definitive work.

Gras, Vernon, ed. *European Literary Theory and Practice*. New York: Dell, 1973. See the "Theory" section for Gras's well-chosen excerpts in "existential phenomenology" from primary sources, including Ludwig Binswanger.

Hoy, David. *The Critical Circle: Literature and History in Contemporary Hermeneutics*. Berkeley: University of California Press, 1978. Most useful because of its carefully reasoned defense of Gadamer.

Ingarden, Roman. *The Literary Work of Art*. Translated by G. Grabowicz. Evanston, Ill.: Northwestern University Press, 1973.

Iser, Wolfgang. "Feigning in Literature." In *Identity of the Literary Text*, ed. Mario Valdés and Owen Miller, pp. 204–28. Toronto: University of Toronto Press, 1985. Resourceful and assimilative, the contemporary Iser.

Kaelin, Eugene F. *Art and Existence: A Phenomenological Aesthetics*. Lewisburg, Pa.: Bucknell University Press, 1970. An excellent phenomenology of aesthetics, creative yet securely founded on both essentialist (Husserl, Ingarden) and existentialist (Heidegger, Merleau-Ponty) phenomenology. Highly recommended.

Langellier, Kristin. "A Phenomenology of Narrative in Performance." In *Phenomenology in Rhetoric and Communication*, ed. Stanley Deetz, pp. 83–90. Washington, D.C.: University Press of America for the Center for Advanced Research in Phenomenology, 1981. A good example of how phenomenology has positively influenced drama (and performance).

Magliola, R. *Phenomenology and Literature*. West Lafayette, Ind.: Purdue University Press, 1977. In part 1, treatment of both the Geneva School and Heideggerian hermeneutics (including Binswanger); in part 2, chapters on Hirsch and Husserl, Ingarden, Dufrenne, and Magliola's own appropriation of Heidegger.

Martínez-Bonati, Félix. *Fictive Discourse and the Structures of Literature: A Phenomenological Approach*. Translated by Philip Silver. Ithaca, N.Y.: Cornell University Press, 1981. (Revised and expanded version of the Spanish edition, 1960.) The author's own development and extension of classical phenomenology. Opposes Heideggerian approach.

————. "The Stability of Literary Meaning." In *Identity of the Literary Text*, ed. Mario Valdés and Owen Miller, pp. 231–46. Toronto: University of Toronto Press, 1985. Emphasizing the stability of meaning, Martínez-Bonati here shores up his defense and refutes both structuralism and Heideggerian hermeneutics.

Palmer, Richard. *Hermeneutics: Interpretation Theory in Schleiermacher, Dilthey, Heidegger, and Gadamer*. Evanston, Ill.: Northwestern University Press, 1969. Still a definitive work, upon publication it excited the heated opposition of both American New Critics and European Husserlians because of its championing of Gadamer.

Ricoeur, Paul. *Time and Narrative*. Vol. 2. Translated by Kathleen McLaughlin and David Pellauer. Chicago: University of Chicago Press, 1984. Examination of the rapports between time and narrative in both fiction and literary theory. Includes practical analyses of Virginia Woolf, Thomas Mann, Marcel Proust.

Valdés, Mario J. *Shadows in the Cave: A Phenomenological Approach to Literary Criticism Based on Hispanic Texts*. Toronto: University of Toronto Press, 1982.

White, D. A. *Heidegger and the Language of Poetry*. Lincoln: University of Nebraska Press, 1978.

Phenomenology and Literary Criticism

Carrabino, Victor. *The Phenomenological Novel of Robbe-Grillet*. Parma: C.E.M. Editrice, 1974. One of the few satisfying explanations of why Robbe-Grillet is considered "phenomeno-logical." Demonstrates the connections with Husserl and Merleau-Ponty. Good bibliography.

Flinn, Frank. "The Phenomenology of Symbol: Genesis I and II." In *Phenomenology in Practice and Theory*, ed. W. Hamrick, pp. 223–49. Dordrecht: Nijhoff, 1985. Much inspired by Ricoeur, Flinn offers a phenomenological reading of the two biblical versions of "the Beginning." Proposes to show that phenomenology can contribute what biblical "form criticism" cannot.

Gras, Vernon, ed. *European Literary Theory and Practice*. New York: Dell, 1973. See the "Practice" section for examples (full-length essays) by Staiger, Binswanger, Poulet, and others.

Halliburton, David. *Edgar Allan Poe: A Phenomenological View*. Princeton, N.J.: Princeton University Press, 1973. Inspired most by the Geneva School, this is an example of English-language practical phenomenological criticism at its best.

Hines, Thomas J. *The Later Poetry of Wallace Stevens: Phenomenological Parallels with Husserl and Heidegger*. Lewisburg, Pa.: Bucknell University Press, 1976. An example of independent phenomenological criticism derived directly from philosophical phenomenological thinkers. Shows that the "philosophy in literature" of Stevens resembles assumptions of Husserl and Heidegger.

Iser, Wolfgang. *The Implied Reader: Patterns of Communication in Prose Fiction from Bunyan to Beckett*. Baltimore: Johns Hopkins University Press, 1974. Outstanding criticism of Bunyan, Fielding, Scott, Thackeray, Joyce, and others.

Johnson, Bruce. *True Correspondence: A Phenomenology of Thomas Hardy's Novels*. Tallahassee: University Presses of Florida, 1983. Independent phenomenological criticism, arguing that Husserl and Hardy operate from the same world view, each reflecting it in his own discipline.

Lawall, Sarah. *Critics of Consciousness*. Cambridge, Mass.: Harvard University Press, 1968. Good for a history of the Geneva School's practical criticism; weaker in its discussion of how phenomenology pertains.

MacCary, W. T. *Friends and Lovers: The Phenomenology of Death in Shakespeare's Comedies*. Cambridge: Cambridge University Press, 1985.

Poulet, Georges. *The Interior Distance*. Translated by Elliott Coleman. Ann Arbor: University of Michigan Press (Ann Arbor paperback), 1964.

————. *The Metamorphoses of the Circle*. Translated by Carley Dawson and Elliott Coleman. Baltimore: Johns Hopkins University Press, 1967.

Rooks, Sharon E. "*The Tin Drum*—Novel into Film: A Phenomenological Approach." *Dissertation Abstracts International* 43, 4 (1982): 1158A–59A.

Spanos, William, ed. *Martin Heidegger and the Question of Literature: Towards a Post-modern Literary Hermeneutics*. Bloomington: Indiana University Press, 1980. Practical criticism as well as theoretical essays showing the latest appropriations of Heideggerian thought.

Phenomenology and Controversy

Derrida, Jacques. *Edmund Husserl's "The Origin of Geometry": An Introduction*. Translated and with a preface by J. P. Leavey, Jr. Stony Brook, N.Y.: Nicholas Hay, 1978. Derrida's first published work, it remains the clearest deconstruction of Husserl available.

Graff, Gerald. *Literature against Itself: Literary Ideas in Modern Society*. Chicago: University of Chicago Press, 1979. Graff is a maverick sort of neoclassicist, as anticapitalist as he is anti-Marxist. Attacks phenomenology, hermeneutics (see esp. pp. 130–32), and American New Criticism, too. Perhaps he is best described as a rational, "objective" critic who places himself in the classical-Renaissance-Enlightenment tradition.

Jauss, Hans-Robert. "The Identity of the Poetic Text in the Changing Horizon of Understanding." In *Identity of the Literary Text*, ed. Mario Valdés and Owen Miller, pp. 146–74. Toronto: University of Toronto Press, 1985. A personal account of his whole career. Of particular interest for its response to Mikhail Bakhtin, who has his own view, of course, of "dialogy."

Jay, Martin. "Should Intellectual History Take a Linguistic Turn? Reflections on the Habermas–Gadamer Debate." In *Modern European Intellectual History*, ed. D. La Capra and S. Kaplan, pp. 86–110. Ithaca, N.Y.: Cornell University Press, 1982. A dispassionate, sophisticated, very clear account of the dispute between "universal pragmatics" and Gadamerian hermeneutics. Jay recognizes the dispute as the diachronic matter it is, with the several phases of both philosophers represented.

Ricoeur, Paul. *Freud and Philosophy: An Essay on Interpretation*. Translated by Denis Savage. New Haven: Yale University Press, 1970. An ingenious and thorough phenomenological response to psychoanalysis, partly refutation and partly appropriation.

————. *The Rule of Metaphor*. Translated by Robert Czerny. Toronto: University of Toronto Press, 1977. Involved in almost all of the contemporary debates, this presentation of Ricoeur's theory of language comprises effective responses to deconstruction and structuralism.

Rockmore, Tom, et al. *Marxism and Alternatives*. Dordrecht: Reidel, 1981. Part 4, "The Transcendentalism of Phenomenology," pp. 187–264, proffers a very good description of Soviet Marxism's response to Husserl and Heidegger. Though a Marxist inclination is detectable, the appraisals are well balanced.

Rowe, John Carlos. *The Theoretical Dimensions of Henry James*. Madison: University of Wisconsin Press, 1984. In the pertinent chapter, "Phenomenological Hermeneutics: Henry James and Literary Impressionism," pp. 189–217, Rowe identifies two kinds of phenomenology, one "impressionistic" and the other reader-oriented. Though there is much evidence that Rowe misunderstands phenomenology, he does try, through an analysis of James, to save what is best in the approach while pointing out defects.

JOEL WEINSHEIMER

Hermeneutics

Hermeneutics, in brief, is the theory and practice of interpretation. Its province extends as far as do meaning and the need to understand it. Like the other varieties of critical thought discussed in this collection, hermeneutics is not limited in scope solely or even primarily to literary interpretation. There exists no "hermeneutic school" centered in Paris, Frankfurt, Geneva, or elsewhere; there are no major literary critics whom one could unreservedly designate as specifically "hermeneutical." Moreover, hermeneutics names neither a particular method of interpretation nor a systematic body of theory. Rather, hermeneutics is best understood as a family resemblance persisting over many generations, as a historical tradition of which the theory and practice of literary interpretation are themselves part.

Hermeneutics has its origins in the allegorical interpretation of Homer, beginning in the sixth century B.C., and also in rabbinic interpretation of the Talmud and Midrashim. Influenced by both, Christian hermeneutics is commonly dated from Philo Judaeus in the first century, whose methodized interpretation of the Bible influenced not only Origen, Augustine, and many others before the Reformation but also Dilthey and Betti long afterward. The four-tiered hierarchy of meanings, now best known to literary critics through Northrop Frye's adaptation, is also indebted to Philo Judaeus, as are typological interpretations still employed in churches today.

Hermeneutics begins, then, with the interpretation of canonical texts, including the Homeric epics, and even in our time it has not entirely lost sight of the aim that motivates all scriptural interpretation: to disclose not just fact but truth. Yet now, hermeneutics reaches well beyond theology—into sociology, aesthetics, historiography, law, and the human sciences generally. And since postpositivist philosophy has begun to acknowledge the role of hermeneutic understanding in the natural sciences too, there is good reason to take seriously Gadamer's claim that the scope of hermeneutics is universal.

This broadening of hermeneutics, from a mere exegetical aid to a fundamental, universal mode of understanding involves more than the extension of its boundaries. A fairly clear, though gradual change in the nature of hermeneutical study itself occurs in the late eighteenth century, when the coincidence of classical and biblical modes of interpretation could no longer be taken for granted. "Hermeneutics as the art of understanding does not yet exist in general," Friedrich Schleiermacher writes in the outline of his 1819 lectures; "rather, only various specialized hermeneutics exist."[1] Thus, Schleiermacher recognizes the need for a comprehensive theory, a theory that would unite not only classical and biblical but all interpretive activities, regardless of their subject matter. Schleiermacher is credited with sketching out the first such general hermeneutics.

Schleiermacher's program is significant not only because of its specific cross-disciplinary methods but also—and more important—because his hermeneutics, since it was to cover every sphere of interpretation, was constructed apart from any particular sphere. Schleiermacher was concerned not with the obstacles specific to understanding some particular canon but rather with the fact that understanding itself had become problematic. We cannot assume that the effort of interpretation results naturally in understanding, Schleiermacher contends; quite the contrary, "strict interpretation begins with misunderstanding."[2] His hermeneutics devotes itself to elaborating the means for avoiding misunderstanding, which he considered inevitable. Schleiermacher attempts not so much to understand understanding as to guide it, to methodize it, and to produce artificially the understanding that does not occur naturally.

Correct interpretation, in Schleiermacher's view, requires a regulated re-creation of the creation one seeks to understand. Since no creation is consciously constructed by rule (as we follow but do not think about the rules of syntax in speaking), the re-creator who does reconstruct a text on the basis of its implicit rules can understand it better than its author did. But though rule-governed, the task of reconstruction is by no means mechanical or certain of its results. It involves, first, what is variously called grammatical, historical, or comparative reconstruction. Schleiermacher uses a text as his example of the pattern of interpretation; and just as an element of a text can be understood only in relation to its context, so also the author's text must be understood in relation to his canon, the canon in relation to the language, and the language in relation to history generally. "Posed in this manner, the task is an infinite one, because there is an infinity of the past and the future that we wish to see in the moment of discourse."[3] Since "no inspection of a work ever exhausts its meaning,"[4] it follows that the meaning of every work is potentially infinite and thus that every interpretation is finite and therefore provisional.

Second, the re-creation of the author's creation also requires divinatory reconstruction, without which one cannot undertake contextual reconstruction. *Divinatory reconstruction* is the process through which "one seeks to understand the writer immediately to the point that one transforms oneself into the other."[5] Although the meaning of a work is infinite, the work's meaning is also determinate, because it is the creation of a particular author on a particular occasion. The interpreter of a text thus cannot content himself with what contemporary authors typically thought, or even with what this author characteristically wrote; rather, he must seek to recover what the author means in this specific text. Understanding an original and creative author requires more than consulting the typical and characteristic. It also necessitates immediate understanding and intuitive or empathic understanding of the particular for its particularity; this process Schleiermacher calls "divination." To understand the author as such, the interpreter takes his inspiration from the shared universal traits of human nature, then undertakes a sympathetic leap beyond the common and the shared, even beyond himself, in an effort to become the individual creator whom he interprets.

Schleiermacher's guidelines for correct interpretation are retained and intensified by his biographer and intellectual heir, Wilhelm Dilthey. But Dilthey believed that before one could specify the methods or rules for interpretation, a methodology, a general theory of valid understanding, had to be developed. Occasioning and complicating Dilthey's methodological task were two factors: his acute sense of the achievements of the historical school, including not only Ranke and Droysen but even Hegel; and his no less acute sense of the achievements of natural science and the success of Kant's attempts to legitimate it. We can see both factors at work in Dilthey's contention that hermeneutics

has, beyond its use in the business of interpretation, a second task which is indeed its main one: it is to counteract the constant irruption of romantic whim and sceptical subjectivity into the realm of history by laying the historical foundations of valid interpretation on which all certainty in history rests. Absorbed into the context of the epistemology, logic and methodology of the human studies, the theory of interpretation becomes a vital link between philosophy and the historical disciplines, an essential part of the foundations of the studies of man.[6]

The several "studies of man" Dilthey attempts to buttress with his methodology originated during the Enlightenment when "the general system of history was divided up into individual systems—like those of law, religion, or poetry."[7] Insofar as history means legal, religious, literary, or other history, then history is only one among the many human sciences. With Winckelmann, philosophical and empirical historians began "treating history as the source of all mind-constructed facts."[8] In this view, historical development belongs intrinsically to all the human sciences, and it is only historically that they can be understood. Dilthey affirms and expands Schleiermacher's insight—that the essentially intelligible entities are texts—to include all historical phenomena. Every product of objective mind, every product of culture—even nonverbal records—must and can be understood as a text. Thus, if there is to be validity in interpreting the great book of history—if one is to resist "romantic whim and sceptical subjectivity"—then the very certainty of historical interpretation must itself rest on historical foundations. History is self-certifying; that is, history is a ground of truth.

But for Dilthey history was not a sufficient ground for truth; he also suggests that hermeneutics needs to be "absorbed into the context of the epistemology, logic and methodology of the human studies."[9] This absorption necessitates a rational rather than a historical grounding, and it was to be accomplished in Dilthey's *Critique of Historical Reason*. This unfinished work was intended to show the conditions and limits of historical knowledge just as Kant's first critique had done for pure reason in natural science. Among Dilthey's main ambitions was to distinguish the foundations of the human sciences from those of the natural, and make these bases equally solid. Thus like other neo-Kantians, Dilthey distinguished understanding from explanation and based the human sciences on understanding while attempting to justify understanding epistemologically.

For Kant the main problem in demonstrating the intelligibility of nature was the application of the unifying categories to the manifold of experience, which he solved through the transcendental schemata. Because of the absence of lawlike causality in the historical world, however, Dilthey found that Kant's transcendental solution could not be transposed to explain the validity of knowledge of the historical world. And in fact it did not need to be transferred, because historical knowledge possesses a more immediate ground of unity, intelligibility, and reliability than does an understanding of the natural world. This ground Dilthey discerned in historical life itself.

Life consists of parts, of experiences which are inwardly related to each other. Every particular experience refers to a self of which it is a part; it is structurally interrelated to other parts. Everything which pertains to mind is interrelated: interconnectedness is, therefore, a category originating from life. We apprehend connectedness through the unity of consciousness which is the condition of all apprehension. However, connectedness clearly does not follow from the fact of a manifold of experiences being presented to a unitary consciousness. Only because life is itself a structural connection of experiences—i.e. experiencable relations—is the connectedness of life given.[10]

As the constellation of individual experiences, the historical world exhibits intrinsic connection and relation, instead of the external relation characteristic of causality in the natural world. Experience cannot be subdivided into more elementary units, such as discrete sensations, whose synthesis would then require explanation; rather, historical experience is already coherent. The understanding of it necessitates no imposition of alien unities: Experiences are intrinsically intelligible because they are structurally connected to other experiences. The hermeneutic relation of part and whole inheres not only in the interpretive apprehension of the knowing subject, then, but also in the object known: Historical life itself is an organic, intrinsically intelligible text.

Whereas Schleiermacher contributed substantially to the general methods of the science of interpretation and Dilthey to the methodology of the human sciences broadly conceived, Heidegger's primary intent is not to contribute anything further to either level of science, though he builds on his predecessors' efforts. "Dilthey's own researches for laying the basis for the human sciences were forced one-sidedly into the field of theory of science," Heidegger acknowledges.[11] Nevertheless, if his own analysis of the problem of history arises "in the process of appropriating the labours of Dilthey,"[12] that is because "the 'logic of the human sciences' was by no means central to him."[13] Heidegger learns from Dilthey that hermeneutics names not just the methodology of the human sciences but something more fundamental to *Dasein* (i.e., human being) than any science. Heidegger's project is not epistemological but ontological, and for him understanding is less a way of *knowing* than of *being*. Thus he extends the sphere of hermeneutic understanding beyond individual texts and all other historical entities to an understanding of being itself.

In *Being and Time* hermeneutics figures both as the mode of inquiry and the subject matter inquired about; and these are necessarily—even circularly—interrelated. The cardinal aim of *Being and Time* is to reopen the "question of the meaning of Being in general."[14] Simply, what does it mean to be? Since the answer to this question is a meaning, one must discover that

meaning the way all meaning is discovered: by interpretation. As a mode of
inquiry, interpretation requires something already given. Yet Heidegger's
ontology does not consist merely in describing phenomena (modes of given-
ness); rather, it is also concerned with what has been covered up, which, for
Heidegger, is preeminently the question of the meaning of being. "Covered-
up-ness," Heidegger writes, "is the counter-concept to 'phenomenon.'"[15] For
what is covered up, description does not suffice. Thus Heidegger's phenomenology is hermeneutic: first, because its aim is a meaning; and second, because
this meaning needs to be uncovered through interpretation.

Interpretation operates in the ambiguous space between the hidden and
the open, the concealed and the revealed. Since interpretation cannot begin *ex
nihilo*, it needs a clue; and if hermeneutic ontology can uncover the meaning of
being, then "the meaning of Being must already be available to us in some
way."[16] (If this meaning were not somehow already available, all ontological
interpretation would be impossible, and the whole project of *Being and Time*
would be futile.) If the meaning of being is even vaguely familiar, however,
that fact is in itself highly significant, for it implies that "understanding of
Being is a definite characteristic of Dasein's being."[17] *Dasein* is distinct from
all other beings in that its own being is an issue for it, and if so it has at least a
dim intimation of what it means to be. Thus *Being and Time* interprets the
being of *Dasein* as the clue to the meaning of being.

To take *a* being as the clue to the nature of being is manifestly not a
presuppositionless mode of inquiry; quite the opposite, it is circular. But
though circular reasoning is open to obvious objections, it finds its own kind
of rigor in "working our [its] fore-structures in terms of the things themselves,"[18] and this Heidegger has done. His own inquiry into the being of
Dasein is circular, no doubt, but so is *Dasein* itself: "An entity for which . . .
its Being is itself an issue, has, ontologically, a circular structure."[19] There is
thus an exact coincidence between Heidegger's method and its object:

Like any ontological Interpretation whatsoever, this analytic can only, so to speak,
"listen in" to some previously disclosed entity as regards its Being. And it will attach
itself to Dasein's distinctive and most far-reaching possibilities of disclosure, in order
to get information about this entity from these. Phenomenological Interpretation
must make it possible for Dasein itself to disclose things primordially; it must, as it
were, let Dasein interpret itself.[20]

Dasein—this circular interrelationship between the human being and the
world constituted by his or her understanding of being—interprets itself.
Such interpretation is neither introspective self-interpretation nor interpretation of human beings as objects of the human or natural sciences. Instead,

Heidegger is concerned to elucidate a more primordial kind of interpretation from which all such interpretations are derivative. What he terms "understanding" designates a way of being in the world that is colloquially called "know-how," "knowing the ropes," or being "in the know." This understanding consists not in knowing specific facts but instead in being familiar with an entirety of relations in such a way that within them one can do, make, and know without reflection. Heidegger argues that all interpretation depends on this background of prereflective practices in which there is neither subject nor object.

As understanding, *Dasein* "knows" what everything in its world can be used for, its significance and possibility; and as a being in the world, the same is true of *Dasein* itself. "Understanding 'knows' *what* it is capable of—that is, what its potentiality-for-Being is capable of."[21] Potentiality, possibility, capability refer not only to what *Dasein* can be but also to what it already is. The being of *Dasein* as understanding consists in being able not just to perform given tasks in being able to be. In a sense, *Dasein* never is, but always is to be. In every present, it projects in understanding what other things and itself can be. Paradoxically, its present future being is also past, since *Dasein* projects its being on the basis of historical context or tradition. *Dasein* already (past) understands what it is (present) to be (future).

The making explicit of what *Dasein* can be Heidegger calls interpretation. "In interpretation, understanding does not become something different. It becomes itself. Such interpretation is grounded existentially in understanding; the latter does not arise from the former. Nor is interpretation the acquiring of information about what is understood; it is rather the working-out of possibilities projected in understanding."[22] We need to remember that Heidegger is not here describing literary, historical, or other kinds of reflexive interpretation, though what he says has an obvious bearing on them. "Any interpretation which is to contribute understanding, must already have understood what is to be interpreted. This is a fact that has always been remarked, even if only in the area of derivative ways of understanding and interpretation, such as philological Interpretation."[23] Traditionally, the hermeneutic circle was expressed in spatial terms, of part and whole. Heidegger, by contrast, thinks of it temporally, in terms of a circle between the "already" and "to be." This circularity corresponds to the historical being of *Dasein* from which the interpretive sciences and all other modes of understanding derive. The whole that is projected before the parts are understood is a whole historical world, a familiar network of significances, a past world already understood that is continually modified in interpretation. Simply put, life is interpretation. In coming to be what *Dasein* can be, *Dasein* interprets itself, and this interpretive proliferation of being progresses until *Dasein* itself ceases.

Taking up Heidegger's analysis of understanding in order to explain the nature of biblical interpretation, Rudolph Bultmann developed a theory that stressed the existential appropriation of the meaning of Scripture. To understand the kerygma is, for Bultmann, to discover a possibility for changing one's life, for altering what one is. Understanding the Word of God means understanding it as a call to salvation, that is, an invitation to authentic existence; and understanding a call as such involves not just knowing what it means but heeding it, whether by acceptance or rejection. The New Testament is itself one approach to the kerygma, specifically that of the early Christians, but it is not the only or the definitive one. Scripture is not the Word of God itself but only an initial interpretation of the Word, one expressed in a mythic language appropriate to its initial audience. Yet, since mythic explications of the saving Word are now largely incredible, understanding the kerygma today requires a demythologization. Far from debunking the kerygma or exposing its pretenses, demythologization allows the call to be heard and heeded.

Like the early Christians, modern man can interpret and appropriate the Word of God because he already preunderstands it, already knows what it would mean to be saved, already recognizes the poverty of his existence and believes in the possibility of enriching it. Such belief is the precondition of interpretive understanding. Suppressing this preunderstanding therefore does not promote correct interpretation but simply renders the text nonsensical and unintelligible. Similarly, denying the prior claim of the Word does not permit one rightly to understand it. Rather, the interpreter's preunderstanding needs to be tested and examined. The interpreter needs to allow his very being to be called into question through the same process by which he questions the text. In a sense, for Bultmann the most subjective interpretation, the one that hits closest to home, is thus always the most objective.

This integration of subjectivity and objectivity caused Emilio Betti to charge that Bultmann's hermeneutics is finally subjective, that it not only lacks any means for certifying the correctness of interpretation but also encourages the worst kind of projection. Reminiscent of Schleiermacher and Dilthey, Betti writes, "It is our duty as guardians and practitioners of the study of history to protect . . . objectivity and to provide evidence of the epistemological conditions of its possibility."[24] Betti acknowledges the principle of the "actuality of understanding," namely, that in order to understand a past event one must assimilate it "into one's intellectual horizon within the framework of one's own experiences."[25] But Bultmann's fault, Betti argues, was to neglect another and no less fundamental principle: the autonomy of the object. The object of interpretation is the objectification of a mind not our own; interpretation aims to comprehend what someone other than ourselves did or thought or wrote. The object of interpretation must therefore be understood according to its own logic, not ours. The danger of Bultmann's approach, Betti argues, consists in "deriving only what is meaningful or reasonable to oneself and of missing what is different and specific in the Other or, as the case may be, bracketing it as a presumed myth."[26] For Betti, the other's alienness to the interpreter occasions interpretation in the first place; and just as this alterity necessitates objectivity in interpretation, so also it makes objectivity possible. The possibility of objective interpretation should be preserved by sharply separating the two questions that Bultmann confused, "the question concerning the meaning of an historical phenomenon" and the "completely different question . . . concerning its present [significance] and relevance in changing historical epochs."[27] Both kinds of inquiry are necessary. Perhaps the question of significance is even the more important; but answering it, in Betti's view, requires first the objective determination of meaning in itself.

Betti levels similar charges against Hans-Georg Gadamer, who like Bultmann builds on the insights of Heidegger. In *Truth and Method*, Gadamer, too, is concerned to disclose the grounds of the possibility of true interpretation; but from his point of view it is not Bultmann's but rather Betti's position that appears subjectivist—not despite Betti's objectivism but because of it. From Gadamer's perspective, objectivism and subjectivism amount largely to the same thing. Governing itself by rule, objectivity tries methodically to eliminate bias, prejudice, and all the distortions that go by the name of subjectivity. This Cartesian endeavor assumes that a methodologically purified consciousness guarantees certainty. On one level, objectivity consists in humble self-effacement; but on another, it is marked by a distinct arrogance insofar as it makes individual self-consciousness the locus and arbiter of truth. Though it disclaims subjectivity, objectivity derives from a highly subjectivist understanding of human knowledge.

One may well ask why it is more than a matter of convenience or curiosity to understand another's mind if our own is the sufficient condition of truth. Conversely, if, like Gadamer, we agree with Heidegger that consciousness always *is* more than it knows, then this "more" cannot be understood by trusting solely to the self-governance of consciousness. Not introspection but only interpretation of tradition is capable of understanding the truth that exceeds self-consciousness—exceeds it because (however conscientious) consciousness belongs to historical tradition. It cannot, by pulling on the bootstraps of method, extricate itself from the very history of which consciousness is a part. If there is indeed a truth that exceeds what can be methodologically certified, its disclosure always requires an interpretation of tradition from within tradition, which interpretation (being circular) cannot be called objective.

Instead of an objective or subjective act, Gadamer thinks of interpreting as playing a game. In playing we do not stand outside the game but participate in it. A player who does not fully involve himself in the game we call a spoilsport because toying with a game spoils it. By contrast, taking a game seriously involves belonging to it, and this belonging in turn precludes treating the game as an object separate from oneself. Moreover, in the same process of playing that prevents objectifying the game, the player loses his status as a subject. As part of the game, the participant plays a part that is not merely himself, for he has been assigned a role to perform. Thus, playing is a performance of what is no object by what is no subject. And if interpreting is like playing, as Gadamer argues, then it always involves something like performing a drama, for the player who takes the play seriously interprets it from within, by belonging to and playing a part in it.

The larger drama in which we must play is history. Since human beings exist historically, interpreting historical tradition from within is inevitable. To assert the contrary—that at some point interpretation of tradition is unnecessary—is to assert that at some point consciousness is nonhistorical and self-grounding. But if this Cartesian thesis is mistaken, then all interpretation of tradition (as of everything else) occurs within tradition. Understanding always begins within and returns to an already given horizon of understanding. The hermeneutical circle is distinct from linear induction because not only do the parts lead to understanding the whole but also there must be an understanding of the whole prior to examining the parts. This prior understanding of the whole Gadamer calls a "prejudice," a judgment that precedes inquiry. The necessity of such prejudgment indicates that understanding is possible only insofar as understanding has always already begun. To understand tradition from within tradition means to be prejudiced. But if prejudice is the condition of interpretation, and if true interpretation is nevertheless possible, then though not all prejudices are true, they are not all ipso facto false, either. The function of conscientious interpretation is not to eradicate all prejudices, then, but rather to sort out the true from the false ones; this discrimination can be performed not at the outset, by an act of will, but only in the very process of projection and revision that is interpretation itself.

A true interpretation, in Gadamer's view, has performed this discrimination of false from true prejudices (i.e., those unconfirmed from those confirmed by the text). But true interpretation nevertheless remains within the horizon of prejudice that is the interpreter's world. That world horizon is not fixed and immutable, however, like a circle in which the interpreter is forever circumscribed. Rather, the horizon of understanding is no less capable of changing than the visual horizon. Gadamer images the process by which the interpreter's horizon is broadened as a dialectical fusion of horizons—a dialogue in which, as the interpreter puts questions to the text, the text puts questions to the interpreter. This dialogue is always possible because both the author of the text and its interpreter speak a language, even if a different one. Not only for the author but for the interpreter also, to understand is to find a language to express that understanding. Interpreting, like translation, consists in finding, within the resources of the interpreter's language, a common language that can say both what the text means and what the interpreter understands of it. Interpretation is the process by which the horizon of one's own language is fused with that of another and thereby expanded. In dialogue, a common language is formed that makes understanding possible. For this reason, language cannot itself be objectified. We can and obviously do understand our language, of course, but that means understanding what is said and not the language per se. Language cannot be made an object precisely because language is the means of objectification itself.

Beyond the sphere of objectivity and including it, "Being that can be understood is language," Gadamer writes.[28] The scope of hermeneutic understanding is coextensive with that of being. Gadamer's argument for the universality of hermeneutics implies that there can be no critique of tradition that is not itself traditional, no falsification of another's opinion that does not already presuppose a common language in which the dispute is carried out. All thought depends on a dialogically reached consensus that cannot be called into question as a whole since it is only within this background that questions make sense. But Gadamer is tempted to equate tradition, this common ground, with truth; and it is to avoid this unwitting legitimation of the status quo that Habermas stresses an element of dialogue that Gadamer slights: its critical, emancipating interest. Gadamer assumes, according to Habermas, that every apparent dialogue is real. That is, he ignores the possibility that the participants may be "talking past each other" without realizing it. Such pseudocommunication will result in an illusory consensus, and no amount of further dialogue will be able to penetrate the illusion. Moreover, a consensus that has apparently been reached in free dialogue may actually have been enforced by implicit forms of coercion and domination that are quite unknown to the speakers. This coercion will be least recognizable, in fact, when the forms of domination are woven into the very language that to all appearances unites the parties in unfettered debate. When language itself is a form of sedimented violence, systematically distorted communication cannot be recognized and rectified by participating in it. Rather, only a nonparticipating, external observer can provide correct diagnosis and appropriate therapy.

Habermas suggests the psychoanalyst on the individual level and the critic of ideology on the societal level as instances of observers who operate at the limit of hermeneutic universality, where coming to an understanding through dialogue does not suffice. "The 'what,' the meaning-content of systematically distorted expressions, can only be 'understood' when it is possible to answer, at the same time, the 'why' question, i.e. to 'explain' the emergence of the symptomatic scene by reference to the initial conditions of the systematic distortion itself."[29] Applying the borderline, hermeneutic-explanatory task of the psychoanalyst to the "hidden pathology of societal systems" involves the assumption that "every consensus, as the outcome of an understanding of meaning, is, in principle, suspect of having been enforced through pseudo-communication."[30] The critique of ideology involves a recognition that not every actual consensus is the locus of truth. For this reason, each actual consensus must be evaluated in light of a regulative ideal, "according to which truth would only be guaranteed by *that* kind of consensus which is achieved under the idealized conditions of unlimited communication free from domination and could be maintained over time."[31] This regulative ideal is the methodological correlate of the utopian impulse not just to understand reality but to change it for the better.

Whereas Gadamer takes little interest in modern linguistics or philosophy of language (since, in his view, language cannot be objectified), Habermas does not hesitate to borrow from the insights of Peircean semiotics and the linguistics of Chomsky and Piaget. Insofar as any language can itself be a mode of repression, merely understanding, speaking, and listening to it cannot lead to emancipation. Instead, the analyst needs also to be able to explain the systematic functioning of language; and it is at this point, where understanding alone falls short, that the objectification performed by linguistics becomes necessary. "Linguistics is not hermeneutic," Jonathan Culler asserts. "It does not discover what a sequence means or produce a new interpretation of it but tries to determine the nature of the system underlying the [speech] event."[32] The application of Saussurean linguistics to literary study promoted not interpretation but poetics; and as structural poetics came to dominate the field of literature, the result was not just an avoidance of interpretation but a positive animus against it. "There are many tasks that confront criticism," Culler later wrote, "many things we need to advance our understanding of literature, but one thing we do not need is more interpretations of literary works."[33]

Such statements register a reaction to the proliferation of New Critical "readings" in the 1950s and sixties. But, beyond indictments of this mode of criticism in particular, interpretation came under broader and more developed attack from deconstruction. Deconstructive analysis does not simply demonstrate the impossibility of univocally decoding the secret of a text; it suggests "the possibility that indeed it might have no secret, that it might only be pretending to be simulating some hidden truth within its folds."[34] Of Nietzschean deconstruction Derrida writes, "The hermeneutic project which postulates a true sense of the text is disqualified under this regime. Reading is freed from the horizon of the meaning or truth of being, liberated from the values of the product's production or the present's presence. . . . Truth in the guise of production, the unveiling/dissimulation of the present product, is dismantled. The veil [is] no more raised than it is lowered."[35]

As the archetypal metaphor of interpretation, the unveiling of meaning and truth that Derrida here repudiates is an image as ancient as hermeneutics itself. It appears as early as the fourth century, in the pseudo-Areopagite, and as late as Heidegger. In a crucial passage of his "Defense of Poetry," however, Shelley juxtaposes unveiling with another, and somewhat different, image of interpretation:

Veil after veil may be undrawn [from the poem], and the inmost naked beauty of the meaning never exposed. A great poem is a fountain forever overflowing with the waters of wisdom and delight; and after one person and one age has exhausted all its divine effluence which their peculiar relations enable them to share, another and yet another succeeds, and new relations are ever developed, the source of an unforeseen and an unconceived delight.[36]

Shelley draws no distinction between unveiling and overflowing, since both figure the inexhaustibility of interpretation, yet there is a tension between the two images. As unveiling, interpretation descends from surface to depth. It penetrates the superficial to reach the profound. Since it images the true as the hidden, interpretive unveiling must lift or rend a concealing veil; such interpretation construes its object as an inner kernel or dark secret. Interpretive overflow, by contrast, is like the fountain; it ascends from depth to surface and figures the true as the apparent. Interpretation is the poem's continuing emergence, exposition, or exteriorization.

No one has better explicated, or better integrated, these conflicting models of interpretation than Paul Ricoeur. Throughout Ricoeur's work, whatever the immediate topic, can be discerned two distinct moments: of doubt and of faith. The energy of his thought derives largely from his resisting the temptation to resign these distinct moments to antithesis, to juxtapose them in a facile eclecticism, or, worse, to let one eclipse the other.

The names Ricoeur assigns the two moments vary with the occasion. The "hermeneutics of suspicion," for example, refers to the necessary task of unveiling, of doubting the surface. It involves the suspicion, as Brecht once brutally remarked, that the edifice of culture is built on dogshit. The hermeneutics of suspicion comprehends not only critique of ideology, orthodox Marxist philosophy, and Freudian psychoanalysis but also Husserl's eidetic reduction as well as structural linguistics and anthropology. Common to these modes of skeptical interpretation is the belief that all forms of consciousness and tradition conceal something to which the knowing, speaking subject is not privy, and which therefore necessitates an objective interpretation that the subject has no authority either to confirm or to deny.

On the other hand, Ricoeur suspects that the hermeneutics of suspicion is itself only a half-truth. The bloom is no less real than the manure it feeds on. Ricoeur believes that Hegel, Heidegger, Bultmann, and Gadamer reflect a faith that a preobjective understanding, a shared community, precedes, grounds, and limits all subsequent activities of objectification. All interpretation is the continuing development, the overflow of fullness from that primordial unity.

Addressing himself to Lévi-Strauss, Ricoeur asks, "Can the structuralist explanation . . . be separated from *all* hermeneutic comprehension?"[37] Ricouer answers that there can be "no structural analysis . . . without hermeneutic comprehension of the transfer of sense (without 'metaphor,' without *translatio*), without that indirect giving of meaning which founds the semantic field, which in turn provides the ground upon which structural homologies can be discerned."[38] Ricoeur similarly asks the hermeneutical question of Habermas: "from where do you speak when you appeal to *Selbstreflexion*, if it is not from the place that you yourself have denounced as a non-place? . . . It is indeed from the basis of a tradition that you speak. This tradition is not perhaps the same as Gadamer's. . . . But it is a tradition nonetheless, the tradition of emancipation rather than that of recollection. Critique is also a tradition."[39] Yet, despite his critique of Lévi-Strauss and Habermas, Ricoeur scarcely abandons the structural, critical, or objective moment of interpretation, for this is precisely the standard by which he criticizes Bultmann:

Even if it is true, finally, that the text accomplishes its meaning only in personal appropriation . . . this appropriation is only the final state, the last threshold of an understanding which has been first uprooted and moved into another meaning. The moment of exegesis is not that of existential decision but that of "meaning," which, as Frege and Husserl [and Betti] have said, is an objective and even an "ideal" moment. . . .

The semantic moment, the moment of objective meaning, must precede the existential moment, the moment of personal decision, in a hermeneutics concerned with doing justice to both the objectivity of meaning and the historicity of personal decision. In this respect the problem Bultmann posed is the exact inverse of the problem which contemporary structuralist theories pose. The structuralist theories have taken the "language" side, whereas Bultmann has taken the "speaking" side. But we now need an instrument of thought for apprehending the connection between language and speaking, the conversion of system into event.[40]

Ricoeur's ambition has been to locate the site of this conversion, the multidimensional intersection of *langue* and *parole*, structure and history, objectivity and subjectivity, doubt and faith. In *Freud and Philosophy*, his most intensive meditation on this topic, Ricoeur identifies the symbol as the locus of this intersection.[41]

Symbols lend themselves to an archaeological hermeneutics that searches out origins, the subliminal beginnings of subjectivity in a system of desire that can be studied objectively. But authentic symbols also lend themselves to a teleological hermeneutics that looks not to the primitive past but to a future beyond objectivity. Teleological hermeneutics is not objective because it has no object. It neither discloses nor conceals a dark secret because it does not discover an underlying system but participates in a continuing genesis of meaning, a history where meaning derives from successive rather than simultaneous differences. Whereas in archaeological hermeneutics interpreting the symbol consists in retrospection on its repressed past, in teleological hermeneutics the symbol's meaning depends prospectively on a released future, on what the symbol will come to mean in the continuing history of its interpretation. Most important to remember is that in the overdetermined symbol these two hermeneutics converge. As their remembrance of the archaic past precludes naive faith, so also their prophetic anticipation of the future precludes naive doubt. In interpreting the symbol, skepticism and hope are one.

There is no reason to suppose that the history of hermeneutics comes to a conclusion, or even a climax, in Ricoeur's dialectical mediation of the conflict of interpretations. His own thought is still in the process of development, still open to the future, as is hermeneutics itself. Even in this brief overview it should be clear that hermeneutics raises more questions than it offers answers.

What, then, are the practical consequences of hermeneutics for the literary critic? One obstacle to answering this question is that, as we noted at the outset, hermeneutics names no systematic or unitary body of theory. Retracing its history leads us (as history often does) to the nominalistic conclusion that hermeneutics exists not in general but only in the particular, only in the particular theories championed by their several partisans. To elaborate the practical consequences implied by each of them would not, of course, be possible here. Given the generality of the scope of hermeneutics, what occurs in all understanding and interpretation, there is and can be no identifiably hermeneutic approach to literary interpretation. Since in principle it comprehends every mode of understanding, hermeneutics has no definite characteristics or procedures that would prescribe how one could produce a specifically "hermeneutic interpretation." Thus, for the practical critic, it would seem that hermeneutics has either too many consequences or too few.

This conclusion might be taken as indicating a deficiency in hermeneutics itself, unless one raises a basic question about the relation between hermeneutics and practice: Is it the raison d'être of hermeneutics to guide practical criticism? Answering this question has divided modern hermeneutics into the opposed factions of theorists or methodologists on the one hand and philosophers on the other. Theorists such as Betti, Hirsch, Habermas, and Apel have fruitfully addressed themselves to the issues of methodology, that is, to the theoretical foundations of correct interpretation upon which, presumably, specific methods for guiding interpretation could be erected. Such theorists believe that hermeneutic theory by definition makes a claim on interpretive practice, that the claim to regulate or even just aid practice is the raison d'être of theory.

Hermeneutic philosophy, by contrast, makes no such claim. Neither Heidegger nor Ricoeur nor Gadamer offers recommendations for the literary critic or any other interpreter. Gadamer, for example, states quite bluntly, "I did not intend to produce an art or technique of understanding, in the manner of earlier hermeneutics. I did not wish to elaborate a system of rules to describe, let alone direct, the methodological procedure of the human sciences."[42] This patent refusal to look for practical consequences indicates that Gadamer's hermeneutics is something other than a failed theory of interpretation, one so abstract and remote as to be inapplicable to practice. It is not a theory but a philosophy; it is not prescriptive but descriptive, and what it aims to describe is not how we ought to interpret but how we do so already, unawares. Gadamer's thesis is that understanding, like literature itself, is not ultimately produced by following rules and methods: Interpretive theory, in sum, does not finally regulate interpretive practice.

We come to realize that the demand for practical consequences is not itself neutral but rather has already sided with hermeneutic theory and assumed its basic postulate—namely, that interpretation should and can be governed by self-conscious theoretical methodology. This premise is not obviously false, but as Gadmer has shown it is at least disputable. The contested issue between hermeneutic theory and hermeneutic philosophy is whether understanding always involves an implicit will to power, whether understanding is essentially or only accidentally the attempt to regulate, govern, and dominate interpretation. If it is not such, as Gadamer insists, then there is always a point beyond which theory has no effect on practice, and understanding is not theoretical but rather already involved in the everyday world of practice.

The question whether hermeneutics ought to have practical consequences has not been resolved, and probably it is not likely to be, because of an ambiguity woven into the very conception of hermeneutics. Just as *history* means both the course of events and what is written about them, both the object and the understanding of it, so also *hermeneutics* means both the practice and the theory of interpretation. Perhaps because of this constitutive ambiguity, the continuing need for interpretive theory to guide interpretive practice is not just counterbalanced but is indeed also explained by the fact that practice continually outruns theory. If hermeneutics justifies the search for the practical consequences of theory, it nevertheless also suggests that we might well investigate the theoretical consequences of practice.

Notes

1. F. D. E. Schleiermacher, *"The Hermeneutics*: Outline of the 1819 Lectures," trans. Jan Wojcik and Roland Haas, *New Literary History* 10 (1978): 1.

2. Ibid., p. 8.

3. Ibid., p. 10.

4. Ibid., p. 14.

5. Ibid.

6. *W. Dilthey: Selected Writings*, ed. and trans. H. P. Rickman (Cambridge: Cambridge University Press, 1976), p. 260.

7. Ibid., p. 205.

8. Ibid., p. 159.

9. Ibid., p. 260.

10. Ibid., p. 211.

11. Martin Heidegger, *Being and Time*, trans. John Macquarrie and Edward Robinson (New York: Harper and Row, 1962), p. 450.

12. Ibid., p. 449.

13. Ibid., p. 450.

14. Ibid., p. 61.
15. Ibid., p. 60.
16. Ibid., p. 25.
17. Ibid., p. 32.
18. Ibid., p. 195.
19. Ibid.
20. Ibid., p. 179.
21. Ibid., p. 184.
22. Ibid., pp. 188–89.
23. Ibid., p. 194.
24. Emilio Betti, "Hermeneutics as the General Methodology of the *Geisteswissenschaften*," in *Contemporary Hermeneutics: Hermeneutics as Method, Philosophy, and Critique*, trans. and ed. Josef Bleicher (London: Routledge and Kegan Paul, 1980), p. 73.
25. Ibid., p. 62.
26. Ibid., p. 73.
27. Ibid., p. 68. This Fregean distinction plays an important role in the work of E. D. Hirsch as well.
28. Hans-Georg Gadamer, *Truth and Method*, ed. Garrett Barden and John Cumming (New York: Seabury Press, 1975), p. 432.
29. Jürgen Habermas, "The Hermeneutic Claim to Universality," in Bleicher, *Contemporary Hermeneutics*, p. 194.
30. Ibid., p. 205.
31. Ibid.
32. Jonathan Culler, *Structuralist Poetics: Structuralism, Linguistics, and the Study of Literature* (Ithaca, N.Y.: Cornell University Press, 1975), p. 31.
33. Jonathan Culler, *The Pursuit of Signs: Semiotics, Literature, Deconstruction* (Ithaca, N.Y.: Cornell University Press, 1981), p. 6.
34. Jacques Derrida, *Spurs: Nietzsche's Styles*, trans. Barbara Harlow (Chicago: University of Chicago Press, 1979), p. 133.
35. Ibid., p. 107.
36. Percy Bysshe Shelley, "A Defense of Poetry," in *Critical Theory since Plato*, ed. Hazard Adams (New York: Harcourt Brace Jovanovich, 1971), p. 509.
37. Paul Ricoeur, "Structure and Hermeneutics," trans. Kathleen McLaughlin, in *The Conflict of Interpretations: Essays in Hermeneutics*, ed. Don Ihde (Evanston, Ill.: Northwestern University Press, 1974), p. 55.
38. Ibid., p. 60.
39. Paul Ricoeur, "Hermeneutics and the Critique of Ideology," in *Hermeneutics and the Social Sciences: Essays on Language, Action, and Interpretation*, ed. and trans. John B. Thompson (Cambridge: Cambridge University Press, 1981), p. 99.
40. Paul Ricoeur, "Preface to Bultmann," trans. Peter McCormick, in Ihde, *Conflict of Interpretations*, p. 397.
41. Paul Ricoeur, *Freud and Philosophy: An Essay on Interpretation*, trans. Denis Savage (New Haven: Yale University Press, 1970), p. 282.
42. Gadamer, *Truth and Method*, p. xvi.

Selected Bibliography

Apel, Karl-Otto. *Towards a Transformation of Philosophy*. Translated by Glyn Adey and David Frisby. London: Routledge and Kegan Paul, 1980.
Apel, Karl-Otto, et al., eds. *Hermeneutik und Ideologiekritik*. Frankfurt: Suhrkamp, 1973.

Bartsch, Hans Werner, ed. *Kerygma and Myth: A Theological Debate.* Translated by Reginald H. Fuller. London: SPCK, 1953.

Baumann, J. H. *Hermeneutics and Social Science: Approaches to Understanding.* London: Hutchinson, 1978.

Betti, Emilio. *General Theory of Interpretation.* Translated by Susan Noakes. Forthcoming.

————. "Hermeneutics and the General Methodology of the *Geisteswissenschaften.*" In Bleicher, *Contemporary Hermeneutics,* pp. 51–94.

Bleicher, Josef, ed. *Contemporary Hermeneutics: Hermeneutics as Method, Philosophy, and Critique.* London: Routledge and Kegan Paul, 1980.

Bultmann, Rudolf. *Faith and Understanding.* Translated by L. P. Smith. London: CSM Press, 1969.

Dallmayr, Fred R., and Thomas A. McCarthy, eds. *Understanding and Social Inquiry.* Notre Dame, Ind.: Notre Dame University Press, 1977.

Dilthey, Wilhelm. *Poetry and Experience.* Edited by Rudolf A. Makkreel and Frithjof Rodi. In *Selected Works,* vol. 5. Princeton, N.J.: Princeton University Press, 1985.

————. *Selected Writings.* Translated and edited by H. P. Rickman. Cambridge: Cambridge University Press, 1976.

Frank, Manfred. *Das Individuelle Allgemeine: Textstructurisierung und -interpretation nach Schleiermacher.* Frankfurt: Suhrkamp, 1977.

Gadamer, Hans-Georg. *Philosophical Hermeneutics.* Translated by David E. Linge. Berkeley: University of California Press, 1976.

————. *Truth and Method.* Edited by Garrett Barden and John Cumming. New York: Seabury Press, 1975.

Habermas, Jürgen. "The Hermeneutic Claim to Universality." In Bleicher, *Contemporary Hermeneutics,* pp. 181–212.

————. *Knowledge and Human Interests.* Translated by Jeremy Shapiro. Boston: Beacon Press, 1971.

Heidegger, Martin. *Being and Time.* Translated by John Macquarrie and Edward Robinson. New York: Harper and Row, 1962.

————. *Poetry, Language, Thought.* Translated by Albert Hofstadter. New York: Harper and Row, 1971.

Hirsch, E. D., Jr. *The Aims of Interpretation.* Chicago: University of Chicago Press, 1976.

————. *Validity in Interpretation.* New Haven: Yale University Press, 1967.

Hoy, David. *The Critical Circle: Literature, History, and Philosophical Hermeneutics.* Berkeley: University of California Press, 1978.

Macquarrie, John. *The Scope of Demythologizing: Bultmann and His Critics.* New York: Harper and Row, 1966.

Makkreel, Rudolf. *Dilthey: Philosopher of the Human Sciences.* Princeton, N.J.: Princeton University Press, 1975.

Murray, Michael. *Modern Critical Theory: An Introduction.* The Hague: Nijhoff, 1975.

Palmer, Richard. *Hermeneutics: Interpretation Theory in Schleiermacher, Dilthey, Heidegger, and Gadamer.* Evanston, Ill.: Northwestern University Press, 1969.

Ricoeur, Paul. *The Conflict of Interpretations: Essays in Hermeneutics.* Translated and edited by Don Ihde. Evanston, Ill.: Northwestern University Press, 1974.

————. *Freud and Philosophy: An Essay on Interpretation.* Translated by Denis Savage. New Haven: Yale University Press, 1970.

————. *Hermeneutics and the Social Sciences: Essays on Language, Action, and Interpretation.* Translated and edited by John B. Thompson. Cambridge: Cambridge University Press, 1981.

Rorty, Richard. *Philosophy and the Mirror of Nature.* Princeton, N.J.: Princeton University Press, 1979.

Schleiermacher, Friedrich. *Hermeneutics: The Handwritten Manuscripts*. Translated by Terrence N. Tice. Atlanta: John Knox Press, 1966.

———. "*The Hermeneutics*: Outline of the 1819 Lectures." Translated by Jan Wojcik and Roland Haas. *New Literary History* 10 (1978): 1–15.

Taylor, Charles. "Interpretation and the Science of Man." *Review of Metaphysics* 25 (1971): 3–51.

von Wright, Georg Henrik. *Explanation and Understanding*. Ithaca, N.Y.: Cornell University Press, 1971.

Weinsheimer, Joel. *Gadamer's Hermeneutics: A Reading of "Truth and Method."* New Haven: Yale University Press, 1985.

Wolff, Janet. *Hermeneutic Philosophy and the Sociology of Art*. London: Routledge and Kegan Paul, 1975.

DANNY J. ANDERSON

Deconstruction: Critical Strategy/Strategic Criticism

> [O]ne does not simply practice deconstruction as a method; it is not something that one can pick up or put down or put into play at will. It must be understood as *phrónēsis*, that is, a kind of wisdom that enables one to live through a situation. I mean that deconstruction is a way of living through the finitude of our being in which we always appear to be in the grasp of tradition and cannot get out of it. This is why it is said that knowledge and truth are not at issue in deconstruction; at issue is the problem of power and authority. Deconstruction does not solve this problem; it lives with it in a certain way.
>
> Gerald L. Bruns,
> "Structuralism, Deconstruction, and Hermeneutics"

What is deconstruction? One cannot easily answer this question, for deconstruction works to understand the impossibility of ever "getting it right" when explaining what deconstruction, or anything else, *is*. Instead, an introduction to this polemical mode of analysis must respond to questions such as "What does deconstruction do?" and "What does it produce?" In general terms, deconstruction investigates the nature and production of knowledge, a consideration with far-reaching implications for all aspects of human activity. More specifically, deconstruction aims its critique against a conception of knowledge and meaning as graspable essences that independently precede or follow expression. In opposition to such essences, deconstruction contemplates knowledge and meaning as representations unavoidably enmeshed in the heterodox and contradictory nature of language and interpretation. Though it proposes radical critiques of the interrelations between knowledge and language, between meaning and interpretation, deconstruction does not arrive at a more absolute truth; rather, it attempts to unravel interminably the texture of power and authority at work in knowledge, language, meaning, and interpretation.

Deconstructive criticism shifts the emphasis of analysis to the signifying processes of language and texts, to textuality. In so doing, it also turns back onto itself and levels an equally rigorous consideration of critical writing. As deconstruction contemplates textuality and the critical text, it underscores the inherent contradictions in the canonical conception of literature, method, and even the traditionally upheld hierarchy of the critical text as secondary and subordinated to the literary text. In other words, deconstruction is an attitude that examines the force of power and authority in the text as a desire for mastery—the attempt to master knowledge through language, and meaning through interpretation—a desire that textuality ultimately subverts, for writing always already has begun to deconstruct itself.

Derrida, the Metaphysics of Presence, and Language

One cannot overestimate the role of the French philosopher Jacques Derrida in the relatively recent introduction of deconstruction to contemporary literary criticism. Indeed, Derrida's critique of structuralism in a 1966 Johns Hopkins international symposium brought deconstruction to the attention of American scholars.[1] Although this symposium and the appearance (in French) of Derrida's *Speech and Phenomena*, *Of Grammatology*, and *Writing and Difference* in 1967 serve as approximate dates for the inauguration of deconstruction and underscore its historical relation to structuralism, as Gayatri C. Spivak points out, Derrida is indebted to and continues a specific line of philosophical inquiry that includes Hegel, Nietzsche, Freud, Heidegger, and Husserl.[2] In addition, Susan Handelman emphasizes the similarities among the rabbinic modes of interpretation and concepts of textuality and Derrida's practice of deconstructive reading, a phenomenon that G. Douglas Atkins refers to as the "dehellenization of literary criticism."[3] In this respect, Derrida's contribution consists not of an *ex nihilo* philosophical formulation but of a continuation and ceaseless extension of various critical traditions.

In the broadest perspective, a consistent conception of the working of language and meaning informs all of Derrida's writings. In one case, Derrida formulates the deconstructive notion of language through a critique of Ferdinand de Saussure's *Course in General Linguistics*. According to Saussure's *Course*, writing "exists for the sole purpose of representing" speech, and "the spoken forms alone constitute the object" of linguistics as a science;[4] hence, Saussure assigns priority to spoken forms over written forms. Saussure then creates another hierarchical opposition within the spoken forms: language/speech. For Saussure, language becomes the object of scientific inquiry, a closed system that serves "as a link between thought and sound, under conditions that of necessity bring about the delimitations of units."[5] Saussure then concludes that it all "boils down to this: in language there are only differences. Even more important: a difference generally implies positive terms between which the difference is set up; but in language there are only differences *without positive terms*."[6] Finally, he remarks: "But the statement that everything in language is negative is true only if the signified and the signifier are considered separately; when we consider the sign in its totality, we have something that is positive in its own class."[7]

Derrida's *Grammatology* reconsiders Saussure's reasoning on several accounts. On the one hand, the establishment of the hierarchy speech/writing, privileging the first term of the opposition while attributing a subordinate or parasitic value to the second term, reflects a "metaphysics of presence." From Plato onward, philosophy and linguistics have placed writing in a secondary position with respect to spoken forms. In attempting to elevate linguistics to the level of a science, Saussure's *Course in General Linguistics* repeats the subordination of writing to spoken forms in accordance with the entire Western cultural tradition. According to Derrida, "[t]he history of metaphysics, like the history of the West," depends on "the determination of Being as presence in all senses of the word."[8] Derrida contends that Western philosophy develops from a series of restrictive presuppositions predicated on the illusion of "hearing/understanding-oneself-speak." To this series of presuppositions Derrida gives the name *phonocentrism*, emphasizing the privileging of the spoken word, the illusion of the full presence and unity of meaning in spoken forms.

On the other hand, the drive toward mastery requires the privileging of language over speech in order to provide Saussure with a closed system within which he could postulate the principles of its internal coherence. From the notion of a closed system Saussure derives his greatest insight, that in "language there are only differences *without positive terms*." Even in relation to spoken forms, however, writing abides by Saussure's characterization of language: The written mark, inscribed in durable substance (the *grammè* or *graphème*), is only a difference without positive terms. Derrida notes:

If "writing" signifies inscription and especially the durable institution of a sign (and that is the only irreducible kernel of the concept of writing), writing in general covers the entire field of linguistic signs. In that field a certain sort of instituted signifiers may then appear, "graphic" in the narrow and derivative sense of the word, ordered by a certain relationship with other instituted—hence "written," even if they are "phonic"—signifiers. The very idea of institution—hence the arbitrariness of the sign—is unthinkable before the possibility of writing and outside of its horizon. Quite simply, that is, outside of the horizon itself, outside the world as space of inscription, as the opening to the emission and to the spatial *distribution* of signs, to the *regulated play* of their differences, even if they are "phonic."[9]

In this perspective, written and spoken forms differ in their substance of inscription (i.e., graphic or phonic), and writing better describes linguistic phenomena.

On this basis, Derrida's *Grammatology* attempts to break the hold of phonocentric tradition and deal with language and meaning in terms of writing. Such an inversion of terms, reversing the hierarchy of spoken over written forms, strategically shifts the debate and enables Derrida to confront the play of differences without positive terms in a manner that is unthinkable within a metaphysics of presence. Such a consideration leads to a radical reevaluation of the working of the linguistic sign. Derrida follows the negative characteristic of the sign—absence—to its extreme implications through the analysis of difference without positive terms.

The play of differences supposes, in effect, syntheses and referrals which forbid at any moment, or in any sense, that a simple element be *present* in and of itself, referring only to itself. Whether in the order of spoken or written discourse, no element can function as a sign without referring to another element which itself is not simply present. This interweaving results in each "element"—phoneme or grapheme— being constituted on the basis of the trace within it of the other elements of the chain or system.[10]

Henceforth Derrida focuses his critique on the "element" itself and the "trace within it." In order to be able to consider the negative difference of language, Derrida coins the term *differance*, which is "a structure and a movement no longer conceivable on the basis of the opposition presence/absence."[11]

Derrida accounts for three aspects of difference as a structure and a movement. First, he considers the play of differences among elements: Since in language there are only differences without positive terms and the linguistic sign is arbitrary, the differences among signs constitute signification. Second, Derrida reveals that the systematic play of traces of differences within each element also contributes to signification. As an inverse of the first aspect of differance, the second underscores "the strange 'being' of the sign: half of it always 'not there' and the other half always 'not that.' The structure of the sign is determined by the trace or track of that other which is forever absent."[12]

Meaning is caught up in the system of language where each element has significance only by virtue of its difference from the other elements of the system: Meaning is not present, as an essence, within any linguistic unit.

Finally, differance includes the play of spacing by which the elements relate to each other. Spacing refers to the "simultaneously active and passive . . . production of the intervals," "the becoming-space" of spoken or written discourse that generates the temporal play of differences and defers arrival at the meaning of the word or the thing itself.[13] Atkins explains:

Space as well as time bears in a fundamental way on the concept of difference, for the temporal interval, the deferring into the future of any grasping of the thing, divides irreducibly all spatial presence. In the movement of thought, elements are never fully present because they must always already refer to something other than "themselves"; or, to change perspectives, if perception of objects depends upon perception of their differences, each "present" element *must* refer to an element *other* than "itself."[14]

In fine, whereas Saussure posits language as a system of differences without positive terms, he nevertheless reiterates the assumptions underlying Western metaphysics.[15] Although Saussure at times almost begins to explore the strange "being" of language, his cultural heritage and the force of the desire for scientific understanding within a closed structure lead him to privilege presence over absence. Saussure writes: "Although both the signified and the signifier are purely differential and negative when considered separately, their combination [the sign] is a positive fact."[16] The continual drive to privilege presence, to conceive of meaning as positively present within language, the unity of presence and meaning within the word, is the phenomenon that deconstruction understands as *logocentrism*.[17]

Critical Strategy

The deconstructive attitude toward language and meaning and Derrida's procedure for analyzing Saussure lead to several important observations. First, Derrida does not intend his interpretation of the *Course in General Linguistics* to point out flaws, weaknesses, or stupidities in Saussure's thinking. On the contrary, it is what Barbara Johnson calls a *critique*: "every critique exposes what the starting point [of a theory] conceals, and thereby displaces all of the ideas that follow from it."[18] Though Saussure writes about language, he must also write in a language, and for that reason his own writing is subject to (and indeed possible because of) the working of differance: The meaning of Saussure's text is always already different and deferred; neither he as writer nor we as readers can ever master or control meaning.

On this basis, Derrida points out what a deconstructive interpretation—a reading—should produce:

[T]he writer writes *in* a language and *in* a logic whose proper system, laws, and life his discourse by definition cannot dominate absolutely. He uses them only by letting himself, after a fashion and up to a point, be governed by the system. And the reading must always aim at a certain relationship, unperceived by the writer, between what he commands and what he does not command of the patterns of the language that he uses. This relationship is not a certain quantitative distribution of shadow and light, of weakness or of force, but a signifying structure that a critical reading should *produce*. [19]

In other words, the meaning of a text is at stake in interpretation. Meaning, however, is not a transcendental presence lying beyond, before, or beneath the text that the critic must discern or recover. Instead, a deconstructive reading strives to produce meanings by "teas[ing] out the warring forces of signification *within the text itself*." [20]

Considered from a different perspective, Derrida's reading of Saussure follows a strategic plan or "double gesture." Saussure's theory derives from a series of oppositions: speech/writing, language/speech, sign (positive)/signified-signifier (negative). These are not merely neutral oppositions between equal terms, however, for they are based on a "violent hierarchy. One of the two terms governs the other (e.g., axiologically, logically), or has the upper hand. To deconstruct the opposition, first of all, is to overturn the hierarchy at a given moment." [21] Derrida thus demonstrates that writing already takes into account the phenomena Saussure ascribed to language and that language and signs work by virtue of the unmasterable play of absence, negative differences, and deferral.

Nevertheless, "to remain in this phase is still to operate on the terrain of and from within the deconstructed system. By means of this double, and precisely stratified, dislodged and dislodging, writing, we must also mark the interval between inversion, which brings low what was high, and the irruptive emergence of a new 'concept,' a concept that can no longer be, and never could be, included in the previous regime." [22] In this respect, Derrida's reading of Saussure proceeds to search for terms to write about absence and difference without positive terms, through differance, spacing, phonocentrism, logocentrism. He invokes a series of terms that allow him to consider the working of the chain of concepts put into play by Saussure's text, a working that logocentrism strives to repress and control.

In sum, deconstruction is, by necessity, an interminable analysis, for "the hierarchy of dual oppositions always reestablishes itself." [23] Moreover, deconstruction is strategic: It is not a *neutral* approach to the text but an *intervention* in its signifying process. Deconstructors repeatedly return to the phase of *overturning*, reminding themselves and their readers (often with the phrase *always already*) that the violent hierarchy of the opposition is always other than it seems and that this "otherness" already operates within the opposition: Deconstruction must demonstrate that the opposition is always already *other*, that it works because of the repression of differance within the very terms of the opposition, and that such repression is the mark of the drive toward power and mastery. In the end, a deconstructive reading attempts to displace "the unequivocal domination of one mode of signifying over another."[24] No text is homogeneous; rather, writing, as such, is always already heterogeneous. In the case of Saussure, Derrida analyzes a logocentrist/phonocentrist layer of the text "in order to show immediately that it was in contradiction to Saussure's scientific project."[25] Derrida's analysis, however, even in its strategic evasions of the *closure* associated with the terms of Western metaphysics, is also heterogeneous and, hence, has already begun its own deconstruction.

Strategic Criticism

Deconstruction seeks to mark the circularity that the metaphysics of presence must dissimulate, expel, exclude, and jettison in order to enclose itself within a simulacrum of rectitude, to maintain belief in its grounds for coherence and logic. Through such maneuvers, the language of metaphysics attempts to repress its other, its inherent contradictions and unmasterable play; and throughout the history of metaphysics the exclusion of this other has been related to a series of hierarchical oppositions that overvalue presence and undervalue absence, unable to confront the dynamic interaction between the two terms of such an opposition. Such repression is the force of a desire that enables metaphysics to accept the illusion that meaning and knowledge can be mastered through interpretation and language. Or, as Jonathan Culler writes in reference to the *Grammatology*, "Derrida is working . . . to describe a general process through which texts undo the philosophical system to which they adhere by revealing its rhetorical nature."[26]

The emphasis placed by deconstruction on the rhetorical nature of texts and the displacement of the repression of differences has had the greatest impact on the critical study of the canonical series of texts called "literature." To attribute this impact solely to Derrida, however, is misleading. Before the importation of Derrida's ideas, a group of Yale critics—Geoffrey Hartman,

J. Hillis Miller, Paul de Man, and Harold Bloom—had already begun to question the roots of their own critical practice in the New Criticism. In the words of Hartman:

They questioned [the New Criticism] by a more rigorous application of its own emphasis on the text rather than on the text's historical frame. But even the text as its own frame is questioned by this group, which did not privilege unity by vesting it in the "achieved" or "coherent" form of a literary work. Their tendency, fed by many sources including Freud, was not so much to radicalize ambiguity and to delay closing the interpretation as to see *through* literary form to the way language or symbolic process makes or breaks meaning. To hold that making and breaking together risked, sometimes, giving the impression of enchanting disenchantment; . . . but the main thrust of this American deconstruction that did not know its name was to create a more dialectical and open view of how literature worked. The rhetoric of "tension," refined by the New Critics as irony, paradox, and controlled ambiguity, seemed too self-enclosing a version of literariness. [27]

Indeed, the New Critical presupposition that every detail in the text counts in the signifying or symbolic process is important, but, as Hillis Miller points out, "the accompanying presupposition that every detail is going to count by working harmoniously to confirm the 'organic unity' of the poem or novel may be a temptation to leave out what does not fit, to see it as insignificant or as a flaw." [28] In other words, for both Derrida and the homegrown variety of deconstruction, texts are heterogeneous and a deconstructive reading must account for the workings of heterogeneity as such.

With the imperative to reconsider the heterogeneity of texts, deconstruction disrupts the hierarchical oppositions associated with logocentrism. More specifically, deconstructive reading includes a variety of strategies. Paul de Man, in the often cited essay "Semiology and Rhetoric," interrogates the signifying process of language: He contemplates the way a clear, well-formed question may engender "two entirely coherent but entirely incompatible" meanings. De Man calls our attention to the closing lines of Yeats's poem "Among School Children":

> O chestnut-tree, great-rooted blossomer,
> Are you the leaf, the blossom or the bole?
> O body swayed to music, O brightening glance,
> How can we know the dancer from the dance? [29]

De Man notes that interpretations have traditionally taken the concluding question as a statement of "the potential unity between form and experience, between creator and creation." [30] Certainly, a presupposition of "organic unity" in the text leads readers to unify the entire poem along the lines of the traditional interpretation.

In a strategic turn, however, de Man questions why the last line of the poem must be read figuratively, as a rhetorical question, rather than literally. Readers generally assume that the figurative reading is more knowledgeable; in this case, however, de Man demonstrates that the opposite is just the case: The figurative reading is easier and more naive than the literal reading of the question, which

leads to greater complication of theme and statement. For it turns out that the entire scheme set up by the first [traditional] reading can be undermined, or deconstructed, in the terms of the second, in which the final line is read literally as meaning that, since the dancer and the dance are not the same, it might be useful, perhaps even desperately necessary—for the question can be given a ring of urgency, "Please tell me, how *can* I know the dancer from the dance"—to tell them apart.[31]

The effect of such an inversion, reading the literal rather than the figurative, produces a divergence within every detail that previously supported the notions of "unity between form and experience, between creator and creation." Two contradictory readings of an entire poem thus hinge on the interpretation of the last line, readings that oppositionally engage each other: "the one reading is precisely the error denounced by the other and has to be undone by it."[32] In the final analysis, however, neither reading leads to a more absolute "truth," or meaning. On the contrary, the deconstructive reading produced the signifying structure that the figurative reading conceals in order to assert its dominance; the deconstruction does not add something to the text but demonstrates the play of language that allows it to signify in the first place.

Whereas de Man deals with the language of the text and its signifying process by revealing the repressive effect of a series of hierarchical oppositions—semiology/rhetoric, grammar/meaning, figurative meaning/literal meaning—deconstructive readings often consider the overall logic or organizational patterning of a text. Peter Brooks, for example, in *Reading for the Plot: Design and Intention in Narrative*, examines the functioning of plot as a deconstructive drive in narrative. In order to discuss this drive in narrative, Brooks exploits the dynamics of the Russian formalist dichotomy *fabula/sjuzet*. *Fabula* consists of the events in their linear, temporal order. *Sjuzet*, in contrast, is the way the events are ordered in the text, that is, whether they are organized around a certain perspective or narrated out of cause–effect or linear sequence, anachronically. Such a dichotomy, however, usually depends on the privileging of one of these terms over the other. Culler points out that critics often assert the primacy of the events in the *fabula* and debate "the significance of the character's actions (taking those actions as a given)."[33] Critics may, however, adopt the opposite perspective, treating the events as products of meanings according to the structure of the *sjuzet*, in order to discuss "the appropriateness or inappropriateness of an ending" on the grounds of thematic structure.[34]

Whereas Culler emphasizes the impossibility of "synthesis [between the two perspectives] because what is involved here in narrative is an effect of self-deconstruction," Brooks explores the opposition as a constitutive aspect of narrative, an aspect that he calls "plot."[35] Brooks proposes:

> Plot could be thought of as the interpretive activity elicited by the distinction between *sjuzet* and *fabula*, the way we *use* one against the other. . . . [W]e can generally understand plot to be an aspect of *sjuzet* in that it belongs to the narrative discourse, as its shaping force, but that it makes sense (as indeed *sjuzet* itself makes sense) as it is used to reflect on *fabula*, as our understanding of story. Plot is thus the dynamic shaping force of the narrative discourse.[36]

Moreover, "[t]he irreconcilability of the 'two logics' [the logic of *sjuzet* vs. the logic of *fabula*] points out the peculiar work of understanding that narrative is called upon to perform, and to the paralogical status of its 'solutions.' "[37] Thus Brooks concludes that "contradiction may be in the very nature of narrative, which not only uses but *is* a double logic."[38]

Dom Casmurro (1900), by the Brazilian novelist Machado de Assis, exploits this "double logic" as its principal signifying force.[39] In general, the novel deals with the causes for the estrangement of the main character, Bento Santiago, from his family and friends. When the novel is interpreted within the perspective of the *sjuzet*, infidelity motivates the estrangement. The *sjuzet* consists of the memoirs of Bento Santiago, nicknamed Dom Casmurro. In brief, Bento narrates the story of his relationship with two characters: Capitú, his childhood sweetheart and wife, and his best friend, Escobar. Until Escobar's death, Bento recounts a life of conjugal happiness. At Escobar's funeral, however, when observing the "passionate fixedness" (p. 228, chap. 123) of Capitú's gaze upon the dead man, Bento first suspects her infidelity with Escobar. With great effort Bento convinces himself of his jealousy: "I concluded inwardly that my old passion still darkened my vision and deluded me as always" (p. 232, chap. 126).

Nevertheless, Bento later becomes obsessed with the resemblance of his son, Ezekiel, to Escobar. Although Ezekiel has always demonstrated an immense capacity for imitating others, Bento deduces that the resemblance owes to Ezekiel's paternity:

> Escobar emerged from the grave, from the seminary, from Flamengo; he sat at table with me, welcomed me on the stairs, kissed me each morning in my study or asked me for the customary blessing at night. All of this repelled me. . . . When neither mother nor son were with me, my desperation was extreme, and I would vow to kill

them both, suddenly or slowly—slowly, so as to transfer into their dying, all the moments of my dulled, agonized life. [P. 239, chap. 132]

Their family life becomes unbearable, and Bento eventually confronts Capitú. At the conclusion of the confrontation, Capitú and Bento "involuntarily glanced at the photograph of Escobar, and then at each other. This time her confusion was pure confession. They were one; there must have been some photograph of Escobar as a little boy which would be our little Ezekiel. With her lips, however, she confessed to nothing" (p. 250, chap. 139). Henceforth the family separates, Capitú dies, and Bento has only one more brief encounter with Ezekiel as a young man before the latter dies on an archaeological expedition near Jerusalem.

In the final analysis, Bento remains convinced that his wife and his best friend deceived him. Bento organizes his *sjuzet* in order to demonstrate that he had not been jealous until his unfortunate discovery. After that point, however, he retrospectively confirms his suspicions: "Pell-mell, there rushed to my mind vague, remote episodes—words, meetings and incidents, in all of which my blindness saw no wrong and my old jealousy had been lacking" (p. 251, chap. 140). Bento concludes his memoirs with the following passage:

But this is not, properly speaking, the rest of the book. What remains is to discover whether the Capitú of Gloria [the neighborhood of the conjugal household] was already within the Capitú of Matacavallos [the street of their childhood homes], or if this one was changed into the other as the result of some chance incident. If Jesus, son of Sirach, had known of my first fits of jealousy, he would have said to me, as in his Ch. IX, vs. 1: "Be not jealous of thy wife lest she set herself to deceive thee with the malice that she learnt from thee." But I do not believe it was so, and you will agree with me. If you remember Capitú the child, you will have to recognize that one was within the other, like the fruit within its rind.

Well, whatever may be the solution, one thing remains and it is the sum of sums, the rest of the residuum, to wit, that my first love and my greatest friend, both so loving me, both so loved, were destined to join together and deceive me. . . . May the earth rest lightly on them! [Pp. 262–63, chap. 148]

Thus Bento holds fast to the veracity of his allegations. In sum, the logic of the *sjuzet* allows Bento to convince himself of the surprising tragedy of his life and justify his rejection of everyone he once loved.

In contrast to Bento's interpretation, the "rest of the book" he mentions in closing contradicts the logic of the *sjuzet*. Whereas the force of Bento's argument depends on a *sjuzet* organized to demonstrate a life of believed happiness, the discovery of infidelity, and the retrospective confirmation of the infidelity, he also recognizes the possibility of considering his life in a broader, more historical perspective when he questions the relation of Capitú the childhood sweetheart to Capitú the unfaithful wife. Although Bento immediately rejects any problematic relation here ("one was within the other, like the fruit within its rind") and equally expects his readers to do so ("you will agree with me"), much criticism has tended to read *Dom Casmurro* in the perspective of the *fabula*, accepting the events as prior, "historical" givens and debating whether or not Bento has grounds for distrusting his wife.[40]

When interpreted within the perspective of the *fabula*, at least three series of arguments allow readers to infer that unfounded jealousy motivates Bento's estrangement from his loved ones. First, Bento's conclusions are contrary to his characterization of Capitú and Escobar, both of whom from the outset are loyal and generous friends. Indeed, Bento himself must admit late in the memoirs that he is characteristically jealous: "I must explain to you that I had often had these fits of jealousy, wishing to know what might be inside my wife's head—not outside or above it. It is a known fact that the wandering thoughts of a person can be guilty, half guilty, a third, a fifth, a tenth guilty, since in the matter of guilt the gradation is infinite" (p. 210, chap. 107). Second, the "vague, remote episodes—words, meetings and incidents" that Bento retrospectively adduces to confirm his suspicions necessarily arise from the life he and Capitú closely shared with Escobar and his wife, Sancha. Finally, Bento's personal biases produce a degree of unreliability in his capacity to narrate; in other words, the *sjuzet* results from possible distortions as Bento selects and organizes the historical events of the *fabula* according to his own expressive and persuasive needs. On the one hand, Bento's choice of words, when describing Capitú's reaction during their confrontation, for example, already supposes Capitú's infidelity: "Capitú's stupefaction, and the succeeding indignation were both so natural they would confuse the finest eye-witnesses of our courts" (p. 248, chap. 138). On the other hand, the specific evidence that Bento adduces to prove Capitú's guilt is equivocal at best: Capitú's gaze at Escobar's funeral, Capitú's confusion during their confrontation, and the uncanny resemblance between Ezekiel and Escobar. In sum, when interpreting *Dom Casmurro* in terms of the *fabula* readers may conclude that Bento loses his family and friends because of unfounded jealousy, that his judgments are out of character for Capitú and Escobar, and that the *sjuzet* results from his distortion of the "facts" of the *fabula*.

In the final analysis, however, the meaning of *Dom Casmurro* cannot simply be resolved into the available interpretations of either infidelity or unfounded jealousy. Whereas a traditional formalistic interpretation might cease at this point and emphasize the irony of unresolved ambiguity, deconstruction contemplates the irony itself as the very possibility and condition of signification. Simply to accept such mutually exclusive interpretations as irreconcilable meanings is to ignore the complexity of the plot as constituted by the interplay of the *sjuzet* and the *fabula*. *Dom Casmurro*, rather, signifies because of the incompatible and yet mutually dependent interweaving of these two perspectives. Instead of providing a resolution of meanings, the plot leads back to the enigmatic Bento, both as a character of the *fabula* and as the narrator of the *sjuzet*. In the first chapter of the memoirs Bento explains the title: "Don't consult your dictionaries. *Casmurro* is not used here in the meaning they give for it, but in the sense in which the man in the streets uses it, of a morose, tight-lipped man withdrawn within himself. The *Dom* was for irony: to impute to me aristocratic airs" (p. 4, chap. 1). Within this withdrawn state, Bento the narrator is involved in a search "to tie together the two ends of my life" (p. 5, chap. 2; p. 256, chap. 144). He seeks to restore something that he has lost: "If it were only the others that were missing, no matter. A man consoles himself more or less for those he has lost, but I myself am missing, and this lack is essential" (p. 5, chap. 2). In fine, the plot is an exploration of Bento's "casmurricity" (p. 204, chap. 108), an effect that Bento enacts through the contradictions of plot, the double logic of narrative. At one point Bento comments: "I shall confess everything that bears on my story. Montaigne wrote of himself: *ce ne sont pas mes gestes que j'écris; c'est mon essence.* Well, there is only one way of describing one's essence: it is to tell it all, the good and the bad" (p. 138, chap. 68). Bento finds himself caught up in the double logic of narrative as he endeavors to describe himself as both an essential lack and a positive, graspable essence. In sum, although Bento maintains his belief in the veracity of the logic of the *sjuzet*, readers cannot resolve *Dom Casmurro* into a single meaning; rather, readers must carefully follow the play of essential lack and essence, of *fabula* and *sjuzet*, that constitutes the signifying force of the narrative.

In general terms, deconstructive reading aims at the working of forces that would conceal the play of differences and demonstrates that such differences constitute the very basis of signification. The consideration of the working of these forces requires the reevaluation not only of the language and signifying processes of the literary text but also of the concepts and methods of criticism. In addition, deconstruction highlights a series of difficulties in interpretation that literary texts often thematize, such as the contradictions characters and narrators face when they attempt to read or write and the way that "metafictions" (fictions about their own coming into being) erase the conventional boundary between fiction and reality.

Of all of the terms of difference considered by deconstruction, however, perhaps the most radical perspective seeks to evaluate the interrelations between the creative or "literary" text and the critical text. Barbara Johnson, in two essays in *The Critical Difference: Essays in the Contemporary Rhetoric of Reading*, analyzes how Roland Barthes's *S/Z* reads Balzac's *Sarrasine* and how Derrida reads Jacques Lacan's reading of Poe's "Purloined Letter."[41] Johnson emphasizes the repetition in each text—the literary, the critical, and even the metacritical text—of certain regular deconstructive effects of language: the absence of a mastery that would smother the play of differences. "And the difference between literature and criticism," Johnson writes, "consists perhaps only in the fact that criticism is more likely to be blind to the way in which its own critical difference from itself makes it, in the final analysis, literary."[42]

Geoffrey Hartman's *Criticism in the Wilderness* draws further conclusions from the literary nature of the critical text. Hartman contends

> that literary commentary may cross the line and become as demanding as literature: it is an unpredictable or unstable genre that cannot be subordinated, a priori, to its referential or commentating function. Commentary certainly remains one of the defining features, for it is hardly useful to describe as "criticism" an essay that does not review in some way an existing book or other work. But the perspectival power of criticism, the strength of recontextualization, must be such that the critical essay should not be considered a supplement to something else.[43]

Such a view derives from the deconstructive attitude toward language and meaning. Meaning is not a transcendental value beyond, before, or beneath the text: It emerges through interpretation. Equally, language does not translate an a priori or absolute knowledge into words: Linguistic signifying processes produce knowledge as an effect of the text. In sum, all writing and reading are subject to the slips and slides of meaning, interpretation, language, and knowledge. And criticism, when it recognizes its own textual or literary nature, may strive to read/write on the basis of this uncontrollably productive and creative play: "There is not absolute knowledge but rather a textual infinite, an interminable web of texts or interpretations."[44]

Recognition of the literary nature of criticism, moreover, brings about a change in what deconstructors attempt to do with the critical text. As Atkins states it:

> The deconstructive critic, in practice, tries to avoid the strong ultimate temptation to seek meaning as truth outside or before the work of difference. Such a temptation is inevitable, for we naturally want to resolve contradictions and to break out of the endless chains of substitutions, which "condemn" us to endless interpretation. We desire a haven outside contingency and temporality, which "meaning," "truth," and an originating signified offer.[45]

Although to write we must provisionally assume that we know what we mean as critics, discourse is always already caught up in the warring forces within our own critical text, the play of differences *within* the critical text that both allows us to write and guarantees its deconstructibility.

As a result of the deconstructive critic's resistance to an ultimate closure of meaning, criticism becomes a wandering in the wilderness of interpretation. Hartman writes: "To keep a poem in mind is to keep it there, not to resolve it into available meanings. This suspensive discourse is criticism."[46] Within this suspension, the deconstructive reading strives to stimulate a dialogue between the critic and the text. "What emerges is a battle of wills between text and critic—a dialogue of questions that is a mutual coercion. Mutually dependent on language, critic and text question each other. They are thus caught in an inevitable and ceaseless oscillation in which neither text nor critic dominates, acts as master to the slave-other."[47]

In the dialogue between critic and text, deconstruction never offers an escape from the play of difference. Instead, it pushes language and interpretation to their limits by making their border zones apparent so we may observe that power and authority always already are at work in discourse, attempting to smother difference. Deconstruction demonstrates that "a certain view of the world, of consciousness, and of language has been accepted as the correct one, and, if the minute particulars of that view are examined, a rather different picture (that is also a no-picture . . .) emerges."[48] Deconstruction does not provide the certainty of a more absolute truth; rather, it produces a way to begin discussing what is at stake when power and authority repress difference in order to create the illusion of masterable knowledge and meaning. As Barbara Johnson writes: "It is not, in the final analysis, what you don't know that can or cannot hurt you. It is what you don't *know* you don't know that spins out and entangles 'that perpetual error we call life.' "[49]

Many critics object to deconstruction because of the way in which it places the critical endeavor in the wilderness of interpretation—and leaves us there. And perhaps this is not a totally unjustifiable complaint, for everyone desires some kind of security. Indeed, even to attempt to introduce readers to deconstruction requires the illusion of a certain security—security that I know, that I can explain, and that I can make words demonstrate the attitudes characteristic of deconstruction. In the end, however, the project undermines itself: The illusion of security in knowledge, explanation, and demonstration all derive from the force of power and authority that would make what I write (at this very moment) a heuristic machine that tries to (but cannot) conceal the play of difference within the text. And yet deconstruction aims at distinguishing precisely how the power of heuristics and propaedeutics works to control difference: It lays bare the force of anxiety that would believe writing and reading to be easy and transparent, sufficient for the humanistic enterprise of education.

Many have also criticized deconstruction as a new style of formalism, perpetuating the formalist exclusion of context and history as significant in the production of meaning. Indeed, the intense attention given to language and textuality may at first render such an impression. The concepts of context and history themselves, however, are by no means excludable from deconstruction and undergo radical transformation when considered deconstructively. Similarly, others have complained that deconstructive criticism is repetitious in terms of its critical lexicon and themes. Although Derrida, for example, has continually varied his critical terminology in an attempt to avoid the reduction of his writings to an alternate vocabulary and a solidified technique, the material existence and circulation of his publications make them available for such appropriation. In fact, Derrida himself formulates a "general strategy of deconstruction" in *Positions*.[50] Although such allegations against deconstruction are at times justifiable, they are by no means universally true. Indeed, deconstructive criticism has evolved substantially over time. It has come to depend less on a central critical lexicon and a preferred series of themes and has turned more subtly toward the analysis of power and authority in meaning.

In the final analysis, the value of deconstruction emerges from its lack of an absolute, transcendental value, from the interminable movement of laying bare the unavoidable machinations of power and authority. Stanley Fish in *Is There a Text in This Class?* contends that we read and interpret as communities and that the community establishes the criteria for "appropriate" readings through a rhetoric of persuasion.[51] The institution of criticism, as a communal project, is the ongoing debate over the "appropriate," and as such it produces the inevitable search for a security based on the power and authority that would define the "appropriate." Deconstruction can effectively intervene in this process, not to establish a more "appropriate" power or authority but to enable us to lay bare the terms at stake in the critical debate. Deconstruction may help criticism to continue to ask questions without accepting the dogma of a fixed standard of appropriateness that would govern difference, a solidarity that would deny the possibility of criticism. Thus deconstruction permits us to question strategically, aware of the risk involved in community endeavors and attuned to the responsibility at stake in our decisions, as we wander perpetually through the wilderness of interpretation.

Notes

1. Richard Macksey and Eugenio Donato, eds., *The Structuralist Controversy: The Languages of Criticism and the Sciences of Man* (Baltimore: Johns Hopkins University Press, 1970), includes the proceedings and discussions from the 1966 Johns Hopkins symposium.

2. Gayatri C. Spivak, Translator's Preface to *Of Grammatology*, by Jacques Derrida (Baltimore: Johns Hopkins University Press, 1976), pp. ix–lxxxvii.

3. Susan A. Handelman, *The Slayers of Moses: The Emergence of Rabbinic Interpretation in Modern Literary Theory* (Albany: State University of New York Press, 1982), esp. pp. 163–78; and G. Douglas Atkins, *Reading Deconstruction/Deconstructive Reading* (Lexington: University Press of Kentucky, 1983), pp. 34–48.

4. Ferdinand de Saussure, *Course in General Linguistics*, trans. Wade Baskin (New York: McGraw-Hill, 1959), pp. 23–24.

5. Ibid., p. 112.

6. Ibid., p. 120.

7. Ibid.

8. Jacques Derrida, *Writing and Difference*, trans. Alan Bass (Chicago: University of Chicago Press, 1978), p. 279.

9. Derrida, *Of Grammatology*, p. 44.

10. Jacques Derrida, *Positions*, trans. Alan Bass (Chicago: University of Chicago Press, 1981), p. 26.

11. Ibid., p. 27.

12. Spivak, Translator's Preface, *Of Grammatology*, p. xvii.

13. Derrida, *Positions*, p. 27.

14. Atkins, *Reading Deconstruction*, pp. 17–18.

15. For a detailed consideration of *differance*, consult Derrida, "Differance," in *Margins of Philosophy*, trans. Alan Bass (Chicago: University of Chicago Press, 1982), pp. 1–27.

16. Saussure, *Course*, p. 120.

17. Derrida's selection of Saussure's *Course* for such an investigation of differance and logocentrism cannot be accidental. Indeed, Saussure's importance in the development of structural linguistics and his influence on later French structuralism have placed him in a pivotal position for Derrida's consideration of logocentrism in Western tradition. Perhaps the most cited Derridean critique of structuralism comes from his consideration of the concept of "center of structure" in the writings of the famed anthropologist Claude Lévi-Strauss. Derrida, "Structure, Sign, and Play in the Discourse of the Human Sciences," *Writing and Difference*, pp. 278–93, comments on the contradictory and yet coherent use of "center of structure" in structuralist discourse. Although the "center of structure" produces valuable insights and knowledge, it also restricts knowledge to that which can be understood in a logocentric perspective that privileges presence.

18. Barbara Johnson, Translator's Introduction to *Dissemination*, by Jacques Derrida (Chicago: University of Chicago Press, 1981), p. xv.

19. Derrida, *Of Grammatology*, p. 158.

20. Johnson, Translator's Introduction, *Dissemination*, p. xiv.

21. Derrida, *Positions*, p. 41.

22. Ibid., p. 42.

23. Ibid. Also see Jacques Derrida, "*Hors livre*: Outwork (*Hors d'oeuvre*/Extratext/Foreplay/Bookend/Facing/Prefacing)," in *Dissemination*, pp. 1–59.

24. Johnson, Translator's Introduction, *Dissemination*, p. xiv.

25. Derrida, *Positions*, p. 52.

26. Jonathan Culler, *On Deconstruction: Theory and Criticism after Structuralism* (Ithaca, N.Y.: Cornell University Press, 1982), p. 15.

27. Geoffrey Hartman, *Easy Pieces* (New York: Columbia University Press, 1985), p. 190. Also see Christopher Norris, "The American Connection," *Deconstruction: Theory and Practice* (London: Methuen, 1982), pp. 90–125.

28. J. Hillis Miller, *Fiction and Repetition: Seven English Novels* (Cambridge, Mass.: Harvard University Press, 1982), p. 19.

29. Paul de Man, *Allegories of Reading: Figural Language in Rousseau, Nietzsche, Rilke, and Proust* (New Haven: Yale University Press, 1979), p. 11.

30. Ibid.

31. Ibid., pp. 11–12.

32. Ibid., p. 12.

33. Jonathan Culler, "Story and Discourse in the Analysis of Narrative," *The Pursuit of Signs: Semiotics, Literature, Deconstruction* (Ithaca, N.Y.: Cornell University Press, 1981), p. 178.

34. Ibid.

35. Ibid., p. 183.

36. Peter Brooks, *Reading for the Plot: Design and Intention in Narrative* (New York: Knopf, 1984), p. 13.

37. Ibid., p. 29.

38. Ibid.

39. Joaquim Maria Machado de Assis, *Dom Casmurro*, trans. Helen Caldwell (Berkeley: University of California Press, 1966). Page and chapter numbers for subsequent references to *Dom Casmurro* will be given parenthetically within the text of this essay. Extensive critical literature investigates the complexities of *Dom Casmurro*, and many of the contradictions considered henceforth have been discussed under various guises. Although I will not refer to specific interpretations of *Dom Casmurro*, readers interested in studies complementary to the following comments may consult Paul B. Dixon, *Reversible Readings: Ambiguity in Four Modern Latin American Novels* (University: University of Alabama Press, 1985), and John Gledson, *The Deceptive Realism of Machado de Assis: A Dissenting Interpretation of "Dom Casmurro"* (Liverpool: Francis Cairns, 1984).

40. For comments regarding the trends in criticism on *Dom Casmurro*, refer to Keith Ellis, "Technique and Ambiguity in *Dom Casmurro*," *Hispania* 45 (1965): 76–81; and Dixon, *Reversible Readings*, pp. 28–29. Also see Alfred J. MacAdam, "Machado de Assis: Narrating and Lying," *Modern Latin American Narratives: The Dreams of Reason* (Chicago: University of Chicago Press, 1977), pp. 21–28, for a rhetorical study of the opposition between truth and falsehood in the perspective of the dynamics of narrating.

41. Barbara Johnson, *The Critical Difference: Essays in the Contemporary Rhetoric of Reading* (Baltimore: Johns Hopkins University Press, 1980), pp. 3–12, 110–46, respectively.

42. Ibid., p. 12.

43. Geoffrey Hartman, *Criticism in the Wilderness: The Study of Literature Today* (New Haven: Yale University Press, 1980), p. 201.

44. Ibid., p. 202.

45. Atkins, *Reading Deconstruction*, p. 24.

46. Hartman, *Criticism in the Wilderness*, p. 274.

47. Atkins, *Reading Deconstruction*, pp. 87–88.

48. Spivak, Translator's Preface, *Of Grammatology*, p. xii.

49. Johnson, *Critical Difference*, p. xii.

50. Derrida, *Positions*, pp. 41–46.

51. Stanley Fish, *Is There a Text in This Class?: The Authority of Interpretive Communities* (Cambridge, Mass.: Harvard University Press, 1980), pp. 167–73, 338–71.

Selected Bibliography

The following list, in addition to the works cited in the study, includes selected references to basic texts on deconstruction. Atkins, Eagleton, and Norris discuss deconstruction more broadly, in terms relevant for readers unacquainted with contemporary literary theory. The implications of deconstruction beyond philosophy and literary criticism are explored in Atkins, Culler's *On Deconstruction*, and Eagleton. Also, Atkins, Brooks, Carroll, Johnson, and Miller include deconstructive readings of literary texts. Finally, Lentricchia and Said critically examine the problems involved in deconstructive literary criticism as it becomes an institutionalized mode of analysis in the academy. For a more complete bibliography on deconstruction consult Culler's *On Deconstruction*, Harari, and Norris.

Atkins, G. Douglas. *Reading Deconstruction/Deconstructive Reading*. Lexington: University Press of Kentucky, 1983. An introduction to deconstruction and consideration of its uses in critical readings.

Brooks, Peter. *Reading for the Plot: Design and Intention in Narrative*. New York: Knopf, 1984. A major study of the dynamics of plot with an emphasis on psychoanalysis and the "double logic" of *sjuzet* and *fabula*.

Bruns, Gerald L. "Structuralism, Deconstruction, and Hermeneutics." *Diacritics* 14 (1984): 12–23. A careful consideration of the implications of deconstruction for the act of interpretation.

Carroll, David. *The Subject in Question: The Languages of Theory and the Strategies of Fiction*. Chicago: University of Chicago Press, 1982. A critical reconsideration of contemporary critical perspectives combined with critical readings of the novels of Claude Simon.

Culler, Jonathan. *On Deconstruction: Theory and Criticism after Structuralism*. Ithaca, N.Y.: Cornell University Press, 1982. Detailed study that examines the major topics of Derrida's writings and the practice of deconstruction in general. Includes chapters on reader-response and feminist criticism.

———. "Problems in the Theory of Fiction." *Diacritics* 14 (1984): 2–11. Deconstructive consideration of major narratological categories and speech-act theory.

———. *The Pursuit of Signs: Semiotics, Literature, Deconstruction*. Ithaca, N.Y.: Cornell University Press, 1981. Collection of essays that exemplify a deconstructive evaluation of contemporary critical methods.

de Man, Paul. *Allegories of Reading: Figural Language in Rousseau, Nietzsche, Rilke, and Proust*. New Haven: Yale University Press, 1979. Readings that examine the deconstructive effects of figural language.

———. *Blindness and Insight: Essays in the Rhetoric of Contemporary Criticism*. 1971; rpt., Minneapolis: University of Minnesota Press, 1983. Difficult but brilliant essays that examine the production of knowledge on the basis of contradictions repressed in the establishment of a critical perspective or "insight."

Derrida, Jacques. *Dissemination*. Translated and with an Introduction by Barbara Johnson. Chicago: University of Chicago Press, 1981. Essays that analyze the status of prefaces, the deconstructive effects of language in Plato, and the practice of writing in Mallarmé and Sollers. Johnson's Introduction provides a clear and concise examination of Derrida's deconstructive practices.

———. *Margins of Philosophy*. Translated by Alan Bass. Chicago: University of Chicago Press, 1982. Series of essays that give particular emphasis to language and meaning in philosophy, linguistics, and literature.

———. *Of Grammatology*. Translated and with an Introduction by Gayatri C. Spivak. Baltimore: Johns Hopkins University Press, 1976. Lengthy examination of the metaphysics of presence in linguistics, Rousseau, and anthropology. Spivak's preface is one of the most important critical considerations of Derrida and his place in the history of philosophy.

————. *Positions*. Translated by Alan Bass. Chicago: University of Chicago Press, 1981. Three interviews with Derrida where he outlines his major interests and formulates the general strategy of deconstruction.

————. *Writing and Difference*. Translated by Alan Bass. Chicago: University of Chicago Press, 1978. Collection of essays that deconstructively treat diverse topics such as hermeneutics, psychoanalysis, representation, and structuralism.

Dixon, Paul B. *Reversible Readings: Ambiguity in Four Modern Latin American Novels*. University: University of Alabama Press, 1985. Critical study of the dynamics and contradictions of ambiguity in modern Latin American novels.

Eagleton, Terry. *Literary Theory: An Introduction*. Minneapolis: University of Minnesota Press, 1983. A Marxist introduction to and evaluation of several schools of literary theory, which includes a section on deconstruction.

Ellis, Keith. "Technique and Ambiguity in *Dom Casmurro*." *Hispania* 45 (1965): 76–81. Includes a consideration of principal critical trends in the studies on *Dom Casmurro*.

Fish, Stanley. *Is There a Text in This Class?: The Authority of Interpretive Communities*. Cambridge, Mass.: Harvard University Press, 1980. Series of essays that develop the notion of reader-response criticism and the importance of community and persuasion in the establishment of accepted critical "truth."

Gledson, John. *The Deceptive Realism of Machado de Assis: A Dissenting Interpretation of "Dom Casmurro."* Liverpool: Francis Cairns, 1984. A study of meaning and literary style in *Dom Casmurro*.

Handelman, Susan A. *The Slayers of Moses: The Emergence of Rabbinic Interpretation in Modern Literary Theory*. Albany: State University of New York Press, 1982. Analysis of the dichotomy between Hellenistic hermeneutics and the rabbinic tradition. Traces the emergence of rabbinic interpretation in Freud, Lacan, Derrida, and Bloom.

Harari, Josué V., ed. *Textual Strategies: Perspectives in Post-Structuralist Criticism*. Ithaca, N.Y.: Cornell University Press, 1979. Anthology of essays that demonstrate the diversity of poststructuralist criticism. The Introduction demonstrates the interrelations among the different poststructuralist approaches.

Hartman, Geoffrey. *Criticism in the Wilderness: The Study of Literature Today*. New Haven: Yale University Press, 1980. Deconstructive study of reading and meaning in Anglo-American literary studies.

————. *Easy Pieces*. New York: Columbia University Press, 1985. Hartman's deconstructive analyses of literature, popular culture, and film with a consideration of the impact of deconstruction on literary studies.

Johnson, Barbara. *The Critical Difference: Essays in the Contemporary Rhetoric of Reading*. Baltimore: Johns Hopkins University Press, 1980. Lucid discussion of deconstruction in terms of literary criticism and literary texts.

Leitch, Vincent B. *Deconstructive Criticism: An Advanced Introduction*. New York: Columbia University Press, 1983. An entertaining introduction to deconstructive concepts written in a deconstructive style.

Lentricchia, Frank. *After the New Criticism*. Chicago: University of Chicago Press, 1980. Overview of the development of literary criticism since Northrop Frye. Includes a critical evaluation of poststructuralism, de Man, and Bloom.

MacAdam, Alfred J. *Modern Latin American Narratives: The Dreams of Reason*. Chicago: University of Chicago Press, 1977. Essays that examine the rhetorical dynamics of narrative in modern Latin American literature.

Machado de Assis, Joaquim Maria. *Dom Casmurro*. Translated by Helen Caldwell. Berkeley: University of California Press, 1966.

Macksey, Richard, and Eugenio Donato, eds. *The Structuralist Controversy: The Languages of Criticism and the Sciences of Man*. Baltimore: Johns Hopkins University Press, 1970. Proceedings of 1966 symposium that emphasize structuralism and include Derrida's critique of structuralism.

Miller, J. Hillis. *Fiction and Repetition: Seven English Novels*. Cambridge, Mass.: Harvard University Press, 1982. Deconstructive critique of logocentric notions of repetition followed by seven studies of repetition in specific novels.

———. "Stevens's Rock and Criticism as Cure, II." *Georgia Review* 30 (1976): 330–48. Deconstructive consideration of the interrelation between text and interpretation.

Norris, Christopher. *Deconstruction: Theory and Practice*. London: Methuen, 1982. Concise introduction to the development, ideas, and uses of deconstruction.

Said, Edward W. "Criticism between Culture and System." *The World, the Text, and the Critic*. Cambridge, Mass.: Harvard University Press, 1983, pp. 178–225. Critical study of Derrida and Michel Foucault in the perspective of culture; warns against the danger of reducing literature to textuality and emphasizes the importance of culture.

Saussure, Ferdinand de. *Course in General Linguistics*. Translated by Wade Baskin. New York: McGraw-Hill, 1959. Saussure's major text as compiled by his students; cornerstone text for the development of structuralism and semiotics.

DAVID WILLBERN

Reading after Freud

Psychoanalysis is at once a theory of human development, a process of interpretation, and a therapeutic interaction. Though each aspect can be provisionally separated, none is properly isolable from that matrix of ideas about the body, mind, and emotional history that Freud devised. As a developmental theory, psychoanalysis describes a sequence of acts in the difficult tragicomedy of growing up: how we develop in a process of progressions and regressions through the psychosexual phases of our lives; how we construct psychic and emotional patterns in terms of the parental, social, and cultural images we accept or resist; how we re-create ourselves through our reflections of and interactions with the physical and emotional environments we inhabit. The theory argues that long after childhood we still bear the blessings and burdens of infantile wishes and fears that affect our current styles of being. On the largest scale, concerning the bargains we as individuals make with our culture—the restrictions we accept, the dues we pay—the theory dilates into a critique of civilization.

What I find compelling and enduring about Freudian theory is its insistence on the *human* origins of psyche, family, society, and culture. Psychoanalysis grounds itself on actual events in the lives of people—events both universal (such as being nurtured) and unique (such as being nurtured in a particular time and place). Theory proceeds from the personal, however grandiose some of its ultimate generalizations may be. The primary instance is Freud himself: Psychoanalysis derives from, but is not limited to, his own self-analysis. Psychoanalysis also provides techniques of interpretation that are in themselves especially literary. As Freud demonstrated in *The Interpretation of Dreams* (1900), such techniques involve intense and imaginative scrutiny of the text (of the dream) and careful attention to all responses. To use one of Freud's favorite metaphors, psychoanalysis turns a literary work into an archaeological site, with layer upon layer of significance, whose mysteries are to be unearthed and restored. Meaning is reconstructed as the material pieces emerge from the text, like fragments of ancient pottery. The skillful and experienced reconstructor then arranges the pieces into a recognizable order. Some pieces will be missing, perhaps lost forever; here, informed imagination fills in the gaps. The perfectly recovered and restored object, or the perfectly interpreted text, remains only an ideal.

Psychological criticisms of literature are hardly new. The ancient argument between Plato and Aristotle about the value of myth and drama is fundamentally a conflict between psychological assumptions about mimesis. For Plato, the composition ("inspiration") and, by inference, the reception of poetry were a kind of madness or "phrensy." Because it nourished the emotions and weakened reason, Plato argued, through his dramatic dialogist, Socrates, that poetry should be banned from the ideal state. For Aristotle, the same energies of enactment and response were therapeutic "catharsis" that allowed the controlled expression of powerful feelings. Versions of this ancient argument still persist beneath modern disputes about the place of psychoanalysis in literary studies.[1]

Since Freud, psychoanalysis has assumed an inevitable place in the reading of literature. There has been a radical change in the assumptions modern writers (poets, dramatists, novelists, critics) and readers (poets, dramatists, novelists, critics) make about processes of imaginative composition and response. Some twentieth-century writers, such as Thomas Mann or W. H. Auden, welcomed Freudian insights. Others were not so congenial: Witness the articulate resistances of D. H. Lawrence and Vladimir Nabokov, or the witty cooption of James Joyce, who claimed, "I can psoakoonaloose myself any time I want" (*Finnegans Wake*, 522.34). Through such diverse styles of acceptance and dissent, Freudian psychoanalysis has effected a revolution in our ideas about literature. Many modern critics, such as Kenneth Burke, Lionel Trilling, Geoffrey Hartman, and Harold Bloom, have accepted Freud's ideas as enlightening and enabling. Others have rejected them as erroneous or even dangerous.[2]

In short, reading after Freud is different. Our assumptions about textual production and reception, about linguistic significance, about the representation of character, even about rhyme and rhythm, have radically altered.

Besides its scrutiny of the surface, psychoanalytic criticism typically attends to diverse voices, sub- and countertextual currents of meaning and motivation. Beneath, behind, and before the text, another scene of desire is being represented.

The site of this scene, the bedrock of theory, lies in Freud's concept of dynamically repressed mental actions, or the "unconscious." This concept asserts that the psyche is not unified but divided, and that meanings and motives are kept from consciousness in the interests of self-protection and self-delusion. The idea of the unconscious prefigures our construction of reality in relation to our hidden wishes and fears. Therefore any expression—behavioral, linguistic, or imaginary—is a set of complex and mediated relations between what we "think" we are doing, saying, or dreaming and other, unknown operations. The import of this idea is sometimes not fully felt, even by those who accept it. Furthermore, the unconscious has its deepest roots in the physiological and emotional structures of sexual life. By "sexual" Freud intended an entire array of pleasures and gratifications, organic and relational, beginning in infancy and developing into adulthood. Patterns of expectation, satisfaction, and frustration in early life provide templates for the gradual construction and emergence of self.

In the century since Freud published *The Interpretation of Dreams*, psychoanalytic literary criticism has proliferated and branched widely. In a brief essay I cannot trace all the branches (or climb out on all the limbs). What I will do is examine one root analogy: that between literature and dream. There are other root analogies—most notably between literature and play, and literature and transference—that are explored in works cited in the Selected Bibliography. The analogy to the dream is limited, and basic: It is *elementary* in the fullest sense. It allows me to sketch rudimentary psychoanalytic concepts that pertain to literary production and interpretation.

The briefest conceptual formulation of this core psychoanalytic dynamic is Freud's definition of the dream as "a (disguised) fulfillment of a (repressed) wish." It is chronologically layered, with an immediate motive (the "day residue") joined to an unconscious infantile one. The manifest dream becomes a coproduction of past and present that fantasizes a future (fulfillment). It is a regression in the service of a progression, a compromise formation mediating the urges of a wish and the inhibitions of a repressive force (the "censor"). This model characterizes Freud's theories of dream, joke, art, and literature as conservative governments of subversive energies.

Freud's classic definition is deceptively simple. What, for instance, is a dream? Except within his or her own psychic space, a psychoanalyst never deals directly with a dream. That original phenomenon is hallucinatory and transitory, private and unsharable: It is not "literary." (Strictly speaking, there are no dreams in *The Interpretation of Dreams*.) Once told or recorded, the dream becomes a verbal or written report that changes its original form, and each time it is told or rewritten it undergoes further change: It becomes "literary." Moreover, unlike the original dream, the dream-report exists in a context of analytic interpretation. It has an audience, and an especially attentive one. Within this analytic context, the motives of the dream coexist with the motives of the report, and with the motives of the analyst; the latter may reinforce, confuse, or otherwise complicate the former. Analogizing this interrelated process to the practice of reading has become a crucial aspect of contemporary psychoanalytic criticism.

We should not leave Freud's famous definition of the dream without examining another key term: the "wish." The concept refers first to primitive, infantile, unconscious satisfactions, sensual and emotional. Memories (what Freud called "mnemic traces") of such satisfactions provide the ground in which current wishes take root. In order to express itself, a wish must be related to an (unconscious) infantile experience of pleasure (satisfied desire). Thus a wish represents a memory: a retracing of mnemonic paths to a scene or experience of original satisfaction whereby that satisfaction is re-created in the present. It is an *imagined restoration* of a prior condition or relationship. Although it can involve physical sensation, it is basically a psychological event. Wishes thereby differ from needs or drives, basic appetites that can be materially satisfied, such as hunger.

The Freudian model of the wish is thus layered, like the Freudian model of the dream. A later definition, from Freud's essay "Creative Writers and Day-Dreaming" (1907), clarifies this temporal layering. "The wish," he wrote, "makes use of an occasion in the present to construct, on the pattern of the past, a picture of the future. . . . Thus past, present, and future are strung together, as it were, on the thread of the wish that runs through them."[3] The "thread" of the wish is one the interpreter then uses, like Theseus at Crete, to find his way through the labyrinth of the dream, reach its center, and return along his analytic lines. That center holds, like the Minotaur, a powerful force. One of Freud's most striking characterizations of the "wish" involves a similar mythic analogy. "These wishes in our unconscious," he wrote in *Dreams*, "ever on the alert and, so to say, immortal, remind one of the legendary Titans, weighed down since primaeval ages by the massive bulk of the mountains which were once hurled upon them by the victorious gods and which are still shaken from time to time by the convulsion of their limbs."[4] In this mythic model, repression (the censor) is an Olympic paternal tyrant and the wish is an Oedipal rebel, temporarily defeated but always ready to surface. Freud's allegory suggests powerful tensions within psychic structure and their tendency toward eruption (as in dreams or symptoms). The wish in Freudian psychoanalysis is the Titanic infant within, alive from the deepest past and eager to be awakened. A less dramatic statement of the persistence of infantile energies occurs in Freud's case history of "Dora," where he restates his definition of the wish and concludes: "For the wish which creates the dream always springs from the period of childhood; and it is continually trying to summon childhood back into reality and to correct the present day by the measure of childhood."[5] The immortality of the wish inheres in its timelessness, its refusal to acknowledge temporality. It seeks to remake the present into the past, to resurrect a prior state and restore prior satisfactions. It is therefore both rebellious and conservative, a regressive revision of experience.

Such revision has an important corollary motive: the "correction" of the past from the later perspective of the present. That is, as the wish expresses its powerful nostalgia through the dream, the dream recasts the events and emotions of the wish in a retroactive reconstitution. This interaction of present and past, termed "deferred action" or "deferred revision" and particularly emphasized in the work of Jacques Lacan, is critical to those experiences that have not been fully assimilated in human development: an instance is the reemergence and re-vision of infantile sexuality during adolescence. For Freud, the dream as interpreted in analysis was the geological map of these strata.

The fundamental organizing principle in the production of dreams Freud termed the "dreamwork." In outline, its basic operations are:

1. The *day residue*, some recent impression that occasions the dream. As the point of contact with normal life, it plays "entrepreneur" for the "capital" investment of the unconscious wish.
2. The *infantile memory* (fantasy, experience) that energizes the dream, through the power of the *repressed unconscious wish* to which the day residue must connect.
3. *The censorship*. This was Freud's first way of representing the inhibiting or repressive force in the psyche. It prefigures Freud's theory of repression as a defense and is an early model of the (paternal) superego.
4. The effect of *associational "chains"* that combine elements of the dream or connect the day residue with the repressed with. These chains can be constructed along various paths, through the "poetic" agencies of dream formation.
5. *Displacement*, one of the basic strategies of the dreamwork, through which meaning or affect shifts away from the significant to the apparently trivial, as a means of disguising the latent content of the dream.
6. *Condensation*, another basic dreamwork device. It is an aspect of the whole dream,

always seeking unity through the combination of elements, and a feature of specific dream elements (such as persons or words). It can be thought of as a tangle of associational chains, a knot or "nodal point" of the dream.

7. *Secondary revision* (or elaboration). The last of Freud's fundamental processes of dream formation, it functions as an aesthetic principle of representation, shaping the dream into a comprehensible narrative.

In a successful dream, the wish evades the censor and finds reconstitution and fulfillment through these various defensive transformations of the dream-work. All of the above intrapsychic modes, as Lionel Trilling noted, are essentially artistic.[6] The dream itself is a kind of poem—in a reciprocal analogy to Freud's notion of poetry as a kind of dreaming. Both represent styles of thought and representation closer to "primary process" than to "secondary process" mentation, yet moving along a continuum between these modes. (The term *primary process* refers to a style of thought unbound by conventional notions of space, time, sequence, causality, or logic. It is the style of dreams and hallucinations, typically unconscious, governed by the pleasure principle. *Secondary process* refers to a conventional, conscious style of psychic representation that abides by concepts of order and delayed gratification and correlates to the reality principle.) The dreamwork's eventual production reveals and conceals its origins, through a manifest content that hides yet deviously derives from a latent content. A goal of classic psychoanalytic interpretation is to discover this latent content. Interpretation reorders dream elements, translating apparently arbitrary contiguity to meaningful continuity, parataxis to syntax. In this translation, the concept of *overdetermination* allows for various and even contradictory meanings. Because the expressed dream, like the literary work, exists in a continuing and changing relation between creator and interpreter, its meaning may shift as interpretations develop. Meanings are thus multiple, mutable, and historical. These complexities modify the popular notion of "Freudian symbolism," since the relation of sign to signified in psychoanalysis is a function of individual and cultural contexts, historical as well as linguistic. A snake, for example, may provisionally function as a phallic substitute or as a devouring threat for some observers in some contexts, but need not be always or essentially such a substitute or threat.[7]

The "wish" in Freudian dream interpretation is thus something posited at origin but discovered in conclusion. Uncovered and described through the processes of interpretation, it becomes a construction of the interpreter as well as an admission of the dreamer. In other words, there is a reciprocal process of "interpretation work," an analytic mirror of the dreamwork, that reflects the wishes, defenses, and personal styles of the interpreter. The validity of the original wish can be substantiated by the dreamer, but it must first be reconstructed by the interpreter. Like the overall interpretation, the wish is a coproduction or codiscovery of the dreamer and the analyst. A representation of original desire in psychoanalysis results from a working backward in time to a point that is simultaneously discovered and constructed.[8] In this sense Freud was a psychoarchaeologist who restored structures from the ruins he uncovered. Interpretation as historical recovery is thus matched by interpretation as creative re-presentation. The lost fragments of pottery are incomplete until put together by the discoverer's hand.[9] In that final formation lie the skill and style of the interpreter, as well as the reconstituted integrity of the object. Freud's famous definition of the dream as "a (disguised) fulfillment of a (repressed) wish" needs therefore to be supplemented by the revised statement he made after interpreting the dream of "Irma's injection"—the famous "specimen dream" of psychoanalysis: *When the work of interpretation has been completed*, we perceive that a dream is the fulfillment of a wish" (italics added). Just as the German title of *The Interpretation of Dreams* (*Traumdeutung*), merges dream and interpretation, so does this (re)definition connect the meaning of a dream with the act of interpreting it.[10]

The best way for me to demonstrate an act of interpretation is to read a text. In order to exhibit and examine some possibilities of psychoanalytic literary criticism in a brief space, I have chosen a well-known poem by one of America's finest poets. Before discussing it, I want to place it in a context that will highlight Freud's core analogy between "dream" and "poem." Emily Dickinson, whose famous poem I will examine, also composed a parallel account that she herself labeled a dream.[11]

> In Winter in my Room
> I came upon a Worm—
> Pink, lank, and warm—
> But as he was a worm
> And worms presume
> Not quite with him at home—
> Secured him by a string
> To something neighboring
> And went along.
>
> A Trifle afterward
> A thing occurred
> I'd not believe it if I heard
> But state with creeping blood—
>
> A snake with mottles rare
> Surveyed my chamber floor

In feature as the worm before
But ringed with power—
The very string with which
I tied him—too
When he was mean and new
That string was there—

I shrank—"How fair you are"!
Propitiation's claw—
"Afraid," he hissed
"Of me"?
"No cordiality"—
He fathomed me—
Then to a Rhythm *Slim*
Secreted in his Form
As Patterns swim
Projected him.

That time I flew
Both eyes his way
Lest he pursue
Nor ever ceased to run
Till in a distant Town
Towns on from mine
I set me down
This was a dream.

Not surprisingly, this poem has drawn attention from psychoanalytically minded Dickinson critics.[12] Read after Freud, the text represents a raw phallic fantasy, an uneasy evocation of the phenomenon of male tumescence. Gripped by a mixture of fear and admiration, the (female) speaker makes an effort at domestication and ownership (the leash of string) but discovers this creature to be beyond her control and ultimately beyond her ken. Gestures of intimacy are simultaneously psychological and physical. The discourse of "Propitiation's claw" augurs a symbolic intercourse: "He *fathomed* me" (embraced, sounded the depths). In a quasi-hallucinatory moment, as vision blurs and "Patterns swim," intimacy surrenders to mutual flight and the conventional repression of fantastic reminiscence: "in a distant Town . . ./I set me down/This was a dream."

Read in this way, the poem represents a psychosexual allegory of ambivalent feminine fascination with masculine potency. In this particular case, questions of "manifest" and "latent" content seem almost moot. Though Dickinson retrospectively labeled her poem "a dream," it is not, of course (it is a literary text). Yet it may well have emerged from a dream and been fashioned into a poem. Another text, more conventionally poetic, emerges, I will argue, from a similar intrapsychic constellation. This poem, one of only a handful published in Dickinson's lifetime, is a perennial favorite in student anthologies. Standard readings characterize it as her "snake poem."[13]

> A narrow Fellow in the Grass
> Occasionally rides—
> You may have met Him—did you not
> His notice sudden is—
>
> The Grass divides as with a Comb—
> A spotted shaft is seen—
> And then it closes at your feet
> And opens further on—
>
> He likes a Boggy Acre
> A Floor too cool for Corn—
> Yet when a Boy, and Barefoot—
> I more than once at Noon
>
> Have passed, I thought, a Whip lash
> Unbraiding in the Sun
> When stooping to secure it
> It wrinkled, and was gone—
>
> Several of Nature's People
> I know, and they know me—
> I feel for them a transport
> Of cordiality—
>
> But never met this Fellow
> Attended or alone
> Without a tighter breathing
> And Zero at the Bone—

After Freud, and in the context of Dickinsonian dream imagery, how can we read this poem? As a beginning, I will offer a psychoanalytically oriented paraphrase.

In the first stanza, a mysterious masculine creature appears, "sudden" yet familiar. Then the syntax shifts into neutrality and passivity—the grass "divides," a shaft "is seen"—as though the viewer/speaker is distanced from the event even as it is vividly described. The simile of the comb solicits associations of hair—an anatomical arena further implied by references to feet and to acts of opening and closing. The related phrase, "Unbraiding in the Sun," evokes an image of dis-integration and of distant power.[14] Though embodied in a woman, the poet describes herself as masculine: "when a Boy, and Barefoot."[15] Nineteenth-century slang used "barefoot" metonymically to connote nakedness; the term also highlights an anatomical appendage. Repetitively ("more than once"), at noon (the hour of erect hands), the speaker found this fellow, now "a Whip lash" (recalling the rider of line 2). Bending down to grasp it, he(she) found only a wrinkle, and absence.

My paraphrase of the poem presses a Freudian translation toward the momentous (re)discovery of genital difference. A woman, fascinated with the phenomenon of male sexuality, imagines herself "a Boy, and Barefoot"— eventually to discover that the potent appendage she stoops to secure is gone, marked only by a wrinkle. Her feelings are highly ambivalent: both ecstatic and anxious. She feels "a transport/Of *cordiality*" (note the identical term from Dickinson's phallic dream-poem, "In Winter in my Room"), as well as "a tighter breathing/And Zero at the Bone." Like the poem itself, this last phrase is overdetermined. It refers to fear and coldness . . . an uncanny *frisson* of terror and excitement—as well as to anatomical fact. She is not a barefoot boy, with an easily secured appendage of mastery; in fact she possesses (or feels she possesses) an absence, a lack: "Zero [no/thing] at the [pubic] Bone." Though the latest book on the subject does not discuss this poem, here is the "anxiety of gender" at its deepest level. [16]

A reading after Freud, then, reconstructs Emily Dickinson's famous poem about a snake as a poem about the female discovery of genital difference, perceived as an anxious absence. The traditional psychoanalytic terms here are *castration anxiety* and *penis envy*. Does this then mean that the poem is not about a snake, or not about the anxious relation of human to Nature (transcendentalism modulated by terror), or not about the idea of mortality (for the snake augurs breathlessness and "the Bone"), or that it does not present a modern version of Edenic myth (woman and serpent in the garden)? Are these standard readings to be supplanted or erased by psychoanalytic interpretation? Of course not. To assert that Dickinson's poem symbolically figures her disunited relation to her body hardly contradicts the thesis that it presents her alienated relation to Nature. A psychoanalytic reading deepens and expands the issue of "Nature" here, to include concepts and figurations of the *poet's* nature; her psychological sense of her self and her body image. Without rejecting "external" readings (the snake as other), such an explanation adds an "internal" reading (the snake as self-representation). A reading after Freud locates the poem in both symbolic arenas, external and internal. As Vivian Pollak writes of Dickinson's nature poetry, "she projects her socially conditioned sexual anxieties into her imagination of nature." [17]

Cynthia Griffin Wolff, Dickinson's latest biographer, remarks that "the besetting anxiety" of the poet's life, expressed in a theme that "runs like a

crimson thread" throughout her work, is the issue of loss and separation.
Wolff's commentary on "A narrow Fellow" is especially useful in demonstrating the place of psychoanalytic assumptions in current literary criticism. Her
close attention to the sounds of the verse expresses itself in a striking image:
"If the first line is said aloud," she writes, "the tongue is forced to flicker
almost obscenely in the mouth." She traces a traditional juxtaposition of
wilderness and culture (through the metonymies of "grass" and "comb") to a
psychological observation of the poem's temporal trajectory as it moves into
the past, "recollecting the more vulnerable time of childhood when . . .
primitive fears and thought patterns still lurk very close to consciousness."
She briefly notes that the poet's boyish persona may imply anxiety about "male
sexuality or even phallic brutality," reinforced by the images of exposed feet
and toes. Then, exiting the interpretive arena of primitivity and sexuality, she
concludes that this poem lacks the support of traditional transcendental
assumptions; it "stands alone" with no secure foundation in natural or theological symbol systems. Without the theocentric "semiotic system of latter-
day American Puritanism," Wolff concludes, "only the broken shards of
magnificence remained."[18]

This brief and suggestive reading of Dickinson's poem exemplifies a style
of literary criticism informed by a psychoanalytic awareness of temporal
layering, linguistic possibility, and sexual symbolism. Yet it uses this awareness superficially; it does not dig deeply enough. Without diluting the power
of Wolff's large assertion about the disintegration of Puritan semiotics, a
psychoanalytic eye can still discern some bodily bases for her own metaphors. I
would even say that her sublime translation of apparent physical loss into the
destruction of an entire system of meaning is a fair paraphrase of the extended
effects of Freud's idea of "castration anxiety," fully understood. That is,
"castration" stands as a terminological sign for a larger theme: the uncanny
separation or division of self from nature, or of subject from signifier, or of part
from whole. Castration, in short, is a type of metonymy: It figures a division
inside the body or self that mirrors a division *between* self and other, self and
world. As Jim Swan puts it, "castration anxiety . . . signifies the failure of a
dialectic between a symbolic process and its absence."[19] It posits a crisis of
representation, which if unresolved perpetuates an insoluble dilemma.

Psychoanalytic criticism can merge with other kinds of readings without
supplanting them: It can underpin without undermining. My psychoanalytic
reading of Dickinson's poem would not simply substitute one poetic significance (snake) with another (penis). This would be to replace a fallacy of naive
realism with a fallacy of phallic fantasy. Freudian theory, like Dickinson's

poem, is about the *representation* of self, body, others, emotions, and relationships in the enactments of behavior and discourse—the ways we transfer and translate wish and event into memory and utterance. Dickinson's poem occurs on a threshold between inner and outer, dreaming and waking, symbolism and realism. A rigorous identification that fixes the "narrow Fellow" as either snake or phallus obscures one remarkable feature of the poem: The creature is never named, only signified. The poem describes a creature that may be realistically identified as a snake or fantastically identified as a phallus, but that is not finally identifiable. It is a poem about something hidden, mutable, liable to disappear. It is about a powerful absence, or a presence that manifests itself as an absence. Its subject, I might write, is a ~~snake~~, or shifting signs of a snake, or the dialectic of presence and absence as manifested in the natural body.

When this dialectic of presence and absence is located on the site of the genitals, psychoanalysis typically encounters resistance. Freud's concept of *penis envy* is one of the most challenging and challenged of his ideas and the frequent fulcrum of arguments to discredit his theories. That the idea arouses ardent antipathy is of course no measure of its validity or invalidity. Beyond emotional reaction, however, there are cogent critiques of the concept, based in philosophy, politics, and linguistics. First, Freud's mapping of psychosexual development privileges the visible *presence* of male genitals over the apparent invisibility or *absence* of female genitals: the little boy obviously possesses something that the little girl obviously does not possess. Philosophically, then, Freudian theory privileges the epistemology of vision, and further assumes the privilege of presence over absence within the dialectic of both. But it is not merely the presence of a missing appendage that the Freudian girl desires (or envies), it is the presence of a particularly socially *valued* appendage: the crude emblem of power in a patriarchal culture. As long as power is inequitably apportioned within a "phallocentric" gender system, those who lack the sign of the phallus lack social power. Politically, then, orthodox Freudian theory presumes a predominant style of social arrangements. "Normal" gender differentiation involves a process of socialized subordination, just as normal genital sexual organization involves a hierarchy of erotogenic pleasures. Within a culture, gender roles, like language, preexist and prefigure individual identities. (Implicitly, of course, Freudian politics relies on Freudian philosophy.) The question of whether Freudian psychoanalysis is an apology for or a critique of patriarchal cultural arrangements cannot be easily answered.[20] Finally, phallocentrism leads to "phallologocentrism," or the assumption that language itself is based on the totemic signifier of the phallus. To the extent that Lacanian psychoanalysis relies on this assumption (and the issue of this reliance is problematic), it can be challenged by the Saussurean linguistic system underlying Lacan's use of signifiers and signifieds. For Saussure, the signifier is arbitrary. If the phallus is then an arbitrary master signifier, no matter how conventionally potent, other master signifiers (and other conventional social or gender arrangements) are possible. Under the sign of the phallus, conventional femininity must be a masquerade. Although anatomy may not be destiny, it can inscribe powerful cultural definition. Feminist challenges to Lacanian linguistics address this complex issue.[21]

Although psychoanalytic approaches to literary texts can thus engender complex questions of psychology, philosophy, politics, and linguistics, a typical objection to psychoanalytic criticism is that it is "reductive." To conclude, for example, that Emily Dickinson's "snake" poem is really about her missing penis surely sounds reductive. But is it? First of all, I would object to the collapsing of my reading into a single sentence. But any reading can be similarly collapsed or reduced. For instance: "The poem is really about failed transcendentalism." Or: "The poem is really about death." Are these reductive assertions? What does it mean to be reductive? Perhaps we can recuperate the term.

It literally means "to lead back," and it shares its etymology with *education*, *deduction*, and *seduction*. Psychoanalytic interpretation leads back through the temporal strata of an individual psyche, but in no simple linear design and with no simple goal to unearth a traumatic origin. As it attempts to trace the paths of an emerging past while observing the revisionist energies of an active present, it follows convoluted and stratified pathways of individual and social development. To shift the metaphor from labyrinth to laboratory, we could say that psychoanalytic *reduction* is an effort to arrange and analyze the constituent elements of a complex organic molecular compound. In brief, it is possible to rescue "reduction" from its connotations of mere degradation or subjugation, just as it is possible to apply the term, with its various connotations, to any style of critical discourse.

Underlying the conventional charge of psychoanalytic reductionism, however, may lie some unspoken assumptions. To object, for instance, that "everything comes down to the body," or that everything comes down to the family, or to infancy, or to sexuality, is initially and implicitly to assume that the body, the family, infancy, and sexuality are somehow unworthy as aesthetic foundations or irrelevant to critical discourse. Some of this discontent may be fueled by uneasiness with talk about the body, and some of it may derive from a questionable assumption that everyone (always) already knows about these matters, and what else is new? Resistance, like understanding, takes many forms. Any criticism that writes about genital difference or privileges "the phallus" as a primary linguistic signifier is going to have to deal with both understanding and resistance, often simultaneously. (Recall your own initial reaction to my reading of "A narrow Fellow.") In terms of its epistemological bases, one could argue that psychoanalysis is ultimately a theory of the body, as it represents itself and is represented in individual and cultural experience. To quote Erik Erikson, who paraphrased Freud, "the ego is anchored in the ground-plan of the body."[22] My reading of Dickinson's poem is a demonstration and elaboration of this thesis.

Finally, what is the *use* of a psychoanalytic reading of a poem? Like any literary critic, the psychoanalytic reader makes choices about the uses to which he or she puts insights. One use of my reading of "A narrow Fellow," for instance, would be to trace the poem to its personal origins: to characterize Dickinson's intense "anxiety of gender" in specific terms, to note her occasional boyish poses, her self-imaginations as both Eve and Satan, her terrific ambivalence toward masculinity and patriarchal custom, her characteristic eroticization of danger as a way of playing with excitement and anxiety. A post-Freudian reader could theorize that Dickinson's identification with a male persona not only answered fantastically her perception of genital deprivation but also relieved her momentarily of "the deadly necessity of growing into a woman" in nineteenth-century Puritan New England.[23] In short, psychoanalysis can press a literary text into a psychobiographical account of its author.[24]

Conversely, Dickinson's intense evocations of moments of psychic epiphany and disturbance can be viewed not as symptoms but as analyses. In this view the poet becomes a psychologist, a student of mental states whose insights vie with Freud's.[25] Her reclusive withdrawal from the world becomes not a neurotic defense but a conscious choice: a strong act of will in a society where female possibility was constrained by debilitating patriarchal practice. Within her chosen confines, Dickinson's inner life was full and fulfilling. For some current readers, Emily Dickinson has become a feminist heroine.[26]

Yet to suggest that her alternatives were either neurotic defense or heroic resolve distorts the realities of psychic and social life as understood by psychoanalysis. For conscious acts of choice are intermingled with unconscious motives of wish and defense. Moreover, *defense* does not necessarily mean *neurotic* but refers to styles of variously successful adaptation in the world. Emily Dickinson's personal and poetic styles were simultaneously defensive and enabling. Confined to her father's house by whatever private needs and social exigencies, she still managed a household, gardened, baked, and wrote. She left a rich poetic legacy, composed in her second-floor bedroom, on a two-by-two writing desk, on hundreds of sheets of small paper. She discovered release within confinement and strove toward larger unities through the discrete disunities of her fragmented poetic form, where isolated phrases depend ambiguously on dashes—or the vacancy of margins—for syntactic control.

Traditional psychoanalytic criticism reaffirms the connection between poem and poet; in the case of Emily Dickinson the personal connection seems essential.[27] Other uses of psychoanalysis in literary interpretation put litera-ture in the service of psychology. "A narrow Fellow" can be read as a symbolic representation of the discovery of sexual difference and the mystery of gender. As an imaginary chronicle of a basic discovery (or the repetition of such discovery), and the onset (or rearousal) of anxiety, it recasts the Freudian concept of penis envy and the translation of loss into imaginative re-presenta-tion. In the difficult terms of Jacques Lacan, it is about "the phallus [as] the privileged signifier of that mark in which the role of the logos is joined with the advent of desire."[28] Lacan's definition of the phallus as "privileged sig-nifier" points to the emergence of language (a "mark," the representation of "logos") from the awareness of absence, or lack, or *want* ("the advent of desire"). We dream, play, speak, or write in order to fulfill a wish, to restore a lost relation to ourselves, to others (present or absent), to the world.

Like Dickinson's ~~snake~~, Lacan's phallic signifier is most powerful when hidden, operating below the surface of meaning and of consciousness. Lacan's *phallus* refers to an object, or a relationship, on the threshold of the imaginary and symbolic registers: something dreamed in the original (maternal) arena and then relegated to desire (instituted by the father). "A narrow Fellow" describes—or attempts to describe—an ungraspable phenomenon: It demon-strates language reaching after a hidden, alienated, yet familiar reality. It is thus an emblem of the largest issues of poetry and representation that current criticism, psychoanalytic and otherwise, explores. In abstract theoretical terms that yet characterize Dickinson's vivid poem, Elizabeth Wright para-phrases Lacan: "Language imposes a chain of words along which the ego must move while the unconscious remains in search of the object it has lost."[29]

Let us return to the dream-poem, "In Winter in my Room." The fascinat-ing, frightening appearance and metamorphosis of the "Worm" causes the poet-dreamer to flee. Like the snake, she "projects" herself to another place. That other place then becomes precisely the scene of *writing*: Her phrase, "I set me down," refers not merely to stasis or posture but to the written record of the subject. The gesture of flight modulates into the gesture of recollection; repression transmutes into revision. Dickinson's dream-poem is thus an abrupt demonstration of the emergence of writing from repression that Jacques Derrida describes in his reading of Freud's theory of composition.[30]

Psychoanalytic readings of literary texts do not proceed along a one-way street. There can be no simple, univocal "application" of psychoanalytic theory to literature, like taking a tool to a poem to discover what makes it tick. The poetry of Emily Dickinson offers rich examples of the intrinsic psychological dimensions of literature: Her investigations of mental phenomena are often as valid and valuable as those of Freud, though in a different style of representation, and at different levels of conscious control. (My own view is that she was at least as much victim as she was heroine. Not simply a lucid mapper of the geography of psychic dislocation, at times she was lost in it.)

On the two-way thoroughfare of psychoanalytic criticism, traffic can be hazardous. It's risky to take a reading out in public these days, especially one so fundamentally Freudian as my analysis of Dickinson's "A narrow Fellow." Some critics, for example, may object to the phallocentricity of my "masculist" interpretation. To the more conventional forms of publication anxiety may now be added the critic's acute awareness of the self-implications of his or her psychological assertions. For instance, after writing the preceding paragraph I noticed, on rereading, the potential sexual symbolisms of my operative metaphor, "taking a tool" to a poem. Not only does my cliché evoke images of violation (of which psychoanalysis has frequently been charged), but it also suggests that I brought into the poem just that (phallic) meaning I then discovered in it. Literary criticism has always been an unacknowledged form of autobiography. When the issues under discussion concern primitive wishes and fears, images of the body, and representations of person and family, a criticism informed by psychoanalysis may find itself self-reflexive: The page shimmers and becomes a mirror.

At this point the literary critic faces her or his own version of reading after Freud: the self-conscious awareness of *transference*.[31] For whom do we write? To whom? What relation to the text we *write*, and the text we write *about*, are we (re)establishing in the moment of composition? Emily Dickinson wrote almost two thousand poems; she allowed only eleven to be published. To whom, for whom, was she writing her "letter to the World" (see *Complete Poems*, poem #441)? For some authors, an imagined audience can be no less compelling than an actual one. For all authors, actual and imagined audiences must merge. To whom do we speak? This is a cardinal question we ask, after Freud. In the acts of reading and writing we construct imagined relations with a text, with an author, with a tradition, with a profession, or with an image of ourselves as writers—relations that emerge from and connect to significant relations in our past. Harold Bloom's concept of necessary "misreading" has its psychoanalytic analogy in the meaningful misidentifications of transference.[32] The critic's task and problem are to *represent a text*, both in its own terms and in his or her own terms. "The critic," writes Murray Schwartz, "is a reader who makes a difference by using himself to represent another."[33] Through this critical effort to re-present an other through the self-conscious use of self, the psychoanalytic critic expresses a primary human desire: the wish for insight and communication. As well as presenting elementary concepts in psychoanalytic theory, I have intended this essay to challenge you to reconsider the necessary yet knotty interrelations of body and language and to frame questions of your own. For psychoanalysis, or psychoanalytic literary criticism, is as much a process of questions as a repository of answers.

Notes

1. See Plato's *Ion*, and *Republic*, Bks. 9–10; and Aristotle's *Poetics*.

2. Currently, the banner of articulate dissent is most grandly displayed by Frederick Crews, in a series of essays now collected in *Skeptical Engagements* (New York: Oxford University Press, 1986).

3. *The Standard Edition of the Complete Psychological Works of Sigmund Freud*, ed. Strachey et al., 24 vols (London: Hogarth Press, 1954–74), 9:147–48. Hereafter cited as *SE*.

4. *The Interpretation of Dreams*, *SE* 5:553.

5. "Fragment of an Analysis of a Case of Hysteria" (1905), *SE* 7:3–123.

6. Lionel Trilling, "Freud and Literature," *The Liberal Imagination* (1950); rpt. in *Freud: A Collection of Critical Essays*, ed. P. Meisel (Englewood Cliffs, N.J.: Prentice-Hall, 1981), pp. 95–111.

7. For an extended discussion of the mythological meanings of snake symbolism, see Philip Slater, "The Serpent and the Oral-Narcissistic Dilemma," in his *The Glory of Hera: Greek Mythology and the Greek Family* (Boston: Beacon, 1968), pp. 80–122.

8. For an explanation of this procedure by a practicing psychoanalyst, see Roy Schafer, "Psychoanalytic Interpretation," *The Analytic Attitude* (New York: Basic Books, 1982), pp. 183–92.

9. For a similar image, from the same period as *Dreams*, see Freud's "Dora" case, *SE* 7:12.

10. My essay on "The Inter-penetration of Dreams," *Diacritics* 9 (1979): 98–110, demonstrates how this merger or interconnection actually occurs in Freud's dream interpretations.

11. *The Complete Poems of Emily Dickinson*, ed. Thomas H. Johnson (Boston: Little Brown, 1960), pp. 682–83 (poem #1670).

12. The first was Clark Griffith; see *The Long Shadow: Emily Dickinson's Tragic Poetry* (Princeton, N.J.: Princeton University Press, 1964), pp. 177–83, 284 ff.

13. Dickinson, *Complete Poems*, pp. 459–60 (poem #986). The poem was published in a Springfield, Massachusetts, newspaper in February 1866, under the editor-imposed title of "The Snake." For representative standard readings, see Charles Anderson, *Emily Dickinson's*

Poetry: Stairway of Surprise (New York: Holt, Rinehart and Winston, 1960), and Greg Johnson, *Emily Dickinson: Perception and the Poet's Quest* (University: University of Alabama Press, 1985), pp. 35–37.

14. A new book on Dickinson's poetry describes her personal relation to the conventional image of the sun as an emblem of masculine potency: see Wendy Barker, *Lunacy of Light: Emily Dickinson and the Experience of Metaphor* (Carbondale: Southern Illinois University Press, 1987). Cynthia Wolff reads the unbraiding whiplash as an implication of male sexuality, "like a bundle of worms": see her new biography, *Emily Dickinson* (New York: Knopf, 1986), p. 490.

15. Dickinson's first editor, a woman, changed "Boy" to "child": see Rebecca Patterson, "Emily Dickinson's 'Double' Tim: Masculine Identification," *American Imago*, 28 (1971): 333.

16. See Vivian Pollak, *Dickinson: The Anxiety of Gender* (Ithaca, N.Y.: Cornell University Press, 1984). It is illuminating to juxtapose this poem—one of Dickinson's best and best known—with her famous personal definition of poetry: "If I feel physically as if the top of my head were taken off, I know *that* is poetry" (reported in a letter by her contemporary, Thomas Higginson; quoted in Thomas Johnson, *The Life of Emily Dickinson*, 2 vols [Cambridge, Mass.: Harvard University Press, 1965], pp. 474–75). Her image correlates orgasmic excitement, violation, and bodily loss, in a nineteenth-century version of a contemporary phrase, "It blows my mind."

17. Pollak, *Dickinson*, p. 118.

18. Wolff, *Emily Dickinson*, pp. 384–85, 489–90.

19. Jim Swan, "*Mater* and Nannie: Freud's Two Mothers and the Discovery of the Oedipus Complex," *American Imago* 31 (1974): 57. For castration as a type of metonymy, see Jacques Lacan, "The Signification of the Phallus" (1958), *Ecrits: A Selection*, trans. Alan Sheridan (New York: Norton, 1977), pp. 281–91.

20. The work of Juliet Mitchell focuses most directly on this point: see her book *Psychoanalysis and Feminism: Freud, Rank, Laing and Women* (New York: Random House, 1974). For a brief overview of feminist critiques of psychoanalysis, see Jacqueline Rose, "Femininity and Its Discontents," *Sexuality and the Field of Vision* (London, 1986), pp. 83, 103. A good introduction to the place of these critiques in current pedagogy is Constance Penley, "Teaching in Your Sleep: Feminism and Psychoanalysis," in *Theory in the Classroom*, ed. Cary Nelson (Urbana: University of Illinois Press, 1986), pp. 129–48.

21. A direct confrontation with psychoanalytic phallocentrism is in Jane Gallop's chapter, "Of Phallic Proportions: Lacanian Conceit," in her *The Daughter's Seduction: Feminism and Psychoanalysis* (Ithaca, N.Y.: Cornell University Press, 1982), pp. 15–32. For the theory behind many of Gallop's conjectures, see Luce Irigaray, "This Sex Which Is Not One" and "When Our Lips Speak Together" (1977), *This Sex Which Is Not One*, trans. Catherine Porter and Carolyn Burke (Ithaca, N.Y.: Cornell University Press, 1985); and "The Blind Spot of an Old Dream of Symmetry" (1974), *Speculum of the Other Woman*, trans. Gillian C. Gill (Ithaca, N.Y.: Cornell University Press, 1985), pp. 13–129.

22. Erik Erikson, *Childhood and Society* (New York: Norton, 1958), p. 50. Freud wrote that "the ego is first and foremost a bodily ego; it is not merely a surface entity, but is itself the projection of a surface" (*The Ego and the Id* [1923], SE, 19:16). The last remark suggests how the ego, indeed psychoanalysis itself, is, like flesh, on the boundary between biology and sociology: mediating between organism and culture.

23. The phrase is Rebecca Patterson's: see "Emily Dickinson's 'Double' Tim," p. 339.

24. Dickinson has been the subject of several full-length psychological studies. The first was *The Long Shadow* by Clark Griffith. Following an earlier suggestion by Anna Wells ("Was Emily Dickinson Psychotic?" *American Imago* 19 [1962]: 309–21), he inferred that the poet was seriously mentally disturbed. He noted the Freudian concept of "penis envy" as a way to signify her relation to herself and masculine values. A decade later, John Cody, a practicing psychiatrist, studied Dickinson's precarious mental life and her damaging relation to her mother: see

After Great Pain: The Inner Life of Emily Dickinson (Cambridge, Mass.: Harvard University Press, 1971). Her boyish poses, ambivalent identifications, and regressive personae are noted by Rebecca Patterson, "Emily Dickinson's 'Double' Tim"; and Margaret Homans, "Emily Dickinson and Poetic Identity," in *Modern Critical Views: Emily Dickinson*, ed. Harold Bloom (New York: Chelsea House, 1985), pp. 128–48. The best overall account of Dickinson's "crisis of sexual identity" is Vivian Pollak's *Dickinson*. Cynthia Griffin Wolff's new biography may become the standard work; it is reasonably well informed by psychoanalytic theories of development, repression, and creativity.

25. Though her judgment of Dickinson's mental stability is complex, Pollak sees the poet as "a brilliant self-clinician" who "anticipates . . . Freud on the relation between defense mechanisms and disease processes" (*Dickinson*, p. 211 n). Adrienne Rich asserts that Dickinson was "a great psychologist": "*the* American poet whose work consisted in exploring states of psychic extremity"; see " 'Vesuvius at Home': The Power of Emily Dickinson," *Parnassus* 5, 1 (1976): 49–74, quotation from p. 67.

26. See Rich, " 'Vesuvius at Home' "; Sandra Gilbert and Susan Gubar, *The Madwoman in the Attic: The Woman Writer and the Nineteenth-Century Imagination* (New Haven: Yale University Press, 1979); Suzanne Juhasz, *The Undiscovered Continent: Emily Dickinson and the Space of the Mind* (Bloomington: Indiana University Press, 1983); and Bloom, Introduction to *Modern Critical Views*, pp. 1–8. Bloom ranks Dickinson with Shakespeare and Freud as unprecedented, strongly original writers: "Her agon," he asserts, "was waged with the whole of [patriarchal] tradition."

27. See Jonathan Morse, "Memory, Desire, and the Need for Biography: The Case of Emily Dickinson," *Georgia Review* 35 (1981).

28. Lacan, "Signification of the Phallus," p. 287. This seminal essay has also been translated by Jacqueline Rose, as "The Meaning of the Phallus," in *Feminine Sexuality: Jacques Lacan and the école freudienne*, ed. Juliet Mitchell and Jacqueline Rose (London: W. W. Norton, 1982), pp. 74–85.

29. Elizabeth Wright, *Psychoanalytic Criticism: Theory in Practice* (London: Methuen, 1984), p. 111.

30. See Jacques Derrida, "Freud and the Scene of Writing" (1967), *Writing and Difference*, trans. Alan Bass (Chicago: University of Chicago Press, 1978). Reprinted in Meisel, *Freud*, pp. 145–82.

31. For helpful discussions of the psychoanalytic concept of transference and its relation to literature, see Schafer, *Analytic Attitude*, and two essays by Murray M. Schwartz: "Where Is Literature?" *College English* 6 (1975): 756–65, and "The Literary Use of Transference," *Psychoanalysis and Contemporary Thought* (New York: International Universities Press, 1981).

32. See Harold Bloom, *A Map of Misreading* (Oxford: Oxford University Press, 1975).

33. Schwartz, "The Literary Use of Transference."

Selected Bibliography

Freud: Primary Sources

Start by reading Freud. A good place to begin is *The Interpretation of Dreams* (1900). This book, to which Freud returned on numerous occasions throughout his career for emendation and elaboration, remains the core text of psychoanalytic textual interpretation. Beyond *Dreams*, I have listed below several important representative texts. Each is cited from the *Standard Edition* but is also available in paperback form, from Collier, Signet, or Avon presses.

"Creative Writers and Day-Dreaming" (1908). *The Standard Edition of the Complete Psychological Works of Sigmund Freud*. Edited by James Strachey et al. 24 vols. London: Hogarth Press, 1954–

74. 9: 143–56. Hereafter cited as *SE*. Freud's central paper on literary creativity. In it he develops analogies among dream, play, and literary composition and makes intriguing suggestions about the sources of aesthetic pleasure. Reprinted in *On Creativity and the Unconscious* (see below).

"Fragment of an Analysis of a Case of Hysteria" (1905) *SE* 7:3–123. The famous "Dora" case. A student should read at least one of Freud's several published case histories: I recommend "Dora," or "The Rat-man," or "The Wolf-man." "Dora" is an early and incomplete case, but it addresses central questions in Freud's theories and relations to women. See the Bernheimer-Kahane casebook cited below in the section "Feminist Revisions of Psychoanalysis."

The Interpretation of Dreams (1900). *SE* 4,5. A preeminent text of twentieth-century literary interpretation, it introduces the Oedipus complex and explains Freud's basic models of the mind.

Introductory Lectures on Psycho-Analysis (1915–16). *SE* 15, 16. These lectures represent Freud's first effort to communicate his ideas publicly. Designed to be delivered to students, they are organized sequentially and logically and trace the development of psychoanalytic theory to 1915. Above all, Freud's unmistakable voice sounds through.

On Creativity and the Unconscious: Papers on the Psychology of Art, Literature, Love, and Religion. Edited by Benjamin Nelson. New York: Harper and Row, 1958. A convenient collection of several of Freud's papers on psychoaesthetics, including "Creative Writers and Day-dreaming," "The Uncanny," "The Theme of the Three Caskets" (on Shakespeare), and "Three Contributions to the Psychology of Love"—all important texts in psychoanalytic criticism.

"Some Psychical Consequences of the Anatomical Distinction between the Sexes" (1925). *SE* 19:243–59. A synthesis of Freud's thinking to this point on crucial matters of bodily and psychic structure.

Three Essays on the Theory of Sexuality (1905). *SE* 7:125–247. Freud's sketch of human development through psychosexual stages, and the residual mental structures generated in such development.

Freud: Secondary Sources

Erikson, Erik. *Childhood and Society*. New York: Norton, 1963. An excellent narrative and demonstration of basic psychoanalytic concepts.
———. "The Dream Specimen of Psychoanalysis" (1954). Rpt. in *Psychoanalytic Psychiatry and Psychology: Clinical and Theoretical Papers*, ed. Robert Knight and Cyrus Friedman, 3:131–70. New York: International Universities Press, 1954. An extensive reinterpretation of Freud's "dream of Irma's injection" from chapter 2 of *The Interpretation of Dreams*. Erikson places the dream in Freud's personal and social history, and provides a wide-ranging framework through which to contextualize psychoanalytic readings.
Gilman, Sander, ed. *Introducing Psychoanalytic Theory*. New York: Brunner-Mazel, 1982. An anthology of essays by theorists and clinicians on contemporary psychoanalytic theory.
Holland, Norman. *The I*. New Haven: Yale University Press, 1985. An ambitious effort to correlate Freudian, post-Freudian, and cognitive psychology in a current theory of the self. Psychoanalytic concepts are well explained.
Klein, George. *Psychoanalytic Theory: An Exploration of Essentials*. New York: International Universities Press, 1976. A handbook of psychoanalytic theory by a lucid interpreter.
Lacan, Jacques. "The Agency of the Letter in the Unconscious or Reason since Freud." *Ecrits*, trans. Alan Sheridan, pp. 146–78. New York: Norton, 1977.
———. "The Signification of the Phallus." *Ecrits*, pp. 281–91. This essay and the one cited

above, along with Lacan's famous meditation on the mirror ("The mirror stage . . . "), are good places to begin an encounter with this provocative writer.

Lemaire, Anika. *Jacques Lacan* (1970). Translated by David Macey. London: Routledge and Kegan Paul, 1977. A good introduction and explication of basic Lacanian ideas.

Miner, Marion [Joanna Field]. *On Not Being Able to Paint*. London: Heinemann, 1950. An excellent personal account of the relation of art to self, and the emergence of individual style in aesthetic expression.

Schafer, Roy. *The Analytic Attitude*. New York: Basic Books, 1982. A collection of essays by a practicing analyst, many of which pertain directly to literary experience.

Silverman, Kaja. *The Subject of Semiotics*. New York: Oxford University Press, 1985. An intelligent review and critique of many fundamental concepts underlying various styles of Freudian and post-Freudian psychoanalysis.

Winnicott, D. W. *Playing and Reality*. New York: Methuen, 1971. A valuable introduction to basic concepts in post-Freudian "object-relations" psychology, with immediate applications to aesthetic creation and response.

Wollheim, Richard. *Freud*. New York: Viking Press, 1971. Among the best of the brief introductions to Freud and Freudian theory.

Feminist Revisions of Psychoanalysis

Bernheimer, Charles, and Claire Kahane, eds. *In Dora's Case: Freud-Hysteria-Feminism*. New York: Columbia University Press, 1985. An anthology of contemporary essays on this fascinating and problematic case.

Chodorow, Nancy. *The Reproduction of Mothering: Psychoanalysis and the Sociology of Gender*. Berkeley: University of California Press, 1978. An important sociological revision of psychoanalytic developmental theory.

Irigaray, Luce. "Psychoanalytic Theory: Another Look." *This Sex Which Is Not One* (1977). Translated by Catherine Porter and Carolyn Burke. Ithaca, N.Y.: Cornell University Press, 1985. This essay, originally published in a French medical encyclopedia in 1973, just before Irigaray's major work, *Speculum of Another Woman* (1974), is a more accessible introduction to the themes of that work—fundamentally a critique of Freudian and Lacanian phallocentrism, and an effort to reconstitute a feminine order of representation.

Kolodny, Annette. "A Map for Re-reading; or, Gender and the Interpretation of Literary Texts." In *The (M)Other Tongue: Essays in Feminist Psychoanalytic Interpretation*, ed. Shirley Nelson Garner, Claire Kahane, and Madelon Sprengnether. Ithaca, N.Y.: Cornell University Press, 1985. Though not strictly psychoanalytic, a fine introduction to the issues; the entire volume raises important questions about past and current critical practice.

Kristeva, Julia. *Desire in Language: A Semiotic Approach to Literature and Art*. Edited by L. Roudiez. New York: Columbia University Press, 1980.

———. *The Kristeva Reader*. Edited by T. Moi. New York: Columbia University Press, 1986. As a feminist theoretician and practicing psychoanalyst, Kristeva's ideas are consistently challenging. Her work intersects several current loci of contemporary criticism, including psychoanalysis. Her style can be difficult.

Strouse, Jean, ed. *Women and Analysis: Dialogues on Psychoanalytic Views of Femininity*. New York: Dell, 1974. A good location for the continuing conversation of psychoanalysis and feminism.

Psychoanalytic Literary Criticism

Felman, Shoshana. *Jacques Lacan and the Adventure of Insight: Psychoanalysis in Contemporary Culture*. Cambridge, Mass.: Harvard University Press, 1987. A collection of essays primarily on literary texts, this volume is also a perceptive introduction to the ways in which Lacanian theory has redirected current critical attention.

Holland, Norman. *The Dynamics of Literary Response*. New York: Norton, 1968. This book and Lesser's *Fiction and the Unconscious* remain central statements of the psychoanalytic study of literary process.

————. "Literary Interpretation and the Three Phases of Psychoanalysis." *Critical Inquiry* 3 (1976): 221–33. A sketch of major shifts in psychoanalysis and psychoanalytic criticism since Freud.

Lesser, Simon. *Fiction and the Unconscious*. Chicago: University of Chicago Press, 1957.

Schwartz, Murray M., and David Willbern, "Literature and Psychology." In *Interrelations of Literature*, ed. Jean-Pierre Barricelli and Joseph Gibaldi, pp. 205–24. New York: Modern Language Assn., 1982. An overview of major concepts in psychoanalytic theory and representative critical applications.

Skura, Meredith. *The Literary Use of the Psychoanalytic Process*. New Haven: Yale University Press, 1981.

Wright, Elizabeth. *Psychoanalytic Criticism: Theory in Practice*. London: Methuen, 1984. Of several recent works in the field, Skura's and Wright's are among the best. Each offers a different organizational mode and perspective. Skura designs her book around five basic analogical models: the literary text as case history, as fantasy, as dream, as transference, and as psychoanalytic process. Wright's design is more conventional and very thorough. She traces the development of psychoanalytic thought from classic Freudian "id psychology" to "ego psychology," to "object-relations," to the structural psychoanalysis (based on Saussurean linguistics) of Lacan, to the poststructural psychoanalysis of Derrida and Bloom.

Anthologies, Bibliographies, Dictionaries

Keill, Norman. *Psychoanalysis, Psychology, and Literature: A Bibliography*. 2 vols. Metuchen, N.J.: Scarecrow, 1982. An extensive storehouse of specific references to psychoanalytic interpretations of authors and texts, primarily from 1900 to 1980.

Kurzweil, Edith, and William Phillips, eds. *Literature and Psychoanalysis*. New York: Columbia University Press, 1983. A revised version of an earlier anthology, this remains an excellent introduction to the varieties and values of psychoanalytic criticism.

Laplanche, J., and J.-B Pontalis. *The Language of Psycho-Analysis* (1967). Translated by Donald Nicholson-Smith. New York: Norton, 1973. See also Charles Rycroft, *A Critical Dictionary of Psychoanalysis*. New York: Basic Books, 1968. These are two very useful glosses on the psychoanalytic vocabulary. Laplanche and Pontalis, *Language*, is now the standard explication, providing an annotated history of core terms in Freudian and post-Freudian usage. Rycroft's *Dictionary* is less extensive and scholarly than *Language*, yet it distills essential theoretical terms and concepts in a slim volume.

Meisel, Perry, ed. *Freud: A Collection of Critical Essays*. Englewood Cliffs, N.J.: Prentice-Hall, 1981. See also Joseph Smith and William Kerrigan, eds. *The Literary Freud: Mechanisms of Defense and the Poetic Will*. vol. 4, *Psychiatry and the Humanities*. New Haven: Yale University Press, 1980. These are two excellent collections of essays on psychoanalysis and its literary uses. Meisel's *Freud* contains germinal essays by Kenneth Burke, Lionel Trilling, and other modern writers. The Smith and Kerrigan volume contains current essays by contemporary critics.

CHERYL B. TORSNEY

The Critical Quilt: Alternative Authority in Feminist Criticism

> You can't talk about *a* female sexuality, uniform, homogeneous, classifiable into codes—any more than you can talk about one unconscious resembling another. Women's imaginary is inexhaustible, like music, painting, writing: their stream of phantasms is incredible.
>
> Hélène Cixous, "The Laugh of the Medusa"

Just as we cannot reasonably discuss a single female sexuality, neither can we discuss *a* feminist literary criticism. Although the underlying impetus for the various "schools" may be similar—to recognize and valorize the female experience in reading, writing, and responding—the permutations are various, making the feminist critical field resemble a pieced quilt. Behind the top is the batting, that which gives the quilt its utilitarian substance, the insulating material that each piece of the top shares in common with each other piece: the conviction that one can read, write, and interpret as a woman. The pieced top, however, is that which presents the alternatives. The blocks may vary as to pattern or fabric, in structure and texture. Not every block need be stitched by a woman, nor are contiguous blocks necessarily complementary. Yet even in its theoretical difference, each block is stitched to sister blocks. They share and make a space, creating the feminist critical quilt, offering myriad alternatives to androcentric criticism. So, instead of the metaphor, for example, of the well-wrought urn in which each element reinforces the value of the single artifact, feminist criticism offers us a critical quilt of plurality, strong and varied, pieced in community. As Annette

Kolodny states, "Only by employing a plurality of methods will we protect ourselves from the temptation of . . . oversimplifying any text."[1]

To understand the nature of this feminist critical quilt and its alternative authority, we must first understand its history. Feminist literary criticism is traceable to the revitalization of the woman's movement during the late 1960s, when bra burnings and freedom yearnings were ignited by the likes of Betty Friedan, Gloria Steinem, and Germaine Greer. In this acutely political climate, feminist literary criticism, whose goal was to reveal "the misogyny of literary practice," was born.[2] Although, as Elaine Showalter notes, "There is no Mother of Feminist Criticism," critics like Simone de Beauvoir, Mary Ellman, and Kate Millett were among the first to reveal that throughout literary history women have been conceived of as "other," as somehow abnormal or deviant.[3] As a result, female literary characters have been stereotyped as bitches, sex goddesses, old maids. For the first time in history, criticism posited a female reader for whom stereotypes of womanhood were offensive. And for the first time criticism recognized that women, as both readers and writers, had been excluded from literary history. Elaine Showalter calls this early political criticism, which focuses on female readers and their responses, the "feminist critique," a historically grounded inquiry focusing on "images and stereotypes of women in literature, the omissions and misconceptions about women in criticism, and woman-assign [*sic*] in semiotic systems."[4]

The apotheosis of this politically grounded feminist criticism is Judith Fetterley's influential *Resisting Reader*, a text that the author claims is more than a piece of criticism or an academic exercise. Quoting Adrienne Rich, she asserts: "it is an act of survival."[5] In her study Fetterley indicts many "classics" of American writing, components of any introductory or advanced course in literature, among them "Rip Van Winkle," "A Rose for Emily," *A Farewell to Arms*, *The Great Gatsby*, and *The Bostonians*, for seducing women readers into collaborating with male writers and, in so doing, reading woman as enemy and identifying "against herself."[6] For example, Fetterley's reading of "Rip Van Winkle" demonstrates that the female reader is excluded from the experience of the story: from the drinking and political chatter at the inn, from the hunting in the woods, from the male camaraderie of sport and drink. Dame Van Winkle "is made a masculine authority figure and damned for it."[7] A woman reading "Rip Van Winkle" is coerced into identifying with Rip instead of with his wife, who stands for community, family, work—the values on which postrevolutionary society flourished.

Fetterley also attacks phallocentric readings of Faulkner's "Rose for Emily," which suggest that the story allegorizes the conflicts between the North and the South or old and new orders. It is, she argues, "a story of the patriarchy North and South, new and old, and of the sexual conflict within it."[8] In Fetterley's reading, Miss Emily is not the grotesque; rather, the grotesque is the disparity between the cultural myth of the "lady" and the cultural reality "of the severely limited nature of the power women can wrest from the system that oppresses them."[9]

Once the feminist literary critics had precedents, for reading as women rather than as men, they directed their interest to woman as producer of literary artifacts.[10] In style and tone feminist criticism moved from being overtly political to being essentially literary. The focus of this second-stage feminist literary criticism shifts from hypothesizing a female reader to accepting a woman reader as a donnée "to provide leverage for displacing the dominant male critical vision and revealing its misprisions."[11] In describing this critical trend, Jonathan Culler turns to Jane Tompkins's "Sentimental Power: *Uncle Tom's Cabin* and the Politics of Literary History," which rescues Stowe's novel from the ranks of despised sentimental novels by rereading it as a retelling of "the culture's central myth—the story of the crucifixion—in terms of the nation's greatest political conflict—slavery—and of its most cherished social beliefs—the sanctity of motherhood and family."[12] During this period interest in genres formerly dismissed as subliterary was encouraged, resulting in such works as Cheryl Walker's *Nightingale's Burden*, a study of American women's poetry of the nineteenth century, much of which appeared in magazines and gift books, and Nina Baym's *Women's Fiction: A Guide to Novels by and about Women in America, 1820–1870*, a study of the domestic novel.[13]

This new ability to escape the limitations imposed by male readings encouraged feminist critics to rediscover an entire women's literature "whose historical and thematic coherence, as well as artistic importance, has been obscured by the patriarchal values that dominate our culture."[14] Feminist criticism challenged the canon by writing women's literary history in texts such as Patricia Meyer Spacks, *The Female Imagination* (1975); Ellen Moers, *Literary Women* (1976); Elaine Showalter, *A Literature of Their Own* (1977); and Sandra M. Gilbert and Susan Gubar, *The Madwoman in the Attic* (1979).[15] These works deal with the concept of a female aesthetic—in all of its colors, ages, nationalities, and sexual preferences.

During this stage critics began to wonder why "*Huckleberry Finn* had produced a veritable Mark Twain industry, while *The Awakening* had left Kate Chopin without either a standard edition or a definitive, scholarly biography until Per Seyersted's *Kate Chopin* appeared in 1969."[16] Thus a full-scale effort to recover women's texts, like *The Yellow Wallpaper* by Charlotte Perkins Gilman, *Life in the Iron Mills* by Rebecca Harding Davis, and *Their Eyes Were Watching God* by Zora Neale Hurston, was initiated. These rediscovered and consequently reprinted works made their way into course syllabi, fighting for and gaining places in the canon. [17] At this time new and serious attention began to be paid minority literature by black, working-class, lesbian, and native American women, and women of Spanish, Italian, Jewish, and Italian extraction. Women writers began to perceive their places in women's literary history and to trace their family trees. Alice Walker's *In Search of Our Mothers' Gardens*, which contains her important essay "Looking for Zora," and Wendy Martin's *American Tryptich*, which examines the relationships among the poetry of Anne Bradstreet, Emily Dickinson, and Adrienne Rich, were written to situate contemporary writers in a distinctly feminist or, for Walker, "womanist" tradition. [18]

If the second historical trend in feminist literary criticism can be said to describe "a literature of our own," the aim of the most recent stage is to propose "a criticism of our own," a project that entails a "radical rethinking of the conceptual grounds of literary study." [19] In Elaine Showalter's scheme, the rediscovery of a women's literary tradition overlaps the most recent trend, an interdisciplinary investigation of various gender issues through a new, gender-filtered lens. She calls this newest variety of criticism, one more self-contained and experimental than the first, gynocriticism, a type of criticism that treats the psychology of female creativity, linguistics, female language, and women's literary history. [20] Showalter summarizes: "The program of gynocritics is to construct a female framework for the analysis of women's literature, to develop new models based on the study of female experience, rather than to adapt male models and theories." [21] Jonathan Culler describes the current trend in feminist literary criticism in similar terms, saying that the test of this recent criticism is to deconstruct our culture's automatic privileging of male over female, rational over emotional, serious over frivolous, or reflective over spontaneous. [22]

This most recent feminist literary criticism remains, like its predecessors, political in tone, yet it has integrated feminist critiques from other disciplines to vary the patterns established by the earlier trends. [23] In America the newest feminist literary criticism has, for the most part, continued to be practical. Literary critics have used the new feminist readings of the world—of history, linguistics, psychology—to read texts and to write the histories of feminist literary criticism. In France, for the most part, criticism has become theoretical and polemical though American critics have jumped to add swatches of this French critique to their own critical scrap bags for practical use. The newest trends are interdisciplinary, findings in one discipline being applied in others, multiplying and varying the patterns available in the critical quilt.

Critics like Elaine Showalter, for example, have seized upon research undertaken by anthropologists to provide metaphors and paradigms for women's writing. Showalter draws upon the work of Shirley and Edward Ardner, Oxford anthropologists, whose study of the Bakweri culture of Cameroon offers an alternative to the Victorian paradigm of complementary spheres, where women's lives in the home complement rather than infringe upon their husbands' lives in the workplace. In this new model, women experience the dominant culture, even that part of it off-limits to them through their familiarity with myth and legend, but men cannot partake of the "wild zone" of the "muted" women's culture. Showalter uses the Ardners' research to explain the sociohistorical position of women's writing.[24]

Revisionist historians, as well as anthropologists, have contributed to the multipatterning of the feminist literary quilt by identifying and describing particular women's cultures, research that has proved invaluable for recovering and studying "lost" women's writing, such as letters, diaries, and domestic fiction. In *The Bonds of Womanhood*, for example, Nancy Cott studies women's culture in New England from 1780 to 1835 because it offers a limited though, she senses, a universal test case, for it produced a profusion of documents: diaries, memoirs, and letters, all of which bore testimony to the beliefs and daily habits of women.[25] Similarly, Carroll Smith-Rosenberg, through an investigation of letters and diaries of American women written in the nineteenth century, has shown that "a female world of varied and yet highly structured relationships appears to have been an essential aspect of American society."[26] Men were all but absent from this female world, where intense relationships among women provided them with much emotional sustenance throughout their lives. Research by historians like Cott and Smith-Rosenberg has been widely used by feminist literary critics, for example, by Mary Kelley in *Private Woman, Public Stage*, to describe specific characteristics of women's writing.[27] Feminist revisions of history have also been employed in new treatments of the lives of women writers: For instance, Sharon O'Brien, in her award-winning essay " 'The Thing Not Named': Willa Cather as a Lesbian Writer," cites, among others, Cott and Smith-Rosenberg to evidence the world of single-sex relationships inhabited by Cather and Sarah Orne Jewett.[28]

The development of practical feminist literary criticism has been perhaps most significantly influenced by the work done in psychology by Nancy

Chodorow and Carol Gilligan, who have challenged traditional Freudian thought. Reconsidering Freud's theories in feminist terms, Gilligan outlines how a problem in Freudian theory "became cast as a problem in women's development."[29] Freud argues, she observes, that because of a girl's anatomical inability to experience castration anxiety, and thus the drive to resolve her Oedipus complex, a woman develops abnormally.[30] According to Freud, women "show less sense of justice" and are less rational than men because their responses are influenced by the emotions.[31] For Gilligan and Chodorow, gender identification is a product of the social environment, specifically of a mother's nurturing style, rather than an inborn response. Both psychologists contend that as a result of mothers' encouraging their daughters to identify with them and discouraging their sons from identifying with feminine qualities, girls grow up to value nurturing and affiliation and boys to devalue these same traits in preparation for their lives as men. Because of their identification with their mothers, girls' ego boundaries are flexible and less defensive than boys'.[32]

This Freudian revision has been incredibly influential in literary circles, spawning much solid practical literary criticism. As Judith Kegan Gardiner notes, Gilligan's theory is well suited to practical use by contemporary feminist criticism since it "describes female morality as narrative and contextual, and novels obviously provide an admirable ground on which to construct systems that are narrative and contextual."[33] Elizabeth Ammons, for example, cites Gilligan's image of the web as representative of women's epistemology (as opposed to hierarchy, a linear, progressive image, representing man's) to argue that Sarah Orne Jewett's *Country of the Pointed Firs* is not "plotless" as androcentric critics have argued; rather, the novel is "webbed, net-worked. Instead of being linear, it is nuclear: the narrative moves out from one base to a given point and back again, out to another point, and back again, out again, back again, and so forth, like arteries on a spider's web."[34] Similarly, Jean Wyatt, in her discussion of *Jane Eyre*, explains the reader's response to the heroine's joy at her marriage as Jane's "recovery of the bliss, comfort, and unity of that initial boundary-free connection with another," that other being the mother.[35] To ground her argument, Wyatt cites Chodorow's discussion of the symbiotic mother–daughter relationship, which endures throughout life since mothers frequently see daughters as extensions of themselves. As final examples of the practical use of these new psychological paradigms, we can cite N. Katherine Hayles's use of Gilligan's theory in "Anger in Different Voices: Carol Gilligan and *The Mill on the Floss*," in which the critic compares "Gilligan's narrative strategies with those at work in

another narrative about mutual misunderstanding, conflict, and reconciliation, George Eliot's *The Mill on the Floss*"; and Shirley Nelson Garner's
Chodorovian thesis in " 'Women Together' in Virginia Woolf's *Night and
Day*," that "Woolf's novel encodes [the] perception . . . that women, because
they have been mothered by women in infancy, retain primary emotional
bonds with each other even though their adult sexual orientation may be
toward men."[36]

In addition to writing practical criticism using interdisciplinary evidence, American critics have also recently been engaged in writing metacriti-
cism. Their attempt to historicize feminist critical theory has helped to effect
the institutionalization of the feminist critical quilt.[37]

Among these critics is Jonathan Culler, who calls feminist criticism "the
name that should be applied to all criticism alert to the critical ramifications
of sexual oppression, just as in politics 'women's issues' is the name now
applied to many fundamental questions of personal freedom and social justice."[38] He divides the history of feminist criticism into three modes or
moments:

> In the first moment or mode, where woman's experience is treated as a firm ground for
> interpretation, one swiftly discovers that this experience is not the sequence of
> thoughts present to the reader's consciousness as she moves through the text but a
> reading or interpretation of "woman's experience"—her own and others'—which can
> be set in a vital and productive relation to the text. In the second mode, the problem is
> how to make it possible to read as a woman: the possibility of this fundamental
> experience induces an attempt to produce it. In the third mode, the appeal to
> experience is veiled but still there, as a reference to maternal rather than paternal
> relations or to woman's situation and experience of marginality, which may give rise
> to an altered mode of reading. The appeal to the experience of the reader provides
> leverage for displacing or undoing the system of concepts or procedures of male
> criticism, but "experience" always has this divided, duplicitous character: it has
> always already occurred and yet is still to be produced—an indispensable point of
> reference, yet never simply there.[39]

"Feminist Criticism in the Wilderness," Elaine Showalter's influential essay,
provides another model of feminist literary history. Obligatory reading for
anyone seeking to understand the nature of women's writing, the essay
delineates four models explaining the difference between men's and women's
writing: biological, linguistic, psychoanalytic, and cultural. Showalter herself proposes the cultural field as the most encompassing and meaningful of
the locations of difference.[40]

One of the most succinct and helpful introductions to the bibliography
and history of feminist literary criticism can be found in the *Classroom Guide*

accompanying the groundbreaking and controversial *Norton Anthology of Literature by Women* by Sandra M. Gilbert and Susan Gubar.[41] Their conception of the development of the feminist literary critique comprises the stages of critique, recovery reconceptualization, and reassessment, in both feminist history as a whole and the history of feminist literary criticism in particular.

Throughout the history of feminist literary criticism the Anglo-American tendency, Showalter notes, has been to concentrate on women's experience as readers and writers, whereas in France the critical tendency has been more theoretical, centered, as it is, on psychoanalytic revisionism.[42] Among the most prominent of the most recent critics are Hélène Cixous and Luce Irigaray, both former students of Jacques Lacan, who attack language itself as phallocentric, as representing the word of the father and thus inappropriate for use by women.[43] Cixous is best known for her manifesto "The Laugh of the Medusa," which describes "l'écriture feminine" as "both the means and the product of releasing the libido repressed by a masculine economy that represents woman only as lack, as the castrated, deficient mirror of man."[44] It is only through writing, a subversive activity for women, that they may inscribe their femininity as "the very possibility of change."[45] In their writing, she argues, women create "the space that can serve as a springboard for subversive thought, the precursory movement of a transformation of social and cultural structures."[46] Cixous warns, however, that

it is impossible to *define* a feminine practice of writing . . . for this practice can never be theorized, enclosed, coded. . . . it will always surpass the discourse that regulates the phallocentric system; it does and will take place in areas other than those subordinated to philosophic-theoretical domination. It will be conceived of only by subjects who are breakers of automatisms, by peripheral figures that no authority can ever subjugate.[47]

In "The Laugh," Cixous heralds the arrival of a New Woman, who, as opposed to the woman "still impressed by the commotion of the phallic stance," "will not fear any risk, any desire, any space still unexplored in themselves, among themselves and others or anywhere else."[48]

Luce Irigaray practices *l'écriture feminine* in order to reread Freud. Her effort is neither to supplant the phallus with the clitoris nor even to assign to woman any symbolic representation at all, since any such representation must take place within a phallocentric universe. Rather, she is interested in "disrupting and modifying"[49] the phallocratic order, which sees women as commodities, as the medium of exchange, in a male economy: "Women are marked phallically by their fathers, husbands, procurers. And this branding determines their value in sexual commerce. Woman is never anything but the locus of a more or less competitive exchange between two men, including the competition for the possession of mother earth."[50] All of Freudian theory is suspect, she maintains, since it may not even be possible "to pursue a limited discussion of female sexuality so long as the status of woman in the general economy of the West has never been established."[51] In *Speculum of the Other Woman*, Irigaray deconstructs Freud in detail from a feminist perspective, subverting concepts such as penis envy ("For the 'penis-envy' alleged against woman is—let us repeat—a remedy for man's fear of losing one"), the Oedipus complex ("The desire of Oedipus has misunderstood, repressed, and censored, the libidinal attachment between the growing girl and her mother"), and the ego ("Women's 'ego' . . . is largely 'unconscious' and subject to the 'conscience' of fathers, men-fathers, which functions as her super-ego").[52] In her own descriptions of women, Irigaray employs images of fluids and caves— images of intangibility and emptiness. These analogies "resist definition, and are therefore less subject to phallocentric reappropriation"—in other words, to recuperation and definition by masculine language, according to Elizabeth L. Berg.[53]

Although considered more theoretical than practical, French feminist criticism has been employed effectively by American critics for practical purposes. For example, two recent discussions of Charlotte Perkins Gilman's "Yellow Wallpaper" appeal to the notion of *l'écriture féminine*. In her argument Janice Haney-Peritz recognizes that the mad narrator's discourse resembles that of her husband, and that realization drives the reader to ask Irigaray's first question: " '[H]ow can women analyze their exploitation, [and] inscribe their claims' within an order prescribed by the masculine?" In response the woman can resubmit herself to a masculine logic and in so doing make "visible . . . what should have remained hidden: the recovery of a possible operation of the feminine in language." In Gilman's fiction, Haney-Peritz proposes, such an uncanny effect is manifest.[54] In a second recent essay, Paula A. Treichler uses Irigaray's notion that because women must function in the father's symbolic system, language, they live under a death sentence. Treichler explains that in Gilman's story the reader recognizes that the narrator lives under the terms of a "death sentence" since "she is constituted and defined within the patriarchal order of language and destined . . . to repeat her father's discourse 'without much understanding' " until she recognizes the subversive feminist discourse of the yellow wallpaper.[55]

As Stevens's jar alters surrounding Tennessee landscape, so the feminist critical quilt has forever changed the pattern of critical inquiry. The tenets of the criticism, frequently alluding to research in fields other than literature, have produced radically new readings of texts written by men as well as those written by women. We have already considered Fetterley's landmark study, *The Resisting Reader*, whose clear, convincing readings are at work in many classrooms. For other extended examples, let us consider first the case of Shakespeare, second that of Emily Dickinson, and third that of Kate Chopin. The first two cases offer examples of the different textures feminist criticism now offers, and the last suggests how interpretations of one work already reflect the changes undergone by feminist literary criticism.

Feminist psychoanalytic critic Madelon Gohlke finds in Shakespeare structures of male dominance and fear of feminine betrayal. This she calls "a matriarchal substratum or subtext within the patriarchal text."[56] Coppélia Kahn adopts this theory of "maternal subtexts in patriarchal literature" in her discussion of Shakespearean tragedy. Though this method does not present a female perspective, she admits, it does demonstrate that male readings of female characters "must be based on infantile fantasies of what they once were."[57] She notes the advantage of such feminist interpretation as follows:

To read Shakespearean tragedy or any other patriarchal literature as the account of specifically masculine dilemmas of self-definition, it might seem, is to privilege male experience and allow its voice to speak for women as well, accepting just those assumptions which we as feminists are at pains to challenge. The crucial difference, however, between the feminist reader in pursuit of the maternal subtext and Maynard Mack or A. C. Bradley is that they take it for granted that the male experience portrayed in Shakespearean tragedy is universal, while the feminist reader consciously notes the gender perspective of this genre, and tries to learn from it about the working myths of patriarchal culture.[58]

To exemplify her approach, Kahn presents a reading of the maternal subtext of *King Lear*. The play, Kahn contends, revolves around a man whose attempt to exercise patriarchal authority fails; "his reaction to the failure of this attempt reveals the hidden presence of the mother in his psyche, in the shape of a repressed identification with her."[59] As support for this assertion, Kahn cites the mother–child relationship Lear searches for with his daughters and remarks his designation of his passion as "hysteria," then thought a disease of the womb and so limited to women. The sin of Lear's daughters is not only their refusal to mother him but also their turning the formerly powerful patriarchal figure into a woman.

Strategies for studying women writers long in the canon have also taken radical turns as a consequence of feminist theory. Consider, for example, Emily Dickinson. Long read as a charming spinster, the weird Belle of Amherst, who wrote "nice" though often morbid poems, Emily had a particular penchant for punctuation to match her eccentric personality. The Dickinson myth made any serious treatment of her poetry difficult. Moreover, reliance on the truth of the myth split Dickinson studies, according to Suzanne Juhasz, into two disparate camps: the critics who chose to see Dickinson as a woman and those who preferred to read her as a poet.[60] Feminist criticism, first and most important, demonstrates that Dickinson is a woman poet, that her writing clearly reflects her gender, as Juhasz contends. Other scholars in Juhasz's collection also reconsider Dickinson from a feminist perspective: Karl Keller's essay treats Dickinson within the context of American puritanism; Sandra Gilbert's essay considers the roles the poet wrote for herself (e.g., The Woman in White, The Belle of Amherst). Barbara Mossberg also rereads Dickinson's biography from a feminist perspective. Joanne Dobson and Adalaide Morris deal with imagery in the poetry, and Margaret Homans, Christanne Miller, and Joanne Feit Diehl consider Dickinson's language. Juhasz's collection thus offers a fine introduction to a variety of feminist critical approaches to a canonical woman writer.

As feminist critical theory gained converts, texts written by women have been increasingly represented in otherwise traditional course syllabi. One of the most successful narratives resurrected by women's studies has been Kate Chopin's *Awakening*, a novel that provides an instructive example of the history of feminist critical theory. When first rediscovered, the novel was read as an exposé of a young woman's heroic though tragic triumph over her husband and patriarchal society in her fight for personal independence.[61] Understood as a manifesto favoring sexual freedom, the novel sounded sympathetic chords with readers in the late sixties and early seventies. More recently, with theories of women's communities gaining in currency, readers have begun to read Edna as developing her sense of self not in relation to her sexual adventures with Robert Lebrun and Alcée Arobin but rather in relation to a circle of women composed of Adèle Ratignolle and Mademoiselle Reisz.[62] Other recent readings have taken other tacks entirely. For example, Sandra Gilbert chooses to read the novel as a reworking of the myth of Aphrodite.[63] Although obscure until the late sixties, *The Awakening* is now stocked in most college bookstores, is included in the traditional anthologies of American literature, and is taught in classes focusing on American literary history.

In addition to offering challenging new readings of texts for classroom use, feminist literary criticism has also suggested new paradigms and metaphors to complement theory and promote practice. The metaphor of quilting, for example, has presented itself as amazingly apt.

As a way of remaining communally bound and supported, quilting neatly responds to Chodorow's and Gilligan's readings of the female experience of maturation. It is not surprising, then, that quilting and quilts appear so frequently in women's writing—in letters, essays, poetry, fiction—from the eighteenth century in the correspondence of colonists to today in the fiction, for example, of Alice Walker or in the poetry of Joyce Carol Oates, Marge Piercy, and Marilyn Nelson Waniek.[64] Frequently quilting, especially the activity of piecing and the narrative content of the finished pieced quilt—the story behind each piece of fabric—serves as a theme in women's writing; however, some critics also see it as a metaphor for composition. Women, for example, were more likely to write shorter works, like regional stories and poems, essays and letters, than long novels. The poems and stories—the pieces—were often collected into gift books, the quilts. Elaine Showalter, for one, has described the art of Sarah Orne Jewett's and Mary Wilkins Freeman's regional stories as having a quilted composition.[65] In Jewett's case, the stories are the pieces and the collection, *The Country of the Pointed Firs*, the quilt.

Multipatterned and multicolored, stitched by women and men from various racial and national cultures with various critical predispositions, the feminist critical practice forms a sort of critical quilt, an alternative to the critical methods of the past. Moreover, like a pieced quilt, feminist literary criticism is clearly meant for everyday use, in readings of all genres in all periods. Feminist literary criticism is now institutionalized with courses, textbooks, and MLA sessions; literary students should become comfortable with its patterns and textures, adding it to their critical repertoire rather than struggling to kick it off.

Notes

1. Annette Kolodny, "Dancing through the Minefield," in *The New Feminist Criticism*, ed. Elaine Showalter (New York: Pantheon Books, 1985), p. 161.

2. Showalter, Introduction, *New Feminist Criticism*, p. 5.

3. Elaine Showalter, "Women's Time, Women's Space: Writing the History of Feminist Criticism," *Tulsa Studies in Women's Literature* 3, 1–2 (Spring/Fall 1984): 29. See also Simone de Beauvoir, *The Second Sex*, which popularized the notion of woman as "other"; Ellman's *Thinking about Women*; and Millett's *Sexual Politics*.

4. Showalter, "Feminist Criticism in the Wilderness," *New Feminist Criticism*, p. 245.

5. Judith Fetterley, *The Resisting Reader: A Feminist Approach to American Fiction* (Bloomington: Indiana University Press, 1978), p. viii.

6. Ibid., p. xii.

7. Ibid., p. 10.

8. Ibid., pp. 34–35.

9. Ibid., p. 45, 44.

10. For the purpose of this essay I have made feminist literary criticism appear as though it has had a linear development, a pattern that flies in the face of feminist theories of how

women experience time. I am aware that the historical trends I identify are oversimplified, the distinctions among them blurred.

11. Jonathan Culler, *On Deconstruction: Theory and Criticism after Structuralism* (Ithaca, N.Y.: Cornell University Press, 1982), p. 57.

12. Ibid., pp. 56–57, citing Jane Tompkins, "Sentimental Power: *Uncle Tom's Cabin* and the Politics of Literary History," *Glyph* 8 (1981): 89. In later reprintings of the essay, however, Tompkins modifies her assertion to read that the novel retells "the culture's central *religious* myth" (italics added).

13. Cheryl Walker, *The Nightingale's Burden: Women Poets and American Culture before 1900* (Bloomington: Indiana University Press, 1982); Nina Baym, *Women's Fiction: A Guide to Novels by and about Women in America, 1820–1870* (Ithaca, N.Y.: Cornell University Press, 1978).

14. Showalter, Introduction, *New Feminist Criticism*, p. 6.

15. Patricia Meyer Spacks, *The Female Imagination* (New York: Knopf, 1975); Ellen Moers, *Literary Women: The Great Writers* (1976; rpt., Oxford: Oxford University Press, 1985); Elaine Showalter, *A Literature of Their Own: British Women Novelists from Brontë to Lessing* (Princeton, N.J.: Princeton University Press, 1977); Sandra M. Gilbert and Susan Gubar, *The Madwoman in the Attic: The Woman Writer and the Nineteenth-Century Imagination* (New Haven: Yale University Press, 1979).

16. Sandra M. Gilbert and Susan Gubar, *A Classroom Guide to Accompany the Norton Anthology of Literature by Women* (New York: Norton, 1985), p. 8.

17. Charlotte Perkins Gilman, *The Yellow Wallpaper* (Old Westbury, N.Y.: Feminist Press, 1973). The effort to reissue long-out-of-print works by women continues, most notably by the Feminist Press, Beacon Press, Rutgers University Press, and the Virago series of Penguin Books.

18. Alice Walker, *In Search of Our Mothers' Gardens: Womanist Prose* (New York: Harcourt Brace Jovanovich, 1983); Wendy Martin, *An American Tryptich: Anne Bradstreet, Emily Dickinson, and Adrienne Rich* (Chapel Hill: University of North Carolina Press, 1984).

19. Showalter, Introduction, *New Feminist Criticism*, p. 8.

20. Showalter, "Feminist Criticism in the Wilderness," p. 248.

21. Elaine Showalter, "Toward a Feminist Poetics," *New Feminist Criticism*, p. 131.

22. Culler, *On Deconstruction*, p. 58.

23. Although I treat only anthropological, historical, and psychological research relevant to practical feminist criticism, the findings of feminists in art, religion, and linguistics, to suggest only a few other fields, are not to be overlooked.

24. Showalter, "Feminist Criticism in the Wilderness," p. 262.

25. Nancy Cott, *The Bonds of Womanhood: "Woman's Sphere" in New England, 1780–1835* (New Haven: Yale University Press, 1977), pp. 10–11.

26. Carroll Smith-Rosenberg, "The Female World of Love and Ritual: Relations between Women in Nineteenth-Century America," in *The Signs Reader: Women's Gender & Scholarship*, ed. Elizabeth Abel and Emily K. Abel (Chicago: University of Chicago Press, 1983), pp. 27–28.

27. Mary Kelley, *Private Woman, Public Stage: Literary Domesticity in Nineteenth-Century America* (New York: Oxford University Press, 1985).

28. Sharon O'Brien, " 'The Thing Not Named': Willa Cather as a Lesbian Writer," *Signs* 9, 4 (Summer 1984): 584–85.

29. Carol Gilligan, *In a Different Voice: Psychological Theory and Women's Development* (Cambridge, Mass.: Harvard University Press, 1982), p. 7.

30. Ibid.

31. Ibid.

32. Nancy Chodorow, *The Reproduction of Mothering: Psychoanalysis and the Sociology of Gender* (Berkeley: University of California Press, 1978), pp. 150, 166–67.

33. Judith Kegan Gardiner, "Gender, Values, and Lessing's Cats," *Tulsa Studies in Women's Literature* 3, 1–2 (Spring/Fall 1984): 116.

34. Elizabeth Ammons, "Going in Circles: The Female Geography of Jewett's *Country of the Pointed Firs*," *Studies in the Literary Imagination* 16 (Fall 1983): 85. See, too, Josephine Donovan, "Sarah Orne Jewett's Critical Theory: Notes toward a Feminine Literary Mode," in *Critical Essays on Sarah Orne Jewett*, ed. Gwen L. Nagel (Boston: G. K. Hall, 1984), who argues that Jewett's cyclical plots result from women's perception of time as repetitive.

35. Jean Wyatt, "A Patriarch of One's Own: *Jane Eyre* and Romantic Love," *Tulsa Studies in Women's Literature* 4, 2 (Fall 1985): 211.

36. N. Katherine Hayles, "Anger in Different Voices: Carol Gilligan and *The Mill on the Floss*," *Signs* 12, 1 (Autumn 1986): 24; and Shirley Nelson Garner, " 'Women Together' in Virginia Woolf's *Night and Day*" in *The (M)Other Tongue: Essays in Feminist Psychoanalytic Interpretation*, ed. Shirley Nelson Garner, Claire Kahane, and Madelon Sprengnether (Ithaca, N.Y.: Cornell University Press, 1985), pp. 318–19.

37. I am well aware that this essay, too, must be situated within this recent trend.

38. Culler, *On Deconstruction*, p. 56.

39. Ibid., p. 63.

40. Showalter, "Feminist Criticism in the Wilderness." It is in the same essay that Showalter historicizes feminist criticism by two rather distinct goals as discussed above: the feminist and the gynocritical, a coinage that has become current in the field, "feminist" describing a mode concerned with the feminist as reader, and "gynocritical" describing the mode concerned with woman as writer.

41. Gilbert and Gubar, *Classroom Guide*, pp. 1–14. When the long-awaited anthology finally appeared, it was greeted by much fanfare. As massive as any other traditional college anthology, this new text contains works in English by women of many ethnic groups and from many historical periods, from the Middle Ages to today. Since its release, however, objections have been raised: It presents itself as a ghetto for women's writing, its texts have been selected according to Gilbert and Gubar's psychoanalytic agenda in *The Madwoman in the Attic*, and the sheer mass of the text makes it look patriarchal. Nevertheless, the investment in such a text on the part of a publishing house of Norton's reputation indicates that women's writing is being not only integrated but also institutionalized in our university curricula.

42. In "Women's Time, Women's Space," Elaine Showalter cautions, however, against "a hostile polarization of French and American feminist discourse" (p. 35). She explains that "American feminist criticism is as theoretically sophisticated as its continental sister, while the sheer brilliance and ambition of post-structuralist feminist writing has made its presence in the academy impossible for even the most unreconstructed critics to ignore" (pp. 35–36).

43. Since I am proposing a distinction, albeit somewhat artificial, between Anglo-American and French trends, I am forgoing a discussion of Jane Gallop, an American who rereads Lacan, and former Lacanian Irigaray, from a French perspective. Anyone investigating contemporary feminist psychoanalytic theory, however, should study Gallop's work, especially *The Daughter's Seduction*.

44. Abel and Abel, Introduction, *The Signs Reader*, p. 9. For discussion of the distinctions among the various theories, including Julia Kristeva's, which I do not discuss here, see Ann Rosalind Jones, "Writing the Body: Toward an Understanding of *l'écriture féminine*," in Showalter, *New Feminist Criticism*, pp. 361–77.

45. Hélène Cixous, "The Laugh of the Medusa," trans. Keith Cohen and Paula Cohen, in Abel and Abel, *The Signs Reader*, p. 283.

46. Ibid.

47. Ibid., p. 287.

48. Ibid., p. 296.

49. Luce Irigaray, *This Sex Which Is Not One*, trans. Catherine Porter with Carolyn Burke (Ithaca, N.Y.: Cornell University Press, 1985), p. 68.

50. Ibid., pp. 31–32.

51. Ibid., p. 67.

52. Luce Irigaray, *Speculum of the Other Woman*, trans. Gillian C. Gill (Ithaca, N.Y.: Cornell University Press, 1985), pp. 53, 80, 89.

53. Elizabeth L. Berg, "The Third Woman," *Diacritics* 12, 2 (Summer 1982): 17.

54. Janice Haney-Peritz, "Monumental Feminism and Literature's Ancestral House: Another Look at 'The Yellow Wallpaper,'" *Women's Studies* 12, 2 (1986): 117, quoting Mary Jacobus's translation of Luce Irigaray's *Ce sexe qui n'est pas un*.

55. Paula A. Treichler, "Escaping the Sentence: Diagnosis and Discourse in 'The Yellow Wallpaper,'" *Tulsa Studies in Women's Literature* 3, 1–2 (Spring/Fall 1984): 72, quoting Luce Irigaray, "Veiled Lips," trans. Sara Speidel, *Mississippi Review* 33 (Winter/Spring 1983): 99–101.

56. Coppélia Kahn, citing Madelon Gohlke's essay, "'I wood thee with my sword': Shakespeare's Tragic Paradigms," in Kahn's "Excavating 'Those Dim Minoan Regions': Maternal Subtexts in Patriarchal Literature," *Diacritics* 12, 2 (Summer 1982): 32, n.1.

57. Kahn, "Excavating," p. 36.

58. Ibid., p. 41.

59. Ibid., p. 37.

60. Suzanne Juhasz, Introduction to *Feminist Critics Read Emily Dickinson* (Bloomington: Indiana University Press, 1983), p. 1.

61. For a short history of critical interpretation of *The Awakening*, see Tonette Bond Inge's bibliographical essay, "Kate Chopin," in *American Women Writers: Bibliographical Essays*, ed. Maurice Duke, Jackson R. Bryer, and M. Thomas Inge (Westport, Conn.: Greenwood Press, 1983), pp. 47–69.

62. For this reading I am indebted to the colleagues of my NEH Summer Seminar group on Women's Writing and Women's Culture, directed by Elaine Showalter.

63. Sandra M. Gilbert, "The Second Coming of Aphrodite," *Kenyon Review*, n.s. 5, 3 (Summer 1983): 42–66.

64. See Walker's short story "Everyday Use"; Oates's poem "Celestial Timepiece"; Piercy's poem "Looking at Quilts"; and Waniek's poem "The Century Quilt."

65. Elaine Showalter, lecture delivered at the Georgetown Conference on Critical Theory, Summer 1985. Showalter's metaphor shares much with Elizabeth Ammons's use of the web metaphor to describe the composition of the same work. (See n. 34, above).

Selected Bibliography

Abel, Elizabeth, and Emily K. Abel. Introduction. *The Signs Reader: Women, Gender & Scholarship*. Chicago: University of Chicago Press, 1983. This short essay provides the rationale for choosing the essays that compose the volume. "To accentuate the revisionary force of feminist scholarship, we looked for essays that raise theoretical issues and expand traditional disciplinary boundaries" (p. 2). These essays include feminist critiques of historiography, sociology, literary criticism, theology, the natural sciences, and feminism itself.

Ammons, Elizabeth. "Going in Circles: The Female Geography of Jewett's *Country of the Pointed Firs*." *Studies in the Literary Imagination* 16 (Fall 1983): 83–92. A clear, concise essay discussing Jewett's structuring of the novel "around two essentially female psychic patterns: one of web, the other of descent" (p. 83), and using Carol Gilligan's and Nancy Chodorow's research to support her (Ammons's) conclusions.

Baym, Nina. *Women's Fiction: A Guide to Novels by and about Women in America, 1820–1870.* Ithaca, N.Y.: Cornell University Press, 1978. The guide to women's fiction of the 1820s, 1830s, and 1850s with some consideration of the 1860s and 1870s, a type often called "sentimental" or "domestic." Provides plot summaries and describes conventions of women's fiction and offers a helpful chronological bibliography and bibliographical note on secondary material.

Beauvoir, Simone de. *The Second Sex.* Translated and edited by H. M. Parshley. 1953. Reprint, New York: Random House (Vintage Books), 1974. A pioneering work, which investigates how woman has been defined as Other by biology, psychoanalysis, and historical materialisms (Bk. 1) and how today's woman experiences the various stages of life.

Berg, Elizabeth L. "The Third Woman." *Diacritics* 12, 2 (Summer 1982). A helpful review of Sarah Kofman's *L'énigme de la femme: la femme dans les textes de Freud*, and Luce Irigaray's *Speculum de l'autre femme* and *Amante marine de Friedrich Nietzsche.*

Chodorow, Nancy. *The Reproduction of Mothering: Psychoanalysis and the Sociology of Gender.* Berkeley: University of California Press, 1978. One of the two most important and influential reinterpretations (along with Carol Gilligan's *In a Different Voice*) of female psychology. Chodorovian "mothering theory" has become indispensable to critics examining women's involvement with literature as both readers and writers.

Cixous, Hélène. "The Laugh of the Medusa." Translated by Keith Cohen and Paula Cohen. In *The Signs Reader*, ed. Elizabeth Abel and Emily K. Abel, pp. 279–97. Chicago: University of Chicago Press, 1983. The manifesto that calls women to write about themselves, about other women, and about bringing other women to writing. This influential essay self-reflexively manages to do everything it encourages others to do.

Cott, Nancy F. *The Bonds of Womanhood: "Woman's Sphere" in New England, 1780–1835.* New Haven, Conn.: Yale University Press, 1977. A fascinating study of "women's experience, consciousness, and outlook in the decades leading to the 1830s" (p. 9), using both personal documents and contemporary published sources on the subject of women's behavior. This examination of women's sphere includes chapters on work, domesticity, education, religion, and sisterhood.

Culler, Jonathan. *On Deconstruction: Theory and Criticism after Structuralism.* Ithaca, N.Y.: Cornell University Press, 1982. Culler's chapter "Reading as a Woman" situates feminist criticism in a reader-response framework and then writes the history of its development through three "moments."

Donovan, Josephine. "Sarah Orne Jewett's Critical Theory: Notes Toward a Feminine Literary Mode." In *Critical Essays on Sarah Orne Jewett*, ed. Gwen L. Nagel, pp. 212–25. Boston: G. K. Hall, 1984. Discusses the typical Jewett plot in terms of Jewett's literary theory. Donovan asserts that Jewett believed the artist to be "a relatively passive transmitter of 'things as they are,' who ideally imposes as little artifice as possible upon the material, and who does not consciously follow literary precedents but evolves formal devices appropriate to her own purpose" (p. 213).

———. "Toward a Women's Poetics." *Tulsa Studies in Women's Literature* 3, 1–2 (Spring/Fall 1984): 99–110. Donovan argues that "women's aesthetic and ethical judgments, when authentic, are rooted in a woman-identified, or woman-centered epistemology. . . . To understand women's art one must have a knowledge of women's experience and practice" (p. 99).

Ellman, Mary. *Thinking about Women.* New York: Harcourt Brace and World, 1968. One of the first texts to take phallic criticism (indeed, the work that coined the term) to task. Elucidates a long list of feminine stereotypes, among them passivity, instability, materiality, irrationality, using examples from Jane Austen to Norman Mailer.

Fetterley, Judith. *The Resisting Reader: A Feminist Approach to American Fiction.* Bloomington: Indiana University Press, 1978. An important piece of practical criticism, this work offers feminist readings of representative works in the American fictional canon from Washington Irving to Norman Mailer.

Gallop, Jane. *The Daughter's Seduction: Feminism and Psychoanalysis.* Ithaca, N.Y.: Cornell University Press, 1982. Designed as "a contribution to French psychoanalytic feminist thought from the vantage point of these English-speaking shores," Gallop's important study reads the relationship between Lacanian psychoanalysis and feminist theory.

Gardiner, Judith Kegan. "Gender, Values, and Lessing's Cats." *Tulsa Studies in Women's Literature* 3, 1–2 (Spring/Fall 1984): 111–24. Using Doris Lessing as an example, Gardiner explores the practical value of new psychoanalytic "mothering" theories of Juliet Mitchell, Carol Gilligan, and Nancy Chodorow.

Garner, Shirley Nelson. " 'Women Together' in Virginia Woolf's *Night and Day.*" In *The (M)Other Tongue: Essays in Feminist Psychoanalytic Interpretation,* ed. Shirley Nelson Garner, Claire Kahane, and Madelon Sprengnether, pp. 318–33. Ithaca, N.Y.: Cornell University Press, 1985. This essay treats female friendship and sexual attraction in Woolf's novel using feminist theory and biographical evidence.

Gilbert, Sandra M. "The Second Coming of Aphrodite." *Kenyon Review,* n.s. 5, 3 (Summer 1983): 42–66. The thesis of this fine essay is that Edna Pontellier fantasizes herself an Aphrodite, that the novel "shows, from a female point of view, just what would 'really' happen to a mortal, turn-of-the-century woman who tried to claim for herself the erotic freedom and power owned by the classical queen of love" (p. 45).

Gilbert, Sandra M., and Susan Gubar. *A Classroom Guide to Accompany the Norton Anthology of Literature by Women.* New York: Norton, 1985. A particularly helpful manual with chapters discussing the history of feminist criticism and the teaching of literature by women.

————. *The Madwoman in the Attic: The Woman Writer and the Nineteenth-Century Imagination.* New Haven, Conn.: Yale University Press, 1979. Nominated for the 1979 National Book Critics Circle Award in Literature, *Madwoman* is already a classic rereading of Jane Austen, Mary Shelley, the Brontës, George Eliot, and Emily Dickinson. Gilbert and Gubar are grounded in psychoanalytic theory and the influence theory of Harold Bloom.

Gilligan, Carol. *In a Different Voice: Psychological Theory and Women's Development.* Cambridge, Mass.: Harvard University Press, 1982. A feminist revision of Lawrence Kohlberg's gender-differentiated theory of moral development, this study highlights the paradox and constraints of Kohlberg's system: "the very traits that traditionally have defined the 'goodness' of women, their care for and sensitivity to the needs of others, are those that mark them as deficient in moral development" (p. 18).

Gilman, Charlotte Perkins. *The Yellow Wallpaper.* Old Westbury, N.Y.: Feminist Press, 1973. Influential reprint of the nineteenth-century narrative retelling the history of one woman's descent into madness.

Haney-Peritz, Janice. "Monumental Feminism and Literature's Ancestral House: Another Look at 'The Yellow Wallpaper.'" *Women's Studies* 12, 2 (1986): pp. 113–28. Discusses the possibility that the narrative told in Gilman's story is John's rather than his mad wife's in claiming problems associated with reading the text as a "feminist monument."

Hayles, N. Katherine. "Anger in Different Voices: Carol Gilligan and *The Mill on the Floss.*" *Signs* 12, 1 (Autumn 1986): 23–39. Fascinating analysis of the repression of anger in Eliot's novel using Gilligan's narrative strategies as a standard of comparison.

Inge, Tonette Bond. "Kate Chopin." In *American Women Writers: Bibliographical Essays,* ed. Maurice Duke, Jackson R. Bryer, and M. Thomas Inge, pp. 47–69. Westport, Conn.: Greenwood Press, 1983. One of the valuable bibliographic essays in a collection that includes articles on writers from Bradstreet, Rowlandson, and Kemble-Knight to Moore, Sexton, and Plath.

Irigaray, Luce. *Speculum of the Other Woman*. Translated by Gillian C. Gill. Ithaca, N.Y.: Cornell University Press, 1985. This important collection contains three long essays: "The Blind Spot of an Old Dream of Symmetry," a feminist revision of Freud; "Speculum," meditations on language, imagination, and philosophy; and "Plato's *Hystera*," a revision of Plato's myth of the cave.

———. *This Sex Which Is Not One*. Translated by Catherine Porter with Carolyn Burke. Ithaca, N.Y.: Cornell University Press, 1985. Collection of intriguing essays on Freud and Lacan, and Marx.

Jones, Ann Rosalind. "Writing the Body: Toward an Understanding of *l'écriture feminine*." In *The New Feminist Criticism*, ed. Elaine Showalter, pp. 361–77. New York: Pantheon Books, 1985. A lucid discussion of the theories of Julia Kristeva, Luce Irigaray, Hélène Cixous, and Monique Wittig, which reveals "theoretical and practical problems."

Juhasz, Suzanne. Introduction. *Feminist Critics Read Emily Dickinson*. Bloomington: Indiana University Press, 1983. An indispensable collection firmly situating Dickinson in the context of her gender and employing cultural, psychological, historical, and literary contexts.

Kahn, Coppélia. "Excavating 'Those Dim Minoan Regions': Maternal Subtexts in Patriarchal Literature." *Diacritics* 12, 2 (Summer 1982): 32–41. This essay begins as a review of Dorothy Dinnerstein's *Mermaid and the Minotaur*, Adrienne Rich's *Of Woman Born*, and Nancy Chodorow's *Reproduction of Mothering*, but its purpose is "to argue that searching out [the] maternal subtext is a valid enterprise in feminist criticism" (p. 36).

Kelley, Mary. *Private Woman, Public Stage: Literary Domesticity in Nineteenth-Century America*. New York: Oxford University Press, 1985. By placing the domestic writers of nineteenth-century America—the best known being Fanny Fern, E. D. E. N. Southworth, Harriet Beecher Stowe, Susan Warner, and Augusta Evans Wilson—in their cultural context, Kelley attempts to answer "the question of how the literary domestics could have been so visibly onstage in their own time and yet remain invisible to the historical audience" (p. xii).

Kolodny, Annette. "Dancing through the Minefield." In *The New Feminist Criticism*, ed. Elaine Showalter, pp. 144–67. New York: Pantheon Books, 1985. A "summary outline" of the triumphs of feminist literary criticisms since the 1970s, and a political inquiry into why feminist criticism is dismissed in some circles.

Martin, Wendy. *An American Tryptich: Anne Bradstreet, Emily Dickinson, and Adrienne Rich*. Chapel Hill: University of North Carolina Press, 1984. A valuable study, which succeeds in the project "to demonstrate the continuing influence of early American thought on contemporary feminism" (p. ix). Solid feminist literary biography.

Millett, Kate. *Sexual Politics*. Garden City, N.Y.: Doubleday, 1970. Focuses on the political aspect of sex in history and as it appears in the works of D. H. Lawrence, Henry Miller, Norman Mailer, and Jean Genêt.

Moers, Ellen. *Literary Women: The Great Writers*. 1976. Reprint, New York: Oxford University Press, 1985. One of the first studies to explore the women's tradition in British, French, and American literature. Includes a dictionary catalogue of literary women.

Oates, Joyce Carol. "Celestial Timepiece." *Invisible Woman*, pp. 50–51. Princeton, N.J.: Ontario Review Press, 1982.

O'Brien, Sharon. "'The Thing Not Named': Willa Cather as a Lesbian Writer." *Signs* 9, 4 (Summer 1984): 576–99. This essay is divided neatly into sections, which examine definitions of a lesbian writer, whether evidence exists for Cather's closet lesbianism, and how her sexual orientation affected her fiction.

Piercy, Marge. "Looking at Quilts." *Circles on the Water: Selected Poems of Marge Piercy*, pp. 170–71. New York: Knopf, 1982.

Showalter, Elaine. "Introduction: The Feminist Critical Revolution." In *The New Feminist Criticism: Essays on Women, Literature, and Theory*, ed. Elaine Showalter, pp. 3–17. New York: Pantheon Books, 1982. A short history of feminist literary criticism and summary of the essays included in the volume. These essays are divided into three sections: "What Do Feminist Critics Want? The Academy and the Canon"; "Feminist Criticisms and Women's Cultures"; and "Women's Writing and Feminist Critical Theories." The volume also contains an extremely helpful 21-page bibliography.

———. "Feminist Criticism in the Wilderness." *The New Feminist Criticism*, pp. 243–70. Attempts to define varieties of feminist literary criticism according to where critics locate differences: in biology, in language, in psychology, in culture. One of the most influential essays to date on the subject.

———. *A Literature of Their Own: British Women Novelists from Brontë to Lessing*. Princeton, N.J.: Princeton University Press, 1977. One of the groundbreaking studies that helped to establish a women's tradition in literature. In discussing writers such as Charlotte Brontë, George Eliot, Olive Schreiner, Virginia Woolf, and Doris Lessing, Showalter distinguishes three stages of women's writing: the feminine phase (1840–80); the feminist phase (1880–1920); and the female phase (1920–present). The text includes helpful biographical and bibliographic appendixes.

———. "Toward a Feminist Poetics." In *The New Feminist Criticism*. In this reprint of her 1979 essay on the obstacles facing an open discussion of feminist literary theory, Showalter introduces the notions of the feminist critique and gynocritics and reprises the feminine, feminist, and female categories of writing proposed in *A Literature of Their Own*. This essay is also, however, a political call, which may seem a bit outdated given the great strides taken in the past ten years by feminist literary criticism. Here Showalter urges "women scholars in the 1970s" to seize "a great opportunity, a great intellectual challenge." "The anatomy, the rhetoric, the poetics, the history, await our writing" (p. 141), she declares.

———. "Women's Time, Women's Space: Writing the History of Feminist Criticism." *Tulsa Studies in Women's Literature* 3, 1–2 (Spring/Fall 1984): 29–43. An effort to write the history of feminist literary criticism by situating it "in women's time"—"in terms of the internal relationships, continuities, friendships, and institutions that shaped the thinking and the writing of the last fifteen years" (p. 30).

Smith-Rosenberg, Carroll. "The Female World of Love and Ritual: Relations between Women in Nineteenth-Century America." In *The Signs Reader*, ed. Elizabeth Abel and Emily K. Abel, pp. 26–55. Chicago: University of Chicago Press, 1983. This oft-reprinted essay, which opened the premier issue of *Signs*, the important feminist studies journal, explains the rich homosocial culture to which women in the eighteenth and nineteenth centuries belonged.

Spacks, Patricia Meyer. *The Female Imagination*. New York: Knopf, 1975. The first treatment of a women's tradition in literature. Spacks discusses works ranging from George Eliot's *Daniel Deronda* to Mrs. Gaskell's *Wives and Daughters* to Mary Maclane's *The Story of Mary Maclane* to Doris Lessing's *Golden Notebook*.

Treichler, Paula A. "Escaping the Sentence: Diagnosis and Discourse in 'The Yellow Wallpaper.'" *Tulsa Studies in Women's Literature* 3, 1–2 (Spring/Fall 1984): 61–77. A fascinating reading of Gilman's story using feminist linguistic and psychoanalytic theory to argue that the "male-identified self disguises the true underground narrative: a confrontation with language" (p. 61).

Walker, Alice. "Everyday Use." In *The Norton Anthology of Literature by Women*, ed. Sandra M. Gilbert and Susan Gubar, pp. 2366–74. New York: Norton, 1985. A wonderful story of a hardworking black mother and her two daughters: one rather dull and scarred from a fire, the other well educated and beautiful. When the latter returns to the poor home to collect some family quilts, which she wants to display in her home, her mother decides that her less beautiful daughter is right—the quilts are for everyday use.

———. *In Search of Our Mothers' Gardens: Womanist Prose.* New York: Harcourt Brace Jovanovich, 1983. In her preface Walker writes: "Womanist is to feminist as purple to lavender" (p. xii). This collection presents previously published nonfiction written between 1966 and 1982.

Walker, Cheryl. *The Nightingale's Burden: Women Poets and American Culture before 1900.* Bloomington: Indiana University Press, 1982. Walker treats "the phenomenon of women's poetry as a sign of women's culture" in her discussion of poets like Anne Bradstreet, Helen Hunt Jackson, Emily Dickinson, Ella Wheeler Wilcox, Lizette Woodworth Reese, and Louise Guiney.

Waniek, Marilyn Nelson. "The Century Quilt." *Southern Review* 21 (Summer 1985): 825–26.

Wyatt, Jean. "A Patriarch of One's Own: *Jane Eyre* and Romantic Love." *Tulsa Studies in Women's Literature* 4, 2 (Fall 1985): 199–216. A reader-response approach to Brontë's novel, Wyatt's article asserts that "part of *Jane Eyre's* appeal lies in the way it allows girls (and women) to work out fantasies of desire and rage against fathers that stem from the power and inaccessibility of a father in a traditional Western family structure and his ambiguous position in regard to his daughter's sexuality" (p. 200).

MICHAEL RYAN

Political Criticism

Marxist criticism is both broader in scope and more focused
than other schools of literary criticism. It is broader because it seeks to
combine textual analysis with the study of social and historical contexts.
Many Marxist critics aim for an ideal of "totality," which means that such
criticism tries to give an account of everything that a literary text means in its
given, determinate social situation. The ideal of totality also implies that
Marxist criticism should be able to include all other forms of criticism in its
general project. It does this primarily by adding a social meaning to what
other schools of criticism would confine to literary meaning. Whereas reader-
response criticism posits a general reader, Marxist criticism describes differen-
tiations among readers according to class; whereas formalist criticism attends
to the style of a literary text in itself, Marxist criticism asks what the
ideological significance of different formal strategies is; whereas psychoanalytic criticism seeks out the personal psychological meaning of a text, a
Marxist critic would investigate the links between social power and the
psychoanalytic "construction" of human agents or subjects; and whereas a
deconstructive critic would be concerned with the rhetorical operations that
disable a central theme or meaning, the Marxist would use this critical
strategy to talk about how a particular dominant ideology or way of thinking
was undermined in a text that supposedly promoted it.

Marxist criticism is more focused than other approaches because it has a
very definite aim, which excludes many varieties of literary criticism in their
pure form. That aim is political: the purpose of Marxist criticism is to enable

an understanding of the social and cultural world that will contribute to its transformation. Marxists study literature as part of a larger political project, but in consequence they sacrifice a purely "literary" study of literature. Their focus on a political understanding of culture necessarily excludes a broader investigation into nonpolitical or aesthetic phenomena. Marxist criticism has been expanding over the past two decades, and its political focus has become more emphatic. It is no longer possible to speak of "Marxist criticism" as a category apart from a broader critical undertaking that includes work being done by non-Marxist radicals and that might most suitably be called either "political criticism" or "cultural criticism." This new, expanded radical mode is "cultural" because it covers not only standard works of literature, the traditional object of literary study, but also such arenas of culture as film, television, popular literature, and the symbolic elements of everyday life, and because increasingly it studies its objects in terms not only of their reference to social history or economic reality but also of their role in the replication of social power through culture. It is "political" because it leaves behind the traditional neutral or objective stance of criticism and is directed explicitly toward an intervention into current political debates, rather than toward a distant future social transformation. Moreover, traditional Marxist criticism has been combined with newer critical developments, such as feminism and poststructuralism, giving rise to hybrids that escape traditional categoriza-tion. What used to be called Marxist criticism—the description of the historical and social referents of texts—is no longer recognizable as such in the new critical forms. In its place has developed a rather sophisticated mixture of critical approaches, from phenomenology and hermeneutics to semiotics and structural psychoanalysis, which are harnessed to the service of Marxist crit-icism but which force it beyond its traditional boundaries.

A major consequence of this expansion is the appearance of works of criticism that provide a much richer and more complicated account of litera-ture and social life than was possible within the bounds of traditional Marxist criticism. Catherine Belsey brings Marxist criticism, psychoanalysis, and semiotics together in her *Critical Practice*, and Donna Przbylowicz relies on a wide variety of approaches, from phenomenology to psychoanalysis, in her nonetheless Marxist study of Henry James, *Desire and Repression*. Another consequence of this expansion is that the criticism usually leveled against the Marxist approach to literature—that it is reductive—is finally laid to rest. The criticism is that Marxist critics reduce an autonomous cultural and aesthetic realm to material, usually economic, determinants that lie outside the aesthetic realm. Marxism in general does underscore the way consciousness is shaped by social circumstances, and early Marxist criticism did tend to overcompensate for the way belleletristic criticism ignored the role of class and of economic circumstance in shaping culture by giving economic determination or historical context so much emphasis that all textual specificity was lost. That tendency has been rectified in the current era, largely as a result of the influence of the Frankfurt School, French structuralism, and Russian formalism. Marxist criticism began to become concerned with the ideological function of literary forms and with the necessary interconnection between textual specificity and supposedly extratextual matters such as the reproduction of social power. With the expansion of Marxist criticism came another refinement of the traditional approach: Instead of simply charting the success of capitalist ideology in literature, it began to notice ways in which supposedly ideological texts cut against the grain of the ideals and principles of capitalism. Texts have come to be recharacterized as sites of struggle and contestation rather than as simple conduits of power. This sort of reframing has been particularly important for Marxist feminists who have argued persuasively for the location of examples of female resistance within supposedly successful exercises in patriarchal ideology. Finally, the expansion of Marxist criticism into political or cultural criticism through the incorporation of numerous other methods and approaches is not simply a symptom of New Left eclecticism. It points toward a new recognition on the part of radicals that the different dimensions of power are interconnected, from capitalist economic and patriarchal sexual power to the power of language to shape reality or the power of desire to promote subjugation.

Thus the old Marxist ideal of "totality," a description of the entirety of social reality, has been at once disaggregated and reconstructed as a discontinuous set of connections among such diverse realms as the economic, the psychoanalytic, the semiotic, and the aesthetic. What this means is that Marxist criticism, by transforming itself into political and cultural criticism, has managed to differentiate itself radically from other forms of literary criticism. It now offers a wider, more comprehensive method than is available in any other critical approach, from deconstruction and reader response to psychoanalysis and semiotics. By drawing together the textual and the social, political criticism moves beyond, while comprehending, the specific concerns with reference, subjective meaning, or representational structure that characterize other critical schools.

Perhaps the major influence on Marxist criticism in the contemporary era was the theory of ideology advanced by the French structuralist–Marxist philosopher Louis Althusser. The work of his student, Pierre Macherey, especially his book, *Theory of Literary Production*, was especially influential.

This approach studies literature as an attempt to resolve basic contradictions of a society—for example, the early nineteenth-century distinction between the ideology of the road of class mobility supposedly open to "all talents" and the reality of limited access to class privilege. The ideology was necessary to justify capitalism, but it generated expectations that were threatening to that very economic system. This contradiction was resolved culturally through a morality of constraint and limitation (most noticeable in the novels of Dickens and Eliot), as well as through a philosophy of cynical opportunism (noticeable in the work of Balzac and Stendhal). The term *ideology* describes the beliefs, attitudes, and habits of feeling and behavior that a society inculcates in order to generate an automatic reproduction of its structuring premises. Ideology is what preserves social power through culture in the absence of direct coercion. Literature that is ideological promotes an imaginary relation to one's real material conditions of existence. Nevertheless, ideology always puts on display the fissures and contradictions it tries to efface. Ideology attempts to appear seamless and self-evident, but it also cannot help but describe the very problems it attempts to resolve. Thus, conservative poets like Yeats and Wordsworth, for example, attempt to transcend social class reality by advancing idealizations of nature or art in formal patterns that are highly symbolic or metaphoric, yet literal readings of their metaphoric images (peasants, aristocratic Anglo-Irish estates) display the very social contradictions the poems were meant to resolve or transcend.

Much contemporary Marxist criticism is framed in terms of the Althusserian conception of ideology. This is particularly true of two of the most influential Marxist critics, Fredric Jameson and Terry Eagleton. In *The Political Unconscious*, Jameson argues that literature is a socially symbolic act that resolves determinate historical contradictions. As ideology, literature consists of strategies of containment that curtail a full understanding of the social totality. The reconstruction of such a totality is for Jameson a major task of Marxist criticism, and he sees contemporary poststructuralist methods such as deconstruction, which break down texts into their motivating aporias, as merely first steps toward such an eventual reconstruction. Ultimately, all critical methods can be made part of this larger project. Jameson also argues that there is a political subtext to every piece of literature. All literature is somehow implicated in class struggle, and a full understanding of literature must take history into account. Jameson differs from other Marxist critics in that he does not grant any specificity to other critical methods; they are all marginal undertakings, and they acquire meaning only when combined into one larger project of Marxist understanding.

I and others disagree with this contention. Methods like deconstruction, for example, which emphasize the indeterminacy of reference, put the very possibility of a totalistic reading into question, and it is not sufficient to declare that it and similar critical approaches can be subsumed to a totalizing project. It would be more fruitful to ask what they propose as an alternative to the model of totality, which they convincingly argue is itself ideological. Susan Wells (in *The Dialectics of Representation*), for example, takes issue with Jameson's exclusion of indeterminacy and intersubjectivity while arguing for the interdependence of the typical and the indeterminate registers of literary discourse: "The deepest indeterminacy marks the most referential moment of a text, and the most compelling reference beckons out of the deepest indeterminacy." She rejects the skeptical extremism of deconstructive critics like Paul de Man, but she argues that Marxist criticism stands to gain by taking deconstruction seriously. In her reading of *The Duchess of Malfi*, for example, she effectively demonstrates that so typical a work, which deals with broad social issues such as the relation between the public and the private, cannot be understood without taking the indeterminacy introduced by the madness of the Duchess's mad brothers into account. Whereas traditional Marxist criticism makes too simple a distinction between the subject understood as a monad and social structure, Wells calls for a more rhetorical understanding which would anchor itself in the relations of reflexivity between subjects. This effects the relations between both text and world and text and reader. Ultimately, it entails opening our own methodological presuppositions to critical reflection, acknowledging the element of subjective indeterminacy that resides in even the most universalizing or typical of Marxist critical discourses.

Terry Eagleton's *Criticism and Ideology* was the first systematic attempt to elaborate a critical approach based in Althusser's work. It is a sustained theoretical meditation on Althusserian principles of reading. One of its sections—"Ideology and Literary Form"—consists of a series of readings of texts according to their specific historical and class contexts. Class sensibility, according to Eagleton, appears as literary form. Yet Eagleton is not a reductionist; his approach follows Macherey in consistently locating the fissures and conflicts within apparently successful ideology. His later efforts in practical criticism, such as *The Rape of Clarissa*, a reading of Richardson, also incorporate poststructuralist methods into the Marxist critical project. But Eagleton remains a traditionalist to the extent that he continues to resist the more radical implications of those methods for a rewriting and expansion of Marxist criticism. He adheres to a fairly formal and abstract conception of ideology, and he has been rightly criticized for this by other Marxist critics like John

Frow (in *Marxism and Literary History*) and Tony Bennett (in *Formalism and Marxism*). Frow counters the Althusserian tendency toward abstract theoreticism by arguing for a concept of discursive power. In one of his most convincing analyses, he demonstrates how five different translations of Homer constructed entirely different texts as a result of the different discursive formations in which they were located. Bennett's work is important for proposing a convincing critique of Althusserianism that emphasizes the practical and political dimensions of literature. The abstractness of Althusserian categories like "ideology" detracts from the agonistic character of literature, its anchoring in a field of cultural struggle where the meaning of the world is fought over. Bennett's reliance on Russian thinkers like Bakhtin is instructive, because it is these thinkers who have been most responsible for influencing current criticism away from abstract considerations of ideology and toward more practical political concerns. Richard Terdiman's *Discourse Counter-Discourse*, for example, examines the way dominant discourses and antagonistic, counterhegemonic discourses contended with each other in literature and popular journalism in nineteenth-century France. Culture, for Terdiman, is a field of struggle in which the meaning of the social world is at stake. Cultural signs are traversed by contending interests who attempt to control them for their own ends. This sort of criticism marks a departure from traditional Marxist criticism, which sees culture as a simple site of domination. "For every discourse," Terdiman argues, "a contrary and transgressive counter-discourse." Satiric journalism represents an "attempt to disrupt the circuit in which the dominant construction of the world asserted its self-evidence," and the prose poem indicates an excess that escapes the utilitarian and commercial rationalism of the bourgeoisie, which was opposed by the radical middle-class intelligentsia.

Yet I do not wish to give the impression that Althusserian approaches are entirely without an explanatory power that can help illuminate the political dimension of culture. James Kavanagh's *Emily Bronte* is an Althusserian "symptomatic reading" that treats *Wuthering Heights* as an unsuccessful attempt to efface a conflict both in the patriarchal family and in class relations of the time. Whereas traditional criticism has attempted to understand the text as a coherent whole, Kavanagh argues that "if we are to explain Emily Bronte's work, we cannot efface the violence, the contradiction, the sense of transgression which mark its troubled discourse." Kavanagh focuses on the rupture introduced in the narrative and in the family by Heathcliff. Contemporary psychoanalysis is brought to bear in a description of the family as an ideological apparatus whose function is to repress desire and construct appropriate subjects for capitalism. The formal narrative resolution thus intersects with a resolution in the crisis of the family in a capitalist industrial economy. Brontë's resolution permits the family to continue to exist in an economic environment that is hostile to it. Thus Althusserian categories, despite their abstractness, can permit a dynamic and historical understanding of the political function of culture. This is also clear in Abdul JanMohamed's *Manichean Aesthetics: The Politics of Literature in Colonial Africa.* JanMohamed examines the social pathology of colonialism, "the manichean allegory of black and white, good and evil, salvation and domination, civilization and savagery, superiority and inferiority, intelligence and emotion, self and other, subject and object." Although the colonialist rejects the colonized, he yet depends on him for his identity, and the native feels attracted to the culture of the whites while yet rejecting it in favor of a more traditional indigenous culture that is nevertheless stagnant. JanMohamed sees in the emblems of unity that writers like Dinesen and Achebe propose symptoms of imaginary ideological resolutions that attempt to efface the fundamental dichotomies of colonial culture. He affirms the presence of real distinctions between colonial literature, which is more complicated but whose world is simpler, and African literature, whose vision is simpler but whose world is much more complicated. And Jan-Mohamed defends the realist specificity of African literature, which he sees as contesting the universalizing tendency of colonial literature. In this instance as well, it is clear that an Althusserian understanding of ideology is not antithetical to a political critique of culture.

Not all Marxist criticism is defined by the Althusserian debate. It is also characterized by interventions into the realms of traditional literary history and sociohistorical scholarship. Lukács is usually the model for this sort of work. Walter Cohen's *Drama of a Nation* is a primarily historical analysis of the relation between the public theater and political life in Elizabethan England and Spain. The theaters flourished as a result of state absolutism, which necessitated a sense of national unity that the public theater could help assemble. Cohen examines both the literary and the ideological prehistory of the theaters as well as their institutional bases as forms of artisinal production. He is also sensitive to the changing ideological functions of the plays as the historical situation changed. Thus *The Merchant of Venice* is read as an attempt to work out a compromise between the new bourgeois self-interest and the older aristocratic ideal of largesse or social responsibility. The decline of the public theater and of absolutism alike engenders works like those of Jonson, characterized by a reactionary sensibility, in which "the hierarchical class perspective prescribed by neoclassical concepts of decorum, combined with the exigencies of satiric form, reduces human life to fixed social categories, generally precluding complexities or character development." Cohen thus succeeds in bringing together in mutually determining ways literary form and social history. Marxist historical criticism also takes the form of attempts to reframe the dominant way of describing historical eras. Generally, this entails locating radical potentials in literary works previously branded as ideological or conservative. For example, Jonathan Dollimore's *Radical Tragedy*, which deals with Jacobean drama, argues that the Jacobean plays were part of a shift in world view that helped bring on the Puritan Revolution. The plays themselves were in their form enactments of radical perceptions, which troubled the stability of the old aristocratic order.

Along with Althusserianism, the movement that has had the greatest impact on Marxist criticism in the current era has been feminism. A strong current of Marxist feminist criticism has sprung up over the past decade, and it has made itself particularly felt in radical film and cultural studies. Lillian Robinson's *Sex, Class, and Culture*, published in 1978, was an important book for many feminist radicals. It is one of the richest and most wide-ranging works of contemporary Marxist criticism, covering such diverse topics as popular fiction, television, literary classics, and working-class women's writing. The book establishes a model for the new nontraditionalist modes of cultural criticism. Also a polemical book, it argues that criticism must be directed toward a revolutionary transformation of society. Robinson's understanding of culture is shaped primarily by political considerations. For example, she reads Austen's novels as staking out a new ideological function for the family in a world in which the new bourgeoisie was threatening to displace the landed aristocracy. And she understands the women warriors of Renaissance romance epics as tokens of a "feminization" of social relations made necessary by the emergence of bourgeois civil society.

Judith Newton's *Woman, Power, and Subversion: Social Strategies in British Fiction, 1778–1860* constitutes a more focused historical argument regarding the role of the ideology of "woman's sphere" in the consolidation of capitalist social relations in nineteenth-century England. Women's fiction of the era plays into this ideology while rebelling against it. Newton's argument is that women's power in society (as domestic producers) was reduced during this period while men's public power in the new commercial world was increased. Middle-class women became more subordinate to bourgeois men, and the ideology of the domestic women's sphere helped compensate for this inequality while aiding the resolution of the severe crisis of capitalism in the early decades of the century by promoting a social ideal of harmony and coopera-

tion. Newton's purpose is to accord more power to women and more significance to the women's question than has generally been the case. She also reads
supposedly ideological fiction in a more complicated manner than is usual.
Women writers, she argues, subvert masculine models of power as enforce-
ment by emphasizing women's power defined as capability and autonomy. In
other words, while seeming to accept male dominance, women writers like
Emily Brontë and George Eliot also engaged in indirect or covert subversions
of male power. This duality accounts for "the peculiar dominance in these
novels of tension, disguise, and ultimately disjunctions of form." The fantasies of power evident in the female quest narratives are evidence of "incipient
revolutionary energies."

Newton and Deborah Rosenfelt also edited an anthology of "materialist-
feminist criticism" entitled *Feminist Criticism and Social Change*, which includes essays on French feminism, the literary canon, the theory of ideology,
and specific literary works. Newton and Rosenfelt argue against feminist
essentialism, which posits "woman" as a category independent of material
determinations and differences. They argue for an alternative dialectical view
that sees all gender as a social and historical construct, that refuses to
dichotomize good oppressed women and unproblematically bad dominant
men, and that studies both the mechanisms of oppression and the sources of
female agency and progressive change:

A materialist-feminist analysis offers a more complex and in the end less tragic view of
history than one polarizing male and female, masculine and feminist; constituting
gender relations as simple and unified patriarchy; and constituting women as universally powerless and universally good. A materialist-feminist analysis actively encourages us to hold in our minds the both-ands of experience; that women at different
moments in history have been both oppressed and oppressive, submissive and subversive, victim and agent, allies and enemies both of men and of one another. Such an
analysis prompts us to grasp at once the power of ideas, language and literature; their
importance as a power of ideological struggle; and their simultaneous embeddedness
in and difference from the material conditions of our lives.

The emphasis on "constructedness" is one of the major contributions of this
criticism, as are the related points that culture is a field of struggle over not
only the definition but also the very determination of reality and that literature as a historical construct that participates in the social construction of
reality is inseparable from other discourses like advertising and film. Thus, in
the volume, Paul Lauter writes on the shaping of the American literary canon,
and Michelle Barrett discusses the cultural production of gender. Newton's
discussion of *Villette* focuses on both the oppressive and the enabling features

of the text's white-middle-class ideology. And Leslie Rabine's essay on Harlequin romances provides a positive reading of the genre which, rather than replicate the traditional condemnation of the popular, draws out the mixture of patriarchal power and implicit feminist protest in the novels.

Rabine's essay points to the broadening of criticism beyond traditional literary boundaries that has occurred in recent years. At least since the Frankfurt School, popular culture has been an object of political criticism. But in recent years the lessons of high literary theory have been brought to bear on the field with the result that more enabling, less condemnatory readings have emerged. In the current era, the Marxist critic who led the way in this regard is Raymond Williams, who has produced books on television and the sociology of culture. His approach is sociological in a traditional sense, however, and the work is markedly less political and less formally oriented than that of younger scholars like Tony Bennett and Tania Modleski. Modleski's *Loving with a Vengeance: Mass-Produced Fantasies for Women* argues for a nuanced understanding of apparently ideological cultural artifacts like Harlequin romances and soap operas that sees them as attempts to invest oppressive situations with a sense of dignity. Modleski acknowledges the conservatism of these products—the way romances train women in self-betrayal, for example—but she also engages in a negative hermeneutic that sees in such things as rape fantasies hidden evidence of feminine anger and revolt against male power. She reads the "bad" female villainess in TV soaps as attempting to gain control over traditional female passivity. These fantasies are women's way of dealing with domestic enslavement. In keeping with the tendency of current political criticism, Modleski incorporates astute formal analysis into her sociological approach. Thus she notes of the soap opera that its form is distinctly suited to a female sense of pleasure in that it is not oriented toward a narrative conclusion and in that its temporality is comparatively slower paced.

Marxist or political criticism has been nearly hegemonic in the area of film studies in the past decade. In no other area of criticism is the approach so much taken for granted as a method. Film studies has been distinguished by remarkable theoretical work (Stephen Heath, *Questions of Cinema*), historical research (Dana Polan, *Power and Paranoia*), feminist criticism (E. Ann Kaplan, *Women and Film*) and specific textual analyses (Bill Nichols, *Ideology and the Image*). The field has also, like literary criticism, been characterized by attempts to amalgamate Marxist criticism with poststructuralist, psychoanalytic, and sociological methods (Doug Kellner and Michael Ryan, *Camera Politica: The Politics and Ideology of Contemporary Hollywood Film*).

Critical methods have also come to be applied to nonliterary texts, and this criticism is most evidently political, since its aim is often the immediate transformation of given social reality. Richard Ohmann's *English in America*, which includes a reading of the Pentagon papers, was one of the first works of this variety. The radical critic who has gained the most notoriety for this sort of work is Edward Said. In *Orientalism*, he examines the political assumptions regarding nonwhite Middle Eastern peoples embedded in the scholarship on the area carried out by European and American "orientalists." Using the concepts of Michel Foucault, Said argues that knowledge is itself a means of exercising domination. The other major practical orientation that has emerged within the field of political criticism is the reconstruction of the study of literature itself in the institutions of higher learning. Paul Lauter's *Reconstructing American Literature* is an exemplary piece of work along these lines. The contributors propose alternate syllabi and curricula for the study of American literature which take hitherto excluded or marginalized kinds of literature (slave narratives, for example) into account.

I tend to agree with these last critics that Marxist criticism has to have an immediately practical relevance, and I also side with those who claim that it must come to terms with and use recent developments in such fields as philosophy and psychoanalysis. Consequently, in the major debate that has emerged over the past decade between the Lukácsian or Althusserian traditionalists and the poststructuralists and feminists, I take the latter position. The traditional categories of economic power can no longer be separated from those of sexual or racial power in the analysis of culture. And the poststructuralist insights into undecidability and indeterminacy, rather than being subsumed to a Marxist totality that is in no way modified by them, should be the bases for a significant modification of categories that have lost their usefulness. Perhaps the primary category that requires reconsideration is ideology. The extent to which the concept has had to be modified in recent years, to include the possibility of resistance, subversion, and so on, should itself indicate that it has real shortcomings. Ideology is no longer adequate for describing the discoveries critics have been making regarding the internally dissonant and indeterminate character of literary texts, texts that are now seen as being both ideological and counterideological at once. If counterhegemonic potentials can be found in so-called ideological texts, then those texts are not, strictly speaking, ideological, if by *ideological* is meant texts that promulgate ideas that tend to preserve unjust social power. What would be an alternate way of describing such texts?

I suggest that Marxist critics discard the concept of ideology and concentrate instead on the specific mechanisms of representation, the specific rhetorical forms used in literary texts and cultural artifacts to construct an experiential world that relates in a variety of ways (some contestatory, some conservative) to the social world of institutions, values, and subjects. Instead of assigning an inherent "ideology" to a text, one would speak instead of different means of representation, what values they imply, and what implications they have for shaping desire and knowledge. What has been called ideology is in its materiality made up of techniques of projective representation, strategies for constructing imaginary worlds that transcode actual representational processes of the social world while reinforcing those processes or reconstructing them. The alternate to ideology is not a nonrepresentational clarity of revealed truth or reality, a daylight into which one steps as out of a fog; it is quite simply alternate ways of representing and thereby constructing the social world.

A focus on the rhetoric of representation also opens up the possibility of a productive indeterminacy of meaning, and this permits poststructuralism or deconstruction to be brought to bear in an enabling way on Marxist criticism. Deconstruction suggests that "ideology" consists of the stabilization of meaning, which occludes the way meaning is constructed rhetorically. Attention to that rhetoric removes the ground of determinacy for such meaning constructs. Thus, to the traditional Marxist focus on such material determinants as economics and class can be added the way the materiality of discourse operates to construct meaning and to posit social worlds. This also opens up a more political understanding of the sort I have noted in several works of contemporary criticism. For rhetoric entails struggle; it is a matter of different contending ways of constructing the social world. And this applies not only to literary texts but to the discourse of criticism itself. One rhetorical frame will posit a text as conservative or ideological, whereas another will construct a different text entirely, one that contains subversive or counterhegemonic moments, for example. The poststructuralist concept of indeterminacy is thus an enabling one for a Marxist criticism that seeks to transcend the mere charting of the perniciousness of capitalism and its culture. In order to get beyond both, a different, more forward-looking approach is needed, one that exploits the indeterminacy of meaning and the productive power of rhetoric.

Selected Bibliography

Belsey, Catherine. *Critical Practice*. London: Methuen, 1981. An informed if not entirely thorough introduction to some of the major critical approaches that make up political criticism. It does successfully demonstrate how poststructuralist methods can be allied with Marxist criticism.

Bennett, Tony. *Formalism and Marxism*. London: Methuen, 1979. A comparison and amalgamation of Russian formalism and Marxism. It contains an excellent account of formalism, and Bennett offers one of the most astute criticisms of Althusser.

Cohen, Walter. *The Drama of a Nation*. Ithaca, N.Y.: Cornell University Press, 1985. A detailed and meticulous analysis of the interrelations and analogies between English and Spanish drama in the Renaissance. It is remarkable for its combination of historical scholarship and close textual analysis.

Dollimore, Jonathan. *Radical Tragedy*. Chicago: University of Chicago Press, 1984. This study covers some of the same ground as Cohen's *Drama of a Nation*, but it does so from a different tradition, that of Althusser and his followers. It is somewhat short on textual analysis, though its mix of theoretical and historical approaches is excellent.

Eagleton, Terry. *Criticism and Ideology*. London: Verso, 1977. A major work by a major critic, this book is a central theoretical statement of the Althusserian position.

————. *The Rape of Clarissa*. Minneapolis: University of Minnesota Press, 1982. This study concentrates on one novel, but it is expansive in its combined use of both Marxist and poststructuralist methods in the same analysis.

Frow, John. *Marxism and Literary History*. Cambridge, Mass.: Harvard University Press, 1986. One of the most thorough theoretical works produced in recent years, Frow's book covers several major problems in contemporary criticism, and it contains an extremely helpful analysis of canon formation.

Jameson, Fredric. *The Political Unconscious*. Ithaca, N.Y.: Cornell University Press, 1981. Working within the Hegelian tradition, Jameson brings together in one method a number of divergent approaches. As well as containing a major statement of the Marxist position, it contains some fine analyses of individual authors from Balzac to Conrad.

JanMohamed, Abdul. *Manichean Aesthetics: The Politics of Literature in Colonial Africa*. Amherst: University of Massachusetts Press, 1983. A comparative account of three white colonialist writers and three black African writers. It brings to bear Jameson's method and contains some extremely good analyses of texts.

Kavanagh, James. *Emily Bronte*. London: Blackwell, 1985. A short but extremely dense and detailed analysis of *Wuthering Heights*, which relies primarily on Althusser but is also based in psychoanalysis.

Modleski, Tania. *Loving with a Vengeance: Mass-Produced Fantasies for Women*. Hamden, Conn.: Archon, 1982. A brief but far-ranging analysis of the way popular cultural fantasies play a role in the subordination of women but also in their liberation from the oppressive conditions of patriarchal capitalism.

Newton, Judith. *Women, Power, and Subversion: Social Strategies in British Fiction, 1778–1860*. Athens: University of Georgia Press, 1981. A combination of Marxist and feminist theory, this book also is a fine piece of historical scholarship. The readings are interwoven with history.

Newton, Judith, and Deborah Rosenfelt, eds. *Feminist Criticism and Social Change*. New York: Methuen, 1985. A major anthology of theoretical and practical critical pieces relating to Marxist feminism.

Przbylowicz, Donna. *Desire and Repression: The Dialectic of Self and Other in the Late Works of Henry James*. University: University of Alabama Press, 1986. An eclectic study of James that considers the late novels from the perspective of several different critical and philosophical approaches.

Robinson, Lillian. *Sex, Class, and Culture*. Bloomington: Indiana University Press, 1986. One of the first works of Marxist feminist criticism. The studies range over numerous topics, all linked together by a common thread of political commitment.

Said, Edward. *Orientalism*. New York: Pantheon Books, 1978. One of the first major works of political criticism to branch out into issues of mainstream social policy. Said combines an archival analysis of the study of the Orient with a political analysis of ongoing social processes.

Terdiman, Richard. *Discourse Counter-Discourse*. Ithaca, N.Y.: Cornell University Press, 1985. A study of the way discourse operates to sustain social power in nineteenth-century French fiction and journalism. It combines refined theoretical discussion with meticulous textual analysis.

Wells, Susan. *The Dialectics of Representation*. Baltimore: Johns Hopkins University Press, 1985. This book is an insightful theoretical meditation that anchors theory in history and in practical criticism. It concentrates on the debates of the Marxists and poststructuralists.

DON BIALOSTOSKY

Dialogic Criticism

Dialogic critics believe that individual voices take shape and character in response to and in anticipation of other voices. In their own responsiveness to the voice of Mikhail Bakhtin, these critics characterize themselves as "dialogic," even as they diversify themselves by their loyalties to the many other voices that have shaped their reading of Bakhtin and called out their writing about him. One might recognize dialogic critics in the *Arts and Humanities Citation Index* by their citing of Bakhtin or of his colleagues P. N. Medvedev and V. N. Vološinov or in the subject index of the same reference work by their adopting such characteristically Bakhtinian key words as *dialogic, polyphonic, heteroglossia, double-voiced, reported speech, chronotope, alterity, carnival,* or *carnivalesque.* But a reading of the critics that this search turned up would quickly discover that their emphases varied with their prior interests in Marx or Vygotsky or Dostoevsky or Derrida and with their efforts to communicate Bakhtin's significance to narratologists, Slavicists, linguists, novel theorists, poeticians, or composition specialists. One would soon recognize that the diversity of these critics' choices to focus on Bakhtin or Vološinov, on the dialogic or the carnivalesque, on Bakhtin's Marxist works or his religious works, reflects a diversity in "Bakhtin" himself, a heterogeneity that challenges the simple identification of him with the "dialogic" even as it confirms his dialogic account of internally divergent selves shaped in response to a world of fundamentally divergent voices. [1]

The "dialogic" Bahktin, then, is a figure advanced by some of Bakhtin's recent readers, and dialogic criticism is the enterprise they have brought forward in his name. Bakhtin himself did not use the terms *dialogic* or *dialogue* in the titles of any of his works, but his most influential and authoritative expositors in France and the United States, Tzvetan Todorov and Michael Holquist, both chose to bring his work forward under the sign of the dialogic. The first major books to headline the term, Todorov's *Le Principe dialogique* (translated as *The Dialogical Principle*) and Holquist's edition of Bakhtin's *Dialogic Imagination*, brought Bakhtin's work in translation to their respective publics and influenced numerous subsequent articles and reviews to feature the rubric. Katerina Clark and Holquist do not attach the term to Bakhtin's name in the title or the chapter titles of their biography, *Mikhail Bakhtin*, but they do frame their account of his life with discussions of his "dialogism," opening with it as a metalinguistic alternative to personalism and deconstruction (pp. 9–12) and closing with it as a metaphysical alternative to all monologic belief systems (pp. 347–50).

As Paul de Man suggests in his critique of Todorov's and Holquist's enthusiastic receptions of Bakhtin, "Dialogue and Dialogism," the metaphysical and religious associations of dialogism that take it "well beyond the limited confines of literary theory" (p. 110) have indeed influenced the literary theorists who have introduced Bakhtin to the West. Those inescapable religious and philosophical associations have led critics to articulate Bakhtin's dialogism with Gadamer's dialogic hermeneutics and Buber's dialogic principle (see Christiane Warner, "Etant ou *energeia*," and Nina Perlina, "Bakhtin and Buber"), but I believe that such associations would not have deeply interested *literary* expositors of Bakhtin if he had been brought forward primarily as a religious and philosophical thinker, author of the as yet untranslated and fragmentary early work "Author and Hero in Aesthetic Activity," a text that has profoundly shaped both Todorov's and Holquist's understandings of Bakhtin's overall intellectual project.

It is Bakhtin's work on language, literature, and culture that has earned him the attention of literary critics and led them occasionally to speculate about "dialogism" as a philosophical and religious stance. Most dialogic criticism responds to the rich elaborations of the dialogic principle in his work and resists an upward collapse of them into a worship of the abstracted principle itself or a hero worship of Bakhtin as its messiah. In his work, the dialogic principle has become productive because he has elaborated its implications in response not only to the predominant modern genre, the novel, but to the major twentieth-century movements in poetics, linguistics, psychology, and social thought, movements whose classical roots and contemporary vitality make his responses to them pertinent to our own continuing dialogues with them. In introducing Bakhtin to the West, Todorov as well as Clark and Holquist sometimes isolate and celebrate the essence and origin of his dialogism, but they too recognize the importance of these diverse responses and help us to connect them with the literary kinds and the classical and contemporary critical enterprises to which they continue to speak. Bakhtin's dialogic criticism "can be enthusiastically received by theoreticians of very diverse persuasion" (de Man, "Dialogue and Dialogism," p. 107), not, as de Man implies, because those theoreticians have relaxed their rigor and succumbed to the will to believe in a hero who has transcended intractable theoretical problems but because Bakhtin has productively addressed himself to many of those problems that have engaged critics of diverse theoretical persuasions from classical times to the present day.

Bakhtin explicitly situates himself in relation to the classical figures of Western poetics, but his implied relations to them run even deeper. He acknowledges his affinity with the Socratic practices of the Platonic dialogues and declares his opposition to the classical genre hierarchies of Aristotelian poetics, but his response to Plato influences the fundamental distinction with which he elaborates his dialogic poetics; his opposition to Aristotle informs not just his overall antiauthoritarian stance but also his detailed articulation of a counterpoetics.

Like Plato, Bakhtin represents ideas embodied in the people who voice them, but unlike Plato he does not project a regulatory realm of disembodied ideas; his interest focuses on the dialogic representation of one voice-idea by another rather than on a dialectical discipline that ultimately transcends voices to contemplate ideas in themselves. Bakhtin also shares Plato's interest in poetic diction as the imitation of ideologically charged speech—the poet's speech, his characters' speeches, and the mixed diction in which the poet speaks and reports his characters' speeches—and he shares Plato's particular fascination with the mixed mode of diction (see *Republic* 3). But whereas Plato studies mixed diction to purge it of philosophically unacceptable voices, Bakhtin studies it to elaborate the various ways in which one voice can reinforce or oppose, absorb or repel the tendencies of another.

Bakhtin's "Exposition of the Problem of Reported Speech" in *Marxism and the Philosophy of Language* works out the formal and historical variations of mixed diction understood as "speech within speech, utterance within utterance, and at the same time also *speech about speech, utterance about utterance*" (pp. 115–59). It is worth repeating Bakhtin's insistence there that the dialogically central phenomenon of reported speech is "distinctly and fundamentally different from dialogue" (p. 116) understood as a dramatic form of presentation in which the speeches of various participants are presented without mediation of a narrator. Like Plato's mixed diction, reported speech is narrated speech, and its dialogic interest is in the interplay between the reporting speech's representation of the reported speech and the reported speech's resistance to or cooperation with the speech that reports it. As Plato recognized and Bakhtin demonstrates, the identities of individual voices and of institutions are reproduced, preserved, dissolved, and undermined in these interactions. Soul making and city making are at stake in what our reported speech reveals about the voices we assimilate to or distance from ourselves.

Bakhtin's analysis of "Types of Prose Discourse" in *Problems of Dostoevsky's Poetics* similarly elaborates the possible forms of cooperation, opposition, and interaction among diverse voices, but it broadens the inquiry from reported speech to cover the wider category of double-voiced discourse or "discourse with an orientation to someone else's discourse," even if that other's discourse is outside rather than within the utterance in question (pp. 181–204). This broadening permits analysis of stylization, parody, hidden polemic, dialogue and hidden dialogue, "discourse with a sideward glance at someone else's word" (p. 199), and a number of other dialogic genres and practices especially important to the understanding of artistic prose, a category that cuts across fictional and nonfictional genres to include rhetorical and scholarly prose in its purview. Even lyric poetry and drama, the genres least double-voiced in their pure forms, can become "prosified" or "novelized" as their discourse shows signs of taking someone else's discourse into account (p. 200).

In making diction its principal category and the novel its central genre, Bakhtin's poetics reverses Aristotle's privileging of plot and drama. But here again, as in his response to Plato's theory of diction, it is not just Bakhtin's position but also his rich elaboration of it that sustains critical attention. His *Problems of Dostoevsky's Poetics* is structured as a full-scale rearrangement of Aristotle's hierarchy of plot, character, thought, and diction that devotes chapters to developing the importance of character ("the hero"), thought ("the idea"), and diction ("discourse") and to displacing plot and plot-governed classical genres like tragedy with the multivoiced and open-ended genre of the Menippean satire. Bakhtin does not merely deconstruct Aristotle's hierarchies by making marginal Aristotelian topics central; he articulates a world of artistic practices beyond the boundaries Aristotle established with the same thoroughness with which Aristotle settled the territory within those boundaries. Bakhtin brings into focus a "classical" tradition of anticlassical discursive practices and analyzes their principles, doubling the field covered by poetics instead of undermining its ground.

The persisting influence of Aristotle's *Poetics* in modern criticism and the recently revived interest in Plato's theory of diction have made Bakhtin's responses to these *loci classici* interesting now. Structuralist narratology has preserved the Aristotelian subordination of diction to plot in its subordination of discourse to story. Rhetorical criticism and speech-act theory have challenged this subordination and emphasized narrative as a transaction between narrator and listener, but they have not developed an account of the relation between the narrator's discourse and the character's discourse as Bakhtin has done. Some recent theorists, notably Gérard Genette, Meir Sternberg, and Paul Hernadi, have returned to Plato's theory of diction to open areas closed by traditional Aristotelian theories,[2] but none of them has elaborated the territory of mixed diction as thoroughly and extensively as Bakhtin has done. No theoretical work since Wayne Booth's *Rhetoric of Fiction* has done as much to free discussion of the novel from Aristotelian prejudices in favor of dramatically unmediated representation or to inform that discussion with productive distinctions and questions about the dynamics of novelistic language. This is not to say that insightful critics have not recognized double-voiced phenomena like those Bakhtin articulates in accounts of free indirect discourse or Hugh Kenner's "Uncle Charles Principle," for example; but many of them have recognized the fullest development of those insights to date in Bakhtin's recently translated work of the 1920s and thirties.[3]

If Bakhtin's responses to the classical voices of Plato and Aristotle have kept his work alive in the critical conversations still involved with them, his responses to the modern masters Marx, Saussure, and Freud have similarly engaged his work with the work of their contemporary advocates and critics. His contribution to the avowedly Marxist works published under the names of Vološinov and Medvedev won him an immediate reception in Marxist critical circles eager for a Marxist theory of language, an unreductive sociological poetics, and an answer to formalism; the anti-Stalinist subtext of his book on Rabelais made "carnival" the rallying cry of activist Marxists intent on the liberation of the body and the lower classes from puritanical repressions.

Robert Young has recently narrated these movements "Back to Bakhtin" in Marxist criticism. His notes provide the best available bibliography of Marxist appropriations and criticisms of Bakhtin, and his argument points out the unresolved opposition between Marxist critics' commitment to a dialectical model of history and discourse and their attraction to Bakhtin's dialogic model. Though dialectic projects the possibility of teleological development in history and of transcendence or subsumption of limited positions in more comprehensive ones, "dialogism cannot be confused with dialectics. Dialogism cannot be resolved; it has no teleology. It is unfinalizable and open ended. . . . dialogism . . . defines itself by its refusal of all forms of transcendence, all attempts to unify" (pp. 76, 80). Young points out that Marxist critics' claims for Bakhtin's transcendence of poststructuralism opt for dialectical rather than dialogical arguments, but he also notes that the works published in Vološinov's and Medvedev's names present their own contributions in dialectical, not dialogical, terms. His conclusion is that Marxist critics can find thought compatible with the dialectical method only in the works signed by Vološinov and Medvedev and that Bakhtin's dialogism excludes the works published in his own name from Marxist discourse. Critics committed to Bakhtin's dialogics, on the other hand, will continue to articulate their differences with Marxist dialectics and with the several voices of Marxist criticism that have reaccented Bakhtin's words to their purposes.

Among those voices, Fredric Jameson's, Terry Eagleton's, and Raymond Williams's have been the most influential and dialogically interesting. Jameson's first published response to Bakhtin in his review of *Marxism and the Philosophy of Language* defends Bakhtin's "great theme of . . . dialogue" against reduction to a dialectical binary opposition (p. 540), but his subsequent appropriation of the dialogical in *The Political Unconscious* precisely reduces it to a binary dialectical class antagonism between contradictory terms, as Young and Dominick La Capra recognize.[4] Though dialogics has significant relations to the more pluralistic model of "the active presence in the text of a number of discontinuous and heterogeneous formal processes" that Jameson employs at a higher level of analysis (*Political Unconscious*, p. 99), he reduces Bakhtin's multivalence to this orthodox duality and confines Bakhtin's applicability to the historically and culturally special cases of carnival and festival.

Eagleton centers his reading of Bakhtin on precisely those cases, though, as Young demonstrates, he is ambivalent about the theory of carnival with which Bakhtin accounts for them. Eagleton's Marxism is as rhetorical and activist as Jameson's is dialectical and contemplative, and Bakhtin's notion of carnival appears to support Eagleton's populist argument for the liberation of the lower classes along with the lower bodily strata identified with them. But Eagleton is also aware that "any politics which predicates itself on the carnivalesque moment alone will be no more than a compliant, containable liberalism" ("Wittgenstein's Friends," p. 90) subject to the authorities to obtain its festival permit. Eagleton can echo a notion of the dialogic close to Jameson's dialectical class antagonism when he writes, "For Mikhail Bakhtin, truth is itself a 'dialogic' concept; but the 'dialogue' in his case is a sharp, unremitting struggle between antagonistic class idioms" (p. 83), but he can also come close to the nuanced dialogic alternative to such contradictory idioms when he recognizes that "to analyze the ideological force of an utterance is, inseparably, to interpret its precise rhythm, inflection, intonality, and to refer it to its determining social context" (p. 80).

Though Eagleton is drawn to Bakhtin's emphasis on the materially embodied utterance whose tone does its evaluative work in relation to the voices of its concrete listeners and heroes in concrete social situations (see "Discourse in Life and Discourse in Art"), he is also eager to contain the polymorphous possibilities of such concrete dialogic relations within a dialectically stabilized politics that can authorize tonal power in the service of a revolutionary rhetoric. Eagleton's own discursive practices range from the dialogically rich but dialectically indeterminate engagements with other concrete voices in his essays on Benjamin and Wittgenstein's friends to the propagandistic subordination of other voices to his revolutionary program in *Literary Theory*. His gift for tone troubles the stability of his political program as poetry troubles Plato's philosophical kingdom and carnival troubles the official world it parodies. His critical practice wavers between the dialectical program of making proletarian philosophers kings and the dialogic program of giving the poets the keys to the city.

Young's exile of the dialogic from proper Marxist criticism, Jameson's subordination of it to the service of the class struggle, and Eagleton's ambivalent attraction to it as itself a liberating practice show that some Marxist critics have had difficulty coming to terms with Bakhtin's dialogism. Marxist critics generally have had less difficulty assimilating Bakhtin's critique of Saussurean linguistics and mobilizing it against latter-day Saussurean structuralists and poststructuralists. Raymond Williams, for example, has adopted *Marxism and the Philosophy of Language* as a crucial and neglected alternative to the objectivist Saussurean structuralism that had inappropriately been synthesized with Marxist theories of language. Williams prefers Bakhtin's account of the "usable sign" as a product of the "continuing speech activity between real individuals who are in some continuing social relationship" to Saussure's model of the sign as an abstract element "in the reified accounts of an 'always-given' language system. . . . usable signs are, on the contrary, living evidence of a continuing social process, into which individuals are born and within which they are shaped, but to which they then also actively contribute in a continuing process. This is at once their socialization and their individuation" (*Marxism and Literature*, p. 37).

Williams here restates precisely the dialogic principle to which Young objects when the latter complains that "Bakhtin's dialogism means that the subject is constituted by both self and other, but the speaker is still allowed to accent words and to compete with other accentuations for his or her own purposes. For all his dispersal of the unity of the subject and the author, Bakhtin contrives to privilege the individual over the system" (p. 85). Williams, however, recognizes, as Young does not, the Bakhtinian definition of individuality that makes an opposition between the individual and the social system meaningless:

individuality, by the fully social fact of language (whether as "outer" or "inner" speech), is the active constitution, within distinct physical beings, of the social capacity which is the means of realization of any individual life. Consciousness, in this precise sense, is social being. It is the possession, through active and specific social development and relationships, of a precise social capacity, which is the "sign-system." [Pp. 41–42]

Williams's quotation marks around "sign-system" emphasize his awareness that the linguistic system, like the social system, is a construct posterior to the concrete process of social relations it models. "Men relate and continue to relate," he writes, "before any system which is their product can as a matter of practical rather than abstract consciousness be grasped and exercise its determination" (p. 42).

Young nevertheless wants to posit a system in order to explain—as he thinks Bakhtin cannot—"how a dominant ideology manages to operate successfully" ("Back to Bakhtin," p. 85), but Williams's dialogic understanding of the "dominant" in its relation to the dominated again gives concrete social relations priority over a systematically abstracted hierarchy of dominance:

The reality of any hegemony . . . is that, while by definition it is always dominant, it is never either total or exclusive. At any time, forms of alternative or directly oppositional politics and culture exist as significant elements in the society. We shall need to explore their conditions and their limits, but their active presence is decisive, not only because they have to be included in any historical . . . analysis, but as forms which have had significant impact on the hegemonic process itself. . . . any hegemonic process must be especially alert and responsive to the alternatives and opposition which question and threaten its dominance. [*Marxism and Literature*, p. 113]

The dominant, in Williams's terms, characterizes itself in part by its answers to the cultural and political voices it would dominate, by its hidden polemics with them, and its reaccentuation of their embedded voices. Even when a dominated class is not allowed to speak for itself, its voice deforms the discourse of the class that works to dominate it.

Williams does not cite Bakhtin in his chapters on hegemony and the dominant as he does in his chapter on language. His account of hegemonic relations, however, enacts his pervasive affinity with dialogic criticism in *Marxism and Literature* by focusing on the specific and active relations of diverse socially situated voices and by resisting their reduction to passive terms in an objectified language or a synchronic social system like the one Saussure posits (for other accounts of Bakhtin's critique of Saussure, see Marc Angenot, "Bakhtine"; Susan Stewart, "Shouts on the Street"; and Holquist, "Answering as Authoring").

Like Bakhtin's critique of Saussure, his critique of Freud is conducted in Marx's name but informed by the dialogic principle. He represents the dynamics of parts of "the soul," like those of classes in "the city," as active interrelations of diverse social languages, reinterpreting Freud's censored conscious as an official language compatible with the ruling ideology of a person's class and Freud's unconscious as an unofficial language distant from and repressed by that ruling ideology. Susan Stewart summarizes the two principal achievements of Bakhtin's critique of Freud: It "substantially predicts Jacques Lacan's reformulation of Freudianism in light of linguistic theory, particularly the translation of the unconscious into a form of language" ("Shouts on the Street," p. 49), and it "stresses the shaping power of the specific dialogic situation of the psychoanalytic interview" (p. 50). Though original in their own time, these contributions had both been developed by others before Bakhtin's work on Freud reached the West, and that work itself does little more than summarize Freud's position and announce a Marxist alternative to it. Less productively elaborated than his engagements with Marx and Saussure, Bakhtin's direct engagement with Freud has also generated less subsequent elaboration. (The implications of his other works for a Lacanian Freudianism, however, have been productively developed by Julia Kristeva.)

Bakhtin's very choice to engage Freud in the first place, however, and to challenge Freud's claims from a Marxist point of view exemplifies a principle of dialogic criticism that Bakhtin criticized the Freudians for neglecting. "Neither Freud nor any of his followers," Bakhtin complained, "has ever made the slightest effort to elucidate precisely and concretely the Freudian position on contemporary psychology. . . . It became the habit of Freud and his students to quote only themselves and refer only to one another. . . . The rest of the world hardly even exists for them" (*Freudianism*, pp. 67–68). The positive value this criticism implies is the commitment to articulate one's own position with the "rest of the world," with the others whose different interests and alternative claims have already spoken for the objects of one's own interest. Bakhtin imagines those others always already in the field, but his dialogic principle recognizes them not as obstacles to be overcome or as uninitiated aliens to be ignored but as provocations to articulate his own views with theirs. One's own position or intellectual identity is never independent of its responses to other positions or identities, nor is it complete as long as it has not responded to all of those positions and identities with which it shares the world. As a self-conscious practice, dialogic criticism turns its inescapable involvement with some other voices into a program of articulating itself with all the other voices of the discipline, the culture, or the world of cultures to which it makes itself responsible.

Bakhtin himself carried out this program, as I have shown, in response to significant voices of classical criticism and poetics as well as to major voices in modern theory (Nietzsche is a significant exception). He projected his own voice in diverse argumentative tones and genres as the objects and audiences to which he responded changed, disseminating it not only in his own name but in the names of others and making it available for appropriation in several disciplines for diverse purposes. His readers in the West have been quick to appropriate Bakhtin's voice and develop its further articulations with Lacan's psychoanalysis (Kristeva, Bové), with Lukács's theory of the novel (Aucoutourier, Belleau, Corredor, Jha), with Wayne Booth's *Rhetoric of Fiction* (Booth, *Rhetoric of Fiction*; Bialostosky, "Booth's Rhetoric"), with Chatman's narratology (Bialostosky, "Bakhtin versus Chatman"), with Halliday's sociolinguistics (Thibault, White), with Jameson's genre theory (Thomson), with Wittgenstein's philosophy (Eagleton, "Wittgenstein's Friends") and Benjamin's criticism (Eagleton, *Walter Benjamin*), with Vygotsky's developmental psychology (Emerson), with Derrida's account of writing (Torode and Silverman), and with formalism (Bennett, Shukman, Walton). Those who have aspired to be his authoritative expositors have made gestures of resistance to this dispersion of his voice, attempting to disburden it of "further association of ideas" and of the "embarrassing multiplicity of meanings" it has accumulated (Todorov, *Dialogical Principle*, pp. xii, 60) or to see him whole instead of in his various appropriations by others (Clark and Holquist, *Mikhail Bakhtin*, p. 3), but they have also helped to disseminate his voice in their own appropriations of it. His account of reported speech would entail that even the most self-effacing exposition of his own or anyone else's words must be colored by the themes and accents of the reporting voice as well as of the reported one: Todorov's and Clark and Holquist's accounts of Bakhtin introduce not only his voice but their own voices, and our engagement with Bakhtin is the richer for it.

My own current work elaborates a self-conscious practice of dialogic criticism that recognizes dialogics as an art of discourse on the same order as the arts of rhetoric and dialectic and compares it as a critical program to the programs for the practice of critical discourse that have been advocated by Todorov, La Capra, Leavis, Jameson, Lentricchia, Eagleton, de Man, and others. I propose dialogical articulation with other voices as an alternative aim of discourse to rhetorical victory over or dialectical transumption of them. Dialogics as an art of discursive practice supplements the dialogic principle as a theory of discourse; whereas the dialogic principle models the possible relations among voices in diverse areas of inquiry, dialogics projects a world of fully articulated relations among voices and a practice of actualizing multiple relations among internally divergent voices in such a world.

Bakhtin privileges the novel as the genre that most fully actualizes such relations by artistically organizing the diverse voices of a contemporary world into mutually revealing responsiveness, and he would allow "novelized" criticism and "novelized" critical theory to work toward the same kind of organization within their own domains of discourse. A final articulation of the diverse voices of any discursive domain is, of course, impossible, but a community of discourse self-consciously working toward such an articulation would enjoy an active and demanding life. Its members would respect the diversities within their own voices and the divergences among the several voices in the community, but they would also demand answers from those other voices and make themselves answerable to them. Neither a live-and-let-live relativism nor a settle-it-once-and-for-all authoritarianism but a strenuous and open-ended dialogism would keep them talking to themselves and to one another, discovering their affinities without resting in them and clarifying their differences without resolving them.

If their psychic defenses, their class interests, and their specific speech communities all restrict the range of voices the members of such a community can bear to listen to, they need not grant those restrictions the last word. Just as a newly translated voice can transform a speech community to which it was previously inaccessible, so a new and unexpected voice can disarm defenses, reinterpret interests, and compel reexamination of previously neglected voices. In just this way the belated advent of Bakhtin's voice in the West has not only won its own response but has altered the way in which many of his readers respond to previously established voices and has moved them to reconsider other voices they had formerly ignored altogether.

The dialogic criticism he has provoked does not, at its best, merely reproduce and apply his distinctive critical terms but engages them in answering and interrogating "the rest of the world." Indeed, that criticism makes us aware that simple reproduction and application of another's terms are as impossible as simple monologism. Just as the most repressive hegemony cannot purge the last trace of the voices it would dominate, so even the most derivative disciple reaccents the master's voice in repeating it, revealing two voices in a single utterance and opening a dialogic loophole into which yet another voice can enter. Dialogic critics, then, cannot help being other than Bakhtinians.

Notes

1. See the first section of the Selected Bibliography for a list of English translations of works published in Bakhtin's name and works attributed to Bakhtin published in the names of Vološinov and Medvedev. See Holquist and Clark, *Mikhail Bakhtin*, for a discussion of Bakhtin's unusual publishing practices. See Robert Young, "Back to Bakhtin," for a recent argument for separating the "own-name" works from those published in the names of Medvedev and Vološinov. Complete bibliographic references for works mentioned in the text and notes can be found in the Bibliography. Whenever possible, page references are given parenthetically in the text.

2. See Gérard Genette, *Introduction à l'architexte* (Paris: Seuil, 1979); Meir Sternberg, "Proteus in Quotation-Land: Mimesis and the Forms of Reported Discourse," *Poetics Today* 3 (Spring 1982): 107–56; Paul Hernadi, *Beyond Genre* (Ithaca, N.Y.: Cornell University Press, 1972), pp. 187–205. See also my "Narrative Diction in Wordsworth's Poetics of Speech," *Comparative Literature* 34 (1982): 305–29.

3. For a critical overview of recent discussions of free indirect discourse that notes the importance of Bakhtin's contribution, see Brian McHale, "Free Indirect Discourse: A Survey of Recent Accounts," *PTL* 3 (1978): 249–87. Hugh Kenner discusses the "Uncle Charles Principle," which calls attention to the effect of a character's diction on a narrator's speech, in *Joyce's Voices* (Berkeley: University of California Press, 1978), pp. 16–17.

4. See Robert Young, "Back to Bakhtin," p. 76, and Dominick La Capra, "Bakhtin, Marxism, and the Carnivalesque," pp. 265–66.

Selected Bibliography

English Translations of Works Attributed to Bakhtin

Bakhtin, M. M. *The Dialogic Imagination: Four Essays by M. M. Bakhtin.* Edited by Michael Holquist. Translated by Caryl Emerson and Michael Holquist. Austin: University of Texas Press, 1981. Includes "Epic and Novel," "From the Prehistory of Novelistic Discourse," "Forms of Time and Chronotope in the Novel," and the major essay "Discourse in the Novel."

———. *Problems of Dostoevsky's Poetics.* Edited and translated by Caryl Emerson. Minneapolis: University of Minnesota Press, 1984. This authoritative translation should be consulted in preference to the earlier Rotsel translation. It also contains a foreword by Wayne Booth, an important editor's preface on the problems of translating Bakhtin, three fragments from the 1929 edition of *Problems*, and Bakhtin's notes toward revising the 1961 edition on which this translation is based.

———. *Rabelais and His World.* Translated by Hélène Iswolsky. Bloomington: Indiana University Press, 1984. Source for the widely cited Bakhtinian topos of the carnivalesque.

———. *Speech Genres and Other Late Essays.* Translated by Vern W. McGee. Edited by Caryl

Emerson and Michael Holquist. Austin: University of Texas Press, 1986. Contains previously untranslated material on Goethe and speech genres, as well as tantalizing notes from late in Bakhtin's life.

Medvedev, P. N., and M. M. Bakhtin. *The Formal Method in Literary Scholarship*. Translated by Albert J. Wehrle. Baltimore: Johns Hopkins University Press, 1978. Reprint. Cambridge, Mass.: Harvard University Press, 1985. A critique of Russian formalism in a Marxist idiom.

Shukman, Ann, ed. *Bakhtin School Papers*. Oxford: RPT Publications, 1983. Includes early essays by Bakhtin published in Vološinov's and Medvedev's names as well as two essays by Medvedev. Contains a translation of "Discourse in Life and Discourse in Poetry" that should be compared with the translation in Vološinov, *Freudianism: A Marxist Critique*.

Vološinov, V. N. *Freudianism: A Marxist Critique*. Edited by Neal H. Bruss. Translated by I. R. Titunik. New York: Academic Press, 1976. The important essay "Discourse in Life and Discourse in Art" is published as an appendix to this volume.

―――. *Marxism and the Philosophy of Language*. Translated by L. Matejka and I. R. Titunik. New York: Seminar Press, 1973. Reprint. Cambridge, Mass.: Harvard University Press, 1986. Important for its critique of Saussurean linguistics and its account of the problem of reported speech.

Selected Contributions to Dialogic Criticism

Angenot, Marc. "Bakhtine, sa critique de Saussure et la recherche contemporaine." *Études françaises* 20 (1984): 7–19. Appears in a special issue of this journal on the uses of Bakhtin.

Aucouturier, Michel. "The Theory of the Novel in Russia in the 1930s: Lukács and Bakhtin." In *The Russian Novel from Pushkin to Pasternak*, ed. John Garrard, pp. 227–40. New Haven: Yale University Press, 1983.

Belleau, André. "Relire le jeune Lukács." *Signum* 1 (1982): 115–33. Reads the early Lukács in light of Bakhtin's dialogic principle.

Bennett, Tony. *Formalism and Marxism*. London: Methuen, 1979.

Bialostosky, Don H. "Bakhtin versus Chatman on Narrative: The Habilitation of the Hero." *University of Ottawa Quarterly* 53 (1983): 109–16. Appears in a special issue on the work of Bakhtin.

―――. "Booth's Rhetoric, Bakhtin's Dialogics, and the Future of Novel Criticism." *Novel* 18 (1985): 209–16.

―――. "Dialogics as an Art of Discourse in Literary Criticism." *PMLA* 101 (1986): 788–97. Enters the conversation begun by Todorov's "A Dialogic Criticism?" and proposes an art of dialogics distinct from both rhetoric and dialectic.

Booth, Wayne C. "Freedom of Interpretation: Bakhtin and the Challenge of Feminist Criticism." In *Bakhtin*, ed. Gary Saul Morson, pp. 145–76. Chicago: University of Chicago Press, 1986. Offers a feminist critique of Bakhtin and Rabelais.

―――. *The Rhetoric of Fiction*. 2nd ed. Chicago: University of Chicago Press, 1983. The afterword to the 2nd edition repeatedly engages Bakhtin as does Booth's foreword to Emerson's translation of *Problems of Dostoevsky's Poetics*.

Bové, Carol Mastrangelo. "The Text as Dialogue in Bakhtin and Kristeva." *University of Ottawa Quarterly* 53 (1983): 117–24. Appears in a special issue on the work of Bakhtin.

Carroll, David. "The Alterity of Discourse: Form, History, and the Question of the Political in M. M. Bakhtin." *Diacritics* 13.2 (1983): 65–83. A comprehensive and thoughtful review of the major translated works of Bakhtin that articulates them with the postmodern themes of Lyotard, Lacoue-Labarthe, and Nancy.

Clark, Katerina, and Michael Holquist. *Mikhail Bakhtin*. Cambridge, Mass.: Harvard University Press, 1984. The authoritative account of Bakhtin's intellectual life and milieu.

Consult it on the question of Bakhtin's authorship of works published under the names of others.

Corredor, Eva. "Lukács and Bakhtin: A Dialogue on Fiction." *University of Ottawa Quarterly* 53 (1983): 97–107. Appears in a special issue on the work of Bakhtin.

de Man, Paul. "Dialogue and Dialogism." *The Resistance to Theory*, pp. 106–14. Minneapolis: University of Minnesota Press, 1986.

Eagleton, Terry. *Literary Theory: An Introduction*. Minneapolis: University of Minnesota Press, 1983.

———. *Walter Benjamin; or, Towards a Revolutionary Criticism*. London: Verso, 1981. Chapter 5 moves toward a revolutionary criticism via Bakhtin's carnival.

———. "Wittgenstein's Friends." *New Left Review* 135 (1982): 64–90. Eagleton's most open and interesting engagement with Bakhtin.

Emerson, Caryl. "The Outer Word and Inner Speech: Bakhtin, Vygotsky, and the Internalization of Language." In *Bakhtin*, ed. Gary Saul Morson, pp. 21–40. Chicago: University of Chicago Press, 1986.

Holquist, Michael. "Answering as Authoring: Mikhail Bakhtin's Trans-linguistics." In *Bakhtin*, ed. Gary Saul Morson, pp. 59–71. Chicago: University of Chicago Press, 1986. Makes an important distinction between the Bakhtinian utterance and the Saussurean *parole*.

———. "The Politics of Representation." In *Allegory and Representation*, ed. Stephen J. Greenblatt, pp. 163–83. Baltimore: Johns Hopkins University Press, 1982. Situates *Marxism and the Philosophy of Language* in relation to contemporary theories of ideology and representation.

———. "The Surd Heard: Bakhtin and Derrida." In *Literature and History: Theoretical Problems and Russian Case Studies*, ed. Gary Saul Morson. Stanford: Stanford University Press, 1986.

Jameson, Fredric. *The Political Unconscious*. Ithaca, N.Y.: Cornell University Press, 1981. Assimilates Bakhtin's dialogics to the class struggle and ignores it in discussing the discontinuous and heterogeneous languages to be found in the novel.

———. Review of V. N. Vološinov, *Marxism and the Philosophy of Language*. *Style* 8 (1974): 535–43.

Jha, Prabhakara. "Lukács, Bakhtin, and the Sociology of the Novel." *Diogenes* 129 (Spring 1985): 63–90.

Kristeva, Julia. "The Ruin of a Poetics." In *Russian Formalism*, ed. Stephen Bann and John E. Bowlt, pp. 102–19. New York: Barnes and Noble, 1973. An introduction to the French translation of *Problems of Dostoevsky's Poetics*, this essay articulates Bakhtin with Lacan and introduces the non-Bakhtinian term *intertextuality* to interpret Bakhtin's account of dialogic relations.

———. "Word, Dialogue, and Novel." In *Desire in Language*, ed. Leon S. Roudiez, pp. 64–91. New York: Columbia University Press, 1980. First published in French in 1967, this is the earliest critical response to Bakhtin in the West. Its reading is colored by structuralism and aware of affinities between Bakhtin and Derrida.

La Capra, Dominick. "Bakhtin, Marxism, and the Carnivalesque." *Rethinking Intellectual History: Texts, Contexts, Language*, pp. 291–324. Ithaca, N.Y.: Cornell University Press, 1983. See also La Capra's critique of Jameson's use of Bakhtin in the essay on Jameson in this volume.

MacCannell, Juliet Flower. "The Temporality of Textuality: Bakhtin and Derrida." *MLN* 100 (1985): 968–87.

Morson, Gary Saul, ed. *Bakhtin*. Chicago: University of Chicago Press, 1986. Contains essays from and responses to a special issue of *Critical Inquiry* 10 (1983) on Bakhtin as well as some previously untranslated work of Bakhtin's. See Morson's introductory dialogue "Who Speaks for Bakhtin?" (pp. 1–19) for an introduction to Bakhtinian topoi.

Perlina, Nina. "Bakhtin and Buber: Problems of Dialogic Imagination." *Studies in Twentieth Century Literature* 9 (1984): 13–28. This articulation of Bakhtin's dialogism with Buber's appears in a special issue of *STCL* devoted to Bakhtin.

Shukman, Ann. "Between Marxism and Formalism: The Stylistics of Mikhail Bakhtin." In *Comparative Criticism: A Yearbook*, ed. E. S. Shaffer, 2:221–34. Cambridge: Cambridge University Press, 1980.

Stewart, Susan. "Shouts on the Street: Bakhtin's Anti-Linguistics." In *Bakhtin*, ed. Gary Saul Morson, pp. 41–57. Chicago: University of Chicago Press, 1986.

Thibault, Paul. "Narrative Discourse as a Multi-level System of Communication: Some Theoretical Proposals Concerning Bakhtin's Dialogic Principle." *Studies in Twentieth Century Literature* 9 (1984): 89–117. Appears in a special issue of this journal on Bakhtin.

Thomson, Clive. "Bakhtin's 'Theory' of Genre." *Studies in Twentieth Century Literature* 9 (1984): 29–40. Discovers affinities between Bakhtin's and Jameson's accounts of genre. Appears in special issue of this journal on Bakhtin edited by the author.

———, ed. *Bakhtin Newsletter*. Nos. 1 and 2 available for $8.00 each from Clive Thomson, Department of French Studies, Queen's Univeristy, Kingston, Ontario, Canada K7L 3N6. Provides the most extensive annotated bibliography available of Bakhtin criticism in Europe and North America as well as bibliography of translations of his work.

Todorov, Tzvetan. "A Dialogic Criticism?" Translated by Richard Howard. *Raritan* 4 (1984): 64–76. Opens the topic of the implications of dialogics for criticism.

———. *Mikhail Bakhtin: The Dialogical Principle*. Minneapolis: University of Minnesota Press, 1984. Compiles Bakhtin's observations on several topics in the human sciences.

Torode, Brian, and David Silverman. *The Material Word: Some Theories of Language and Its Limits*. London: Routledge and Kegan Paul, 1980. The final chapter articulates *Marxism and the Philosophy of Language* with Derrida's work.

Walton, W. Garrett, Jr. "V. N. Voloshinov: A Marriage of Formalism and Marxism." In *Semiotics and Dialectics: Ideology and the Text*, ed. Peter V. Zima, pp. 39–102. Amsterdam: John Benjamins B. V., 1981.

Warner, Christiane. "Etant ou *energeia*: Le sujet dans l'oeuvre de H.-G. Gadamer et M. Bakhtine." *Texte* 3 (1984): 141–58.

White, Allon. "Bakhtin, Sociolinguistics, and Deconstruction." In *The Theory of Reading*, ed. Frank Gloversmith, pp. 123–46. New York: Barnes and Noble, 1984.

Williams, Raymond. *Marxism and Literature*. New York: Oxford University Press, 1977. Develops the most dialogic of Marxist literary theories.

Young, Robert. "Back to Bakhtin." *Cultural Critique* 2 (Winter 1985/86): 71–92. Reviews and thoroughly annotates Marxist appropriations of Bakhtin.

KARLIS RACEVSKIS

Genealogical Critique: Michel Foucault and the Systems of Thought

What made Michel Foucault one of the most original and powerful thinkers of our time is also what makes some of his arguments so difficult to follow. It is therefore helpful, when first approaching his work, to keep in mind a few general principles that have consistently guided his purpose over the years. Thus all of his writings can be viewed as attempts to elaborate an answer to the simple question, "Why do we think what we think?" That is, what are the circumstances that make it possible for us to think in a particular way, of particular things; and what are the limitations imposed on the subjects and scope of our thinking? Obviously, such a question turns out to be not so simple after all, and it soon becomes clear that such an attempt to think about thought can quickly lead to contradictory, confusing, even impossible situations. And, indeed, the work of Foucault is characterized by paradoxes and the sort of implications that occasionally verge on the absurd. At the same time, considering that Foucault's intention is to understand that which conditions understanding itself, paradox and unreason can be seen as both the goals and the tools of his investigations. This is not to say that Foucault is purposefully irrational or absurd. On the contrary, he is systematic and meticulous in his research and, although his writing does occasionally acquire an almost poetic expressiveness, his approach to the subjects he investigates can appear positivistic at times. The difficulty lies with the seemingly impossible task Foucault undertakes: The subject of his investigations is, by definition, not available for direct observation. Hence the need to devise the kinds of strategies that promise a new perspective on what is only too familiar—on our ways of thinking and doing; hence also the perplexity or scandal such strategies will cause for those who are comfortable with the familiar ways of doing and thinking.

Foucault's attempt to get at the systematicness of our thought has several important implications. First, it is obvious that Foucault's approach is predicated on the understanding that there exists a dimension, which he variously refers to as *savoir*, *episteme*, or archive, that oversees, indeed controls, the conscious, normal, and rational functioning of thought at a given time in a given society. His approach also suggests that thinking is to be considered not a haphazard or fortuitous phenomenon but a process that is dependent on some organizational principle, on a plan or a timetable that need only be discerned. And third, his approach implies the understanding that there exists the possibility of uncovering the pattern, of revealing or understanding the traces marking the evolution and development of these systems, a possibility that is to be exploited by the critical activity of the intellectual. These three implicit assumptions relate, respectively, to Foucault's archaeological method, his genealogical purpose, and his own self-conscious involvement in his critical project. Foucault's archaeology, his genealogy, and his definition of the intellectual's role will also be the three major themes around which I shall structure the present survey of Foucault's work.

The Archaeological Method

Taken as a metaphor for Foucault's methodology, the term *archaeology* sums up quite well the principal aspects of Foucault's approach: Archaeology is a science that digs into the presently available sedimentations to find the traces left by past civilizations and to reconstruct the succession of historical paradigms by paying particular attention to sharp demarcations separating different epochs. It is a science that goes beneath the surface of a traditional history of ideas to find objects of knowledge and to reconstruct the processes through which human subjects have made themselves into objects of knowledge. For Foucault, the materials to work with are the discourses that exist as the sedimented layers of our past, accumulated in an "archive." These discourses are to be understood as the material manifestation of a thought that is preserved, transmitted, and still affects our present-day thinking.

Foucault is particularly fascinated by the peculiar nature, the tenacity and pervasiveness, of discursive power: Discourses not only shape thought but have a telling effect on bodies as well. To understand fully and to appreciate this power, it is not enough to consider the explicit significance, the purposeful meaning of discourse; it is the systematic configuration of discourses that is most revealing because the patterns they form are determined by relations they entertain with nondiscursive practices, with institutions, customs, and the everyday practices of a people. It is therefore important to study as many documents as possible for the period under investigation in order to make a pattern appear and to see the fundamental changes that take place as one era gives way to another. Each age thus has an *episteme* that determines and limits its ability to conceive and represent reality; this episteme gives rise to a *savoir*, to a general capacity for understanding and assimilating the various fields of human knowledge that characterize a given age.

The transition from one episteme to another is abrupt, unpredictable, and unexplainable. When an epistemological break occurs, it changes the basic configuration of the process through which knowledge is legitimated. According to Foucault, one such break ushered in the classical age in the seventeenth century, another one occurred at the end of the eighteenth century announcing the modern era, and it is quite likely that we are currently going through another transitional period. In addition, in his last books dealing with the history of sexuality, Foucault refers to yet another break that separated antiquity from the Christian civilization.

Although Foucault has sometimes been characterized as a philosopher of discontinuity, it is important to note that, paradoxically, these breaks serve mainly to underline the continuity in human affairs: The two periods separated by a break become comparable in terms of cognitive processes that adopt different strategies but serve the same purpose for each age. In other words, the break does not change everything but rearranges certain elements of the methodology through which humans gain in understanding of reality and try to justify their attempts to establish their control over it.

On the other hand, Foucault rejects the notion of continuity as basically misleading and finds that any attempt to explain historical events in terms of causes and effects is a delusion made possible by the positing of some "transcendental subject," of a metaphysical concept such as the destiny, spirit, or character of an age or of a people. Thus, for Foucault, there are no hidden meanings to be uncovered. Discourses are studied as material manifestations, as concrete traces of events; indeed, they are themselves to be considered as events and are to be understood in terms of the relationships they enter into with other discourses, of the place they occupy within a whole field of discursive practices. What concerns Foucault, then, is the link between discourse and reality, not in a representational sense but in an operative one. Since discourses have a concrete effect on reality, they are to be regarded as material forces that have something to do with the life and death of human beings.

Furthermore, discourses are not to be studied and appreciated for their capacity to represent the nondiscursive practices of a particular people at a particular moment in history. The official explanation and program a society provides for itself are by no means indicative of what is really happening in this society; the nature and effects of the practices can very well be the opposite of what is proclaimed officially. This discrepancy is not due to any delusion or ideological cover-up but exists in the very nature of things—indeed, for Foucault, such a principle of noncorrespondence is axiomatic. The notion of ideology is therefore irrelevant because it implies the existence of two accounts relating to social reality, one true, the other false. From a Foucaultian perspective, discourses are neither true nor false—they simply are. What is of interest are the "truth-effects" they produce and the specific "regime of truth" to which they belong.

The archaeological approach then proceeds along two paths. On the one hand, it seeks to reveal the isomorphic relationship between discourses by discovering the theoretical models they have in common; on the other, it studies the relations between discourses and nondiscursive domains, such as institutional practices and sociopolitical conditions. Contrary to the traditional historical approaches, which attempt to subsume everything under an all-encompassing explanatory design, this particular archaeological strategy will serve to bring out divergences, inconsistencies, and irregularities in order to capture the singularity of discursive events and to study the manner of their functioning, not in order to find their causes or those responsible—there are no strategists to be found behind the strategies—but because the purpose is to understand how discourses can have an effect on bodies, on the everyday lives of men, women, and children. That is why Foucault is particularly interested in what he calls the "buried knowledges," in the sorts of histories and subjects that are usually excluded from official accounts of a culture, in subjects such as insanity, penal methods and institutions, and sexuality.

These major areas of Foucault's investigations—madness, delinquency, and sexuality—also correspond to three fundamental concerns underlying his genealogical investigations: truth, power, and individual ethics. The first orientation studies the constitution of individuals as subjects of knowledge; the second examines the relation of individuals to fields of power; the third analyzes the making of individuals into moral agents and the constitution of individual ethics.

The Genealogical Purpose

Foucault's genealogical purpose derives from his intention to do an "ontology of the present" and is based on the understanding that the present is a product of history: What we are (or, more precisely, our understanding and conception of ourselves and our place in the world) has been shaped by discourses that precede us, that were here before we were born. Since any cultural object or objectification is the end product of a process that is fundamentally historical, our being is a function of our becoming. Genealogy, a concept Foucault borrows from Nietzsche, refers thus to the method of tracing a lineage, of locating antecedents and explaining the emergence of cognitive entities. As we have seen, however, Foucault's approach does away with such explanatory devices as cause and effect, design, and destiny and brings out the heterogeneous complexity and aleatory deployment of forces that work to shape events; as a consequence, these are seen as contingent, unexpected, and momentary irruptions in a field of forces whose effects are thoroughly unpredictable because no conscious purpose is there to guide or control it.

The effect of such an approach is eminently critical because it clearly brings out the insufficiency and arbitrary nature of official rationalizations that claim to explain the purpose behind the history or the nature of a society. Foucault brings out the contrast between such grandiose elaborations and the nitty-gritty practices that mark individual existences in a society by showing that one has nothing to do with the other—or, rather, that it is precisely because the two realities are antithetical that they coexist so well. Thus, the existence of an objectively ascertainable rationality requires the existence of something called madness; the objectification of criminality has given rise to a whole network of power relations that permeate society; and sexuality, as the fundamental constituent of morality, has become the basis for an individual's moral perception of himself or herself. The reconciliation of reason with unreason, of humanism with the penal system, of the sexual and the moral, is made possible by a discourse whose purpose is to provide a human being with a "soul": It is what makes one understandable in terms of the nature of his or her "being" and renders individuals amenable to the effects of power. The being of the individual is constituted by a particular knowledge, but the body is subjected to the effects of power actualized by social relations and institutional settings and applied in the name of this knowledge. For the modern age, this knowledge has been constituted by the so-called human sciences, the disciplines that have served to legitimate humanism.

The principal subject of Foucault's genealogical critique is Western humanism. This mode of thought has produced models for conduct and for life in society that have become obsolete or that reinforce systems of oppression and domination. The major event marking the advent of the modern age is the emergence of the concept of "man." As a result, Western cultural discourse becomes fundamentally anthropomorphic in nature and models its particular regime of truth on its image of man. The "validity" of this image is established according to the tautological procedure of the human sciences, which take the limitations inherent in empirical knowledge as the very proof of this knowledge's truth. The knowledge thus constituted claims an unimpeachable prerogative to impose its norms as the universally applicable ideal for humanity. From a Foucaultian perspective, the legacy of the Enlightenment translates into a strategy of domination made possible by a discourse of civilization and progress that veils the reciprocal relations between truth and power.

Of course, the human sciences, in contrast with the objective sciences, have a low epistemological profile; that is, their claim to scientific objectivity is relatively weak since they need to found their legitimacy in institutional practices linked to economic conditions, political requirements, and social regulations—to an entire state apparatus and sociocultural establishment. This intimate relationship between humanism and its various institutions illustrates a connection between knowledge and power that is axiomatic for Foucault: Knowledge is made legitimate by power. With the advent of the modern age, the social fabric becomes suffused with power–knowledge strategies. The hegemonic rule of the human sciences provides the necessary environment for the creation of a society in which everyone's existence is submitted to a disciplinary code establishing the dos and don'ts of everyday behavior at school, in the workplace, in hospitals, in the barracks, and in prisons. The existence of individuals is regulated by micromechanisms of power and by microtechniques of discipline unobtrusively operating under the cover of an official discourse of scientific truth and humanitarian concern.

Western humanism, we have seen, legitimates its epistemological prerogative in terms of values derived from the Enlightenment. Though Foucault's critique is aimed at both humanism and the Enlightenment, it is directed not at the values themselves but at the manner of exploiting them. Foucault opposes the institution and preservation of a hypostatized ideal that may have little to do with present conditions. However, though these vestiges of a bygone age are to be resisted, what is still relevant is the intention that moved the Enlightenment thinkers to raise some fundamental questions about the social existence of human beings. Because these universal and perennial concerns must be made to fit a reality that is constantly changing, it is important to do an ontological study of the present circumstances, to investigate the antecedents that have brought us to the present juncture and that determine its shape and outlook. The notion that knowledge is perfectible and is somehow involved in a process that brings its practitioners ever nearer to the truth is a basic delusion inherited from the Enlightenment. As this belief is discredited, it becomes possible to situate critical investigations at the intersection of discursive effects and sociopolitical mechanisms—in the space usually covered up and made inaccessible by the discourse of humanism and its claim of universal validity.

To illustrate the potential of a genealogical critique, I will consider briefly the case of the humanities. Admittedly, the implications of a Foucaultian approach for cognitive or educational practices are yet to be fully gauged; nevertheless, we can already discern a number of consequences such a critique brings to the study and the teaching of the disciplines composing the humanities. Its effect is, first, to disrupt the unity of purpose justifying an educational or a cultural enterprise like the humanities: It will bypass the traditional rationales that either hark back to a sanctified tradition of Great Book Writing or promise the full realization of humaneness through the absorption of the consecrated canon. It will focus instead on the circumstances attending the emergence of the humanities as a legitimate object of educational and social concern. Instead of seeking to evaluate the legitimacy of the humanities in reference to some notion of human essence, a Foucaultian critique will consider the humanities as a singular event that is defined by what Foucault calls a "polyhedron of intelligibility," that is, a context of discursive and nondiscursive facets outlining the reality of the object of knowledge known as "humanities."

A Foucaultian approach will lead us to consider the practice of the humanities in terms of the specific logic, strategy, rationales, historical antecedents, moral imperatives, institutional prescriptions, and socioeconomic conditions that oversee and promote the discipline. We are looking no longer for a content, an aesthetic or a moral core defining the essential nature of the humanities, but for the prescriptive codes that organize the practice of the humanities: Foucault's approach teaches us to look for the disciplinary strategies, the management and marketing techniques that oversee and promote the humanities both inside and outside the university; it calls our attention to the economic and political forces influencing this promotion; and it refers us back to the historical antecedents that have shaped the institutions that promulgate and regulate the humanities.

Second, a Foucaultian approach will seek to describe the regime of truth that oversees the production of discourses needed to justify such practices as the humanities. These are the rationales that operate in the context of a domain authorizing distinctions between the true and the false. Although each age enacts its own particular regime of truth, it inevitably claims to derive it from a system of values it certifies as eternal and universal—whence the need to separate content from context and to consider them as two fundamentally different and not necessarily related issues.

Talk of "content" inevitably brings with it notions of essence, of human expression and meaning. For Foucault, there is no other dimension to be discovered or deciphered; there is no deeper significance to be found in discourse. The evidence is readily available, provided we are willing to apply ourselves to the task of gathering and sorting out all of the pertinent information. It must be remarked, however, that it is also because of this refusal to deal with the questions of representation and expression that Foucault's critique is least amenable to studying texts as texts. It disqualifies itself implicitly from exegetic or interpretive tasks. This is not to say that Foucault was unconcerned about literature. Indeed, he was highly intrigued by the question of writing and was especially attracted to the work of such writers as Beckett, Blanchot, Bataille, Butor, and Robbe-Grillet. Moreover, he dealt expressly with certain aspects of literary expression in his book on Raymond Roussel. He was fascinated by Roussel's experimentation with language and found that the latter's work gave an unusually expressive account of the order of words and things, of life and death, of light and language that makes up the geometry of being. Roussel's experimental writing had achieved the capacity to make manifest a dimension transcending the act of writing, a dimension involving the very question of the author's being. At the same time, Foucault makes it clear that he places his *Raymond Roussel* clearly apart from all his other works. Though he was certainly not indifferent to the issue of literary expression, the question that concerned him above all was not, after all, the philosophical or aesthetic significance of a writer's involvement with language but the ethical and the practical consequences of the intellectual's involvement with his or her society.

The Role of the Intellectual

The critical enterprise of Michel Foucault cannot be considered separately from Foucault's own perception of his role and function as intellectual. His approach to the systems of thought he seeks to survey takes into account both the limits imposed on him and the obligation to explore the limitations of knowledge and morality. In short, Foucault's ethic is a function of his critical project: It makes him conceive of his role as critic in terms of a responsibility toward himself as well as toward others. The realization of this interdependence manifests itself in several ways in Foucault's writings: as an instinctive compassion for the victims of oppression and exclusion, as a resistance to the truths imposed by the prevalent cultural mode, as a desire for anonymity, and as a reliance on the wisdom of collective thought. It follows that Foucault's attitude toward knowledge and the realm of discourse is ambiguous. On the one hand, he is clearly fascinated by the accumulated wealth of discourses that both preserve past thought and continue to shape our present thinking. On the other, he also feels stifled by this massive knowledge to which he has been subjected since his childhood, and he finds oppressive a discursive tradition that has had such an all-powerful role in shaping his capacity to imagine and to think. In addition, he is very much aware of the potentially dangerous and threatening nature of discourses and of the harm they are capable of perpetrating. The distrust that Foucault evinces toward certain applications of psychiatry and of Marxist thought, for example, stems from some very personal experiences and from the realization that discourses can impose their truths by means of brutal strategies of subjection.

To be sure, though it is certainly desirable to resist those forms of culturally instituted knowledge that are oppressive because of their collusion with certain hegemonic forms of institutional or state power, it is not really possible to free oneself from the pervasiveness of thought that dominates one's life and determines one's very being. Indeed, it is an aspect of our existence that not only needs to be recognized but must also be valorized. By granting this aspect a priority over conscious forms of knowledge, Foucault recognizes the legitimacy of collective wisdom and places his trust in the anonymous elaboration of systems of thought by a history that follows its own laws.

For Foucault, writing becomes a way of escaping himself, of dismantling his identify, because it is in the activity of thinking and writing that he discovers the otherness that is constitutive of his being. Foucault's understanding of his own intellectual role and obligations is exemplified by the notion of the "specific" intellectual. It is a stance that he opposes to that of the traditional "universal" intellectual, the man of wisdom who poses as judge and prophet and whose all-encompassing vision and profound knowledge grant him the authority to expostulate on the whys and wherefores of human existence. The specific intellectual has no claim to wisdom or truth but has the specific task of surveying, investigating, and elucidating the field of his or her specialization. It is basically the task of the critic.

The critic's major responsibility is to "problematize" the processes through which truth is produced. Thus Foucault sees his own principal purpose as the elaboration of a genealogy of *problématiques*. It is a project intended to bring out the problematic aspects of the procedures that oversee the production, dissemination, and application of truths. The purpose is to reveal all the unstated presuppositions, the unquestioned and dubious rationales, and the self-serving interests that attend the production of truth. At the same time, the critic is aware that the procedures in question depend on circumstances outside the realm of anyone's perception or understanding— even the critic's. Yet the critic's activity can have a powerful effect, as the example of Marx demonstrates. Marx's theoretical conceptualizations were very much a product of the dominant episteme of his time; nevertheless, Marx exerted a profound influence on the history of Western thought because he inaugurated a new kind of discursive practice.

The specificity of the intellectual's task is also made manifest by the concern he or she has for specific, concrete issues: The intellectual does not simply cogitate and construct theories but gets involved in the actual struggles of real people, especially of those who are the victims of particular regimes of truth. Again, the critic approaches these struggles without an a priori theoretical understanding or rationalization but with the intention of elucidating the situation after he or she has been able to experience it. No program is to be outlined or course of action proposed. These are determined by community action.

The principal reason for which the specific intellectual can never pretend to be "above it all" is that he has an obligation ceaselessly to problematize his own position. The specific intellectual cannot have recourse to the alibi of some universal principle that would elevate him to a superior vantage; the intellectual is accountable only to himself.

The Critical Reception

The writings of Michel Foucault have been considered controversial from almost the very beginning. Ever since the appearance of *Les mots et les choses* in 1966, a work that brought both fame and notoriety to its author by announcing the impending disappearance of man, Foucault's writings have elicited endless debates about the merits and legitimacy of his critical accomplishment.

The most common criticisms have been directed at some of Foucault's basic theoretical concepts. One of the earliest ones concerned the notion of epistemological breaks. Their unexplainable and unpredictable occurrence as well as the all-powerful and uniform nature of the episteme were viewed as among the more objectionable aspects of his theory. Another notion that has elicited a considerable amount of critical comment has been his concept of power, which has been found too vague and too general to serve a useful critical purpose. In addition, some critics—especially Marxists and feminists—find that Foucault's interpretation of power fails to take into account power that is one-directional, acts as a force of oppression, and is to be resisted. According to these critics, Foucault's theory does not make it possible to work out concrete strategies of resistance.

In the United States, the debate around the critical merit of Foucault's writings has frequently contrasted his intellectual approach with that of Derrida. The two thinkers themselves engaged in a brief debate only once, in the midsixties, on the subject of Descartes. Ever since then, however, it has become a commonplace to oppose the two as the representatives of two allegedly irreconcilable philosophical modes of thought. The deconstructionist argument, simply put, consists of asserting that it is not possible to do a critique of reason from within reason and that distinctions between the Same and the Other are but the products of the Same. From a Foucaultian perspective, deconstruction can be seen as a sophisticated game of words uniquely concerned with the inherent logic of language. By concentrating exclusively on textual relations of meaning, deconstruction ends by denying the possibility of connecting texts and reality. We have seen that, for Foucault, what matters is precisely the connections linking discourses to the reality of structures of power.

Whether the distinctions between Foucault and Derrida are as sharp as the rhetoric of polemical disputes would have us suppose is of course open to debate. It is also important to note that the arguments opposing the two French philosophers are relevant only in the Anglo-American context. Deconstruction is mainly an American phenomenon. In France, the impact of Derridean thought has been negligible compared to the considerable fame and influence of Foucault. Furthermore, Foucault and Derrida have been lately joined together as two major representatives of the so-called structuralist age and are both attacked as promoters of unhealthy intellectual habits by critics who seek to reinstate good sense and the "right" values.

In France, the fundamental issue concerning the validity of Foucault's critique is its relation to Marxism. Foucault is naturally associated with the general intellectual and cultural movement that ousted Marxism from the unquestioned eminence it had enjoyed in France, especially during the postwar period. Foucault's own attitude toward Marxism is complex. On the one hand, it is clear that Foucault's thinking has been influenced by Marxist thought in a number of ways; on the other, he also considers Marxism— especially the kind that has rigidified in dogmatic stances and has been appropriated by political parties and regimes—to be obsolete and to have been a monumental failure in its concrete applications. This critical stance with regard to Marxism has subjected Foucault to various accusations. Sartre labeled Foucault's writings "probourgeois," and Habermas has accused him of being a neoconservative. From an epistemological perspective, Marxists find unacceptable Foucault's notion of the anonymous strategies of power–knowledge effects and his rejection of the concepts of ideology and of social classes.

Feminist criticism has expressed similar misgivings about Foucault's theories and their effect on the existing sociocultural paradigm. Thus Foucault has been accused of supporting the phallocratic patriarchal arrangement and of being insensitive to the feminist viewpoint, especially in the volumes that compose the *History of Sexuality*. We should, however, recall that Foucault himself has said that he was not able to speak for women because he was not qualified to do so and that he always supported feminist causes.

Whether Foucault's work has been helpful or not to the powers that be is probably a question that will be debated for a long time to come. What is clear, however, is that his writings have been most controversial from the point of view of traditional perspectives. Foucault's antihumanistic and anti-Enlightenment stance has been identified as basically anarchistic or nihilistic, destructive, and antisocial. Foucault himself pointed out that he has been denounced for being sometimes a blatantly obvious, sometimes a cryptically secret, adherent of political denominations of both the extreme Right and the extreme Left. When asked about political preferences, he replied that politics did not interest him, that he was concerned with ethics. Foucault himself thus suggested the best way of dealing with the question of his political and intellectual identity: If it is to be pursued in terms of the traditional categories, then it is a question best left unanswered.

It is this aspect of Foucault's thought that I have personally found appealing. My own approach to Foucault is characterized by an attempt to bring out the innovative and the most disruptive aspects of his thought, and my intention has been to underline the eccentric and unorthodox position Foucault occupies with reference to conventional academic and political thinking. I have found that Foucault's self-reflexive problematization of his own involvement with his writing can benefit from insights provided by the theory of Lacan, and in my book (*Michel Foucault and the Subversion of Intellect*) I have used some Lacanian notions to help illustrate the concept of the subject in particular. Foucault's emphasis on the pretentiousness of our intellectual claims, on the dogmatism of rationality and scientism, and on the power of discourses to subjugate has contributed, I believe, to making discourses more tenuous and has enhanced the potential that exists for beneficial uses of intellectual inquiry. I agree with Foucault's viewpoint that the danger today lies not so much in the direction of fewer restraints but in that of dogmatism. Yet I do not think Foucault should be construed as a liberator in any absolute sense. If anything, he makes us aware of all the relations and influences that keep us bound to a collective destiny. He teaches us to give history its due and to accept its force and potential for effectuating change; in a sense, he has set history in motion once more by reducing human agency to a more modest stature. Foucault's writings invite us to exercise and to enjoy our intellectual capacities, a pleasure intensified by the realization that the work of intellect can be more than an academic exercise and can have something to do with the ethical issues of power and knowledge that determine our relations to ourselves as well as to others.

Selected Bibliography

Works by Michel Foucault

L'archéologie du savoir. Paris: Gallimard, 1969. *The Archaeology of Knowledge*. Translated by Alan Sheridan. London: Tavistock; New York: Pantheon, 1972. A work of theory outlining the methodology of archaeological investigations. A major purpose is to resist and reject the conceptualization characterizing the conventional history-of-ideas genre.

Ceci n'est pas une pipe. Montpellier: Fata Morgana, 1973. *This Is Not a Pipe*. Berkeley: University of California Press, 1983. On the work of the painter René Magritte.

Le désordre des familles. Lettres de cachet des Archives de la Bastille. Presented by Arlette Farge and Michel Foucault. Paris: Gallimard-Julliard, 1982.

Folie et déraison: Histoire de la folie à l'âge classique. Paris: Plon, 1961. Abridged ed.: *Histoire de la folie*. Paris: Union Générale d'Editions, 1961. Rev. ed. with new preface and two appendices, "Mon corps, ce papier, ce feu" and "La folie, l'absence d'oeuvre," retitled *Histoire de la folie à l'âge classique*. Paris: Gallimard, 1972. *Madness and Civilization: A History of Insanity in the Age of Reason*. Translation of the abridged ed. by R. Howard. New York: Random House, 1965. Madness seen as the strange and disquieting territory that has both eluded understanding and resisted orderly processes of socialization in the Western experience. The creation of psychology covered up these inadequacies.

Herculine Barbin dite Alexina B. Paris: Gallimard, 1978. The memoirs of a hermaphrodite, presented by M. Foucault.

Histoire de la sexualité

Vol. 1: *La volonté de savoir*. Paris: Gallimard, 1976. *The History of Sexuality*, vol. 1. *An Introduction*. Translated by Robert Hurley. New York: Pantheon, 1978; London: Allen Lane, 1979. An outline of a projected series of six volumes and a discussion of the pervasiveness of power-knowledge strategies in a culture intent on imposing its norms in the name of truth.

Vol. 2.: *L'usage des plaisirs*. Paris: Gallimard, 1984. *The Use of Pleasure*. Translated by

Robert Hurley. New York: Pantheon, 1985. Having abandoned his original plan, Foucault is now concerned with the problem of ethics or of the manner in which an individual constitutes him/herself as a moral subject of his/her own actions. Starting with Greek antiquity, Foucault studies the manner in which sexual behavior affected one's relation to oneself, to others, and to truth.

Vol. 3: *Le souci de soi*. Paris: Gallimard, 1984. An analysis of Greek and Latin texts of the first two centuries A.D. that elaborate an art of living dominated by a preoccupation with the self.

Vol. 4: *Les aveux de la chair*. Paris: Gallimard, 1986. The experience of the flesh in the first centuries of the Christian era and the role of a hermeneutics of desire are the principal themes.

Maladie mentale et personnalité. Paris: Presses Universitaires de France, 1954. 2d. rev. ed.: *Maladie mentale et psychologie*, 1966. *Mental Illness and Psychology*. Translated by Alan Sheridan. New York: Harper and Row, 1976. This early discussion of the role knowledge plays in establishing distinctions between the pathological and the normal announces one of the major themes of later works.

Moi, Pierre Rivière, ayant égorgé ma mère, ma soeur et mon frère. . . . Un cas de parricide au XIXe siècle. Paris: Gallimard-Julliard, 1973. *I, Pierre Rivière, having slaughtered my mother, my sister and my brother. . . . A Case of Parricide in the 19th Century*. Translated by F. Jellinek. New York: Pantheon, 1975; London: Peregrine, 1978. Collective work; edited, with one essay and introduction by Foucault.

Les mots et les choses. Une archéologie des sciences humaines. Paris: Gallimard, 1966. *The Order of Things. An Archaeology of the Human Sciences*. With a Foreword to the English edition by Michel Foucault. Translated by Alan Sheridan. London: Tavistock; New York: Pantheon, 1970. Foucault called this his most difficult book. By analyzing three distinctive discourses of knowledge—one on living beings, another on language, and a third on wealth—Foucault discerns two basic epistemological breaks marking the history of Western thought. One occurs in the seventeenth century and inaugurates the classical *episteme*; the other takes place around 1800 and marks the beginning of the modern period. The present age is characterized by a form of knowledge for which Man is both the object and guarantor of its truths. Foucault also suggests the possibility of a third epistemological disruption currently taking place and signaling the disappearance of "Man."

Naissance de la clinique: Une archéologie du regard médical. Paris: Presses Universitaires de France, 1963. Rev. ed., 1972. *The Birth of the Clinic: An Archaeology of Medical Perception*. Translated by Alan Sheridan. London: Tavistock; New York: Pantheon, 1973. A study of the social, economic, technological, and institutional forces that contributed to form the experience of the medical gaze in the nineteenth century.

L'ordre du discours. Leçon inaugurale au Collège de France prononcée le 2 décembre 1970. Paris: Gallimard, 1971. "Orders of Discourse." Translated by Rupert Swyer. In *Social Science Information* 10 (1971): 7–30. Reprinted in the Pantheon edition of *The Archaeology of Knowledge* as "The Discourse on Language." The central theme concerns "the prodigious machinery of the will to truth" that conditions the evolution of knowledge in our culture and "its vocation for exclusion."

Raymond Roussel. Paris: Gallimard, 1963. This work is unique in Foucault's oeuvre because of its literary theme and the spellbinding effect the subject had on him. Foucault found in Roussel some of the obsessions that have marked his own approach to language and to the act of writing.

Surveiller et punir. Naissance de la prison. Paris: Gallimard, 1975. *Discipline and Punish: Birth of the Prison*. Translated by Alan Sheridan. London: Allen Lane, 1977; New York: Pantheon, 1978. A study of the institutions, techniques, and justifications that have marked the application of justice in the classical and modern ages. The epistemological conditions that have led to the establishment of the modern economies of punishment have also served to organize disciplinary regimes overseeing the socioeconomic integration of individuals.

Anthologies of Selected Works and Interviews

Bouchard, Donald F., ed. *Language, Counter-Memory, Practice. Selected Essays and Interviews by Michel Foucault.* Translated by Donald F. Bouchard and Sherry Simon. Ithaca, N.Y.: Cornell University Press and Oxford: Blackwell, 1977.

Fontana, Alessandro, and Pasquale Pasquino, eds. *Microphysique du pouvoir.* Turin: Einaudi, 1977. The transcript of two courses (7 and 14 January 1976) and an interview. The English version of these texts is to be found in Colin Gordon's anthology (see below).

Gordon, Colin, ed. *Power/Knowledge: Selected Interviews and Other Writings, 1972–1977.* Translated by Colin Gordon, Leo Marshall, John Mepham, Kate Soper. Brighton: The Harvester Press and New York: Pantheon, 1980.

Morris, Meaghan, and Paul Patton, eds. *Michel Foucault: Power, Truth, Strategy.* Sidney: Feral Publications, 1979. Contains three interviews with Foucault, "The Life of Infamous Men," and notes taken at a lecture at the Collège de France in 1973, on "Power and Norm."

Rabinow, Paul, ed. *The Foucault Reader.* New York: Pantheon, 1984. An anthology of some representative texts and interviews.

Works on Michel Foucault

Clark, Michael. *Michel Foucault: An Annotated Bibliography. Tool Kit for a New Age.* New York: Garland Publishing, 1983.

Cooper, Barry. *Michel Foucault: An Introduction to the Study of His Thought.* New York and Toronto: Edwin Mellen Press, 1982.

Cousins, Mark, and Athar Hussain. *Michel Foucault.* New York: St. Martin's Press, 1984. An exposition of Foucault's main works. The purpose is to be faithful to Foucault's analytical intentions and to avoid polemical issues associated with a crisis in left-wing politics or in philosophy.

Critique 471–472 (1986). "Michel Foucault: du monde entier." The contributors include Pierre Boulez and Jürgen Habermas; a complete bibliography of Foucault's writings is appended.

Le Débat 41 (1986). In addition to the commentaries and tributes, this special issue on Foucault contains a bibliography of his works and his 1979 conferences at Stanford University.

Deleuze, Gilles. *Foucault.* Paris: Minuit, 1986. An essay on the themes of *savoir, pouvoir,* modes of subjectivization, and the "death of man" by a longtime friend and admirer of Foucault who is also one of France's most eminent philosophers.

Diamond, Irene, and Lee Quinby, eds. *Feminism and Foucault.* Boston: Northeastern Press, 1988.

Dreyfus, Hubert L., and Paul Rabinow. *Michel Foucault: Beyond Structuralism and Hermeneutics.* Chicago: University of Chicago Press, 1982. 2d rev. ed., 1983. *Michel Foucault. Un parcours philosophique.* Translated by Fabienne Durand-Bogaert. Paris: Gallimard, 1984. According to the authors, Foucault has developed a "new method for studying human beings," a method that has the advantage of avoiding the "pitfalls" of both structuralism and hermeneutics.

Frow, John. "Limits: The Politics of Reading." In *Marxism and Literary History,* pp. 207–35. Cambridge, Mass.: Harvard University Press, 1986. A cogent analysis of the famous confrontation with Derrida over the passage from Descartes's *Meditations.*

Gane, Mike, ed. *Towards a Critique of Foucault.* London: Routledge and Kegan Paul, 1987.

Guedez, Annie. *Foucault*. Paris: Editions Universitaires, 1972. Concerning Foucault's place in the field of knowledge.

Humanities in Society 3 (1980). "On Foucault." Articles by Jonathan Arac, Paul Bové, Héctor Mario Cavallari, Karlis Racevskis, and Michael Sprinker.

Humanities in Society 5 (1982). "Foucault and Critical Theory: The Uses of Discourse Analysis." Articles by Robert D'Amico, David Carroll, Michel de Certeau, Ian Hacking, Mary Lydon, Richard T. Peterson, Mark Poster, and Paul Rabinow.

Kremer-Marietti, A. *Foucault*. Paris: Seghers, 1974. A study of Foucault's methodology and major concepts.

Lemert, Charles C., and Garth Gillian. *Michel Foucault: Social Theory as Transgression*. New York: Columbia University Press, 1982. An analysis of Foucault's social theory and critique in terms of a strategy of transgression that the authors consider a central feature of his work.

Magazine littéraire 207 (1984). An interview, a lecture, and a dozen critical reactions and appreciations constitute the *dossier* compiled by François Ewald.

Major-Poetzl, Pamela. *Michel Foucault's Archaeology of Western Culture: Toward a New Science of History*. Chapel Hill: University of North Carolina Press, 1983. Drawing a parallel between Foucault's approach to culture and some advanced modes of scientific thinking.

Megill, Allan. *Prophets of Extremity: Nietzsche, Heidegger, Foucault, Derrida*. Berkeley: University of California Press, 1985. The four thinkers are considered in terms of a commonality of themes and within the context of the modernist/postmodernist debate.

Merquior, José-Guilherm. *Foucault*. London: Collins-Fontana, 1985. *Michel Foucault ou le nihilisme de la chaire*. Paris: Presses Universitaires de France, 1986. An attempt to discredit Foucault.

Michel Foucault: Une histoire de la vérité. Paris: Syros, 1985. A collection of tributes by R. Badinter, P. Bourdieu, J. Daniel, Fr. Ewald, A. Farge, B. Kouchner, Ed. Maire, Cl. Mauriac, and M. Perrot. The principal theme is Foucault's fascination with truth.

Minson, Jeffrey. *Genealogies of Morals: Nietzsche, Foucault, Donzelot and the Eccentricity of Ethics*. New York: St. Martin's Press, 1985. A discussion of the virtues and shortcomings of Foucault's genealogical enterprise from a socialist perspective.

Poster, Mark. *Foucault, Marxism and History. Mode of Production versus Mode of Information*. Cambridge: Polity Press, 1984. Essays that bring out the value of Foucault's work from the perspective of social theory and social history.

Racevskis, Karlis. *Michel Foucault and the Subversion of Intellect*. Ithaca, N.Y.: Cornell University Press, 1983.

Rajchman, John. *Michel Foucault: The Freedom of Philosophy*. New York: Columbia University Press, 1985. *Michel Foucault: la liberté de savoir*. Paris: Presses Universitaires de France, 1986. The purpose is to show that Foucault reconciles his political commitment with his intellectual lucidity by transmuting epistemological insights into an ethics of freedom.

Shapiro, Michael J. "Michel Foucault and the Analysis of Discursive Practices." In *Language and Political Understanding: The Politics of Discursive Practices*, pp. 127–64. New Haven: Yale University Press, 1981. A most helpful discussion of the notion of "discursive practices" and its role in Foucault's work.

Sheridan, Alan. *Michel Foucault: The Will to Truth*. London: Tavistock, 1980. *Discours, sexualité et pouvoir*. Paris: Mardaga, 1985. A retelling of Foucault's writings supplemented with extensive quotations.

Smart, Barry. *Foucault*. London: Tavistock, 1985.

———. *Foucault, Marxism and Critique*. London: Routledge and Kegan Paul, 1983. A thorough discussion of the relation of Foucault's work to Marxist theory and analysis.

Telos 67 (1986). Although the main theme of the issue is the sociopolitical aspect of French intellectual trends today, fully one-half is devoted to a discussion of Foucault's political stance.

Veyne, Paul. "Foucault révolutionne l'histoire." In *Comment on écrit l'histoire*, pp. 203–42. Paris: Seuil, 1978. This appendix to the second edition of Veyne's book is an especially lucid account of Foucault's historiographical innovations.

White, Hayden. "Michel Foucault." In *Structuralism and Since: From Lévi-Strauss to Derrida*, ed. John Sturrock, pp. 81–115. Oxford: Oxford University Press, 1979. White places Foucault in the tradition of "dialectical philosophy," which, according to him, is characterized by the formalization of the tropological qualities of language. Accordingly, Foucault's work is shown to be a function of the catachrestic bent of Foucault's thought.

Notes on Contributors

DANNY J. ANDERSON teaches Mexican literature and the contemporary Spanish American novel at the University of Texas at Austin. He has written articles on contemporary Hispanic novels and has completed a book on a contemporary Mexican writer entitled *Vincente Lenero: The Novelist as Critic*.

G. DOUGLAS ATKINS is professor and coordinator of graduate studies in English at the University of Kansas. He has received grants from the Clark Library, ACLS, the School of Criticism and Theory, and NEH and won the Burlington Northern Faculty Achievement Award for Outstanding Classroom Teaching. He has published widely in eighteenth-century studies and recent criticism and theory, including *The Faith of John Dryden* (University Press of Kentucky, 1980), *Reading Deconstruction/Deconstructive Reading* (University Press of Kentucky, 1983, a *Choice* Outstanding Academic Book for 1984–85), *Writing and Reading Differently: Deconstruction and the Teaching of Composition and Literature* (coedited, University Press of Kansas, 1985), and *Quests of Difference: Reading Pope's Poems* (University Press of Kentucky, 1985). He is presently completing a book on Geoffrey Hartman.

DON BIALOSTOSKY is professor of English at the University of Toledo. He has published *Making Tales: The Poetics of Wordsworth's Narrative Experiments* (University of Chicago Press, 1984) and is completing a book on dialogics and criticism. He serves on the editorial board of the *Bakhtin Newsletter* and contributes the United States entries to its occasional bibliography of Bakhtin criticism.

RICHARD F. HARDIN is professor of English at the University of Kansas. He is the author of a book on the Elizabethan poet Michael Drayton (University Press of Kansas, 1973) and editor of a collection of essays on pastoral literature. Among his most recent scholarly articles are " 'Ritual' in Recent Criticism: The Elusive Sense of Community" and "Milton's Nimrod."

LORI HOPE LEFKOVITZ is the author of *The Character of Beauty in the Victorian Novel* (UMI Research Press, 1987) and has published essays on theory, nineteenth-century literature, and Judaism and feminism. She teaches English at Kenyon College.

ROBERT MAGLIOLA holds the Distinguished Chair Professorship of the Graduate School of Tamkang University, Taiwan. Previously he was professor of comparative literature at Purdue University and the cochair of its special doctoral program in philosophy and literature. He has written *Phenomenology and Literature* (Purdue University Press, 1977), *Derrida on the Mend* (Purdue University Press, 1984), and chapters for several anthologies. He has published widely in journals on philosophy, literature, and Buddhology.

LAURA MORROW is associate professor of English at LSU in Shreveport. The recipient of grants from the National Endowment for the Humanities, the Folger Shakespeare Library, the American Society for Eighteenth-Century Studies, and the Louisiana Endowment for the Humanities, she is the author of articles and reviews on Restoration and eighteenth-century drama, contemporary drama, Milton, and pedagogy.

PETER J. RABINOWITZ is a professor of comparative literature at Hamilton College. He has written on a wide range of topics, from literary theory to detective fiction, to opera. He is the author of *Before Reading: Narrative Conventions and the Politics of Interpretation* (Cornell University Press, 1987) and is also a professional music critic who contributes regularly to such publications as *Fanfare*, *Ovation*, and *American Record Guide*. He is currently working, with composer Jay Reise, on new models of listening and their implications for musical analysis.

KARLIS RACEVSKIS teaches French language, literature, and civilization at Wright State University. He has published *Michel Foucault and the Subversion of Intellect* (Cornell University Press, 1983). His research interests have taken him from the age of Enlightenment to that of poststructuralism and its aftermath.

MICHAEL RYAN teaches English at Northeastern University and is the author of *Marxism and Deconstruction* (Johns Hopkins University Press, 1982),

Camera Politica: The Politics and Ideology of Contemporary Hollywood Film (with Douglas Kellner), and *Politics and Culture: Essays in Culture Criticism*.

CHERYL B. TORSNEY is an assistant professor of English at West Virginia University, where she teaches courses in American literature and women's writing. The recipient of an ACLS Fellowship and a former Fulbright lecturer in France, she has also participated in an American Antiquarian Society Summer Seminar and an NEH Summer Seminar. Her book, *Constance Fenimore Woolson: The Grief of Artistry*, is forthcoming from the University of Georgia Press.

JOEL WEINSHEIMER is a professor of English at the University of Minnesota. He is the author of *Imitation* (Routledge and Kegan Paul, 1984) and *Gadamer's Hermeneutics: A Reading of "Truth and Method"* (Yale University Press, 1985) as well as of numerous essays on existential hermeneutics. He also edited, for many years, *The Eighteenth Century: Theory and Interpretation* as well as edited *Jane Austen Today* (University of Georgia Press, 1975).

DAVID WILLBERN is associate professor of English and associate dean of Arts and Letters at SUNY-Buffalo. From 1983 to 1986 he was director of the Buffalo Center for the Psychological Study of the Arts. Among his publications are essays on Shakespeare, Freud, D. H. Lawrence, Robert Duncan, and psychoanalytic criticism. He is currently completing a book entitled *Poetic Will: Shakespeare and the Play of Language*.

JOHN R. WILLINGHAM, professor of English at Benedictine College and emeritus professor at the University of Kansas, is a specialist in American literature and modernist poetry and poetics. He has held offices in the Modern Language Association, the College English Association, and the South Central Modern Language Association. He is the coauthor of several textbooks in English studies and has written articles and reviews in *American Literature*, *Nation*, *The Explicator*, *CEA Critic* and *CEA Forum*, *Choice*, and *American Studies*.